Beginning PHP4 Databases

Andrew Hill

Chris Lea

Deepak Thomas

Christopher Scollo

Harish Rawat

Jim Hubbard

Sanjay Abraham

Wrox Press Ltd. ®

Beginning PHP4 Databases

First Printed in September 2002

Published by Wrox Press Ltd,
Arden House, 1102 Warwick Road, Acocks Green,
Birmingham, B27 6BH, UK
Printed in the United States
ISBN 1-86100-782-5

Trademark Acknowledgements

Wrox has endeavored to provide trademark information about all the companies and products mentioned in this book by the appropriate use of capitals. However, Wrox cannot guarantee the accuracy of this information.

Credits

Authors
Andrew Hill
Chris Lea
Deepak Thomas
Christopher Scollo
Harish Rawat
Jim Hubbard
Sanjay Abraham

Technical Reviewers
Ken Egervari
Basil Simonenko
Richard Stones
Harish Rawat
James Fuller
Sandro Zic
Matt Anton
Luis Argerich

Commissioning Editor
Dilip Thomas

Author Agent
Safiulla Shakir

Editorial Thanks
Indu Britto
Nilesh Parmar
Victoria Blackburn
Kedar Kamat
Niranjan Jahagirdar

Managing Editor
Paul Cooper

Technical Editors
Dipali Chittar
Anand Devsharma
David Mercer

Project Manager
Abbas Rangwala

Production Coordinator
Rachel Taylor
Pippa Wonson

Production and Layout
Manjiri Karande

Illustration
Santosh Haware

Index
Adrian Axinte
Andrew Criddle

Proof Reader
Agnes Wiggers

Cover
Dawn Chellingworth

About the Authors

Andrew Hill

Andrew is Director of Technology Evangelism for OpenLink Software, an enterprise middleware and data access infrastructure firm located in Burlington, MA. Andrew's position puts him squarely between the business and tech fronts of developing technology industries. He has been programming in PHP for a couple of years, coming to the PHP community initially to support the use of ODBC and database agnostic application connectivity. His technology interests also include XML, VSP, Mac OS X, and various other *nix technologies.

Chris Lea

Chris Lea is a developer currently living in Los Angeles, CA. He received a BS in Physics with Highest Honors and Distinction from UNC-CH in 1997, and has been sitting in front of a computer for a great deal of his time since then. Typically he uses Linux, which has been his platform of choice since sometime in college when he first bumped into it. He started with PHP a few years after that and has worked on projects ranging from the entertainment industry to the financial sector. You can find out all you ever wanted to know and more at his personal website http://www.chrislea.com/.

Deepak Thomas

Deepak is a Member of Technical Staff with Oracle corp. in Redwood Shores, CA. Co-author of Professional PHP; he has also contributed to other Wrox titles on Linux and Java both as an author and a reviewer. His interests include Linux, J2EE technologies and website deployment issues.

Christopher Scollo

Christopher Scollo is a veteran web programmer and one of the authors of Professional PHP Programming and Professional PHP4, both from Wrox Press. Originally from New Jersey, USA, he now lives in Munich, Germany where he is the lead developer at Ciao.com. Despite the sedentary nature of his occupation, he is an active fellow with a hearty appetite. Eating well is his favorite pastime, but he also enjoys hiking and cycling with his wife, Nicole Bator.

Harish Rawat

Harish is a software developer at Oracle Corporation. He has over nine years of experience in Systems programming. His technical areas of interest include XML, Java, and Network Protocols. Co-author of Professional PHP; he has also contributed to other Wrox titles on Linux and Java both as an author and a reviewer.

Sanjay Abraham

Sanjay Abraham has been a PHP developer since 1995 and continues to be an avid publicity-shunning open source evangelist prophesizing his wealth of experience to thousands of programmers around the world. His skill sets include Assembly, C, C++, Java, SQL, PHP, Ruby, Perl, Python, and proficient knowledge of advanced algorithms and data structures. His technology interests also include XML, Mac OS X, and various other *nix technologies. He can be reached at spindoctor@linuxmail.org.

Table of Contents

Table of Contents

Table of Contents

Table of Contents

Table of Contents

Table of Contents

Table of Contents

Table of Contents

Table of Contents

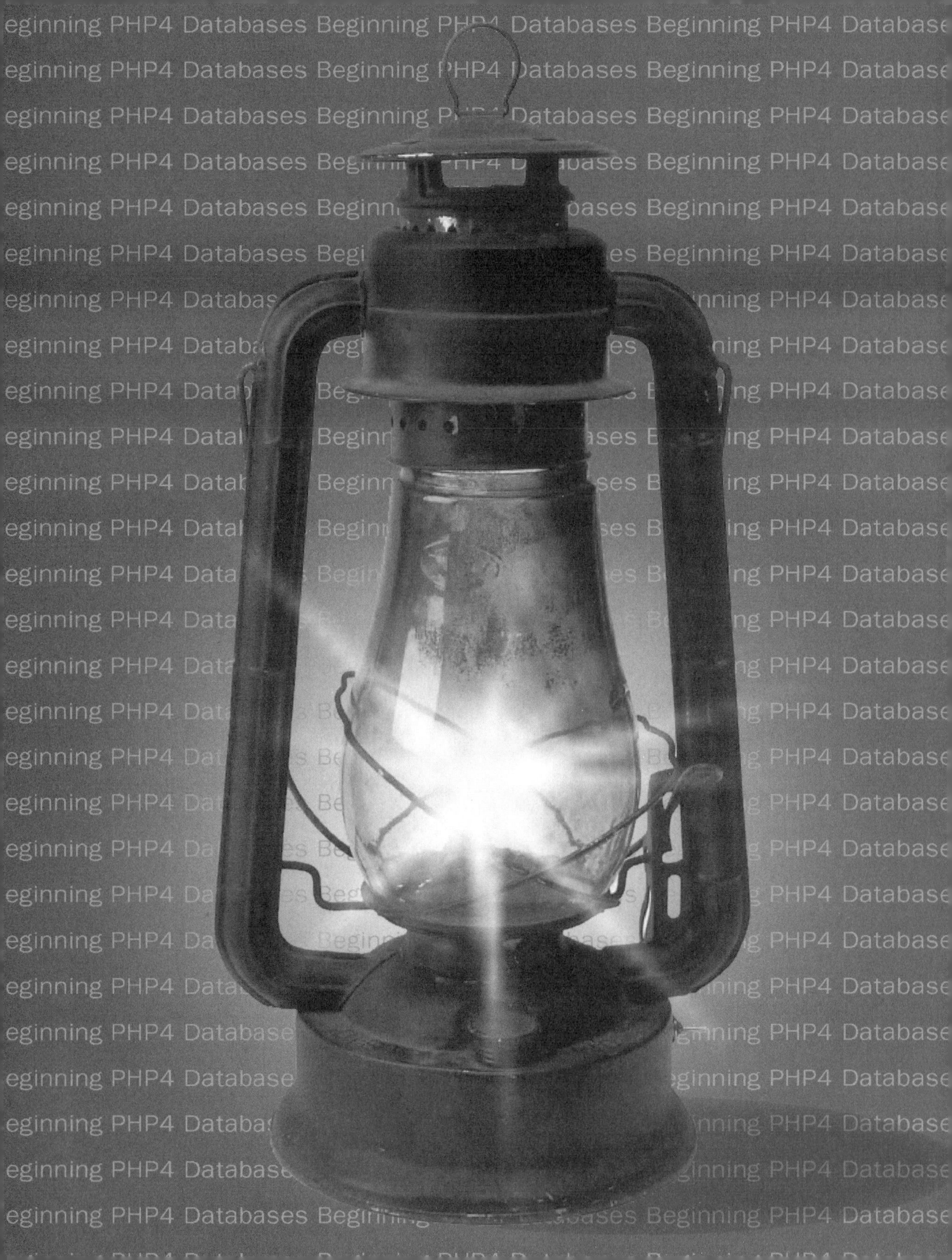

Beginning PHP4 Databases

Introduction

A majority of PHP projects rely on a database back - end more and more applications integrate large databases with web interfaces, we seek to provide the novice database programmer with a solid foundation in the art and science of developing advanced database-driven web applications with PHP.

PHP Introduction

PHP (PHP Hypertext Preprocessor) is a general-purpose scripting language that is especially suited for web development and can be embedded into HTML. It excels when used to write web-based applications. It can be easily used with almost all the important, free or commercial web servers, allowing web applications to be portable and operating system-independent. Besides that, PHP code can be combined very easily with HTML to produce web pages without any programming effort. Thus, the goal of the language is to allow web developers to write dynamically generated pages quickly.

Another very interesting feature of PHP is that one can usually write applications, even complex ones, very fast. If the Perl motto is "There's More Than One Way To Do it" the PHP motto will be "There's a Faster Way to Do it". PHP provides a lot of extensions and built-in functions for very specific tasks that will require a hard-to-find library, or a lot of code in other languages.

With PHP we have the freedom of choosing an operating system and a web server. We also have the choice of using procedural programming, OOP, or a mixture of both. Although not every standard OOP feature is realized in the current version of PHP, many code libraries and large applications (including the PEAR library) are developed entirely using the OOP paradigm.

All these advantages make PHP the scripting language of choice for:

❏ **Website programming and web applications**
This is the most traditional and main target field for PHP. We need three things to make this work. The PHP parser (CGI or server module), a web server, and a web browser. We need to run the web server with a connected PHP installation. Then we can access the PHP program output with a web browser, viewing the PHP page through the server. These scripts can be used to collect form data, generate dynamic page content, or send and receive cookies.

❏ **Command-line scripting**
We can run a PHP script without a server or browser. In this case we only need the PHP parser. This type of usage is ideal for scripts regularly executed using **Cron** (for UNIX) or the **Task Scheduler** (for Windows). These scripts can be used for simple text processing tasks. Also, used in this way, PHP competes with scripting languages like Perl or Python.

❏ **Client-side GUI applications**
PHP is not yet the very best language to write graphics applications, but if we need to use some advanced PHP features in our client-side applications, then PHP-GTK is the best choice. We also have the ability to write cross-platform applications this way. PHP-GTK is an extension to PHP and it is not available in the main distribution.

PHP has had a fairly consistent growth rate of 6.5% per month since the summer of 2000 and in May 2002, PHP was running on a whopping 9,059,850 domains and 1,188,121 IP addresses. For the first time, an open source scripting solution had passed Microsoft's proprietary Active Server Pages (ASP) script to claim the top spot on the Netcraft survey. This, of course, excludes the large number of Intranet sites, which use PHP and which were not included in these statistics.

PHP4

PHP started as a quick Perl-hack, written by Rasmus Lerdorf in 1994. The next couple of years saw it evolve into PHP/FI, which started to get a lot of users. Things started flying when Zeev Suraski and Andi Gutmans came along with a new parser in the summer of 1997, leading to PHP3. This parser defined the syntax and semantics used in both versions 3 and 4.

PHP has been architecturally overhauled since version 3. As a general yardstick, PHP4 is more efficient, more reliable, and much, much faster than PHP3. The performance of PHP4 is particularly noticeable for larger and more complex scripts.

Here is a list of the most important inclusions in PHP4:

❏ **The scripting engine has been redesigned**
The **Zend** engine was rewritten from the ground up to use an efficient 'Compile-Then-Execute' paradigm, instead of the 'Execute-While-Parsing' model employed in PHP3.

❏ **PHP Extensions**
The function modules now referred to as the PHP extensions, have become self-contained. By self-contained, we mean that most of the binaries (in the case of Windows) or the source code (in the case of UNIX) are included in the PHP download for a particular platform. Hence we do not have to separately download the extensions when we need them.

❑ **PHP includes the SAPI web server abstraction layer**

It greatly simplifies the task of adding native support for new web servers. SAPI also leads to enhanced stability and support for multi-threaded web servers. SAPI currently has server implementations for Apache, Roxen, Java (servlet), ISAPI (Microsoft IIS, and soon Zeus), AOLserver, and CGI.

Who is this Book for ?

This book caters to programmers who are curious to learn how to build robust database-driven PHP web applications. Almost antithetically, no prior exposure to databases is expected, meaning that the reader may even be one who wants to understand the basic database concepts. However, experts, who would not need to read the sections explaining database concepts and introducing different types of databases, can get through the book muck quicker. The reader is assumed to have some exposure to PHP programming, at least at a basic level. Still, the book has been kept simple so that none of the content would leave even a learner of PHP in awe.

As suggested by the title, the book packs maximum value for the beginner. We see two categories of such readers:

❑ The experienced PHP developer who is eager to use cutting-edge database technologies, and wants a feel of implementations of the same.

❑ The novice programmer, who this book would help immensely in gaining fluency in database systems, along with the knowledge of how to take advantage of them in PHP applications.

What's Covered in this Book

We shall start with a basic PHP review, with Object-Orientated (OO) programming in good measure. The beginning chapters cover an extensive overview of database systems. An in-depth-understanding of database concepts follows, integrating seamlessly into database abstraction using PEAR::DB. The book reaches a climax with comparative studies of different database applications, including design, coding and testing. A reader can expect to gain extensive exposure to post-relational and XML-native databases, and be able to analytically decide on the applicability of each database system to different requirements.

There are 13 chapters in this book along with three appendices. Also, we have posted an additional chapter on the Wrox website. Here is what you will find in Chapters of this book:

Chapter 1: PHP Fundamentals

This chapter is a PHP fundamentals refresher with an emphasis on OOP. It is targeted to suit the needs of a reader with a decent PHP quotient, at least at beginner level. Also; it digs into the fundamentals of OOP with PHP, which will not only be essential for the rest of the book, but will also be a boost for keeping pace with technology changes.

Chapter 2: Database Fundamentals

Chapters 2-7 concentrate on SQL basics for the database newbie. In particular, Chapter 2 signals the departure of focus from PHP to Database Management Systems. This chapter will briefly cover what is a database and why they are useful in PHP application development. It then details the various database models, database architecture, and the need for Database Abstraction. Database systems like MySQL, PostgreSQL are covered, along with their impacts on PHP, which are significant. By the end of the chapter, the reader should be in a position to make an informed decision on which database to use for a project and build an understanding of database systems to bring into subsequent chapters.

Chapter 3: Understanding Relational Databases

The reader is now aware that there are different basic ways to structure data. Here we look at a more evolved way of structuring data – in tables. With focus on the basic concepts of relational databases like Normalization, Keys, Referential Integrity, and ERD, the chapter describes the process of maintaining organized data in a relational structure.

Chapter 4: The Structured Query Language

This chapter takes the concepts of databases and tables further and explain how to create and modify structures within our databases to organize data into the relational model. It also details how to classify and structure data within a database for efficient storage and rapid retrieval. Further, it looks into database design considerations with regards to application programming and database structure. We look at how an application interacts with the database via SQL to manipulate information in the database.

Chapter 5: SQL: Data Manipulation and Retrieval

This chapter provides the reader with a thorough understanding of:

- ❑ How PHP can embed SQL statements
- ❑ Opening closing and working with database sessions
- ❑ Components of SQL:1999 as supported by various database server implementations, including SQL statement operators, clauses, predicates, conditional evaluation, and combining statements
- ❑ Multi-table SQL statements, including JOINs and UNIONs, as well as complex SQL features such as the CASE statement
- ❑ How databases actually construct result sets using temporary tables, and how programmers may use this to their benefit in planning around some referential integrity feature lacks.

Chapter 6: Data Consistency

What is Data Consistency? In simple terms, your data is consistent, if it behaves the way you want it to in your application. Normally, when the developer writes an application they assume that the database would do what they expect. But there are some common issues that might result in the database throwing incorrect results. This is particularly true in multi-user applications. In this chapter the reader learns the two facets of engineering a development process to success – designing database tables well and using the consistency features of the RDBMS effectively.

Chapter 7: Advanced SQL and PHP

This chapter delves into advanced concepts such as Stored Procedures and Cursors, and explains the various aspects by walking the reader through examples.

Chapter 8: PHP and Relational Databases

This is in some ways a crossroads chapter. After a PHP refresher and a concentrated effort in SQL and relational design, this chapter is situated with the purpose of helping the reader decide on the following issues:

❑   What database to use

❑   Whether to use native PHP functions or an abstraction layer to interact with the database

❑   If a database abstraction layer is to be used, which one

❑   Will the code be mostly procedural or object-oriented

❑   How can the code be modularized

❑   Would a multi-tier development model be used

Chapter 9: Dissecting PEAR::DB

Readers who are in a hurry need not read this chapter to actually start using PEAR:DB. The online documentation provides enough detail about how PEAR is used in applications. This detailed examination is intended to deepen the understanding of PEAR and its abstraction layer. It offers an insight into its functionality, revealing implementation details.

Chapter 10: Case Study: Using PEAR::DB – An Accounts Receivable Application

This case study builds an Accounts Receivable Application that will use a database back-end and the built-in PEAR::DB Access class.

Chapter 11: Case Study: Using Object Databases - A Library Automation System

This case study builds a Library Automation System to be used by library administrators to issue and return items, and by library users to view their accounts and search the library catalog. The chapter demonstrates how PHP can be effectively used to implement object-oriented database applications.

Chapter 12: Native XML Databases

This database is specialized for storing XML data and stores all components of the XML model intact. This chapter talks about what it takes to preserve the data model, explains the actual working of Native XML Databases, reviews associated tools, and discusses different strategies for using a Native XML Database.

Chapter 13: Case Study: Using Xindice – A Recipe Exchange

This chapter builds upon Chapter 12 by creating a full-fledged application based on the native XML technologies, using ASF's native XML database, Xindice, as the back-end data store. Here we design and implement a web application that allows users to exchange recipes of their favorite dishes with other users.

Chapter 14 (online): Case Study: Using Virtuoso

This chapter talks all about the Virtuoso Universal Server developed by OpenLink Software. It is a cross-platform multi-purpose server that has native XML storage and allows XML processing.

This chapter will be provided online, at http://www.wrox.com.

Appendix A: Administration

This is a treatise of database administration, and covers all relevant issues from basics to optimization.

Appendix B: PHP Database Functions

This contains a comprehensive reference listing of database functions corresponding to all contemporary databases. This document can be searched for parameters required, and return type and description of any existing function.

Appendix C: Installing PHP, Apache, and iODBC

This is an installation guide for getting PHP working with the Apache web server with iODBC support on UNIX and Windows systems.

Conventions

To help you get the most from the text and keep track of what's happening, we've used a number of conventions throughout the book.

For instance:

> **These boxes hold important, not-to-be-forgotten information, which is directly relevant to the surrounding text.**

While the background style is used for asides to the current discussion.

Try it Out – A 'Try it Out' Example

'Try it Out' is our way of presenting a practical example.

How it Works

Then the 'How it Works' explains what is going on.

As for styles in the text:

- ❑ When we introduce them, we **highlight** important words
- ❑ We show keyboard strokes like this: *Ctrl-K*
- ❑ We show filenames and code within the text like so: `<element>`
- ❑ Text on user interfaces and URLs are shown as: Menu

We present code in two different ways:

```
In our code examples, the code foreground style shows new, important,
    pertinent code
while code background shows code that is less important in the present
    context or has been seen before.
```

Customer Support

We always value hearing from our readers, and we want to know what you think about this book: what you liked, what you didn't like, and what you think we can do better next time. You can send us your comments, either by returning the reply card in the back of the book, or by e-mail to feedback@wrox.com. Please be sure to mention the book title in your message.

How to Download the Sample Code

When you visit the Wrox site, http://www.wrox.com/, simply locate the title through our Search facility or by using one of the title lists. Click on Download in the Code column or on Download Code on the book's detail page.

The files that are available for download from our site have been archived using WinZip. When you have saved the attachments to a folder on your harddrive, you need to extract the files using a de-compression program such as WinZip or PKUnzip. When you extract the files, the code is usually extracted into chapter folders. When you start the extraction process, ensure your software (WinZip and PKUnzip, for example) is set to use folder names.

Errata

We've made every effort to make sure that there are no errors in the text or in the code. However, no one is perfect and mistakes do occur. If you find an error in one of our books, like a spelling mistake or faulty piece of code, we would be very grateful for your feedback. By sending in errata you may save other reader hours of frustration, and of course, you will be helping us provide even higher quality information. Simply e-mail the information to support@wrox.com; your information will be checked and if correct, posted to the errata page for that title, or used in subsequent editions of the book.

To find errata on the web site, go to http://www.wrox.com/, and simply locate the title through our Advanced Search or title list. Click on the Book Errata link, which is below the cover graphic on the book's detail page.

E-Mail Support

If you wish to directly query a problem in the book with an expert who knows the book in detail then e-mail support@wrox.com, with the title of the book and the last four numbers of the ISBN in the subject field of the e-mail. A typical e-mail should include the following things:

❑ The **title of the book, last four digits of the ISBN,** and **page number** of the problem in the Subject field.

❑ Your **name, contact information,** and the **problem** in the body of the message.

We *won't* send you junk mail. We need the details to save your time and ours. When you send an e-mail message, it will go through the following chain of support:

❑ Customer Support – Your message is delivered to our customer support, and they are the first people to read it. They have files on most frequently asked questions and will answer anything general about the book or the website immediately.

❑ Editorial – Deeper queries are forwarded to the technical editor responsible for that book. They have experience with the programming language or a particular product, and are able to answer detailed technical questions on the subject.

❑ The Authors – Finally, in the unlikely event that the technical editor cannot answer your problem, they will forward the request to the author. We do try to protect the authors from any distractions to their writing; however, we are quite happy to forward specific requests to them. All Wrox authors help with the support on their books. They will e-mail the customer and the editor with their response, and again all readers should benefit.

The Wrox support process can only offer support to issues directly pertinent to the content of our published title. Support for questions that fall outside the scope of normal book support is provided via the community lists of our http://p2p.wrox.com/ forum.

p2p.wrox.com

For author and peer discussion join the P2P mailing lists. Our unique system provides **Programmer to Programmer**™ contact on mailing lists, forums, and newsgroups, in addition to our one-to-one e-mail support system. If you post a query to P2P, you can be confident that many Wrox authors and other industry experts who are present on our mailing lists are examining it. At p2p.wrox.com you will find a number of different lists to help you, not only while you read this book, but also as you develop your applications.

To subscribe to a mailing list just follow these steps:

1. Go to http://p2p.wrox.com/

2. Choose the appropriate category from the left menu bar

3. Click on the mailing list you wish to join

4. Follow the instructions to subscribe and fill in your e-mail address and password

5. Reply to the confirmation e-mail you receive

6. Use the subscription manager to join more lists and set your e-mail preferences

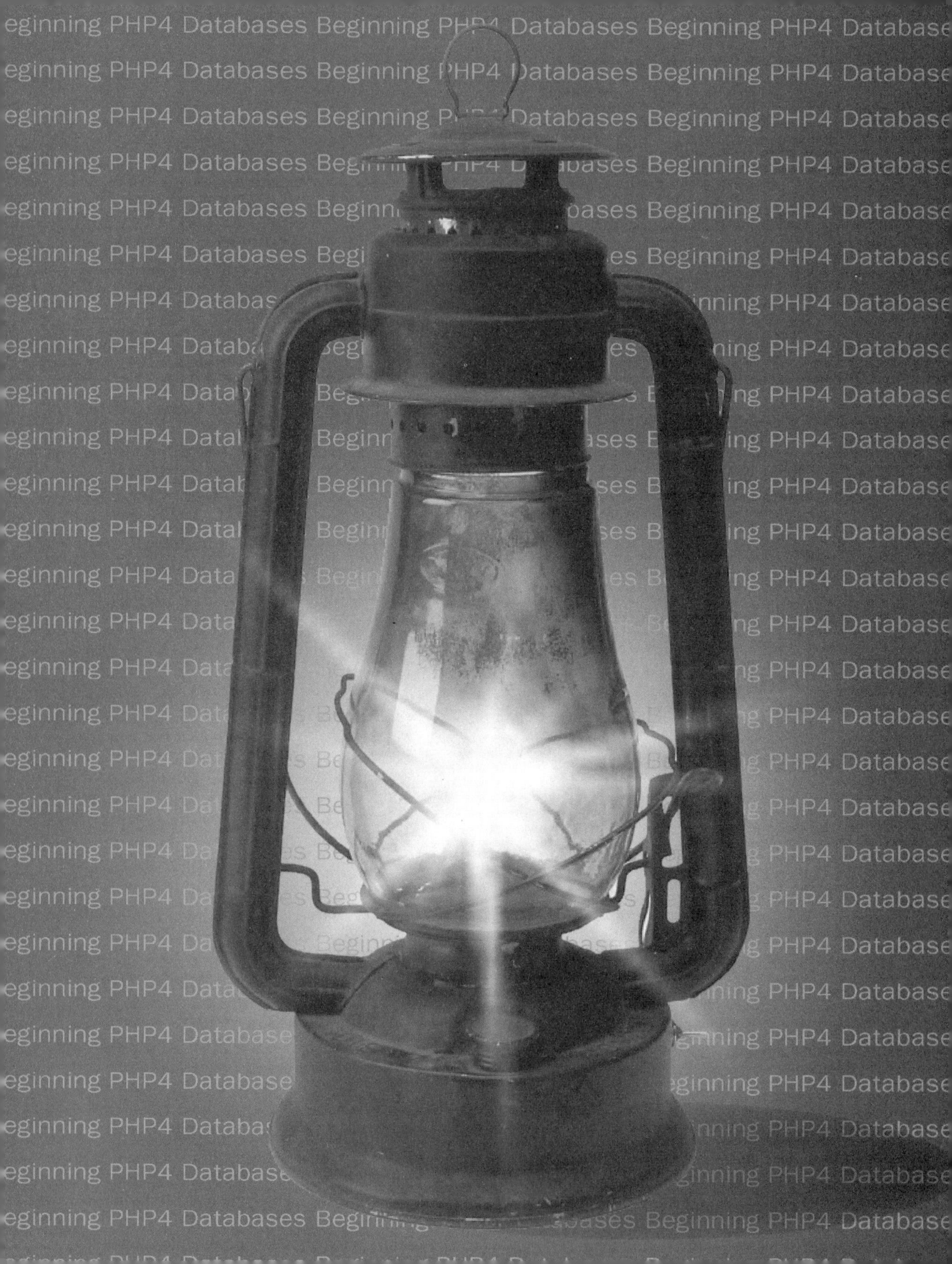
Beginning PHP4 Databases

PHP Fundamentals

This chapter presents an overview of the basic syntax and control structures of the PHP language. It makes very useful reading for those who anyone who does not have much PHP experience. Even otherwise this chapter is recommended as a reference for the basic techniques of object-oriented programming.

PHP programs can be executed either by a web server or by a console program. These programs are stored in standard text files normally with a `.php` extension. However, we can configure the file extension to anything we like, by editing the web server's configuration file. For example, if we want to save PHP files on an Apache web server with a `.phpmm` extension, then we should edit the `httpd.conf` file to recognise that extension:

```
AddType application/x-httpd-php .phpmm
```

The other common extensions are .php3 and .phtml, both of which are now deprecated.

Tag Styles

In the context of a web page, PHP sits embedded within the surrounding markup, which is probably but not necessarily HTML or XHTML. PHP allows for four different tag types to distinguish it from the rest of the markup:

Tag Syntax	Tag Type
`<? ... ?>`	Short tags *This is best for use with SGML processing instructions*
`<?php ... ?>`	XML tags *This is best for use with XML processing instructions*

Table continued on following page

Tag Syntax	Tag Type
`< %  ...  %>`	ASP-style tags
	This is best for use with editors that understand ASP tags but not PHP tags. This is not recommended, particularly on Windows development servers where ASP is also being run.
`<script language="php"> ... </script>`	HTML editor-friendly script-style tags

We will be using the XML-style tags throughout this book since this is the recommendation in most of the coding standards for PHP. However, one can choose the type of tag one wants to use by enabling that specific type under the Language Options section in the php.ini configuration file.

Comments

PHP uses C-style comments (as do Java and JavaScript) as well as Perl-style comments (as does Tcl):

```php
<?php

# This is an example of PHP's Perl-style comment

/* This is an example of PHP's
   C-style multi-line comment */

// This is an example of PHP's C++-style comment
?>
```

Use of Perl/shell-style comments (#) is discouraged.

Data Types

Variables are used as a container to store some data – a variable is like a label that refers to a value. In PHP, all variables are represented by the use of a dollar sign ($) preceding the variable name. A variable name in PHP can be a combination of alpha characters, digits 0-9, and the underscore (_) character. In a variable name, the first character cannot be a digit and no character can be a space. PHP's variables, like Perl's, are loosely typed. The data type of a variable is determined by the first value assigned to it.

There are eight distinct primitive variable types that can be used with PHP for storing data. The eight types are divided into three categories – scalar, compound, and special types.

The scalar types include:

- ❑ Integer
- ❑ Double
- ❑ String
- ❑ Boolean

The compound types include:

- ❑ Arrays
- ❑ Objects

And the special types include:

- ❑ Resources
- ❑ Null

We will look at each of these in detail later on in this section.

gettype() and settype() Functions

We will review a few built-in functions to test the type of the PHP variables and also look at casting data types.

gettype()

We can use the gettype() function to return the data type that PHP has assigned to a variable:

```php
<?php

$variable = "This is a string";
print (gettype($variable));
?>
```

This will print out **string**.

settype()

The settype() function can be used to explicitly set the type:

```php
<?php

$variable = 1;
print (gettype ($variable));
settype ($variable, string);
print (gettype ($variable));
?>
```

This will print out **integer** on the first test using gettype() and **string** on the second test. This is because we explicitly used the settype() fuction after the first test.

Casting

PHP also has casting operators, which allow us to tell PHP to treat a value of one type as if it were another type. Casting is done by surrounding the desired type in parentheses, and applying it to any expression. The code and the embedded comments below illustrate how casting works:

```php
<?php

$value1 = 7.1;
$value2 = "58.1 avg";
$value3 = 8;

$var1 = (integer) $value1;    // assigns 7
print (gettype($var1)."<br>\n"); // prints "integer"

$var2 = (string) $value1;    // assigns "7.1"
print (gettype($var2)."<br>\n"); // prints "string"

$var3 = (object) $value3;    // $var3 becomes an object with 1 attribute
print ($var3->scalar."<br>\n");  // the attribute is 'scalar'. prints 8
?>
```

Types of Casting

PHP allows values to be cast to the following types:

- ❑   int or integer
- ❑   bool or boolean
- ❑   float, double, or real
- ❑   string
- ❑   array
- ❑   object

Casting from one type to another can give unusual results when the source or destination type is non-scalar. Therefore, we should use undefined type casts with caution.

Scalar Types

A scalar data type is so called because it's used to hold a single item of data. This could be a number, a sentence, a single word or character, or another item appropriate to the scalar variable type that contains it.

The four scalar types are:

- ❑   Integer
- ❑   Floating point a.k.a double
- ❑   String
- ❑   Boolean

Integer

Integer values can be specified in decimal, octal, or hexadecimal format, optionally preceeded by a + or - sign. Integers beginning with a leading zero (0) are interpreted as octal. Integers beginning with a leading zero followed by an x (0x) are interpreted as hexadecimal.

Also, all integers in PHP are 32 bits long, and all integers are signed. Therefore the range is from -2,147,483,646 to 2,147,483,647.

If we specify a number beyond the bounds of an integer, or perform an operation that results in a number that is beyond the bounds of an integer, it will be represented as a **float**. In case of division, if both the numerator and denominator are integers, and the result comes out as an integer, then the return value will be an integer; else the return value will be a float.

We can use the is_int() function or its is_integer() alias to test whether a value is an integer:

```
if (is_int($a)) {
    // $a is an integer
}
```

Floating Point

Floating point number is also known as float, double, or real number. The exact size is platform-dependent though a precision of roughly 14 decimal places is common. This conforms to the 64-bit IEEE format. It is important to note that in some cases the floating point arithmetic in PHP is not as precise as one might like. To perform high-precision calculations, we should use the appropriate mathematical functions available in the language.

> PHP provides a library of arbitrary precision math functions (the bc* family) that are useful for these situations. For more information refer the online PHP language manual available at **http://www.php.net/manual/en/ref.bc.php.**

A typical float declaration looks like this:

```
$float_variable = 3.1415;
```

We can use the ceil() function to round up a floating point number:

```
$six = ceil(5.3);        // $six = 6.0;
$ten = ceil(9.999);      // $ten = 10.0;
```

We can use the floor() function to round down a floating point number:

```
$five = floor(5.3);      // $five = 5.0;
$seven = floor(7.999);   // $seven = 7.0;
```

String

String variables are very easy to use in PHP, and there is a wide range of built-in functions to help us manipulate them. A typical declaration looks like this:

```
$string_variable = "Jon Doe is a Professional writer";
```

This is an example of using double quotes to specify a string literal – this is the most common method. However, PHP tries to expand any variables it sees within double-quoted strings. This code:

```
$writing_style = "professional";
$string_variable = "Jon Doe is a $writing_style writer";
print ($string_variable);
```

will print:

Jon Doe is a professional writer

There are a number of escape characters that PHP will recognize in double-quoted strings. Here is a list of the most commonly used ones:

Sequence	Meaning
\n	Linefeed
\r	Carriage return
\t	Horizontal tab
\\	Backslash
\$	Dollar sign
\'	Single quote
\"	Double quote

We can specify string literals with single quotes. However, in this case, PHP does not recognize the above escape characters, and it will not try to expand variables. This example:

```
$writing_style = "professional";
$string_variable = 'Jon Doe is a $writing_style writer\n';
print ($string_variable);
```

will output:

Jon Doe is a professional writer\n.

There is a third method of creating string literals called **heredoc syntax**. It is useful when we have multiple-line strings, and employ the <<< notation. When creating the quotation, one provides an identifier after the <<<, then the string, and finally the same identifier to close. For example:

```
$str = <<<EOQ
  This is a multi-line string.
  Note that I don't have to escape any "quotes" here.
EOQ;
```

As with double quoted strings, variables found in heredoc statements are expanded. In this code sample, the variable $str would have the value 'Getting, there!':

```
$foo = "there!";
$str = <<<EOQ
Getting, $foo
EOQ;
```

There are two very important and potentially problematic issues that must always be remembered when using heredoc syntax:

- ❏ The closing identifier must begin in the first column of the line it is on. It may not be indented with spaces or tabs.

- ❏ After the closing semicolon, there can be no other characters on the same line except for the linefeed (\n) character. This can cause problems when using Windows-based editors, as Windows uses the sequence \r\n as a line terminator, which might make the code fail. Many of these editors have an option that lets us set the line terminator character. If this option is available, then telling it to use UNIX-style terminators should fix the problem.

> **The semicolon at the end of the closing identifier of heredoc is optional, but it is good practice to use it for consistency with the rest of the PHP code.**

Boolean

Boolean variables can have one of the two values – True or False. Like all keywords in the PHP languages, these are case-insensitive. A typical declaration would look like:

```
$boolean_variable = TRUE;
```

Compound Types

The compound types allow us to store more complicated things than a single item of data. Arrays let us store groups of items, and objects are used to group data and the functions that operate on that data.

PHP allows two compound types:

- ❏ **Array** – Arrays let us store groups of items

- ❏ **Object** – Objects are used to group data and the functions that operate on that data

Array

Arrays are an important part of the PHP language. They are in reality optimized ordered maps in PHP. This means that they can be used as real arrays, hashes, dictionaries, lists, and so on interchangeably, without any real work on the part of the programmer. It is one of the things that make development in PHP so much faster than in languages such as C.

A new array can be created with the array() construct. Note that it is, in fact, a true language construct, though it looks just like a function. An array will contain a certain number of comma-separated 'key => value' pairs, where key is either a non-negative integer or a string, and value can be anything. Note that negative integers are allowed but are to be discouraged, simply because they can be confusing to handle. As with most languages, the preferred way of doing things is to begin the index of the array with 0 and go up by one for each index after that.

Here is an example array declaration:

```
$arr_variable = array(0 => 'Person', 'name' => 'jon', 'height' => 'tall');
```

We can also specify arrays using square bracket syntax. The above sample, with square bracket declaration, looks like this:

```
$arr_variable[0] = 'Person';
$arr_variable['name'] = 'Jon';
$arr_variable['height'] = 'tall';
```

If $arr_variable doesn't exist yet, then it is created with the first declaration. Note that unlike Perl, both arrays and scalar variables are designated with the dollar sign ($).

We can use the empty bracket ([]) syntax to push new values into an array. When this syntax is employed, PHP will put the assigned value into the array corresponding to an integer key. Taking the current maximum integer index, and adding one to it determines this integer. If there are no existing integer indices then 0 is used. This means that the above example is equivalent to:

```
$arr_variable[] = 'Person';
$arr_variable['name'] = 'Jon';
$arr_variable['height'] = 'tall';
```

Likewise, the following code snippet:

```
$news_sites[] = "fingertips.com";
$news_sites[] = "wemakenews.com";
$news_sites[] = "flashnews.net";
```

is functionally identical to:

```
$design_sites[0] = "fingertips.com";
$design_sites[1] = "wemakenews.com";
$design_sites[2] = "flashnews.net";
```

Arrays are very versatile and flexible in PHP. One often makes use of multidimensional arrays that use compound square brackets notation, as in C and other languages. A sample declaration for a multidimensional array looks like this:

```
$compound_array['person']['name'] = "Missileman";
$compound_array['person']['occupation'] = "president";
$compound_array['dog']['name'] = "Lassie";
$compound_array['dog']['occupation'] = "none";
```

This could also be declared using the array() construct as follows:

```
$compund_array =
  array('person' => array('name' => 'kalam', 'occupation' => 'president'),
        'dog' => array('name' => 'Lassie', 'occupation' => 'none'));
```

Objects

Objects are another compound type used in PHP. They are instances of classes that group properties and methods together. A simple class declaration looks like this:

```
class SimpleClass
{
  var $mReturn;
  function ShowReturn($str)
  {
    return $this->$mReturn;
  }
} // End class SimpleClass
```

In this example, variable $mReturn is of type object.

Special Types

PHP4 also provides two special types:

❑   Resources

❑   Null

Resources

Resources are created and handled by particular PHP functions, and hold a reference to some external resource (such as a database connection). In earlier versions of PHP, resources were primarily relevant because they sometimes had to be freed manually when no longer in use.

However, since PHP4, this is no longer an issue as there is a built-in garbage collector that takes care of these issues. The garbage collector may clear out the resource before the page is done executing if the resource is no longer needed. This issue is never a problem in a web-based development environment, but can be relevant when we are using something like PHP-GTK to write programs.

The exception to this is the case of persistent database connections that are left available for future use if employed.

A complete list of resource types is available at http://www.zend.com/manual/resource.php.

null

The case-insensitive `null` type represents a variable that has no value. Introduced with PHP4, this type has only one possible value, that is, `null`.

> *This is different than the value 0, `false`, or the empty string "". In each of these cases, there is a value in question. The value 0 is an integer, the value `false` is a Boolean, and "" is a string with length zero.*

A `null` means that the variable has no value whatsoever. Therefore, the following two snippets are checking for different things:

```
if ($value == FALSE) {
  // execute code
}

if ($value == NULL) {
  //execute code
}
```

The first `if` statement is checking to see if `$value` has the Boolean value `false`. The second is checking to see if `$value` has any value assigned at all.

Assigning Variables

Variables can be assigned by value or by reference.

Assigning Variables By Value

Typically, in PHP, new variables are assigned by value. Consider the following snippet:

```
$name = 'Jon';
$second_name = $name;
```

The variables $name and $second_name would both hold the value Jon. However, subsequently changing the value of $second_name would have no effect on $name. This means that it is possible to make many copies of a particular value that are essentially photocopies of each other. But once the copy is made, its value is entirely independent of the orginal variable's vaue – they are all the same, but they are distinct from each other.

Assigning Variables By Reference

Although the standard assignment mechanism in PHP assigns variables by value, it is possible to assign variables by reference using the & syntax as follows:

```
$name = 'Jon';
$second_name = &$name;
```

Essentially, assigning a value by reference creates a pointer to the data in question. Here, $second_name and $name are effectively synonyms for the same data. Changing the value of $name would change the value of $second_name and vice versa.

Variable Variables

A powerful but arguably underused aspect of PHP is the ability to assign variable variables. A variable variable takes the value of one variable, and uses that as the name for a new variable.

Let us examine the following snippet:

```
$name = 'krypton_kooker';
$$name = 'programmer';
```

Here, we create two separate variables. The first is $name which has the value krypton_kooker, while the second is a variable named $krypton_kooker with the value programmer.

This can give us some powerful options as a developer. However, it also gives us the ability to write code that is quite hard to follow. When we use these, it is best to include plenty of comments explaining precisely what is going on.

Constants

Constants can be either numbers or string literals. For example, 'rookie' is a string constant; '45' and '3.59' are numeric constants. Constants can be used in expressions either singularly or in combination with other constants, variables, or function calls returning strings or numbers, as appropriate. Constant identifiers can also be defined in a way similar to C, using the PHP define() function.

Below is an example code for defining a constant:

```
<?php

$rate = 12.5;        // This not truly a constant, since $rate can be changed

define("RATE", 12.5); // Now a constant called RATE has been defined
?>
```

Note that once a constant has been assigned, any attempt to change its value will result in an error. Also, by convention, constants are written using uppercase variables.

Operators

Expressions require operators and operands (parameters). PHP operations can be applied to numbers or strings. As would be expected, PHP has the basic mathematical operations of +, -, *, /, as well as modulus (%), increment (++), decrement (--), and string concatenation (.) operators. There is no exponent operator (**), but there is a pow(base, power) function. These, along with other operators, are discussed below.

String Operators

Two strings are concatenated by joining them into a single string. PHP has two string operators to do this:

❑ The concatenation operator which requires a left and right argument surrounding a period symbol

❑ The concatenating assignment operator which appends the argument on the right side to the argument on the left side

Here is an example:

```php
<?php

//using the concatenation operator
$avg = 39.4;
print "The avg is $avg<br />\n";    //note that <br /> is
                                    //HTML 4.01-compliant although <br> isn't

//using the concatenating assignment operator
$name = "rookie cat";
$msg  = "My name is ";
$msg .= $name;          //concatenates $msg to the end of the current value
                        //of $msg, and assigns the result,
                        //"My name is rookie cat", to $msg. This operation
                        //is the equivalent of: $msg = $msg.$name;
?>
```

Note that the example concatenates three values in the print statement, two of which are already strings. The value of $avg, which is a double, is converted into the string "39.4" during the string concatenation operation. Note that the data type of $avg does not change.

Arithmetic Operators

The four basic mathematical operations (+, -, *, /) are available, along with the % and post- and pre-increment (++) and decrement (--) operators.

The arithmetic operators are summarized in the table opposite:

Operator	Name	Usage	Meaning
+	Add	$A + $B	Add two operands
-	Subtract	$A - $B	Subtract a second operand from a first
*	Multiply	$A * $B	Multiply two operands
/	Divide	$A / $B	Divide a first operand by a second
%	Modulus	$A % $B	Returns the integer remainder when integer A is divided by integer B (the base)
++	post-increment	$A++	Add one to A after evaluating A in some expression
++	pre-increment	++$A	Add one to A before evaluating A in some expression
- -	post-decrement	$A- -	Subtract one from A after evaluating A in some expression
- -	pre-decrement	- -$A	Subtract one from A before evaluating A in some expression

The term operand in the table refers to any numeric value, expression, or variable.

Comparison Operators

PHP4 includes the standard arithmetic operators, as well as a new equality operator. The term operand in the table below refers to any logical value, expression, or variable (that is, TRUE or FALSE), unless otherwise noted:

Operator	Name	Usage	Meaning
==	Equal	$A == $B	Compares the value of two operands and evaluates to true if they are both true.
===	Identical	$A === $B	Compares the 'complete identity' of two operands. If they have the same value and are of the same data type (not just logical), the expression evaluates to true.
!=, <>	not equal	$A != $B $A <> $B	Compares two operands to see if their values are NOT equal. If so, then the expression is true.
<	less than	$A < $B	If A is less than B, then the expression is true.
>	Greater than	$A > $B	If A is greater than B, then the expression is true.

Table continued on following page

Operator	Name	Usage	Meaning
<=	less than or equal	$A <= $B	If A is less than or equal to B, then the expression is true.
>=	greater than or equal	$A >= $B	If A is greater than or equal to B, then the expression is true.
?	Ternary	($A)? $B : $C	If expression A evaluates to true, assign value B. Otherwise, assign value C.

Logical Operators

The standard logical operators are available:

Operator	Name	Usage	Meaning
!	Not	!$A	Negates a true/false value
&&, and	And	$A && $B	Checks for the truth of both operands
||, or	Or	$A || $B	Checks for the truth of at least one of two operands
Xor	Xor	$A xor $B	Checks for the truth of either one operand or the other; not both

Reference Operator

The reference operator (&) allows you to pass variables by reference, or to call functions dynamically through a variable. Passing a variable by reference to a function means that the function accesses the actual global variable instead of using a copy. For function-heavy code, this method reduces memory requirements.

One use of being able to call functions dynamically is for web applications in which we want a different set of menu options to appear for different users. Then we can dynamically decide which function needs to be called instead of having to hard code a function call. This can also make for hard-to-read and hard-to-maintain code if we're not careful. It's best used sparingly.

Passing Arguments To a Function By Reference

Here is an example that demonstrates passing arguments to a function by reference:

```php
<?php

function increment1($x)
{
    return ++$x;
}

function increment2(&$x)
```

```
    {
      return ++$x;
    }

    $i=10;
    print ("\$i = $i<br />");
    print ("increment1(\$i) =" . increment1($i) . "<br />");
    print ("\$i = $i<br />");
    print ("increment2(\$i) =" . increment2($i) . "<br />");
    print ("\$i = $i<br />");
    ?>
```

the output of which is:

```
$i = 10
increment1($i) =11
$i = 10
increment2($i) =11
$i = 11
```

> **To pass arguments to a function by reference, either the function definition or the function call can have the reference.**

Calling a Function By Reference

Here is an example that demonstrates calling a function dynamically (by reference):

```php
<?php
// Calling functions by reference
function Add($x,$y)
{
  $add = $x + $y;
  return $add;
}

function Subtract($x,$y)
{
  $sub = $x - $y;
  return $sub;
}

$func = "Add";
$val = $func(3.5, 4.4);    // Calls add()
print ("value is $val<br>\n");
?>
```

Bitwise Operators

These are operators that allow us to manipulate specific bits within integers. They look somewhat analogous to the logical operators we have already seen. In practice, these are rarely used in PHP programming, since they are typically more complicated to think about than other operators. The reward for this complication is that they are very fast.

If truly blinding speed is a requirement, then we should probably question whether or not PHP is the correct language for our application in the first place. A compiled language like C might suit our needs better.

The bitwise operators are summarized in the table below:

Operator	Name	Usage	Meaning
&	and	$A & $B	Compares bits from A and B that are in the same position. For each pair of bits (A_i, B_i) that are both 1 (on), the resulting bit in that position is also 1. Otherwise the resulting bit is 0.
|	or	$A | $B	Bit pairs where at least one bit is 1 cause the resulting bit to be 1.
~	not	~A	Bits that are 1 changed to zero in the result, and vice versa.
^	xor	$A ^ $B	Bit pairs must be either (1,0) or (0,1) to set the resulting bit to 1. Otherwise the resulting bit is 0.
<<	shift left	$A << $B	The bits of $A are shifted left by $B bits. The bits on the right that are shifted, are replaced by zero. Effectively, this operation multiplies integer value $A by 2 to the power of $B.
>>	shift right	$A >> $B	The bits of $A are shifted right by $B bits. The bits on the left that are shifted, are replaced by zero. Effectively, this operation divides integer value $A by 2 to the power of $B.

Assignment Operators

PHP has a full complement of assignment operators. The table below illustrates a few of them:

Operator	Name	Usage	Meaning
+=	plus equals	$A += $B	Equivalent to $A = $A + $B
-=	minus equals	$A -= $B	Equivalent to $A = $A - $B
/=	divide equals	$A /= $B	Equivalent to $A = $A / $B
*=	multiply equals	$A *= $B	Equivalent to $A = $A * $B
%=	mod equals	$A %= $B	Equivalent to $A = $A % $B
.=	concatenate equals	$A .= $B	Equivalent to $A = $A . $B

Miscellaneous Operators

Other operators in PHP that will come in handy in later examples are:

❑ Array operators: [ ]
For example, `$arr[0]` accesses the first element in array `$arr`.

❑ Variable variable operator: $$
Evaluates a string var's value and creates a new variable with that as the name. For example, if `$varname = "width"`, and `$$varname = 5`, then PHP creates a variable called `$width` and assigns it the value 5. This feature is handy for creating parsers, personalized menus, and other constructs.

❑ Execution operator: ` ` (two backticks)
For example, `$output = `ls - al`;` will attempt to execute the contents of the backticks as a shell command.

❑ Class instantiation operator: `new`
For example, `$tweety = new Bird("tweety", "yellow", "talks");` creates a new object `Bird`.

❑ Object member access operator: `->`
For example, `$tweety->height = "3 inches";`

❑ Error control operator: `@`
For example, `$state = @$cache[$key];` will not issue a notice if the index `$key` doesn't exist.

Operator Precedence

PHP expressions are typically evaluated from left to right, with operator precedence applied if necessary. Operator precedence is shown in the table below, from highest to lowest. All operators in a given row are of the same precedence, and evaluated in order from left to right, if two or more of them occur simultaneously in an expression:

Operator(s)	Notes
New	Instantiation of a new object
[ ]	Array index operator
!, ~, ++, --, (int), (double), (string), (array), (object), @	The operators in brackets are all type-casting operators. @ is the error-control operator
*, /, %	Multiply, divide, modulus
+, -	Add, subtract
<<, >>	Left shift, right shift

Table continued on following page

Operator(s)	Notes
<, <=, >, >=	Less than, less than or equal, greater than, greater than or equal
==, ! =, ===, ! ==	Equal, not equal, identical, not identical
&	Reference
^	Bitwise xor
|	Bitwise or
&&	Logical and
||	Logical or
? :	Ternary
=, +=, -=, *=, /=, .=, %=, &=, |=, ^=, ~=, <<=, >>=	Full set of assignment operators
print	Print function/statement
and	Logical and
xor	Logical xor
or	Logical or
.	String concatenation

> **The general rule of thumb, if you cannot remember the precedence rules, is to use parentheses around groups of operations. This always takes precedence over any other operators.**

Control Structures

A PHP program is a collection of statements. We can tell the program which statements to execute with the use of conditional control structures. We can also tell the program to perform a series of repetitive steps over and over based on some condition. We will look at both of these scenarios in this section. Before we start, we need just a moment to review code blocks.

A code block is a group of statements enclosed by opening and closing curly braces ({ }). PHP will execute the statements within the braces as one group. They are most often used in conjunction with control structures, because this allows executing a group of statements, possibly many times, based on some kind of test. We will see this in use right away.

Conditional Structures

Conditional structures such as if and switch allow different blocks of code to be executed depending on the circumstances at the time of the execution.

if

```
if (expression) {
 statement;
}
```

The if statement is the simplest conditional structure. This allows us to execute a certain piece of code based on a test. Here, expression must provide a Boolean value to the if statement.

Here is an example:

```
if ("Wrox"==$name) {
  print ("\$name equals $name\n");
  print ("All done!\n");
}
```

Here, two lines would be printed out if the variable $a held the value Wrox. However, we might want to be able to tell the program to do something different if the name was not Wrox. This is where the else structure comes into play:

```
if ("Wrox" == $name) {
  print ("\$name equals $name\n");
  print ("All done!\n");
}
else {
  print ("\$name is not Wrox\n");
  print ("All done!\n");
}
```

This gives us a fair amount of control. However, what happens if we want to check to see if the name is either Wrox or FriendsofEd, and act accordingly? There are several ways we could do this, here we can use the elseif control structure:

```
if ("Wrox" == $name) {
  print ("\$name equals $name\n");
  print ("All done!\n");
}
elseif ("FriendsofED== $name) {
  print ("\$name equals $name\n");
  print ("All done!\n");
}
else {
  print ("\$name is not Wrox or FriendsofED");
  print ("All done!\n");
}
```

We can include as many elseif statements as necessary in the if...elseif...else sequences. This lets us test for a variety of different things.

switch

There may be situations where we need to test some variable for a variety of different values; in this case we might be better served by using the **switch** control structure. Then the above example would look like this:

```
switch ($name) {

case "Wrox":
  print ("\$name equals Wrox\n");
  print ("All done!\n");
  break;

case "FriendsofEd":
  print ("\$name = FriendsofEd\n");
  print ("All done!\n");
  break;

default:
  print ("\$name is not Wrox or FriendsofED\n");
  print ("All done!\n)";
}
```

We may use as many `case` blocks as we like; just be sure to add `break` at the end of each one. Otherwise PHP will continue to cascade down each test until it finds either a `break` or a `default` block to execute. The default-block is a special one that will always execute if PHP makes it that far into the `switch` statement.

Note that we do not need to put multiple statements inside curly braces when using `switch`. PHP regards everything between a `case` and its corresponding `break`, or between `default` and end of the `switch` block (}), as a block, and will execute all the statements it finds.

Logically speaking, if...elseif...else structures and switch...case...default structures are identical. Anything we can accomplish with one, we should be able to do with the other. We should choose our structure based on what we are comfortable with, and what will produce the most legible code.

Loops

Loops allow a block of code to execute a given number of times, or until a certain condition is met. They are often used for tasks like accessing records from a database query, reading lines from a file, or traversing the elements of an array. There are four types of loop in PHP: `while`, do ... `while`, `for`, and `foreach`.

while

```
while (expression) {
  statement;
}
```

while can help us perform specific actions many times over, very easily. Again, expression must provide a Boolean to the while structure. Here is an example:

```php
$i = 1;
while ($i <= 10) {
  print ("\$i equals $i\n");
  $i++;
}
```

This will print out:

$i equals 1
$i equals 2
...
$i equals 10

Note that we had to increment the variable within the code block. Otherwise, we would have had an infinite loop situation. The variable $i would have kept the value 1, so the expression $i <= 10 would never have become false.

do...while

```php
do {
   statement;
} while (expression);
```

Closely related to while is the do...while structure. It works the same way, except that the Boolean expression is checked at the end of the loop iteration.

This means that with a do...while loop, we are always guaranteed that the statement will be executed at least once. The above example could be written using this structure, like so:

```php
$i = 1;
do {
  print ("\$i equals $i\n");
  $i++;
} while ($i < 10);
```

Note that the same potential problem with an infinite loop exists as described for the while loop.

for

```php
for (expression1; expression2; expression3) {
   statements;
}
```

Although while and do...while are very useful, the most common kind of loop used is the for loop. It is also the most complex control structure in PHP, though it behaves just like its counterparts in other languages.

When the loop iterates for the first time, `expression1` is evaluated unconditionally. At every iteration of the loop, `expression2` is evaluated as Boolean. If it returns `true` then the loop continues and the statement is executed. Of course, `statement` could be a group of statements nested in a code block. Finally, after the loop iterates each time, `expression3` is executed. The above example would look like this using a `for` loop:

```
for ($i = 1; $i <= 10; $i++) {
  print ("\$i equals $i\n");
}
```

foreach

```
foreach (array_expression as $value) statement;
foreach (array_expression as $key => $value) statement;
```

The special `foreach` operator is designed specifically to help us handle arrays in the simplest way possible. There are two syntaxes for the operator, the second being a minor (but useful) extension of the first:

❑ `foreach (array_expression as $value) statement;`
This syntax simply loops through all the values of the array, and puts the current one in the `$value` variable for use in the statement.

❑ `foreach (array_expression as $key => $value) statement;`
In this syntax, the array key is also put in the `$key` value. If the array has a string key in a particular slot, then that is used. Otherwise, the integer index is used.

A subtle but important note is that the `foreach` operator works on a copy of the `array_expression`, not the array itself. The internal array pointer is always set to the first element, so we do not need to use PHP's `reset()` function before putting the array into the operator.

Here is a simple example demonstrating the use of `foreach`:

```
$person['name'] = "Veliath Punter";
$person['height'] = "Six foot Five"
$person['genre'] = "Punk Rock";

foreach ($person as $key => $value) {
  print "$key is $value\n";            // this will output:
                                       // name is Veliath Punter
                                       // height is Six foot Five
                                       // genre is Punk Rock

}
```

Functions

PHP has a huge wealth of built-in functions that are a part of the language. A great deal of our time as a PHP programmer will be spent writing functions to handle various tasks.

User-Defined Functions

```
function FunctionName($arg_1, $arg_2, ..., $arg_n)
{
  statement1;
  statement2;
  ...
}
```

Any valid PHP code can be put into the code block, including other functions or classes (we will look at them in a moment). Also, any number of arguments can be used for $arg_1, $arg_2, and so on and these arguments can be any type the programmer wishes. However, PHP does not support **function overloading**.

> **Function overloading means that several functions have the same name, but will behave differently depending on the number or type of the arguments supplied to them. As mentioned, the workaround in PHP is to have the same function behave differently, depending on its argument list.**

Typically, the arguments are passed to the function by value once the function has been defined. This means that in the usual case, PHP is working on a copy of the variable that we give to the function:

```
$foo = 2;
function AddTwo($num)
{
  $num += 2;
}
AddTwo($foo);
```

In this snippet, running the AddTwo() function on $foo does nothing. The value of $foo is not changed. However, we may explicitly pass variables by reference using the reference syntax on the argument. Consider this:

```
$foo = 2;
function AddTwo($num)
{
  $num += 2;
}
AddTwo(&$foo);
```

Here, $foo will now have the value of 4, once AddTwo() has been run on it.

At this point, we have not arrived at a very good solution for implementing our AddTwo() function for two reasons:

❑ If the PHP configuration `allow_call_time_pass_reference` is set to `Off` in the `php.ini` file, this will generate an error message. Since this particular configuration grants a speed increase, it is common to find this setup.

❑ The programmer must remember to always pass the argument by reference, or else it won't work as expected. Fortunately, PHP has a way around this as well. If we employ the reference syntax when we define the function, PHP will always force the argument to be passed by reference regardless of whether or not the programmer remembers to do it.

With this in mind, we modify our snippet to:

```
$foo = 2;
function AddTwo(&$num)
{
    $num += 2;
}
AddTwo($foo);
```

Again, `$foo` has the value 4 as expected. But we don't have to pass the argument by reference anymore since we defined the function to always use a reference.

In all of the above examples, the variable `$num` is scoped locally to the function. This means that it will not interfere with a `$num` variable that has been defined globally and is used elsewhere. Also, `$num` can be used as an argument when defining other functions with no trouble.

A last but important issue regarding functions is the ability to define functions with **default variables** for their arguments. Assigning variables to constant values when defining the function does this. For example:

```
function PersonFunction($age , $name = "Jon Doe")
{
    // statements
}
```

Having done this, we can call the function with one or two arguments. If we leave the second one out, the function will simply assume that `$name` is `Jon Doe`. However, if we do supply the second argument then whatever we put in will override the default value.

The only thing to keep in mind is that PHP requires all arguments with default values to be stacked to the right of the argument list. The script will not execute otherwise.

Returning Values

Often, we will want to manipulate data that we give to a function and return our results. This is accomplished by the optional `return` keyword in PHP:

```
function DoubleNumber($num)
{
    return 2 * $num;
}
// will output 6
print (DoubleNumber(3));
```

We can return any of the primitive variable types, including arrays. Also, a function may be able to return more than one type of value, as in the following example:

```
function Divide($a, $b)
{
  if { (0 == $b)
    return FALSE;
  }
  return $a / b;
}
```

Here, the function will return the value of $a divided by $b (which will be an integer or a float), unless $b is zero. In that case, it will return the Boolean value, false. This makes PHP more flexible than strictly typed languages where functions can only return one type of value, and we have to declare that type when we define the function.

It is also possible to return a reference from a PHP function, but we must use the reference operator & when we define the function and assign its return value to a variable:

```
function &ReturnReference()
{
  return $ReferenceVar;
}
$SomeReference = &ReturnReference();
```

Variable Functions

In a way analogous to PHP's variable variables, we can create and use variable functions. This is accomplished by putting parentheses after a variable. When PHP sees this, it looks for a function with the appropriate name to execute:

```
function PrintHello()
{
  return "Hello!\n";
}

$FunctionVar = 'PrintHello';
print ($FunctionVar());    // prints Hello!
```

There is a very wide range of functionality that we can get out of user-defined functions in PHP. This is particularly powerful when used in conjunction with PHP's system of classes and objects, which we will cover in the section after next.

Object-Oriented Programming

Before we start with a technical definition of classes and objects, we should talk for a moment about a more basic issue, the difference between procedural and object-oriented programming (OOP).

Functional vs. OO Programs

The simple examples we have seen so far in this chapter are all procedural. That is to say, there was data, and we manipulated that data with various routines or functions. Sometimes these were functions provided by the language, and sometimes we had written them ourselves. In any case, the important thing to recognize is that the data held in the different variables we saw was not in any way connected or associated to the functions that acted on them. We start with some data, manipulate it in some way, do something with the results, and then the script ends. This is what the term **functional programming** means.

This is a perfectly reasonable top-level approach to writing programs. However, as programs get larger, we may find that it has some drawbacks. First, we may end up doing the same types of things over and over. Second, it is possible that we will have a great many functions and variables all over, and we will want to find a good way to help organize them. Finally, we may want to associate functions and the data they manipulate more closely. When this happens, we should code in an **OO** style.

So what makes OOP different from functional programming? When we code an application with functions, we create programs that are code-centric, applications that call function by function consecutively. The data is first sent as the input, the function does the actual transformation, and then it returns the corresponding output. OOP takes the opposite approach since it is data-centric.

Here is an illustration showing the two paradigms:

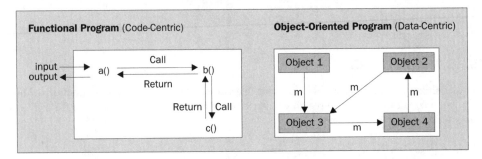

As we can see from the above diagram, input enters the function a(), which then calls the function b() using the output of a(). Function b() then calls c() using the output of b(). Then c() returns its output to b() which then returns its output to a(). Function a() finally produces the program output. Function a() would be the main function of a typical C program. In the object-oriented model, objects request the services of others, easily seen when Object 1 requests the service of Object 3. Object 3 in turn requests the service of Object 4 and so on, until Object 1 receives a reply from Object 3 of the end result, tracing backwards.

What's happening is that each object uses the services provided by the others within the program to receive information so it can do its own work, that is, make its own decisions based on asking other objects for information. The passing of these messages is the flow of the program in itself, the data and the methods or the functionality of the object are contained in one central location.

The difference between the two paradigms is that objects contain all the data and behavior that should exist together, while the data and functions are clearly separated in the functional paradigm. This makes OO code very easy to trace during maintenance and increases the modularity of the project.

Now, this doesn't mean that procedural programs aren't maintainable, because they can be. It just requires a lot more thinking and organization on the architect's part to ensure that everything is located in the proper location. Also ensuring there are no global variables being manipulated in many of the project files if any should exist. The best thing about OOP is that we just make the objects as they make sense, follow some guidelines, and things should be pretty organized. With more complex applications, the use of special patterns can strengthen the design of the systems so we can reap added benefits.

Objects and Classes

OO programs consist of objects. So unlike having functions act on primitives or data structures, objects provide the functionality and behavior for the application. For example, we can have a `Form` object that represents an HTML form on a web page. Inside this form we might have various buttons, text fields, and radio options, which are all modeled as objects as well. To define what these objects are, what they consist of, and what actions they can do, we use the concept of a **class** that defines all this criteria to PHP. To reiterate, a class provides the programmatic definition of the objects that we use in our applications in the same way that a `struct` defines a data structure in C. Let's first talk about classes in more detail.

A class defines a concept or idea that we want to use in the program. For instance, if we want to model the idea of keeping the user's session, we can maintain this information in a `Session` object (or sometimes it can be called `SessionManager`). Classes can model things that are tangible, like forms, sockets, and database connections, and things that are less intangible like proxies, handlers, or listeners. The most important concept is that the class represents a single idea. Usually, classes like `MyEntireProgram` and `TheWorldIsInsideOfMe` do not provide great functionality and should be avoided. This usually indicates the class is doing too many things and can probably be split up into several classes. A general rule is that classes should 'do one thing and do it well'.

Now that we know what classes should do, it's time to talk about what they really consist of. In order to be a class, it must consist of data (the object's members and components) and code (the functionality it provides) called **methods**. This means that a class that is missing one of these things is not really a class, but rather a group of functions or a data structure. If we do not pair the code and data that belong together, there is high probability that our class has been incorrectly defined. Now let's take a look at the components of a class.

For more information on class and object functions within PHP, check out http://www.php.net/manual/en/ref.classobj.php.

Members

These are elements, which we intend the class to contain. For instance, forms contain buttons, text fields, and combo boxes. These items would be considered members of the `Form` class. As with any class, the members might be intangible things like a `DataValidator` for client-server regular expression validation. The members can also be primitive data types like integers, floats, and strings. For instance, the form's `name` and the `action` can also be members of the `Form` class.

Methods

Methods provide the behavior we expect a particular object to perform. For instance, continuing with our current example, forms provide the ability to validate themselves, populate the fields with data from a data store such as a database, process the form to add it to a database or send an e-mail. These methods describe exactly what we intend the forms to do. We wouldn't expect a form to be able to drive a car or do our homework for instance. Although this might sound funny at first, it's true – many programmers simply put methods where they don't belong and this is something that should be avoided.

Constructor

A constructor is responsible for initializing the object's ready state. What this means is that if there is any member (objects or primitive types) that need to be initialized for the methods to work properly, this code usually goes into the class constructor. For instance, we can use the constructor to add all the form elements to the form and specify the regular expression constraints on each form item. One thing to note is that PHP's objects can only have one constructor. This is because PHP does not support a concept called **overloading**. Another thing to note is that it must not return a value.

Here is an example of a Form class. It's not a complete example because the intention is to identify and show the various concepts that we've just learned about:

```php
<?php

class Form
{
```

Here we define a class called Form. Everything within the curly braces is considered to be a method, member, or a constructor of the class. Notice that class name is capitalized. This is generally the style that is used throughout PHP classes to distinguish them from other items in the language; it has been adopted from Java:

```php
    var $name;
    var $elements;
```

Here we define several member variables that are objects or other primitive type variables that this class contains. The $name field stores the name of the form while the $elements member actually contains all the objects that get displayed on the form. It is generally considered good practice to add the members at the top of the class rather than anywhere else, just as in a functional program. This provides a good reference for maintenance later on:

```php
    function Form($name = "The Form")
    {
        $this->name = $name;
        $this->elements = array();
        // add the elements to the form
    }
```

Here is the class's constructor. To define the constructor properly, it must have the same name as the class itself. So the constructor's name is also Form. This is actually one reason why the class name has a capital letter; that makes it easier to distinguish the constructor from the other methods.

The form's name is assigned the value 'The Form' if one is not provided and the elements member was assigned an empty array. Later, we will look at adding objects to this array. The $this keyword is rather unique to OO programs. Think of $this as a variable that points to the object that we are currently writing. Therefore, when we say $this->name, we are referring to the Form object's name variable that we defined above.

The $this keyword allows PHP to distinguish between any local variables and variables (members) that are contained within the object. So the line $this->name = $name is assigning the value of the argument to the object's name member. Although in other languages the $this keyword is optional and is used to clear up naming conflicts and their associated delays, the PHP interpreter did not adopt this feature for increased speed. This might take a little while to get used to, but with practice and the motivation to avoid interpretation errors the usefulness of this syntax becomes apparent.

Here is an example:

```
function Validate()
{
  $boolean = TRUE;
  foreach ($this->elements as $element) {
    // check all the elements and set $boolean to false if
    // any errors occur
  }
  return $boolean;
}

function Process()
{
  // put the data in the elements into the database
}

function Populate()
{
  // populate the elements
}
} //End of class Form
?>
```

These are the object's functions, or rather the methods it provides. Note that these look exactly as they do in a procedural program except for that they are contained within the class { } block. This signifies that they belong to this class; if another part of the program needs to use these functions, they must go through the object first.

Instances

Now that we defined our Form class, we use the following code to define and create a variable that is of the type Form:

```
$form = new Form("My quick form");
```

Here we use the new operator to create a new Form object. When an object has been created using the new operator, it is said that the object has been **instantiated**. It can also be said that the object is called an **instance** of the Form class. A good analogy between instances and classes is that the blueprints and prototypes for a single car can be called a class while all the cars that are on the road that were built using that particular blueprint can be called instances.

Remember our discussion on constructors? That is what we are calling here, passing the name of the form so that the internal name member can be initialized. With PHP's loosely typed variable concept, we don't have to specify the object's type when we create an object. Constructors always allocate the memory for the object. This is actually done automatically, so once we write the constructor for an object that initializes the members, PHP will do this for us.

Calling Instance Methods

Since the object is created into the $form variable, we can freely use the methods provided by the object. For instance, we can call the Validate() method to validate the form using the following code:

```
if ($form->validate()) {
  print ("The form was validated successfully.");
}
```

In this example, we use the -> operator to call the Validate() method that belongs to the $form object. Notice that it takes no parameters. This is one of the benefits of object-oriented programs. Since each object knows and is associated with its member variables, it doesn't need to have any parameters. This serves several benefits. For one, the programmer using the object doesn't need to know how those elements were coded. The internal data is 'hidden' away from the programmer.

The second benefit is that the implementation could have used other objects to store the elements rather than an array. As far as the calling code knows, the object hasn't changed. This makes each object very abstract and provides a nice candy-like interface. It also improves the maintainability of the system. Lastly, this cleans up the code a lot as well. Since each call to the $form object doesn't need to supply rudimentary data every time a method is invoked, this makes our code much cleaner and simplifies our statements greatly.

How This Works

For those that are interested in the 'how', the interpreter actually adds some information before the code is executed. Within PHP, the engine keeps track of what methods belong to which class, but it doesn't actually tie the members to the object itself. Naturally, like any procedural language, it maintains a data structure that is also linked with the class name. Each time the method is invoked, the object's variable is automatically supplied to it. So in this case, the call is modified to:

```
if ($form->Validate($form)) {
  print ("The form was validated successfully.");
}
```

This passes the object back into itself so that the method can access the members of the object that are not declared as local variables. This enables each method to share the same members. So in the class code itself, the $form parameter actually gets transformed into the $this object. Here is the transformation:

```
function Validate($this)
{
  $boolean = TRUE;

  foreach ($this->elements as $element) {
    // check all the elements and set $boolean to false if
    // any errors occur
  }

  return $boolean;
}
```

Since the PHP engine automatically puts the $this variable as the first argument to the Validate() method, it is more easily seen why $this->elements actually exists and why it is done that way (passing the object back into itself). This also provides an explanation about how the object's members in the $this object do not collide with any local variables or function arguments. Remember that the $this parameter is done automatically – so we don't have to define this variable for our methods. In some languages like Python, we actually have to do this. PHP has made this easy for us so we can think of our object's members as being contained within the class definition rather than being closer to the implementation of the interpreter.

Inheritance

Now that the Form class has been defined, we need to define a class for the buttons, text fields, and other form controls that we would like to add to the form. Since PHP does not supply a type for this, we need to define our own class. These classes that we are about to look into have been taken from the eXtremePHP Form Framework (http://www.extremephp.org/). Since the Form Framework actually uses several classes (around 30), some of the classes have been combined and shortened for this example. Therefore, the example is meant to demonstrate OO code clearly rather than present the most refactored solution.

Now, one way to create text fields and submit buttons would be to create different classes that represent each form control and provide the necessary functionality for each one. Although this can work, it's not the best solution. When we think of HTML form controls, most people think of them as being very similar. Generally, the name of the tag and some of the attributes that are assigned represent the only difference between controls, but each control has a name, a value, might have a regular expression constraint, and can display or convert itself into HTML.

To express these commonalities among all form controls that need to be placed inside the Form object, we first make a FormControl class. Later, when we need a very specific control that puts a text field to the screen or creates a submit button, we can create classes called TextField and SubmitButton, which are called subclasses. These classes are said to **inherit** functionality from the FormControl class, meaning they have all the members and methods of that class. FormControl is also said to be the parent, base, or super class to the TextField and SubmitButton classes.

We can define a new subclass for each type of FormControl by only specifying specific information. Since TextField and other subclasses all extend from FormControl, they will possess all the existing functionality from the FormControl– which allows for software reuse. The way this works logically is this – if a TextField is a FormControl, then it should posses all the state and behavior of a FormControl. Notice that the converse is not necessarily true since a FormControl may not contain all the functionality and members of a TextField. This is because a TextField might have additional settings to adjust the field's width, which may not be available to all FormControl objects.

The ability to extend a class by subclassing is the core idea of OO programming. By creating trees of objects, we are able to reuse code, and later we'll see how this makes our programs more generic and easier to work with and maintain.

The Parent Class – FormControl

Here is the code for the `FormControl` class:

```php
<?php

// FormControl.class.php

define("NO_VALUE", md5("novalue"));
define("NEWLINE", "\n");
```

Here we provide several constants that are used by the other classes. The NO_VALUE constant is the value that is used to specify that a form control contains no value. Since `null` values are hard to maintain and keep state across HTML, a value that means nothing is sensible to use:

```php
class FormControl
{
  var $name;
  var $value;
```

Here we provide two member variables for the `name` and `value` of the form. The name provides the unique server-side name that is automatically added to the global variables array and is used when getting the value. The value will be contained within this variable if it is set:

```php
function FormControl($name, $value = NO_VALUE)
{
  $this->SetName($name);
  $this->SetValue($value);
}
```

Our constructor initializes the `FormControl` with a name and there is an optional parameter to specify the value. Usually when we create a new form and we do not wish to populate it with data, we want to provide just a name. In the case where we want the form control to be initialized to a value before it is displayed to the screen, we can use the second parameter `$value`. To initialize these values, we use the `setName()` and `setValue()` methods. These are referred to as **setter** methods and contain assignment code. In some cases, we might also want to have rules defined so that the data maintains its integrity:

```php
function setName($name)
{
  $this->name = $name;
}

function getName()
{
  return $this->name;
}
```

There is also the concept of a **getter** method that returns the value of a member that is in the object. In the above code, we define a setter and getter for the name member. This allows clients that use the object to be able to manipulate and get the object's name. Instead of saying getter and setter all the time, for a pair, we could say that these two methods are both **data accessor methods**:

```php
function SetValue($value)
{
  if ($value == NO_VALUE) {
    global ${$this->name};

    if (!isset(${$this->name})) ${$this->name} = '';
    $this->value = ${$this->name};
  } else {
    $this->value = $value;
  }
}

function GetValue()
{
  return $this->value;
}
```

As with the name member, there is also a getter and setter for the value member. The setValue() method is actually more complicated in that it must handle the special case of the NO_VALUE constant. If the NO_VALUE constant was passed into this function, we check to see if a variable already exists with the FormControl's name. If it does, we can automatically set the value of this form element to that variable. If not, we just make the element contain the empty string. This allows FormControl to maintain state as it was when submitted, and it can be very helpful when the form is not validated correctly. This saves the programmer a great deal of time checking the global values and setting them within the value attribute of the HTML code. This is now done automatically by the class:

```php
function SetConstraint(&$validator, $regex, $errorMessage)
{
  $validator->setConstraint($this->getName(), $regex,
                            $this->getValue(), $errorMessage );
}
```

The SetConstraint() method provides an easy way to add a regular expression check of this form control to an eXtremePHP DataValidator object, $validator. This component is much like the Matcher object in Java or .NET. For the simplicity of this example, we will assume that the $validator object has a method called SetConstraint() as well, and it contains the code to a list of constraints:

```php
function Validate()
{
  return $validator->Validate();
}
```

Once the constraints have been added, they may be also verified using a similar Validate() method:

```
// template method that calls abstract methods.
function ToHtml()
{
  return $this->GetHeaderHtml() . $this->getFooterHtml();
}

// abstract
function GetHeaderHtml() {}

// abstract
function GetFooterHtml() {}
```

The next set of functions provides the base mechanism for displaying the HTML for the `FormControl` component. `ToHtml()` is meant to receive the entire HTML document. In some cases, we might only want to view the header or footer of the HTML, so we can use `GetHeaderHtml()` or `GetFooterHtml()` respectively.

Even though these functions do not provide any functionality, this is actually where the meat of the class is. These methods were left blank intentionally so that they can be redefined in the subclasses of `FormControl`. For instance, a `TextField` has its own HTML that it would like to display as compared to a `SubmitButton`. By overriding these methods (as shown in the next class file), we can provide very specific functionality to each subclass of `FormControl`. We'll take a closer look at overriding methods later on in more detail.

The `ToHtml()` method is actually very powerful in that all subclasses will contain this method. Since every class that inherits `FormControl` will contain the `GetHeaderHtml()` and `GetFooterHtml()` methods, `ToHtml()` makes sure that every class won't need to bother with creating a duplicate `ToHtml()` method. This templates the header and footer methods and the implementer of the subclasses is expected to fill them in.

How do we know when we have to fill them in? Usually in a language that supports full object-orientation like Java, there is a concept called abstract methods that forces any subclasses to implement the methods before the class is compiled. Since the compiler tool will not successfully compile a class where the implementer didn't override the methods, it will be impossible to use this in a program. This is extremely helpful since objects are well-defined in this way and we can guarantee that all the methods in the parent class will work in the subclasses.

However, PHP does not contain this feature so it is up to the designer to indicate that these classes are indeed abstract. This is usually done with an empty body ({ }) for the method. A comment just above the method will also help clarify the intentions of the programmer:

```
function Display()
{
  print ($this->ToHtml());
}

function DisplayHeader()
{
  print ($this->GetHeaderHtml());
```

```
  }

  function DisplayFooter()
  {
    print ($this->GetFooterHtml());
  }
}
?>
```

The last methods simply make it a bit easier to display the HTML to the screen: they have been separated to make it easy to put the HTML into a string. This can be useful if we are to insert it into a database or an e-mail message. If we had tied the HTML generation to the `Display*()` methods, some applications may have been very difficult to write.

The Subclasses

The next file shows how to implement a new subclass, `TextField`, as a subclass of `FormControl`:

```php
<?php

// TextField.class.php

require_once './FormControl.class.php';

class TextField extends FormControl
{
```

Here, we use the `extends` keyword to tell PHP that the `TextField` class inherits from the `FormControl` class. As mentioned before, this means that all the members and methods from the `FormControl` class are now available to this class as well:

```php
function TextField($name, $value = NO_VALUE)
{
  FormControl::FormControl($name, $value);
}
```

Since all `FormControl` objects were expected to have a `name` and `value`, we can use the parent class's constructor to initialize the incoming members rather than rewriting the code again in this class. To do this, we use the class-method call operator to reference the parent function. This is achieved by calling the class name with two colons, followed by the method name we would like to call. Generally, it works like this:

```php
ClassName::MethodName();
```

So in our example, we use `FormControl` to replace `ClassName` and we use the same name for the `MethodName()` because we'd like to call the constructor. By repassing the arguments to the parent method, we can be assured that the `name` and `value` members will be set to this object when it is instantiated. This is a huge benefit to programmers because as long as we know the parent class is bug-free, we can be assured that any subclasses will be dealing with error-free code. Thus, this can save a great deal of time when debugging applications:

```
function GetHeaderHtml()
{
  return '<input type="text" ' .
       'name="' . $this->name . '" ' .
       'value="' . $this->value . '">';
}

function GetFooterHtml()
{
  return '</input>' . NEWLINE;
}
}
?>
```

Remember those two abstract methods `GetFooterhtml()` and `GetHeaderhtml()`? Well, it's our job to implement the code for those in the `TextField` class. In this case, we simply return the `<input>` tag to create a text field in the browser using HTML. Notice the use of `$this->name` and `$this->value`. These fields have been inherited from the `FormControl` superclass, and as such, they are available to use in our code above. As mentioned before, we need not redefine the `ToHtml()` method because it has been made to call these overridden methods automatically.

More on Overriding Methods

So how does the parser know which method to call – the one in the superclass or the subclass? Whenever a subclass defines a method that has been previously defined in its parent, it is overriding its behavior. Now, in the previous case, there was no behavior provided by the superclass because the method was blank. In other examples, however, there are times when we may want to override a method that does have an implementation because its current implementation does not suit the more specific object. Consider three classes where `Baby` is a subtype of `Parent` and `Parent` is a subtype of `GrandParent`, and take this code for example:

```
$babyObject = new Baby("");
$babyObject->SayHello();
```

When an instance of the `Baby` subtype is created and the `SaHello()` method is called, the PHP interpreter will first look to see if the method is defined in `$babyObject` class. If it is, it will execute the code within that method. In this case, if the `SayHello()` method overrides the one in a superclass, the PHP interpreter skips the superclass entirely.

If no method is defined by `SayHello()` within the `Baby()` interface, PHP will then go to the `Parent` class of `$babyObject` and will attempt to execute the same method using the parent's implementation. If this method is defined in the `Parent` class, PHP will begin executing its code and PHP will commence as normal. If in turn the method wasn't found in the `Parent` class, PHP will search the parent class of each current class until there are no parent classes left. At this time PHP will display an error message saying the following:

Fatal error: Call to undefined function: SayHello() in
/websites/babytest.php on line X

The Remaining Subclasses – SubmitButton and HiddenField

As we make more `FormControl` objects, we can appreciate how fast it can be to develop various form components. For demonstration purposes, the next two files will be the `SubmitButton` class and the `HiddenField` class which we will use in the following example. Here is the `SubmitButton` class code:

```php
<?php

// SubmitButton.class.php

require_once './FormControl.class.php';

class SubmitButton extends FormControl
{

  function SubmitButton($value)
  {
    FormControl::FormControl('submit', $value);
  }

  function GetHeaderHtml()
  {
    return '<input type="submit" ' .
        'name="' . $this->name . '" ' .
        'value="' . $this->value . '">';
  }

  function GetFooterHtml()
  {
    return '</input>' . NEWLINE;
  }
}
?>
```

Similarly, the code for the `HiddenField` class that models a hidden value for HTML forms can be written like this:

```php
<?php

// HiddenField.class.php

require_once './FormControl.class.php';

class HiddenField extends FormControl
{
  function HiddenField($name, $value = NO_VALUE)
  {
    FormControl::FormControl($name, $value);
  }

  function GetHeaderHtml()
```

```
  {
    return '<input type="hidden" ' .
         'name="' . $this->name . '" ' .
         'value="' . $this->value . '">';
  }

  function GetFooterHtml()
  {
    return '</input>' . NEWLINE;
  }
}
?>
```

Creating the Form Class

Now that we have created various form controls to be placed onto our Form class, let's take another look how we might build it:

```
<?php

// Form.class.php

require_once './TextField.class.php';
require_once './HiddenField.class.php';
require_once './SubmitButton.class.php';
require_once './Vector.class.php';
```

To use the classes we developed earlier, we need to include them in the main Form class. The Vector class is a utility class that was taken right out of the eXtremePHP library. It operates in 90% of the way Vector objects behave in Java. For those who haven't used Java, a Vector is basically a scalable array. We don't have to worry about indexes and boundaries as the object takes care of all of this information for us. In fact, we won't even realize that it's an array and we'll think of it as a List of objects.

A Vector provides a very consistent way to iterate over the data contained within the array. Called an Iterator, it is analogous to Java Enumeration or C++'s Iterator. This allows us to traverse all the items within the Vector. If we decide to change the Vector into another class that supports Iterator objects, we won't actually have to change any of the traversal code because it supports the same interface. This is very powerful since program maintenance is reduced.

We now define two Vector objects that we will use in our Form. One Vector object, $formControls, will store a list of form controls that we developed earlier. Since PHP variables are loosely typed, it is actually possible to have the first position of the Vector contain a TextField object while the second position contains a SubmitButton object, and so on. This is very useful as we can group all these objects together in a generic fashion:

```
class Form
{
  var $formControls;
  var $parameters;
```

The $parameters Vector will store the name/value pairs for this Form. In this case, we also could have used a Dictionary object or even a HashMap, which resembles an associative array, but again for demonstration purposes this will suffice:

```
function Form($name, $action, $method = "post")
{
  $this->formControls = new Vector();
  $this->parameters   = new Vector();

  $this->SetParameter('name', $name);
  $this->SetParameter('action', $action);
  $this->SetParameter('method', $method);
}
```

Our constructor takes in the name of the form, the PHP page which will process the form when it is submitted, and a $method parameter that can either be POST or GET. This is the same information that would be supplied on an HTML <form> tag. Since the constructor is responsible for putting the object into an unwavering state, we must create new instances of the Vector objects that we defined above. We can use the SetParameter() instance method to set up all the properties that were passed into the constructor.

We now define the data accessor methods GetParameter() and SetParameters() for the <form> tag. In both cases $name and $value are strings. Vector objects have a Set() method where they can not only add a new item to the list, but also set it at a defined index. In this case, we use $name for the index and place the contents of $value at this position. Later we can use the get() method on the $parameters Vector object to retrieve the value at this position as well:

```
function SetParameter($name, $value)
{
  $this->parameters->Set($name, $value);
}

function GetParameter($name)
{
  return $this->parameters->Get($name);
}
```

To make the interface simpler for someone who would like to define several other parameters other than the ones defined in the constructor, there is a SetParameters() method that is intended to take in an associative array and then add each name/value pair within the array to the parameter list:

```
function SetParameters(&$parameters)
{
  foreach ($parameters as $name => $value) {
    $this->SetParameter($name, $value);
  }
}
```

To complete the functionality of parameters, we have a method that easily constructs the HTML code for the parameter list that is meant to be appended to the beginning of an HTML element. Every Vector object has ToArray() that converts its contents back into an associative array. This is helpful when we need to retrieve both the indexes (the parameter names) and the values:

```
function ConstructParameterHtml()
{
  $parameterString = '';

  foreach ($this->parameters->ToArray() as $name => $value) {
    $parameterString .= ' ' . $name . '="' .
              $value . '"';
  }

  return $parameterString;
}
```

After traversing the entire list, we should end up with a string like this "name1=value1", "name2=value2", and so on. Generally, besides the `toArray()` call, there is nothing very interesting here.

Finally we define an `Add()` method so we can add controls to the form. The argument `$control` expects any instance of the `FormControl` class. Because we can take any instance, we don't have to say `AddTextField()` or `AddSubmitButton()` like in a procedural program. We can simply instantiate the class and then pass it into the `Add()` method:

```
function Add($control)
{
  if (get_class($control) == 'submitbutton') {
    $submitName = $this->GetParameter('name') . ucfirst($control->getName());

    $this->Add(new HiddenField( $submitName, $control->GetValue()));
  }

  $this->formControls->Add( $control );
}
```

So what if we really do want to know the type of an object? Well, PHP has a function called `get_class()` that takes in any object and the function will return a string containing the class name. Since all class and function names are case-insensitive, the function will return the entire string in lowercase letters.

In the eXtremePHP framework, there is a special check to see if a `SubmitButton` instance is being passed to the function, so we can use the `get_class()` function to check the instance type of the object dynamically and add a hidden field with the same name with a capital first letter to the form when this happens. Although for our example we don't really use the hidden field for anything, the eXtremePHP framework requires a field to be defined to do some fancy tricks and to generally make programming forms much easier and more reusable.

The lesson learned here is that we can check the types of objects in our code and execute extra code for various conditions:

```
function GetHeaderHtml()
{
  return $this->GetTagHeader('form') . NEWLINE;
}

function GetFooterHtml()
{
  return $this->GetTagFooter('form') . NEWLINE;
}

function GetTagHeader($tagName)
{
  return "<$tagName" . $this->ConstructParameterHtml() . '>';
}

function GetTagFooter($tagName)
{
  return "</$tagName>";
}
```

As with the FormControl, the Form object itself can also get the header and footer HTML. We use some helper methods to generate the HTML more easily. Notice that the getTagHeader() method uses the ConstructParameterHtml() method defined earlier. This method places the string containing the generated attributes right after the tag name. In this case, our form options defined in the constructor will be placed after the <form> tag as they should be:

```
function GetContainedTagsHtml()
{
  $html = '';

  for ($i = $this->CreateIterator(); !$i->isDone(); $i->next()) {
    $control = $iterator->GetCurrent();
    $html .= $control->ToHtml();
  }

  return $html;
}
```

Since Form objects can contain other FormControl objects, it is also required that we generate the entire HTML for each control. The result needs to go in between the <form> and </form> tags. The general strategy here is to create an Iterator on the $formControls member variable (remember, it's a Vector object), and we can traverse all the Form elements as they were added to the Vector. The call to:

```
$html .= $control->ToHtml();
```

is actually very interesting. The ToHtml() method returns the HTML markup for the TextField or the SubmitButton class. Remember that the Vector object can contain a whole bunch of different FormControl instances. PHP is actually smart enough to call the correct code for each of these controls, regardless of what it is. So when a TextField object is the next object in the iteration, the PHP interpreter will execute the GetHeaderHtml() and GetFooterHtml() of the TextField class.

This method calling on a group of similar objects is called **polymorphism**. Regardless of what the object is, since PHP knows all FormControl instances have a ToHtml() method, it will execute the proper code for each control, relieving the programmer from having to decide which method to call. This greatly improves the maintainability of the application since if any new FormControl objects are added, we will not need to modify much of our current code.

How Polymorphism Works

Since the code doesn't specify which code to execute, how does PHP know which method to call? To answer this question, let's look how we might do something like this in a procedural program:

```
if ($control->type == TEXT_FIELD) {
  DisplayTextField($control);
} elseif() {
  DisplaySubmitButton($control);
  ...
}
```

As with most procedural programs, we define data structures for complicated types. In this case $control is a record containing the name, value, and so on, of the form control. By testing its type against various constants, we can determine which method to call to draw the correct component. So if it's a text field, it should call DisplayTextField(). Likewise, if it's a submit button, the code should execute DisplaySubmitButton() and so on. So where is this code in our OO program?

This is what makes OO programs very different procedural ones. Recall that all FormControl objects contain a ToHtml() method and that any subclass of FormControl will also contain this method. So when we iterate through the Vector and call the ToHtml() method on each FormControl, we are guaranteed that each control can deliver this method and return the appropriate HTML for the form control. So how does PHP know which one to call? Let's assume the Vector contains the following values:

```
["formControls"]=> &object(vector)(2) {
  ["collection"]=> array(4) {
    [0]=> object(textfield)(3) {
      ["name"]=> string(4) "name"
      ["value"]=> string(3) "Hey"
    }
    [1]=> object(textfield)(3) {
      ["name"]=> string(5) "stuff"
      ["value"]=> string(3) "You"
    }
    [2]=> object(hiddenfield)(3) {
      ["name"]=> string(12) "Submit"
      ["value"]=> string(6) "submit"
    }
    [3]=> object(submitbutton)(3) {
      ["name"]=> string(6) "submit"
      ["value"]=> string(6) "submit"
    }
  }
  ["size"]=> int(4)
```

Upon the first iteration of the Vector, the call to $i->GetCurrent(); will return the TextField object at index 0. Once a call to ToHtml() has been made, the PHP interpreter finds that a ToHtml() method is found in the base class, FormControl (as explained in the section about overriding methods). Let's take a look at the code for the ToHtml() method once more:

```
function ToHtml()
{
   return $this->GetHeaderHtml() . $this->GetFooterHtml();
}
```

As PHP executes this code, it comes across $this->GetHeaderHtml() first and decides that it has to execute this code. So what is $this really referring to? In this case, $this is still an instance of the TextField class, even though we are currently executing code from the FormControl class. So now that it has to call GetHeaderHtml() from the current TextField object, it checks to see if the method exists. As we already know, it does perform this check and the function returns the <input> HTML code for the text field. The same process happens for the GetFooterHtml() as well and both results are concatenated together and the result is returned to the caller.

Back To the Form Class

Now that we have all three HTML methods defined, we can create the Form class's ToHtml() method as shown below:

```
function ToHtml()
{
   return $this->GetHeaderHtml() .
          $this->GetContainedTagsHtml() .
          $this->GetFooterHtml();
}
```

As with the form controls, the Form needs to be able to display itself. So we defined a Display() method for this purpose:

```
function Display()
{
   print ($this->ToHtml());
}
}
```

Using the Form

In this application, we are going to create a form with two text fields and a submit button. When the form is submitted, the application will simply type out the contents of the two boxes to the screen. Now that all our classes have been written, we can start to build an application at the problem-domain level. This generally means that we can work with objects that make sense to the problem. This is much like building structures with Lego blocks. Generally, this turns out to be really simple, so let's look at the code:

```
$form = new Form("MyForm", $_SERVER["PHP_SELF"]);
$form->Add(new TextField('name'));
$form->Add(new TextField('stuff'));
$form->Add(new SubmitButton('submit'));
$form->Display();
```

Here we create a new instance of the Form object. We give it any random name and use PHP_SELF to tell PHP to use this script to process the form when it has been submitted. At this time, all the internal vectors are initialized so the object's services are ready to be used. So in this case, we add several form controls using the Add() method of the $form object. By creating new instances and passing them to Add(), we are placing the controls onto the form. Lastly, we can invoke the Display() method which displays the generated HTML to the screen. Simple enough:

```
if (isset($_REQUEST['submit'])) {
  print ("You have typed in '" . $_REQUEST['name'] .
      "' into the first box and ");
  print ("'" . $_REQUEST['stuff'] . "' into the second box");
}
?>
```

Assuming the form has been submitted with the words 'Jon Doe' and 'Some Stuff', the display of the application would look like this:

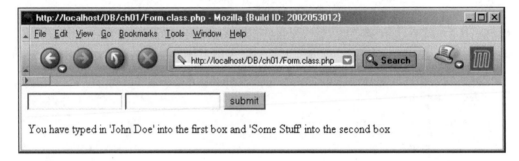

In this section, we have learned the essential concepts to programming OO code using PHP. Although there are many more concepts we need to learn, this should provide us with a good footing to start with as well as utilize OO capabilities within our applications.

Summary

This chapter has been a brief refresher on the PHP language.

First we looked at the basic PHP syntax. Then we saw how we can create variables and skirted through the different types. Later we considered constants. We also looked at the most commonly used operators.

Then we turned our attention to the structures that form the building block of any successful application:

❑ The conditional statements if and switch are used to test a condition and execute different blocks of code depending on the results.

❑ The loops while, do...while, for, and foreach allow repetitive behavior. The foreach loop is specifically designed for traversing the elements of an array.

❑ Functions are reusable units of code that can be invoked as necessary to perform specific tasks. They make code more modular and maintainable.

Then we looked at OOP that is essential for PHP to survive as the web platform of tomorrow. We talked about how it differs from procedural programming and discussed its benefits – increased reusability and maintainability. We learned that objects contain methods, members, and a constructor and that they become instantiated in our program with PHP's operators.

The aspects of OOP that PHP supports make it possible to create large and complex applications in a full OOP framework. It is interesting to note that some of the most popular PHP-based libraries out there, such as PHPLib and PEAR, are implemented as OOP classes.

There is an enormous amount of functionality built into the APIs that are available. In particular, it is always a good idea to read through the references for string manipulation functions, array manipulation functions, regular expressions, and file or directory access functions.

For a detailed treatment of the basics of PHP programming, refer to *Beginning PHP4* (*ISBN 1-861003-73-0*) and *Professional PHP4* (*ISBN 1-861006-91-8*) from *Wrox Press*. The most up-to-date information is always available on the official PHP web site at http://www.php.net/.

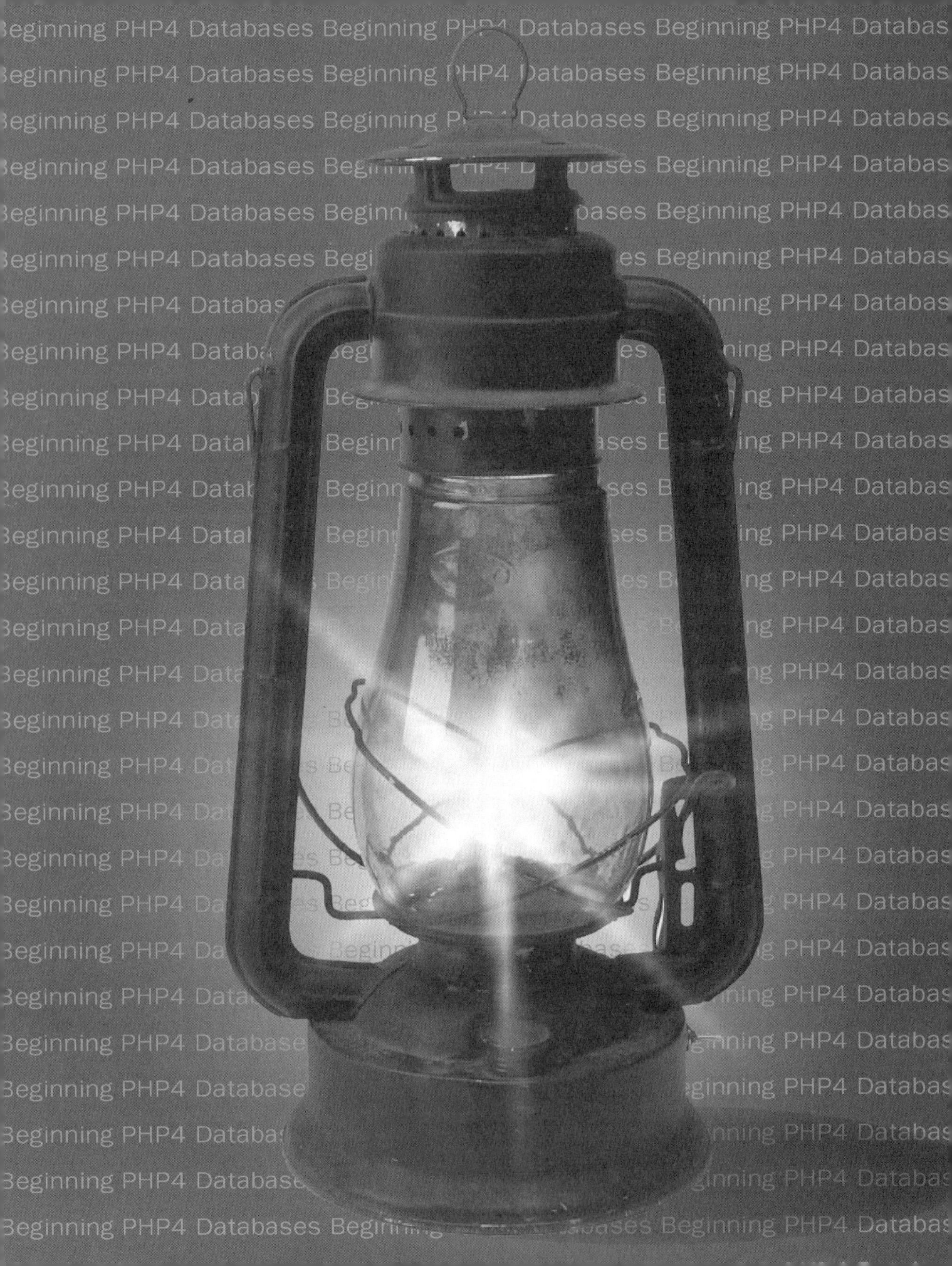
Beginning PHP4 Databases

Database Fundamentals

So far you've seen a refresher on PHP programming, with an emphasis on object-oriented programming. This chapter will depart from straight PHP for a moment, and focus on something you will be using in your web applications – Database Management Systems.

This chapter will briefly cover:

❑ What a database is

❑ Why databases are useful in PHP application development

❑ Details on several database systems in use today and their impact on PHP

❑ Connection methods specific to different database systems

❑ Database abstraction in PHP

❑ An introduction to `PEAR::DB`, a unified API for accessing SQL databases

The purpose of this chapter is to help you make informed decisions on which database to use for a project. Also, it should provide an understanding of database systems that you would be able to put to use in the subsequent chapters.

What is a Database?

Let's begin with a simple definition of a database. A database is an organized collection of interrelated and persistent information. This means that every structured collection of stored data, from the simple list of your friends' phone numbers to the paperwork maintained by the local public library, may be considered a database. In this chapter, we will cover databases, as recognized by computer-based systems.

Databases are structured collections of various records and their relationships with other structured collections. Each record has several attributes associated with it. These are called **fields**, and can be used to store and retrieve rich and meaningful information. In short, a field defines a record, and an instance of a record in a database is called a **row**.

An example of a simple database might be a list of tasks. A task database could be a sheet of paper with your important assignments for the week, with each task comprising a structured record represented as a row, and the details of each task comprising fields for that row, as shown in the example `Task List` database below:

Task	Details	Assigned By	Due By
Grocery Shopping	Buy Food	Andrew	Friday
Birthday Shopping	Buy Flowers	Andrew	Wednesday
Car Maintenance	Change Oil	Susan	Saturday

Where do Databases Fit in?

For our purposes, we can think of databases as working with applications. A software application can typically be broken down into different parts, from a graphical skin called the presentation layer, which acts as an interface between input and output mechanisms, to application logic for processing information. Complementing this breakdown, a database allows both the application and the users of the application to store persistent information that will be created, shared, and changed in the course of the application.

What is a DBMS?

The term DBMS (Database Management System) covers not only the collection of information, but the server application used to store, query, and process the information, called the database engine, as well as the underlying disks to store the data. The term database server is often used to include the DBMS with the server hardware and operating system optimized to run the Database Management System.

Why Use a Database?

Let's discuss the real-world need for databases in web applications. We hear about complex ways to store, change, and retrieve information. The biggest argument for structuring data in some fashion beyond a simple list is the sheer amount of information that exists in the world today. It is estimated that the Internet doubles in size every year, and with it the amount of corporate and individual information persisted and stored in web pages.

Imagine that our `Task List` had an additional field, `Assigned To` as shown in the table below:

Task	Details	Assigned By	Assigned To	Due By
Grocery Shopping	Buy Food	Andrew	Sean	Friday
Birthday Shopping	Buy Flowers	Andrew	Andrew	Wednesday
Car Maintenance	Change Oil	Susan	Andrew	Saturday

This adds just a bit more complexity, but what if this list were for 100 people? It would quickly become unmanageable due to the amount of work required to add and delete items in our list, the amount of time required to find a single record would skyrocket, and errors might be introduced when changing items singularly. Other maintenance and data consistency issues exist too, such as limiting redundant information. Also, think about the unchecked access that could occur using files which are simple documents. What could happen when two people try to change the same data at the same time? How can this data be searched quickly without reading through the whole file? How can data items be interrelated within the file? As you can begin to imagine, data storage in a document-centric way quickly becomes unmanageable.

Secondly, databases play a vital role in web-based applications, as they lend themselves to storing information and enabling separation of the presentation layer from the content, thus reducing dependencies between them.

Publishing data on a web page using PHP will be explored thoroughly in this book. To understand the importance of this, consider the amount of work that would be required to maintain both the HTML formatting and the text content in a single web page, especially where the text needs to change frequently. If we published our task list to the web without a database, changes anywhere would require editing the web page. A quick look at http://www.google.com shows they search over 2 billion web pages. Even assuming that Google finds all possible pages, it's quickly clear that hand editing of web content is extremely costly, and hardly feasible.

For quite some time, many large companies didn't understand this fact and literally had rooms full of service personnel dedicated to editing and updating web pages. Many of these companies might have done a lot better if they had substituted one well written database application in PHP for 100 full time HTML jockeys creating markup for static content.

OLAP vs. OLTP

You will often hear databases classified in one of two categories: **OLAP (On Line Analytical Processing)** and **OLTP (On Line Transactional Processing)**. While some databases can serve as both, specific vendor offerings are often better at one or the other, as will be seen later in the chapter.

OLAP databases can be thought of as persistent stores of information where the data is seldom changed, but is kept around for the purpose of decision making and information retrieval. An example of an OLAP database is a set of financial records for a company; this information should not be changed after it is entered, but it might be very useful to look up revenue trends, calculate profits or losses based on the financial history, or assist in decisions about what a customer base is like based on past sales records. OLAP databases allow grouping of the data by a subject and time, for instance by asking "what if" or "why" questions.

OLTP, on the other hand, is more focused on processes, and is therefore, a dynamic store of information that often emphasizes more real-time data, and answers more "what" questions, providing a snapshot of the current state of the data. To this end, OLTP data is typically structured in a fashion to allow adding records as well as updating and deleting. Our little Task List works as an OLTP example, as we can look at the pending tasks for the week, remove tasks as they are completed if we wish, and add additional tasks as they are assigned.

Database Models

Let's step back a little and discuss database types with emphasis on how information is structured. As mentioned earlier, a simple list is a database just as much as a terabyte-sized enterprise financial repository. While many data requirements can be solved with a simple text file, we saw earlier where text files may fall short. This section will briefly describe the different database models that have developed over the years, including coverage from ordinary flat files to the most current inflection of Native XML Databases. The term **model** here refers to how the database system structures a record. This includes structuring how records are stored as well as how they are retrieved.

> *DBMS that adhere to different models are often abbreviated with those model names:RDBMS – Relational Database Management System and ODBMS (or OODBMS) – Object Oriented Database Management System.*

Hierarchical Database Model

Hierarchical databases were one of the first codified structures due to their simplicity and are still in use today, as file systems for example.

A hierarchical database is also known as a **tree**, with relationships between records thought of as **parent** and **children**. Parent and child records are tied together with pointers, which can be within records or in the file system. If the characterizations of data are known, for example where individual items are stored based on the pointers, a hierarchical database can actually be exceptionally good in terms of performance. The diagram below shows a hierarchical database:

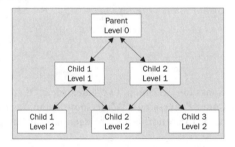

This appears more familiar when we consider that graphically browsing our desktop computer file system typically shows files in a hierarchical view.

Taking our Task List example, a hierarchical model could be shown as below:

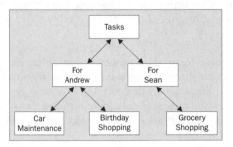

This begins to get cumbersome, both for maintaining and for scanning extensive data. In addition, redundant data may easily creep in. Now, let's modify our flat list of task items so `Andrew` and `Sean` both have a task with the same name:

Task	Details	Assigned By	Assigned To	Due By
Grocery Shopping	Buy Food	Andrew	Sean	Friday
Birthday Shopping	Buy Flowers	Andrew	Andrew	Wednesday
Car Maintenance	Change Oil	Susan	Andrew	Saturday
Car Maintenance	Change Oil	Bob	Sean	Monday

The diagram reflecting this modification is as follows:

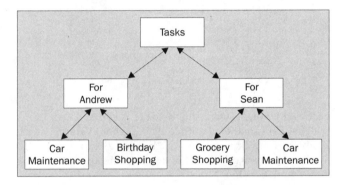

Here both `Andrew` and `Sean` have a `Car Maintenance` item. But since it is stored in two different places within the model, to cater to several people and several tasks, the data starts to become increasingly redundant, which leads to issues in cleanly changing data as well as efficiency problems in speed and storage. Since hierarchical databases existed in the days of tape storage, the files instantiating this model were serialized (converted to binary data) and stored on tape.

You can imagine that it became difficult to quickly find single items and control errors when searching for data required reading all the records on the tape in a single pass. Lastly, this model impedes updating records, as the updater needs to know the full set of records and pointers to reach a specific record for updating.

This might not appear terribly problematic but, as records and pointers change, the path to discrete records also changes. As a result, the actual methods used to update records, with regards to the path, constantly changes and needs to be be managed. Data changes were even more problematic in the days of tape storage as well. Imagine making multiple changes to data where each change requires reading the serialized databases from one tape to another, and changing a couple of items.

As an aside, the advent of XML has returned many database developers to thinking about hierarchial models, as XML is essentially hierarchical. This is one reason we are now seeing many of the enterprise database companies implementing XQuery in their products, as it is a hierarchical traversal mechanism to allow for searches in this model.

Network Database Model

Advances in information storage began to limit dependence on tape, as what we know of as disks began to emerge. Instead of sequential access required by tape, technologists now had the bonus of random access to specific disk locations. With this distributed storage benefit came additional considerations on data access. Developed as a similar model to the hierarchical model, the network model allowed a more multi-relationship view of the data, in that children could have multiple parent items and parent items could have multiple children.

Let's consider another example using our Task List:

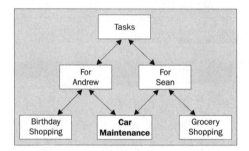

This diagram captures the additional relationship between Sean and Car Maintenance nicely. In addition, changing a single item can affect multiple records. For example, altering the Car Maintenance details above, from Change Oil to Change Oil and Wash Car, affects both Sean and Andrew. While fine in theory, a network model of any size effectively becomes a convoluted web with pointers mapping out every relationship.

The network model adds to the difficulty in traversing the tree to find a single record, which increases the costs of finding data and makes the model less efficient. Also, as the relationships and the items are always changing, there is an additional maintenance penalty to maintain data stored in this model. It doesn't get away from the problems of the hierarchical model completely, although the network model does allow for handling more complex relationships than the hierarchical model.

Relational Database Model

While the hierarchical and the related network models still have application and indeed are in use, OLAP (querying large amounts of data) and OLTP (quickly inserting, updating, and deleting data) functions cannot be easily carried out with those models. In 1970, a researcher at IBM named E.F. Codd published the first papers on relational database management. Codd developed his theories based on simple and powerful mathematical models. Like many successful technologies, the relational model succeeded because it was standards-based, in this case according to the standards of algebra and logic.

The relational model differs from the previous two models in several ways. Perhaps most importantly, the concept of a relation was introduced in this model. This codifies our previous examples of records in that records and their component fields are now grouped together into a relation, also called a table. This obviates the need for pointers by structuring data more logically, and in fact, the relational model does not account for the relationship of records and tables to each other.

Additionally, the relational model allows for a single set of records to be split across multiple tables, which is another departure from the earlier models where all of the records typically comprised a single logical structure.

Lastly, while the hierarchical and network models require records to be extracted by sequentially reading through the database or following a tree to arrive at a data element, the relational model only requires you to know the table name and makes comparisons on a piece of data you might know. With only a table name and these comparisons, discrete questions could be asked that return records, for example:

```
Show all the records where the records are greater than [something]
```

Simply put, the structure of the relational model has uniquely named tables comprised of records in horizontal rows and fields in vertical columns. While this is the standard terminology, you may also hear tables, rows, and fields referred to as relations, tuples, and attributes respectively. In addition, collections of tables can be referred as catalogs; a relational database can have one or many catalogs.

The diagram below illustrates the structural division of the relational model, with records (or rows) inside tables, tables inside catalogs, and catalogs inside a database:

Accessing records in tables for updates, inserts, and deletes is undertaken by asking discrete questions about the possible data in a table using a language called **SQL (Structured Query Language)**.

Conceptually, SQL satisfies all the needs not met by the access mechanisms in the hierarchical and network model. SQL is powerful, simple-to-use, and also very efficient. Additional coverage of the SQL commands used to manipulate database structure and data according to the relational model will be given later in the book. Chapter 3 will first cover how to design your tables to ensure the data stored in them is consistent, efficient, and minimizes redundancy. Chapters 4 and 5 will introduce you to SQL in depth, with Chapter 4 covering the SQL commands used to manipulate the structure of databases, and Chapter 5 introducing you to the manipulation of data.

For the purposes of this chapter, however, it's important to note that SQL combined with the relational model allows a different approach to records in a database. Unlike the hierarchical or network models, and to some extent the object and XML models that will be discussed later, SQL allows manipulation of data in a relational database against multiple records at once.

Importantly, data can now be conceptualized of as sets instead of discrete and individual records, and can be added, deleted, and updated as sets instead of individual records.

Codd's Rules

As stated earlier, Codd first developed the relational model in 1970. In 1985, he published a list of twelve rules for the relational database model entitled "Twelve Principles of Relational Databases". These rules have been followed in all major RDBMS (Relational Database Management Systems) vendor implementations, to some extent. While there has been less emphasis on Codd's rules as the relational database market has matured, the principles still play an important part in designing applications based on RDBMS, understanding the relational model, and even evaluating the completeness of different RDBMSs. As much of the book will focus on Relational Database Management Systems, we will list Codd's rules here for completeness.

> **Rule 0: Relational Database Management Systems must be able to manage data entirely through relational capabilities.**

Rule Zero? OK, there are actually thirteen rules if you include this one, which was incidentally not part of Codd's original paper. Essentially, this rule is a rider on the twelve rules that indicates that a RDBMS cannot use non-relational database models to satisfy the following rules, and still be considered a true RDBMS.

> **Rule 1: The Information Rule: Data must be presented in tables.**

This is really the core of the relational model, as we discussed above. While this is the first real point of differentiation from the other models discussed in the chapter, it is refined by the additional rules below to really highlight how proper table handling by the RDBMS leads to greater control over the data.

To further clarify the table paradigm, it's important to note that there can be no physical relationships between tables, only logical ones.

> **Rule 2: Guaranteed Access: All data should be logically accessible without ambiguity.**

RDBMSs handle this through table structure and naming. Not only do tables and columns have unique names, but there should also be at least one column, or a combination of columns, whose values would be unique for each row of records. Such fields are called candidate keys, and one of them is selected as the table's primary key. The purpose of doing this is to be able to uniquely identify every record in a table based on its primary key. Also, the catalogs (groups of tables) mentioned earlier in the chapter can further distinguish records.

While RDBMS do not mandate that primary keys exist in all tables, support for these keys is expected to be present.

> **Rule 3: Systematic Treatment of Null Values: Fields must be allowed to remain empty.**

Simply put, a field value set to zero is not the same as one that is empty. While seemingly a minor point, it has huge impact on application structure. Most database systems support this 'null' or missing value across all types of data to be stored in the database, although nulls are illegal in the case of primary key fields.

> **Rule 4: Dynamic On-Line Catalog: A relational database must provide access to its metadata through the same methods that are used to access its data.**

Rule 4 mandates that databases must maintain information about themselves including structure and other **metadata** (data about the structure and form of data) within the database management system.

This is most often accomplished by setting aside specific tables as **System Tables** to store the metadata. Chapter 4 will cover SQL commands used to create, interrogate, and change the structure of a database by altering these tables.

> **Rule 5: Comprehensive Data Sub-language: The database must support a language to control functions for data definition, data manipulation, data integrity, and transaction control.**

As mentioned earlier, the Structured Query Language is the lingua franca across all commercial RDBMS implementations. Also of interest is that Codd's rules do not require that the SQL must be the data access and manipulation language used; only that the database engine uses some language to do this.

> **Rule 6: View Updating Rule: A presentation of data may be made to the user in physically distinct combinations called views. Views must support manipulation of data in the view consistent with access to the underlying tables.**

A **view** is an incredibly useful database programming tool.

While perhaps a bit of an oversimplification, a view can be thought of as a "canned" query, analogous to a bookmarked query of an Internet search – potentially changing whenever the search engine is pulled up. As indicated earlier, SQL considers data in sets, and SQL statements are typically written to pull up a set of rows out of all possible rows. While these sets don't necessarily have the same structure of underlying tables the data is pulled from, views save the definition of the set and can greatly reduce the complexity of an SQL statement required by the programmer. We shall be covering views and their use in Chapter 7 of this book.

> **Rule 7: High-level Insert, Update, and Delete: Data can be manipulated in a relational database in sets comprised of data from one or many rows and / or one or many tables.**

Again, this rule highlights that data is thought about in sets instead of in single rows. Changing data via record insertions, changes, and deletions must include support for sets of rows as well as discrete rows. Chapter 5 will cover the SQL syntax commands used to manipulate data in these and other ways.

> **Rule 8: Physical Data Independence: The physical storage and retrieval methods for the data must be abstracted from the user view of the data.**

Simply put, Rule 8 mandates that the disk storage and other underlying hardware should have no affect on the RDBMS from the databases user's point of view, allowing not only the user but the application developer to maintain blissful ignorance of these details.

> **Rule 9: Logical Data Independence: The user view of data should be independent of the database tables view with respect to changes in structure.**

This rule indicates that the user view of the data should be abstracted from the table structure. Most RDMBS don't have a clear implementation of this rule, instead linking table structure to the user view. That being said, SQL's ability to return sets of data only loosely related to the original table structure can be said to satisfy this rule.

> **Rule 10: Integrity Independence: Data manipulation language support must include constraints on user input to maintain integrity of the data.**

This is one of Codd's rules that some database vendors ignore to some extent. Ideally there should be no way to corrupt data using SQL or any other data manipulation language. As a starting place, vendors typically support primary keys, which uniquely identify rows of records. Not allowing null values in these keys helps to maintain integrity, as two empty values would break uniqueness. Additionally, a RDBMS worth its salt will support foreign keys, which is a key column in a table that must be a primary key in another table. Chapter 3 will cover referential integrity and other concepts governed by this rule, but a proper implementation of foreign keys means that changes to a primary key cascades to the record indicated by the foreign key.

As an example, consider a consulting database with a `Client` table containing a single field listing company names, and a `Contractor` table, also containing company names in a `current_site` field:

```
Client
-----------------
company
address

Contractor
-----------------
name
current_site
skill_level
```

In an ideal situation, the `current_site` field in the `Contractor` table would be comprised of foreign keys taken from the `company` field in the `Client` table, and deleting a company from the list of clients would also cascade the deletion to the `Contractor` table. Without this, we either have to handle this referential problem in our application logic or risk our employees getting paid for sitting at home.

> **Rule 11: Distribution Independence: The user view of the data should be abstracted from the location of the data.**

This rule focuses on **distributed** databases. Distributing a database means that the storage-server layer and /or other parts of the RDBMS may exist in multiple locations. Advantages of this include putting heavily accessed tables on separate physical disks or even separate machines to reduce the impact of disk, CPU, and memory performance depending on application needs and patterns of use.

> **Rule 12: No Subversion Rule: The only way to modify the database structure should be the multiple row database language support.**

This rule is often flagrantly violated by modern RDBMS. To paraphrase, this rule mandates that the only way to modify the database structure should be SQL. This is fine, but many RDBMS's support administrative interfaces that enable changes to the database structure, with or without SQL.

We will now return to an overview of the other database models that you may encounter. Moving forward throughout the book and in developing your applications, try to keep Codd's rules in mind, as database systems adherence to these rules will protect your data and give your application layer additional power and control over the database.

Object/Transactional Database Model

The object model, popularly termed OODBMS, was introduced in the mid 1990's and has seen some adoption. Simply, an Object Database System presents the programmer with a multidimensional view of the data. Ideally these views are designed to fit closely to real-world data, with the theory being that storing complex, real-world data is best done in structures that resemble the data they are to store. Object technology also hides the underlying storage from the programmer, only providing the data objects to work with. Creation of storage formats is done automatically on the object structure.

The object model is often referred to as the transactional model due to the multidimensional presentation of data. For example, it can be displayed as a business logic object, or transaction, which means that the arrays may be created, indexed, or referenced by one or many of the data elements. This differs greatly from the relational model in that data does not need to be "broken down" into two-dimensional tables when stored, and can be accessed in the form it is stored without being constructed from tables as the result of a query.

This approach has pros and cons. Among its advantages, the information stored closely maps to the application. As an example, we may consider a business process that allows storage of data with the same structure as the information that is presented to the business. A significant drawback is that these objects remain discrete. So, ad hoc queries to create new results or views on the data that differ widely, may be difficult if not impossible.

Many early object database systems also failed to design the underlying storage well. So, slow object databases entered into a world where relational databases held firm sway. To make matters more difficult, SQL is not a requirement of the object model, which requires language- and database-specific APIs instead, to convert the database objects into a form that can be used by the programming language. Transforming the data object into a usable form typically involves converting the in-memory or on-disk object into a serialized array, or providing a pointer to the array. This serialization can be quite expensive in terms of processor and memory demands. So pure object database management systems are rare.

The lack of SQL has been a huge impediment to widespread adoption of the object model. It also limited the update of object data technology when it was introduced, simply because SQL had become the lingua franca of the database world. While the programming languages in use are moving more and more towards object orientation, SQL is still regarded a core technology and should remain so due to its unique ad hoc querying strengths.

Hybrid (Object-Relational) Database Model

Addressing the shortcomings of the object model, the object-relational model is typically a combination of, as you must have guessed, the object and the relational models. So, what does this mean? In general, object-relational models typically store data as in the relational model, but provide views of this data consistent with the object model. Some object-relational systems actually do the converse of this – storing objects and mapping them to relational model tables. Either way, there is a forced-mapping across the object-relational boundary. This can often result in a limit of the type of data that can be described and stored in the mapped format. Data types will be covered in Chapter 4, but for now, they should be understood as the allowable formats to store and represent bits of information in. As an illustration, our `Task List` could be thought of as a table, with fields named `Assigned-By`, of data type `Name`.

Many relational database vendors have built object technology into their databases to create the hybrid type. These are sometimes referred to as Post-Relational Databases. Object-relational databases have some of the other featues of object databases, such as inhertitance of tables and extending the support for user defined data types and arrays.

Native XML Database Model

The Native XML model can be thought of as a combination of the hierarchical model with the object model. Native XML Databases store XML documents without breaking them down. They provide associated XML technologies like Xpath and XQuery (to navigate the hierarchy) and XSLT (for transforming XML documents into other XML documents) as well as object-relational features for mapping relational data into XML and relational features such as ODBC to aggregate data for transforamation.

Let's take part of our `Task List` and convert it to a hierarchical XML document:

```
<?xml version="1.0" encoding="UTF-8" ?>

<task_detail>
  <assigned_to name= "Andrew">
    <item_category name="Grocery shopping">
```

```
        <item>buy food
        </item>
      </item_category>
      <item_category name="Birthday shopping">
        <item>buy flowers
        </item>
      </item_category>
    </assigned_to>
  </task_detail>
```

This is a very simple example, but it should give you an idea that XML is hierarchical and uses defined tags. While covering XML syntax and rules is out of the scope of this chapter, it's important to note that this example is one of dozens of valid XML documents that could be created to describe the data we are using as an example.

Also, while Native XML is admittedly more of a buzzword and marketing term, XML handling in storage, retrieval, and transformation is a powerful technology that is rapidly growing and providing new inflections in business application. Sensitive to this, as well as the power of XML, most relational database vendors are now implementing XML support.

Overview of Relational Database Systems

Now that we have an idea of the relational model, or the concepts used to implement Relational Database Management Systems, let's dig down into the practical implementation of the RDBMS.

Database Architecture

Before covering some of the significant vendor offerings, let's touch upon the different components of databases, and how they affect us as PHP developers.

Earlier in the chapter we defined a database as a collection of records. Let's recollect the differences between a database and a database server.

A database server is not just the records, but the entire record keeping system, including:

- ❑   Physical disk hardware used to store the records
- ❑   Files used as storage
- ❑   Software used to accesses these files and view or change the data stored in the records

The DBMS acronym is often extended depending on the database model used in the system, for example RDBMS is a Relational Database Management System, ODBMS is an Object Oriented Database System, and so on.

Connection Architecture and PHP

PHP typically contains the application programming logic, but SQL is the language used to act on data within a RDBMS. Let us look at SQL for a moment to understand how it has grown from a server-side language to something that can be used by our programming language.

The Evolution of SQL

For the purposes of this book, we need to think about the different communication protocols and data access methods. When the SQL specification was first presented, it existed in a form called Embedded SQL. As the name implies, the only way to run SQL commands was with SQL stored directly in the computer program, such as C. Around 1990, UNIX database vendors, which included Oracle, Informix, and IBM, formed the SQL Access Group, SAG in short, and created a CLI (Call-Level Interface) specification to allow SQL to be used in a portable fashion. Allowing the use of SQL in application layers addressed the then existing problem of impedance mismatch, by ensuring that the capabilities of the database were not exposed to the application programming language.

The initial SAG CLI was based on a subset of the SQL specification known as ANSI SQL86. The database vendors implemented native client layers that could use this new SQL. In 1992, Microsoft first implemented the SAG CLI in a set of APIs. They called it called ODBC (Open Database Connectivity), which allowed the passing of SQL statements to a database independent of the middleware layer. Thus, it was no longer restricted to any database client. This also had the effect of pushing adherence to the SQL86 specification, since database vendors had extended support of SQL in proprietary ways, ensuring that choosing a database affected many application programming decisions and tying applications to specific databases.

Database Sessions

To use data stored in a DBMS, PHP needs to open and control a database connection.

The database connection in PHP consists of:

1. Connecting to the database server, or to an already open persistent connection

2. Selecting the specific database catalog

3. Selecting records or doing work on data (such as inserting, updating, and deleting records), or optionally reading a record into an array or other variable

4. Disconnecting from the database server

There is an example in the next section of creating a database connection and selecting data. Steps 1 through 4 have been listed in the code comments to help you see what is going on, although this will be covered in greater depth in the next few chapters.

It's also important to note that in a single PHP script, open database sessions are closed upon the termination of the script, like when the page finishes running, but it is still good practice to explicitly close database sessions. PHP also provides the facility to create persistent database connections, which are database connections that remain open when a single script ends. Instead of requesting a new connection, we may request a persistent connection, forcing PHP to check for a connection that remains open from earlier using the same connection attributes. If such a connection exists it will be used, and if not PHP will create a new one.

The Need for Database Abstraction

Given that RDBMS have different API calls to perform similar data handling functions, as application developers we often run into the issue that RDBMS-specific calls in our scripts will lock our application to that RDBMS.

Enter ODBC

ODBC is still widely used today across most UNIX, Mac, and Windows platforms, and in fact continues to grow on non-Windows platforms. Using ODBC allows the developer to swap in and out of different database systems. For instance using a lightweight, free database for development and then deploying an enterprise-level database system.

Unfortunately, it's not possible to abstract all application level considerations from any code using ODBC, simply the database connection. Abstracting your PHP from a database requires handling of abstraction across all features of databases, including differences in data types, referential integrity, table structure, and so on. Many of these items will be covered in the next few chapters, but suffice it to say that there are still some application constraints when using ODBC.

Database Abstraction in PHP

PHP has native APIs for connecting to different databases. These include APIs based on native database connections, as well as ones based on ODBC. Actually, the unified ODBC functions (http://www.php.net/odbc) appear to be true ODBC API functions, but may be used either with ODBC drivers or with native database connections. The native clients are used in a few cases where the API's were so similar that the database-specific calls could be hidden in the unified ODBC functions.

The database systems supported by the unified ODBC API will be covered in the next section.

Database Abstraction with PEAR::DB

PEAR stands for PHP Extension and Application Repository, a library of reusable PHP objects and code snippets enabling reuse of PHP libraries, distribution of C-based PHP extensions, and encouraging consistent coding practices. Essentially, it provides a place to share PHP-style foundation classes. Today, PEAR includes classes for database access, content caching, and mathematical libraries. The **PCS (Pear Coding Standard)** is an emerging standard to encourage interoperability of code libraries in the repository.

With the recent increase in OOP emphasis in the PHP community, PEAR should see even more activity. The PEAR site (http://pear.php.net) is a great resource for new PHP developers.

As one distinct project within PEAR, and indeed the most initially useful part, PEAR::DB is a database abstraction layer coded to comply with the PEAR guidelines. It is the emerging leader in the PHP abstraction space, not in the least because it has been authored by the Core PHPteam. Other abstraction layers are available for use in PHP, such as Metabase, eXtremePHP, and ADODB. PEAR::DB also contains features available in all of them, is very OO, and is in step with PHP development so should prove to be the most flexible solution in the long run.

If you have a default installation of PHP, you should have PEAR::DB support already present, as recent builds of PHP include PEAR by default. On some systems PHP may have been compiled using the -without-pear- switch, so if you encounter problems you can check how your PHP instance was built using the function phpinfo().

This also may change, as the default build state of PHP and the modules it includes is in hot debate currently. As always, YMMV (your mileage may vary) but the phpinfo() function is very useful.

If you find that your PHP installation was built without PEAR support, you may rebuild it using the instructions provided in the PEAR manual at: http://pear.php.net/manual/.

> Those who aren't already familiar with the phpinfo() function, may view the documentation at http://www.php.net/manual/en/function.phpinfo.php.

Please refer to Appendix C for detailed instructions on this.

So, let's briefly explore an example of database connections with PEAR::DB. We won't go into the coding syntax or SQL at this point – see Chapter 4 for an introduction to SQL and Chapter 10 for in-depth coverage on the PEAR::DB library features.

Before we look at some sample PEAR::DB code, let's look at an example of a basic MySQL database connection using the MySQL PHPAPI functions to instantiate a basic database session and return some results to the screen.

Note, the field1 and field2 referenced in the script will simply be column names in your database:

```php
<?php
//set some connection attributes
$username = "my_username";
$password = "my_password";
$hostname = "localhost";
$database = "name_of_database";
//create database link.
$link_id = mysql_connect($hostname, $username, $password) or die (mysql_error());

//select database or catalog.
mysql_select_db($database, $link_id);

//assign the SQL statement to a variable.
/*this could be a static SQL statement, where the the database tables and columns
references in the statement are known when the script is written, or include
variables for parameters
$sql="SELECT field1, field2 FROM tablename";

//return result set to php
$result = mysql_query ($sql, $link_id) or die (mysql_error());
//$result is the result set from the SQL statement.
if (!$result) echo "wait - no result set!";
while (list ($field1, $field2) = mysql_fetch_row ($result))
{
  echo "Field One is $field1 <br>
  Field Two is $field2";
}
/*now free the resources associated with the result set
mysql_free_result($result)- this would occur anyways at the end of the script, but
it's good practice! */
mysql_close();
?>
```

Now, let's look at the same connection using the PEAR::DB abstraction:

```php
<?php

$user = "my_username";
$pass = "my_password";
$hostname = "localhost";
$database = "name_of_database";
//specify which database flavor to use
$dbms="mysql";

/*this is include in PEAR and is required to use PEAR::DB, and must be in the path
of the user that started apache or the include path */
require_once("DB.php");


//connect to the database according to the connect string
$db = DB::connect("$dbms://$user:$pass@$hostname/$database");

//assign the SQL statement to a variable
$sql = "SELECT field1, field2 FROM table";

//return result set to php
$result = $db->query($sql);

while ($row = $result->fetchRow())
{
  echo
  "Field One is $row[0]<br>
  Field Two is $row[1]
  ";
}
//close the database session, disconnect and free the result set
$db->disconnect();

?>
```

Getting the results the PEAR::DB way is a bit more compact than the using the PHP API functions for MySQL, and it does make use of object-oriented coding. The real benefit of the PEAR::DB method is that the entire PEAR::DB example could be pointed to another flavor of database by simply altering the $dbms variable to another database supported by PEAR::DB.

Looking at the DSN connect string from PEAR::DB, we see that:

```
$dbms://$user:$pass@$hostname/$database
```

Is eqivalent to:

```
$mysql://'username':'password'@'localhost'/'database'
```

73

PEAR::DB currently supports the following database system flavors:

- ❏ mysql (MySQL)
- ❏ pgsql (PostgreSQL)
- ❏ ibase (InterBase)
- ❏ msql (Mini SQL)
- ❏ mssql (Microsoft SQL Server)
- ❏ oci8 (Oracle 7/8/8i)
- ❏ odbc (ODBC: Open Database Connectivity)
- ❏ sybase (SyBase)
- ❏ ifx (Informix)
- ❏ fbsql (FrontBase)

It becomes clear how important this is when you consider that the PHP API for each database system is often vastly different depending on the native client connectivity.

We will get deeper into PEAR and SQL further on in the book. The next section of this chapter will highlight some of the features of the common relational database systems you may wish to use with PHP, as well as some of the strengths and drawbacks to consider when selecting your database platform.

Importantly, differences in database features will still be potential issues even when using PEAR::DB, as underlying features may differ too much for PEAR::DB to account for where the database system lacks major features. That being said, using this PEAR database class with ODBC will go a long way towards isolating you from database vendor lock that occurs when vendors compete in feature and SQL syntax support, and both PEAR::DB and ODBC provide a rich feature set that successfully provides database and data handling equal to native connectivity and APIs.

The Players

Relational database vendors offer many database products that run from simple read-optimized text storage to large enterprise-focused clustered server decision support and data-warehouse systems. You should always do some testing and modeling of your application logic, and data handling against the database systems you are considering. To get you started, there are a handful of players in the database industry that have proven to be very useful in different circumstances.

While your requirements may vary, the next section will attempt to briefly summarize the history, major distinguishing features, and the advantages and drawbacks that may affect your database application development. This is not meant to be a comprehensive guide, but to simply give you an informed starting point for your testing.

In addition, many of these database systems are either "free" Open Source products, or are available under a trial license for testing. They are presented in alphabetical order.

The database-specific configuration switches are presented below as well. For full instructions on compiling PHP in your environment, please see http://www.php.net/manual/en/installation.php#install.general. These configure flags are specific to UNIX installations, for example BSD, Linux, Mac OS X, Solaris, AIX, HP/UX, and so on. Under Windows PHP installations, support for database clients is typically a matter of installing the native client or ODBC driver and uncommenting the appropriate line in the `php.ini` file to enable the database connectivity.

Berkeley DBD

Sleepycat Software (http://www.sleepycat.com) maintains the Berkeley database, which is optimized to function as an embedded database. An embedded database is one that is linked directly into an application, or otherwise tightly integrated into the application layer. This means that Berkeley DB will be a very small, file-based, lightweight database and is best used for specialized applications. The Berkeley-style databases are not relational, but instead use a key => value style system of hash tables or b-trees.

To use the file-based, or dbm-style databases, you first need to specify this in the configure options:

```
--enable-dba=shared
```

Then, depending on which Berkley DB table handler version you want, you would configure PHP as follows:

```
--with-db2[=DIR]
```

This includes Berkeley DB2 support. The following option includes Berkeley DB3 support:

```
--with-db3[=DIR]
```

The DIR specified above should point at the Berkeley native client libraries available from Sleepycat. Berkeley DB is licensed under an Open Source license that appears to have the same limits as the GNU GPL. This means that to redistribute an application built with the Berkeley database, one has to release the source code of the application as well.

This is a serious issue – research Open Source licenses before blandly adopting them, or you may lose control over your own application. That being said, Sleepycat Software does provide for distribution under a commercial license. If you do not wish to open the source of your application you may purchase a license from them.

PHP and Berkeley DB

PEAR::DB doesn't support the file-based style Berkeley DB databases, but PHP has specific API's for dealing with the different types of Berkeley DB databases including dbm, gdbm, db2, db3, and cdb. The section of the PHP manual dealing with these functions is available here: http://www.php.net/manual/en/ref.dba.php.

Here is an example of a database session in PHP with a Berkeley DB – note that SQL is not used:

```php
<?php
/*this opens the database connection against the file in the path
the "r" specifies a read-only mode of connecting
the "db3" specifies the file handler, in this case Sleepycat's DB3
*/
$connection= dba_open ("/tmp/some_file.db", "r", "db3");

//error checking for a valid connection, always a good idea
if (!$connection ) {
  echo "ack - couldn't open the database<br>";
  exit;
}

//assign a handler for the first record to the $key variable
$key=dba_firstkey($connection);


//do some work - get the data for the first record
$first_data=dba_fetch($key, $connection);

//display the record
echo "first item in database is $first_data<br>";

//close your connection - always good form
dba_close ($connection_id);

?>
```

It is also just as straightforward to iterate over the entire database file and return all records using a loop:

```php
<?php
/*this opens the database connection against the file in the path
the "r" specifies a read-only mode of connecting
the "db3" specifies the file handler, in this case Sleepycat's DB3
*/
$connection= dba_open ("/tmp/some_file.db", "r", "db3");

//error checking for a valid connection, always a good idea
if (!$connection ) {
  echo "ack - couldn't open the database<br>";
  exit;
}

//assign a handler for the first record to the $key variable
$key=dba_firstkey($connection);

//now, iterate over the remaining rows and echo them
while ($key != false)
{
  //dba_nextkey is just like dba_firstkey above, with an obvious difference
```

```
     $key = dba_nextkey ($connection);

//do some work - get the data for the first record
$data=dba_fetch($key, $connection);

//display the next record
  echo "next item in database is $first_data<br>";

}

//close your connection - always good form
dba_close ($connection_id);

?>
```

DB2

IBM DB2 (http://www.ibm.com/db2/) is distributed under a commercial license. It was one of the first relational database offerings and remains a strong offering by IBM. DB2 runs on most UNIX flavors, as well as OS/390 and AS400 mainframe systems, and Windows. It is very ODBC friendly, and well supported by the unified ODBC functions in PHP. To use DB2 from PHP you will either need to install an ODBC driver on your PHP box or the DB2 client, called DB2 Connect (in the sqllib directory of a default DB2 install).

Setting up ODBC connectivity can be accomplished by referring to the HOWTO section on http://www.iodbc.org. Using the DB2 Connect client requires the compilation option:

```
--with-ibm-db2[=DIR]
```

The DIR is the DB2 base install directory, which defaults to /home/db2inst1/sqllib.

Do not be confused by the -with-db2 option; this is for the Berkeley DB2 database, and not IBM DB2.

PHP and DB2

As mentioned, DB2 is supported by the unified ODBC functions. This means that after configuring for DB2 support you can use the odbc_function() style functions or install a true ODBC driver for additional database abstraction and use the same functions.

They are viewable here: http://www.php.net/manual/en/ref.odbc.php.

As we gave an example of PEAR::DB earlier in the chapter, here is an example of a straight ODBC API connection to DB2. This is a simple example that returns formatted results with the odbc_result_all() function:

```
<?php
include "odbc.putenv.inc.php";
/*
ODBC requires that environment variables be set for the location of:
the ODBC Driver manager, the odbc.ini file at the very least
```

```
for completeness, this is an example of one odbc.putenv.inc.php file:

<?
putenv("LD_LIBRARY_PATH=/usr/openlink/odbcsdk/lib");//location of libiodbc
putenv("ODBCINSTINI=/usr/openlink/bin/odbcinst.ini");//driver setup info
putenv("ODBCINI=/etc/odbc.ini");//DSN information
?>
*/

$dsn="OpenLink_DB2";
$usr="db2";
$pwd="";

//assign the SQL statement to a variable
$sql="SELECT * FROM account WHERE branch = 6";

//create a connection handle
$connection = odbc_connect($dsn, $usr, $pwd) or die (odbc_error());

//do some work -  get the SQL result set
$result=odbc_exec($connection, $sql);

//display the results, autoformat in an html table
odbc_result_all($result);

//close the connection - always good form
odbc_close($result);
?>
```

Here is the result from the above example:

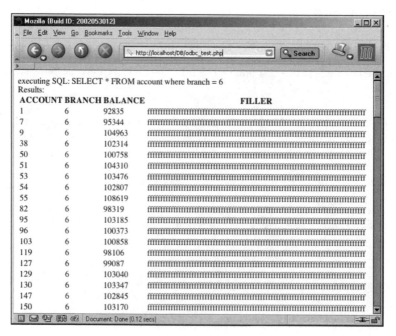

The `odbc.ini` file mentioned contains specific settings for our **Data Source Names**, or DSNs. Here is the content of the `odbc.ini` file:

```
[ODBC Data Sources]
db2   = OpenLink Generic ODBC Driver

[db2]
Driver       = /dbs/openlink/v42/lib/oplodbc.so.1
Host         = oplussol2
ServerType   = DB2
UserName     = db2inst1
Password     = fitzroydb2inst1
Database     = SAMPLE
```

DSN configuration can vary a bit from driver to driver – it's a good idea to peruse the documentation on your ODBC driver thoroughly.

Interbase

Interbase (http://www.borland.com/interbase/) is distributed by Borland and was recently released under an Open Source license, moving from a commercial product. Borland's Interbase Public License is viewable here: http://info.borland.com/devsupport/interbase/opensource/IPL.html.

Interbase is available on most Windows and UNIX platforms. Configuring PHP to use Interbase requires the flag:

```
--with-interbase[=DIR]
```

`DIR` is the Interbase base install directory, which defaults to `/usr/interbase`.

PHP and Interbase

As mentioned earlier in the chapter, `PEAR::DB` supports Interbase using `Ibase` in the `DB::connect()`. The `PEAR::DB` example should work fine for this database as long as you have the client libraries set up properly. As always, check your environment with a `phpinfo()` call if you experience difficulties, and verify that you can connect to the database using its native client before assuming a problem with PHP.

To use PHP's Interbase API instead, functions are available at:
http://www.php.net/manual/en/ref.ibase.php.

Interbase, like Sybase, uses a single quote (`'`) for escaping special characters. To enable this in PHP make the following change to your `php.ini`:

```
magic_quotes_sybase = On
```

Note that Interbase 6 support was added in PHP as of version 4, so earlier versions of PHP will not support Interbase 6.

Informix

Informix (http://www.ibm.com/informix) software was recently acquired by IBM, but this does not mean the the Informix database products are not viable. IBM has publicly stated that the Informix products will not be discontinued for the time being.

Informix is available on most Windows and UNIX platforms. Configuring to use Informix requires the flag:

```
--with-informix[=DIR]
```

As above, DIR is the Informix base install directory. Of note here – the default is nothing, so a default Informix installation will not be found by PHP's configure command without the DIR path.

The Informix client is ESQL/C. Versions of ESQL/C including 7.2x and later should work with PHP. ESQL/C is available as part of the Informix Client SDK and is available from IBM here: http://www-3.ibm.com/software/data/informix/tools/esqlc/.

When configuring your PHP environment for Informix support, set the INFORMIXDIR and INFORMIXSERVER environment variables, ensure that $INFORMIXDIR/bin is in your path before you run the configure, and ensure that the ESQL/C libraries are available to the loader (by setting their location via LD_LIBRARY_PATH or ld.so.conf/ldconfig).

PHP and Informix

As mentioned earlier in the chapter, PEAR::DB supports Informix using Ifx in the DB:connect(). The PEAR::DB example should work fine for this database as long as you have the client libraries set up properly. As always, check your environment with a phpinfo() call if you experience difficulties and verify that you can connect to the database using its native client before assuming a problem with PHP.

PHP also supports an Informix specific API. Documentation on the ifx_functions() is available here: http://www.php.net/manual/en/ref.ifx.php.

Just as in compile time, set the above environment variables in your scripts at runtime using putenv() commands.

Microsoft SQL Server

There is no MS SQL Server (http://www.microsoft.com/sql) native client for non-Windows platforms, so ODBC must be used, for example, configuring -with-iodbc and installing an ODBC driver such as the OpenLink Single Tier Driver for MS SQL (http://www.openlinksw.com).

Since Sybase SQL Server and Microsoft SQL Server began as the same product, it is also possible to use -with-sybase pointing to the Sybase Open Client. Another alternative is to use the Open Source FreeTDS libraries, essentially as a substitute for ODBC. FreeTDS is still somewhat immature, so caveat emptor. As an example, FreeTDS does not work well against MS SQL Server 2000, although it has had some success when used against MS SQL Server 7.

MS SQL Server is a full SQL-92 RDBMS, as well as keeping pace with other industry developments in XML and SQL-to-XML support. It typically stays near or at the head of the pack in commercial enterprise databases, and competes with Oracle and Sybase.

Microsoft initially licensed the SQL Server code base from Sybase and then proceeded to market the product as different from from Sybase SQL Server, with indigenous features as well as tighter Microsoft platform integration. It has excellent support for ODBC and typically enables easy migration from other databases. Its biggest drawback is that it is only available on Windows platforms, so the choice of database server platforms is severely limited.

MS SQL Server is a commercial product.

PHP and MS SQL

As mentioned earlier in the chapter, `PEAR::DB` supports MS SQL Server using `Mssql` in the `DB:connect()`. The `PEAR::DB` example should work fine for this database as long as you have the client libraries set up properly.

Check your environment with a `phpinfo()` call if you experience difficulties, and verify that you can connect to the database using its native client before assuming a problem with PHP.

It is also possible to use PHP's functions for MS SQL Server, listed here: http://www.php.net/manual/en/ref.mssql.php, if you are using a Windows installation of PHP and have the MS SQL Server Client Tools installed. They are provided by Microsoft and are also available on the installation media that your MS SQL Server installation is shipped on.

After installing the Client Tools, enable MS SQL Server support in your PHP instance by adding or uncommenting the following line in your `php.ini`:

```
extension=php_mssql.dll
```

From UNIX platforms, the Sybase functions may also be used if the Sybase Open Client is installed. The documentation can be found here: http://www.php.net/manual/en/ref.sybase.php.

MySQL

Perhaps the best known Open Source database, MySQL (http://www.mysql.org), is freely available on Windows, most UNIX platforms, and the Mac OS X. As its source code is available to everyone, compiling binaries for platforms where they are not readily available is also possible.

MySQL is currently optimized as a read-only database. While it certainly supports write activity such as 'Inserts' and 'Updates', it has historically lacked many of the features that are required for full-fledged database application development, such as stored procedures, triggers, foreign keys and referential integrity, sub-queries, transactions, and complete SQL92 support.

The PHP community has certainly embraced MySQL up to this point. In fact, it's often joked that the native API for web development languages is the MySQL API, as its interface availability is nearly ubiquitous across platforms and web development languages.

After installing MySQL, configuring PHP to use it requires the flag:

```
--with-mysql[=DIR]
```

The `DIR` is the MySQL base directory. A nice feature of PHP is that if no `DIR` is specified, a MySQL library bundled with the PHP distribution will be used.

For read-only speed, MySQL is fast, and if the application you are developing is simply using a database as storage and doesn't require enterprise scalability, such as an information repository like a telephone directory, MySQL may be a good initial choice. MySQL 3.x ideally should not be used for more than learning and testing, as it may not expose new developers to the power of the relational model. Also, MySQL doesn't support views, covered in Chapter 7, limiting the ability of the developer to reduce complexity of SQL by offloading complex queries to the database.

So, if MySQL is one of the more popular databases, it's Open Source, and the relational model features are indeed important, why are there lacks in functionality?

Enter InnoDB, (http://www.innodb.com). Here's an extract from the InnoDB website:

"It is an attempt to provide tansactions, row level locking, hot backup, and foreign keys for MySQL, without compromising on the speed of MySQL. This is done by offloading table handling from the standard MyISAM table handler in MySQL to an InnoDB table handler that builds in the additional features. InnoDB is still somewhat immature, and not all features are available on all platforms, but it looks promising, especially as MySQL 4.x nears completion and integrates InnoDB tables as a standard option. One thing to be aware of is that InnoDB increases the disk space footprint of MySQL substantially to provide these features."

To experiment with transactions and foreign keys in MySQL, InnoDB is the ideal resource. Caution: Tables must be created with InnoDB support.

Explaining the methods to add this support to MySQL is out of the scope of this book, but the InnoDB manual will be an invaluable resource: http://www.innodb.com/ibman.html

PHP and MySQL

As mentioned earlier in the chapter, `PEAR::DB` supports MySQL using `Mysql` in the `DB:connect()`. The `PEAR::DB` example should work fine for this database as long as the client libraries are set properly. As always, `putenv()` should be used in your PHP scripts to ensure that the Sybase environment variables are reflected in the PHP script environment. Verify that you can connect to the database using its native client before assuming a problem with PHP.

The MySQL specific functions for MySQL may also be used. They are documented here: http://www.php.net/manual/en/ref.mysql.php.

Oracle

PHP can be configured to use Oracle (http://www.oracle.com) in a few different ways. First, ODBC drivers exist on all platforms for Oracle. Additionally, Oracle is fairly aggressive in providing their native client libraries across Windows and UNIX platforms.

Oracle also has good SQL support and full support for most relational model concepts. The drawbacks of an Oracle installation include a large installation footprint in disk space and often a large amount of RAM to run. It is a true enterprise solution and many PHP applications are built and deployed against Oracle.

To use a current release of Oracle with Oracle's native Oracle Client Interface (OCI) layer like Oracle 8i or later, use the configure flag:

```
--with-oci8[=DIR]
```

This configures PHP to use the Oracle-OCI8 support. Unlike some of the earlier examples, `DIR` defaults to an environment in the UNIX shell, called `ORACLE_HOME`. This variable is set while installing Oracle and may also be done by hand if the OCI location is known or is installed without the Oracle database server.

To use an earlier version of Oracle, configure PHP:

```
--with-oracle[=DIR]
```

This sets PHP to Include Oracle-oci7 support. Again, `DIR` defaults to `ORACLE_HOME`.

The Oracle database is a commercial product.

PHP and Oracle

As mentioned earlier, `PEAR::DB` supports Oracle using `oci8` in the `DB:connect()`. The `PEAR::DB` example should work fine for this database as long as you have the client libraries set up properly. As always, check your environment with a `phpinfo()` call if you experience difficulties and verify that you can connect to the database using its native client before assuming a problem with PHP.

Again, database-specific PHP functions may be used for Oracle as well. In this case, you have two options:

❑ For early versions of Oracle, the `ora_functions` call may be used:
http://www.php.net/manual/en/ref.oracle.php.

❑ For recent version of Oracle, the `OCI_functions` call may be used:
http://www.php.net/manual/en/ref.oci8.php.

In the UNIX environment, runtime settings using `putenv` need to be specified for two environment variables at a minimum:

❑ `ORACLE_HOME` is the path to your Oracle installation directory

❑ `ORACLE_SID` is the name of the database instance you want to connect to

It also may be very convenient, for resolving permission issues, to add the user that Apache runs as to the Oracle group. This is typically www or `nobody`.

PostgreSQL

PostgreSQL (http://www.postgresql.org) is the "other" well-known Open Source database, running second in adoption behind MySQL. This may be considered odd, especially as PostgreSQL has transaction, stored procedure, and foreign key support that MySQL lacks. PostgreSQL is also an object-relational database, supporting creation of user-defined data types, structured data types like arrays, and table inheritance. Its slower adoption may be considered a function of the Open Source community process, which also saw MySQL garner more mindshare and consequently, more development attention. That may all be changing, however. The Linux vendor RedHat has embraced PostgreSQL strongly and is providing a commercial presence in support services, as well as shipping a version of RedHat with optimized PostgreSQL.

It's also sometimes slower for simple read access, but often quicker for multi-user write access. We will dig further into PostgreSQL as we go on in this book.

Configuring PHP for PosgreSQL requires the following flag:

```
--with-pgsql[=DIR]
```

`DIR` in this case is the PostgreSQL base install directory and defaults to `/usr/local/pgsql`.

PHP and PostgreSQL

As mentioned earlier in the chapter, `PEAR::DB` supports PostgreSQL using `Pgsql` in the `DB:connect()`. The `PEAR::DB` example should work fine for this database as long as you have the client libraries set up properly. `putenv()` should be used in your PHP scripts to ensure that the environment variables are reflected in the PHP script environment. Verify that you can connect to the database using its native client before assuming a problem with PHP.

PHP also has PostgreSQL specific functions. The `pg_functions()` are documented here: http://www.php.net/manual/en/ref.pgsql.php.

Notably, according to the PHP manual, the `pg_function` name will be changed shortly to conform to coding standards. This is yet another reason to use `PEAR::DB` instead of the natively named functions in PHP.

Sybase

This venerable entry from Sybase (http://www.sybase.com) should more correctly be named Sybase Adaptive Server Anywhere, and is one of a few database server products the company provides.

Like Oracle, Sybase enables a couple of different connection options. In both the examples below, `DIR` defaults to `/home/sybase` and should be set to the Sybase home directory. The option below configures PHP to use the Sybase DB-Lib support:

```
--with-sybase[=DIR]
```

This option instead configures PHP to use the Sybase CT-Lib support:

```
--with-sybase-ct[=DIR]
```

It's recommended that you use CT-Lib support, as Sybase has ceased active development of DB-Lib.

As in MS SQL Server, FreeTDS may also be used, and ODBC function support is quite widely available for Sybase, either by using the native Sybase libraries and the unified ODBC wrapper under the covers, or by installing true ODBC drivers from Sybase or another vendor.

As in other databases, certain environment variables should be set at compile time to aid PHP in finding the appropriate Sybase client libraries. The most relevant ones and their default values for Linux are:

```
DSQUERY=SYBASE
SYBASE=/opt/sybase
SYBPLATFORM=linux
LD_LIBRARY_PATH=$SYBASE/lib
PATH=$SYBASE/bin:$PATH
```

PHP and Sybase

As mentioned earlier in the chapter, `PEAR::DB` supports Sybase using `SyBase` in the `DB:connect()`. The `PEAR::DB` example should work fine for this database as long as you have the client libraries set up properly. As always, check your environment with a `phpinfo()` call if you experience difficulties and verify that you can connect to the database using its native client before assuming a problem with PHP.

PHP also supports Sybase specific functions. These are documented at http://www.php.net/manual/en/ref.sybase.php.

As with other databases, `putenv()` should be used in your PHP scripts to ensure that the Sybase environment variables are reflected in the PHP script environment.

Virtuoso

Virtuoso (http://www.openlinksw.com/virtuoso) is the latest offering from OpenLink Software. OpenLink maintains the Open Source iODBC Driver Manager to enable ODBC on non-Windows platforms, as well as providing commercial ODBC drivers for most UNIX, Windows, and Macintosh platforms.

With that in mind, it should come as no surprise that OpenLink Virtuoso uses ODBC as it's native Call Level Interface. So, simply configuring your PHP to use ODBC, and connecting against the native Virtuoso driver will be sufficient:

```
-with-iodbc[=DIR]
```

`DIR` here is the location of the odbcsdk directory included with the iODBC SDK available at http://www.iodbc.org. The `default is /usr/local`.

Virtuoso is a full SQL-92 compliant database, with support for database transactions, triggers, stored procedures, cursors, and so on. Surprisingly, it has a very small disk footprint (approx. 3.5Mb for the binary and under 80Mb for the whole server including sample databases) and runs very quickly with only 24Mb of RAM.

Like MS SQL Server, Virtuoso supports transformation of relational data into XML, as well as supporting all of the current XML protocols such as Xpath, XSLT, and XQuery. Additionally, Virtuoso can act as a **Virtual Database**. What this means is that Virtuoso can transparently link in tables from other relational database systems, providing a single transparent database schema to develop against.

Perhaps the most exiting thing about Virtuoso is it's built-in PHP support. Virtuoso has a non-relational XML native storage as well as relational tables and provides HTTP access against this repository. PHP documents stored directly inside of Virtuoso can be interpreted without the need for a separate web server such as Apache.

Chapter 14 will go in depth into OpenLink Virtuoso's features and show how to port a sample PHP application into native Virtuoso storage, create and use XML from relational database tables, and employ Virtuoso as a high-level database abstraction to integrate multiple back-end databases.

Virtuoso is a commercial product, and is licensed against the number of concurrent client connections against the server. Virtuoso downloads with a 30 day unlimited connection license and may be obtained from http://www.openlinksw.com/virtuoso.

PHP and Virtuoso

As Virtuoso uses ODBC as it's native connection, PEAR::DB support will work fine using Odbc in the DB:connect(). The PEAR::DB example should work fine as long as you have the client drivers set up properly. As always, check your environment with a phpinfo() call if you experience difficulties and verify that you can connect to the database using its native client before assuming a problem with PHP.

We will go into PHP and Virtuoso in depth in Chapter 14, but aside from the PEAR::DB calls, Virtuoso can also be accessed via the unified ODBC functions at: http://www.php.net/manual/en/ref.odbc.php.

Summary

This chapter should have given you a decent understanding of the need for a database. We traced the evolution of modern Relational Database Management Systems and discussed some of the strengths and weaknesses in the common RDBMS available for use with PHP.

The chapter was actually an appetizer for a serious treatment of PEAR::DB and a beginning awareness of the best-practice ways of abstracting your PHP code from the underlying database systems as much as possible.

An awareness of some of the issues should make you think about how to architect connections to a database from PHP, as well as some of the important differences between RDBMS flavors available. In later chapters, we will address the important considerations you need to be concerned with when designing a PHP application for use with a database. In the next chapter we will encounter normalization and then spend a couple of chapters learning some SQL.

Moving forward throughout the book, try to keep in mind that even with database abstraction you will need to know data types and database-specific SQL syntax occasionally and be aware of the database you are developing against.

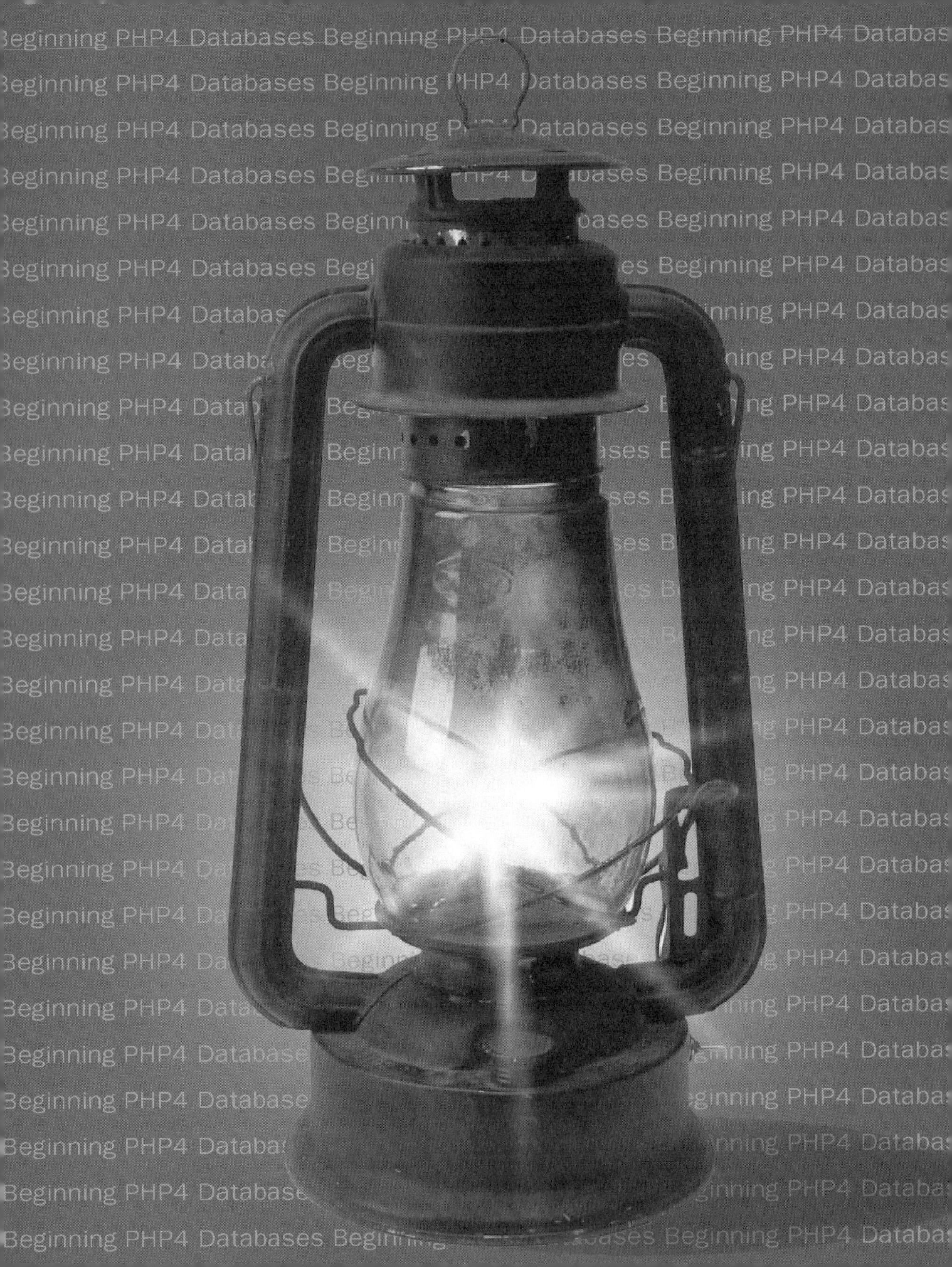
Beginning PHP4 Databases

Understanding Relational Databases

As we have briefly seen in the previous chapter, there are many possible ways to structure data, such as trees, lists, and objects. In relational databases, data is structured as relations. Relations are expressed as sets of **tuples**, which are implemented in the form of tables. Conceptually, tables are easy to grasp, since it is a form that is familiar to most people. Anyone who has read a spreadsheet, a train timetable, or even a television guide is already familiar with the organization of data into columns and rows.

In this chapter, we will lay out the basic concepts of relational databases and describe the process of organizing data in a relational manner. The topics covered in this chapter are:

- ❑ **Schema normalization**
  The process by which redundancy and inconsistency are eliminated from the database

- ❑ **Keys**
  Fields or combinations of fields that are used to identify records

- ❑ **Referential integrity**
  A state of consistency for database schemata

- ❑ **Entity relationship diagrams**
  Models used to design databases

Tabular Data

As mentioned earlier, a table is a data structure that uses columns and rows to organize the data. As an example, consider the following ledger sheet sample of a charity containing details of the donations:

Donor	Donation 1	Donation 2	Donation 3
Marco Pinelli	$200 Solar Scholars		
Victor Gomez	$100 Pear Creek	$100 Danube Land Trust	$50 Forest Asia
Seung Yong Lee	$150 Forest Asia		

Tables represent **entities**, which are unique items like people, objects, and relationships about which we wish to store data. Each row represents an instance of the entity. In the above example, each row represents an instance of one donor. In relational database terminology, an instance is known as a **record**, but the terms row or tuple are also used.

Each column represents an **attribute** of the entity, or something about the entity. In this case, each column represents a donation made by the donor, listing the amount of the donation and the project to which the money is donated. In relational database terminology, an attribute is known as a **field**, but the term column is also very common. Adding or removing columns would change both the data stored in the table and the actual structure of the table, whereas adding or removing rows would only change data stored in the table. In other words, removing a column removes information about entities whereas removing a row only removes one instance of an entity but no information about them in general.

As we shall see in the next chapter, each field in a table is assigned a data type. The type indicates what sort of data will be stored in that field: text data, integer data, boolean (true or false) data, and so on. The assigned type then applies to that field's value for every record in the table.

Keys

We create databases because we need to store information. For the information in the database to be useful, we need to be able to perform certain operations on it. These operations fall broadly into two categories: reading the data, and changing the data. Whether one wishes to read a record, update it, or delete it, one first needs to identify the record in a way that distinguishes it from the other records in the table.

This is where keys come in. A **key** is a field or a combination of fields whose value identifies a record for a given purpose. One type of key is a unique key, which can be used to identify a single record. For example, every book has a unique ISBN (International Standard Book Number) that marks the book unmistakably. If a table of information about books includes an ISBN field, then that field can serve as a unique key.

A table might have more than one unique key. Suppose that each book in our table also has a unique product ID. While there is no problem with the existence of more than one unique key, it is considered desirable to have one that stands out as the **primary key** – the key that is considered the foremost means of identifying a record. In this case each of the unique keys is known as a **candidate key**, since each has the possibility of serving as the primary key. It is then up to the database designer to designate the primary key from among the candidate keys.

In our example from the previous section, the Donor field is a candidate key, if we accept (for now) that each donor is unique within the table. We shall revisit the topic of keys later in this chapter.

A Few Inadequacies

At first glance, a simple table such as the one shown in the chapter seems to meet all of our needs for storing data. When designing and filling the table, we may add as many fields and records as we like to accommodate large amounts of data. But after some examination, we are likely to encounter quite a few failings with our table. What if a donor makes more than three donations? We can add more fields to the table, of course, but to change the structure of a database once it is in use is extremely inconvenient. Also it is difficult to know in advance how many donations would be enough. What if one donor makes dozens of donations?

What if we wish to store more information about a project, such as a description? Or even more information about a donation, such as the date? Again, while it is conceivable that additional columns could address this issue, such a solution would be awkard and wasteful. If columns named DonationDate1 and DonationDate2 are added, the same uncertainty over the appropriate number of columns exists. Adding a description after every project name produces a lot of redundant data, since each project appears in the table multiple times. Every time a new donation is made, the description of the project would have to be repeated. Such redundancy is very inefficient as seen in the following table:

Donor	Amount1	Project1	Description1	Amount2	Project2	Description2
Marco Pinelli	$200	Solar Scholars	Powering schools with solar panels			
Victor Gomez	$100	Pear Creek cleanup	Cleaning up litter and pollutants from Pear Creek	$100	Danube Land Trust	Purchasing and preserving land in the Danube watershed
Seung Yong Lee	$150	Forest Asia	Planting trees in Asia			

The underlying problem is that a table is two-dimensional. It consists of columns and rows. Real-world data is usually multi-dimensional. We wish to store not only the data relevant to the donors and donations, but also data that relates to details in the table, such as additional information about the projects.

There is a solution to our problem. Relational databases allow us to create multiple tables of related data. The database designer uses the relationships between these tables to represent multi-dimensional data. This is also why they are called relational databases.

Let's now look at the process of normalization in relational databases.

Normalization

A **schema** (pl. schemata) is the basic organization of the database – the structure of the tables and the relationships among them. The term **normalization** refers to a series of steps used to eliminate redundancy and reduce the chances of data inconsistency in a database's schema. There are six forms of normalization described in relational database theory:

- ❑ First Normal Form
- ❑ Second Normal Form
- ❑ Third Normal Form
- ❑ Boyce Codd Normal Form
- ❑ Fourth Normal Form
- ❑ Fifth Normal Form

In practice, database designers mainly concern themselves with the first three forms. The last three are somewhat atypical in the practical world, but remain important in the realm of academic database theory.

First Normal Form

For a schema to meet the requirements of the **First Normal Form (1NF)**, every record within a table should have the same "shape", which means that every field should contain a single value only, and each row should contain the same fields. Duplicated fields (or groups of fields) should be removed.

In our charity donation example, the repeated donation fields, like Amount1 and Amount2, are a violation of First Normal Form. Some of the records (such as the one with Victor Gomez) use all of the fields, while others (such as Marco Pinelli), use only a few of them. These records clearly do not have the same shape. We will now change the table so that each record represents a single donation, thereby eliminating the duplicated fields:

Donor	Date	Amount	Project	Description
Marco Pinelli	13Dec2002	$200	Solar Scholars	Powering schools with solar panels
Victor Gomez	15Dec2002	$100	Pear Creek cleanup	Cleaning up litter and pollutants from Pear Creek
Victor Gomez	15Dec2002	$100	Danube Land Trust	Purchasing and preserving land in the Danube watershed
Victor Gomez	15Dec2002	$50	Forest Asia	Planting trees in Asia
Seung Yong Lee	16Dec2002	$150	Forest Asia	Planting trees in Asia

This arrangement is a significant improvement over our previous schema, since it offers greater flexibility. No matter how many donations `Victor Gomez` contributes, our new table can easily accommodate it simply by adding records.

An additional requirement of First Normal Form is that each record be uniquely identifiable. As we learned earlier in the chapter, this is accomplished with a primary key. In our original table, the `Donor` field could serve as the primary key. There was only one record per donor, and knowing the donor name was all that one needed to locate the specific record for that donor.

Our new table is a little more complicated. The donor name alone cannot serve as a primary key, since there may be multiple records for the same donor. For example, the name `Victor Gomez` does not uniquely identify any one record. Similarly, none of the values in the `Date`, `Amount`, or `Project` fields is necessarily unique. However, the combination of `Donor`, `Date`, and `Project` is unique. This is known as a **composite key**, a key that is composed of more than one field, as opposed to a **simple key**, which uses only one field. While there are many records for `Victor Gomez`, there is only one record for the same on `15Dec2002` for the `Forest Asia` project.

Composite primary keys are often the ideal solution for uniquely identifying records in a table. However, in our particular example, the composite key that we have chosen may be disadvantageous too. Although there are no two records in the table with the same combination of values for `Donor`, `Date`, and `Project`, we need to ask ourselves if it is impossible that the same donor could make more than one donation to the same project in a day. Though unlikely, it does seem possible, and we want our database schema to account for all possibilities. In such a situation, even a composite key is inadequate.

The primary keys that we have seen so far are *natural* or *logical keys* – keys that are derived from data that already existed in the table, such as the `Donor` field in our original table. When neither a simple key nor a composite key can be derived from among the fields in the table, it is common practice to create a new field dedicated to the purpose of serving as primary key. Such a key is known as an artificial key, or a **surrogate key**. Surrogate keys are fields whose values are changed automatically, to a value previously unused in that field with each new record. Let's add a surrogate key to uniquely represent each donation in the table. We'll place it at the beginning of the table, since that is where primary keys are conventionally kept:

DonationID	Donor	Date	Amount	Project	Description
1	Marco Pinelli	13Dec 2002	$200	Solar Scholars	Powering schools with solar panels
2	Victor Gomez	15Dec 2002	$100	Pear Creek cleanup	Cleaning up litter and pollutants from Pear Creek
3	Victor Gomez	15Dec 2002	$100	Danube Land Trust	Purchasing and preserving land in the Danube watershed

Table continued on following page

DonationID	Donor	Date	Amount	Project	Description
4	Victor Gomez	15Dec 2002	$50	Forest Asia	Planting trees in Asia
5	Seung Yong Lee	16Dec 2002	$150	Forest Asia	Planting trees in Asia

It is very common for a surrogate key to have a name that both describes the type of entity the table represents (such as a donation) and indicates that the purpose of the field is to identify the record (such as the ID).

This table now meets the requirements of First Normal Form. To summarize those requirements once more:

❑ All records in a table should have the same shape, or number of fields. Repetitive fields or groups of fields should be eliminated.

❑ Each record should be uniquely identifiable within the table.

Second and Third Normal Forms

Second Normal Form (2NF) and **Third Normal Form (3NF)** are very similar. Both are primarily concerned with eliminating data redundancy within a table. For a schema to be in Second Normal Form, it must meet the following requirements:

❑ The schema must meet all requirements of First Normal Form

❑ All non-primary-key fields which are dependent on part but not all of a primary key should be removed and placed in a separate table

For a schema to be in Third Normal Form, it must meet the following requirements:

❑ The schema must meet all requirements of Second Normal Form

❑ All fields which are dependent on a non-primary-key field should be removed and placed in a separate table

The first point of each list is important to note. The steps of normalization are cumulative. A schema cannot conform to Third Normal Form if it does not also conform to Second Normal Form, which in turn means that it must conform to First Normal Form.

The second points of the two lists are similar and may be combined like this:

> **All non-primary-key fields which are not fully dependent on the primary key should be removed and placed in a separate table.**

For example, the `Date` field is an attribute of the donation itself. It describes something about the donation, and therefore the `Date` field is considered to be dependent on the donation's primary key, the `DonationID`. Similarly, the `Project` field modifies the donation. It describes the project that the donation is for. However, the `Description` field does not directly modify the donation; it describes the project. It is thus dependent on the project, which is not the primary key of the table. Therefore, the `Description` field should be removed from the `Donation` table and placed in a separate table specific to the projects:

Name	Description
Solar Scholars	Powering schools with solar panels
Pear Creek cleanup	Cleaning up litter and pollutants from Pear Creek
Danube Land Trust	Purchasing and preserving land in the Danube watershed
Forest Asia	Planting trees in Asia

In the `Donation` table, we now have:

DonationID	Donor	Date	Amount	Project
1	Marco Pinelli	13Dec2002	$200	Solar Scholars
2	Victor Gomez	15Dec2002	$100	Pear Creek cleanup
3	Victor Gomez	15Dec2002	$100	Danube Land Trust
4	Victor Gomez	15Dec2002	$50	Forest Asia
5	Seung Yong Lee	16Dec2002	$150	Forest Asia

Not only does the introduction of a new table simplify our original table's design considerably, it also offers a new level of flexibility. We now have a place where we can store additional information about the project, such as the project's director or date of inception. In other words, our schema is no longer two-dimensional. The new table enables us to handle not only details about the donations, but also details about the projects to which donations are made. Now that we have introduced more than one table, it should be noted that the tables' names must be unique within the database.

We need to ensure that our new table also complies with the First Normal Form. It obviously does not have any duplicated fields. Does it have a primary key to uniquely identify each record? The project's name is unique within the table, but again we must ask, is it possible for two projects to have the same name? It is conceivable that the Pear Creek cleanup might be an annual event, and might be regarded as a new project each year, with the same name as the previous year's project. To be safe, it is a good idea to introduce a surrogate key to the `Project` table to serve as the primary key:

ProjectID	Name	Description
1	Solar Scholars	Powering schools with solar panels
2	Pear Creek cleanup	Cleaning up litter and pollutants from Pear Creek
3	Danube Land Trust	Purchasing and preserving land in the Danube watershed
4	Forest Asia	Planting trees in Asia

Foreign Keys

Now that the Project table has a reliable primary key, it makes sense that the Donation table should refer to the ProjectID rather than the name of the project, since the whole point is to definitively identify the project to which the donation was made:

DonationID	Donor	Date	Amount	ProjectID
1	Marco Pinelli	13Dec2002	$200	1
2	Victor Gomez	15Dec2002	$100	2
3	Victor Gomez	15Dec2002	$100	3
4	Victor Gomez	15Dec2002	$50	4
5	Seung Yong Lee	16Dec2002	$150	5

In the Donation table, the ProjectID field is what is known as a **foreign key**. It is a field which refers to the primary key of another table. Like primary keys, a foreign key may be either simple or composite, depending on whether the foreign table's primary key is simple or composite. A table may contain any number of foreign keys, since a table may contain data that relates to any number of foreign tables.

To further normalize our schema, we should create a Donor table, since it is likely that we will want to store more information about the donor. We will use a surrogate key, since it is not uncommon for different people to share the same name. In general, fields that represent the names of entities such as the names of people or companies, make poor primary keys due to the possibility of repeated values.

To demonstrate the flexibility of the added data dimension, we'll add a Country (of residence) field to the new table, but it can be easily imagined that organizations would probably also store many other details, such as contact information and the like:

DonorID	Name	Country
1	Marco Pinelli	Italy
2	Victor Gomez	United States
3	Seung Yong Lee	South Korea

The `Donation` table can now refer to the unique `DonorID` as a foreign key:

DonationID	DonorID	Date	Amount	ProjectID
1	1	13Dec2002	$200	1
2	2	15Dec2002	$100	2
3	2	15Dec2002	$100	3
4	2	15Dec2002	$50	4
5	3	16Dec2002	$150	4

A Key To Keys

With all of the choices of keys that we have discussed in this chapter, a quick review will help us at this stage. A key may be:

❑ **Primary or Foreign**
A primary key uniquely identifies each record in its table. A foreign key uniquely identifies a record in some other table.

❑ **Simple or Composite**
A simple key is composed of a single field. A composite key is a combination of fields whose values together identify the record.

❑ **Surrogate or Logical**
A surrogate (or artificial) key consists of unique, arbitrary values that abstractly represent the records in the table. A logical (or natural) key consists of the actual data, which may identify the record.

In the `Donation` table, the `DonationID` field is a surrogate or a primary key.

Boyce-Codd Normal Form

Boyce-Codd Normal Form (BCNF) is hierarchically placed between Third Normal Form and Fourth Normal Form and it is normally considered to be a more restrictive form of Third Normal Form. A table is considered to be in Boyce-Codd Normal Form if every determinant (any attribute whose values determine other values with a row) in the table is a candidate key. If a table contains only one candidate key, the 3NF and BCNF are equivalent.

Fourth and Fifth Normal Forms

Our database schema has come a long way from our original awkward ledger sheet. Third Normal Form is generally considered the acceptable level of normalization for professional database applications. Schemata that conform to Third Normal Form have consistent arrangements of keys and relationships with little to no redundancy within their tables. Hands-on database designers (as opposed to theoreticians) tend to regard Fourth and Fifth Normal Forms as belonging to the realm of academia, although real-world examples do sometimes arise.

Fourth Normal Form (4NF) involves multi-valued dependencies (that may contain multiple values for an entity). For example, a project is an entity within our database schema. Suppose we wish to store information about the project's fund-raising events and milestones (there is no relationship between a fund-raising event and a milestone, but each has a relationship to the project). We will quickly realize that each project may have multiple fund-raising events, as well as multiple milestones. As we are well versed with First Normal Form, we know better than to create a table with fields like `FundEvent1`, `FundEvent2`, and so on. However, we might just end up structuring the table like this:

ProjectID	FundEventID	MilestoneID
1	43	644
1	09	645
1	56	
2	43	679
2	110	780

This is really a violation of First Normal Form, because there is no primary key, but for the purpose of this example, we'll allow it to stand for a moment. If it really bothers you, pretend that there is a `RecordID` surrogate key. The quest for normalization can admittedly be an obsessive pursuit.

The `Solar Scholars` project (ID 1) has three fund-raising events, and only two milestones. Suppose we wish to remove fund-raising event `89` from the project. Should we replace the value `89` with a `Null` (empty) value? Or should we combine the second and third records? This would involve updating one record and deleting the other – an inefficient operation that increases the potential for error.

As you have probably guessed, we should split the table into two. The requirements for Fourth Normal Form are:

❑ The schema must meet all requirements of Third Normal Form

❑ No table should contain more than one multi-valued dependency

`FundEventID` and `MilestoneID` are both multi-valued dependencies. Each is dependent on the `ProjectID` and each represents a fact for which there may be multiple values per `ProjectID` (multiple fund-raising events per `ProjectID`, and multiple milestones per `ProjectID`). Separating the table into two solves the problem as shown in the two tables below.

In the `Project_FundEvent` table, we have:

ProjectID	FundEventID
1	43
1	89
1	56
2	43
2	110

In the `Project_Milestone` table, we have:

ProjectID	FundEventID
1	644
1	6445
2	679
2	780

This also solves the primary key problem. Each table may now have a composite primary key. The combination of `ProjectID` and `FundEventID` is unique. The reason why database designers rarely invoke Fourth Normal Form is that it is usually rendered difficult as a result of the pursuit of unique identifiers early in the schema-building process. Ensuring that primary keys exist for each table makes it difficult for two multi-valued dependencies to occur in one table in the first place.

Fifth Normal Form (5NF) is the most esoteric and the least applicable in the real world, therefore we will not discuss it in depth. It concerns multiple multi-valued facts that are related to each other as well as to another key (as opposed to the multi-valued dependencies mentioned above, which have relationships only to the `ProjectID`, not to each other). Untangling such complex relationships usually requires splitting tables into more than three related tables. Fifth Normal Form attempts to eliminate all remaining redundancy from a schema by decomposing each table to the point where it cannot be decomposed any further. It requires each field to be a candidate key, which is the main reason why it is generally considered unattainable in real-world applications.

Denormalization

Now that we've invested a valuable chunk of our day in learning about normalization, it's time to introduce the concept of **denormalization**, which is exactly what it sounds like: decreasing a schema's level of normalization. As we've learned, normalization eliminates the data redundancy within a table, which greatly reduces the risk that data may become inconsistent. Why would one wish to reverse this process?

Normalization usually comes at a cost: speed of retrieval. Before normalization, if we wanted to know a donor's name, the dates of the donations, and the name of the project, it was all right there in one record for us to pick. After normalization, we have to go traversing through three or four tables for the same information. In most cases, the extra work is worth it, considering the benefits of data consistency and reduced storage usage. However, in a few rare cases, the speed of data retrieval is the factor that trumps all others. In large databases with complex schemas, one might sometimes require data from twelve or more tables in a single query, and the application may need to perform this type of query hundreds of times per minute. In such situations, a fully normalized database may be unacceptably slow.

Denormalization should not be done early, however. It is a last desperate resort that one should turn to only after exhausting all other options (like query optimization, improved indexing, and database system tuning, all of which will be discussed later in the book). Normally, follow the simple rule:

When in doubt, normalize.

One alternative to denormalizing the base tables (the tables that make up a database) is to create a separate reporting table so that the base tables are left unaffected. For example, suppose that in our previous example, we very frequently need to retrieve a donor's name, donation ID, and the date of the donation. The query often proves to be too slow in providing results. This may not seem realistic, given that it only involves two tables and any modern RDBMS would handle this with break-neck speed, but just use your imagination. We might be tempted to re-enter the donor's name to our Donation table:

DonationID	DonorID	Donor	Date	Amount	ProjectID
1	1	Marco Pinelli	13Dec2002	$200	1
2	2	Victor Gomez	15Dec2002	$100	2
3	2	Victor Gomez	15Dec2002	$100	3
4	2	Victor Gomez	15Dec2002	$50	4
5	3	Seung Young Lee	16Dec2002	$150	4

This is a heart-breaking departure from everything we've worked so hard to achieve. See the redundancy? See the wasted space?

With a separate reporting table, our three base tables of Donation, Donor, and Project remain beautifully normalized. The schema as a whole is not fully normalized, because the reporting table itself is redundant, but at least all of the redundancy is concentrated and isolated in one table, whose sole job is to provide quick access to data that comes from multiple sources. Thus in the Donor table we have:

DonorID	Name	Country
1	Marco Pinelli	Italy
2	Victor Gomez	United States
3	Seung Yong Lee	South Korea

The Project table is as follows:

ProjectID	Name	Description
1	Solar Scholars	Powering schools with solar panels
2	Pear Creek cleanup	Cleaning up litter and pollutants from Pear Creek
3	Danube Land Trust	Purchasing and preserving land in the Danube watershed
4	Forest Asia	Planting trees in Asia

The Donation table is as follows:

DonationID	DonorID	Date	Amount	ProjectID
1	1	13Dec2002	$200	1
2	2	15Dec2002	$100	2
3	2	15Dec2002	$100	3
4	2	15Dec2002	$50	4
5	3	16Dec2002	$150	4

The purpose of the three tables shown above is to properly store the organization's data in a way that is consistent and reliable. They are the core tables on which the organization's applications will be based. In contrast, the Report_DonorName_Date table below is solely designed to facilitate a specific report without involving the base tables. We have not abided strictly to normalization with this table in order to provide a single location where the most frequently requested data might be accessed quickly.

The Report_DonorName_Date table is as follows:

DonationID	DonorName	Date
1	Marco Pinelli	13Dec2002
2	Victor Gomez	15Dec2002
3	Victor Gomez	15Dec2002
4	Victor Gomez	15Dec2002
5	Seung Yong Lee	16Dec2002

A reporting table is usually used as a data cache – a place to store amalgamated or semi-amalgamated data for fast access, which reduces demand on the main location where the data are stored in a raw state. Depending on the business requirements of the application, it might even be possible to only fill the Report_DonorName_Date table periodically, say overnight when the system is least busy. Others among us are not quite as lucky, and have to ensure that the data in the reporting table is no older than ten minutes, or even ten seconds. Even then, the reporting table offers a performance advantage. It is better to query the base tables once every ten seconds than hundreds or thousands of times per minute. Triggers, which will be discussed in Chapter 7, can be useful in keeping a reporting table up-to-date.

Denormalization is not pretty, but it is often helpful. If you absolutely must do it, then do it; but make sure you feel guilty about it, just like the professionals. A simple rule for beginners to database design is never denormalize.

Referential Integrity

Many relational database management systems include mechanisms that enforce a database's referential integrity. Referential integrity is another measure of the consistency of the data in a database. Referential integrity is violated when the relation to which a foreign key refers no longer exists.

For example, if one deletes a donor from the `Donor` table, without also deleting the corresponding donations from the `Donation` table, then the `DonorID` field in the `Donation` record would refer to a non-existent donor. In later chapters, we will discuss a few mechanisms that can be used to enforce referential integrity, including triggers, constraints, transactions, and stored procedures.

Entity Relationship Diagrams

With databases as with programming, manufacturing, and many other disciplines, before we build we should design. The database's design process begins with the design process of the application as a whole, including consideration of user requirements, design patterns, and system requirements. For more information on these topics, see Chapter 10.

An entity relationship diagram is used to illustrate all of the entities that an application must handle, and the relationships among the entities. This information is the blueprint for building the database tables.

Entities typically correspond to nouns that are involved with the process being automated. In the charity example explained in the chapter, nouns include donors, projects, and donations. Relationships correspond to the verbs. Take a look, and make note of how they interrelate. A donor *makes* donations. A project *has* multiple donations.

In an entity relationship diagram, entities are shown with their attributes listed below them:

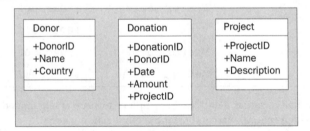

There is no one standard way to represent relationships. Some designers use diamond shapes containing a description of the relationship. Others use lines to connect the entities in a relationship. The line should specifically link each foreign key to its designated primary key as shown in the diagram below:

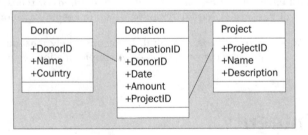

Types of Relationships

Both of the relationships illustrated opposite are one-to-many relationships. Each record in the `Donor` table may correspond to many records in the `Donation` table, however each record in the `Donation` table has only one corresponding record in the `Donor` table. Similarly, each project may have multiple donations, but each donation is made to only one project.

In entity relationship diagrams, the "one" side of the relationship is usually represented with a numeral `1`, and the "many" side of the relationship with either an `M` or the infinity symbol:

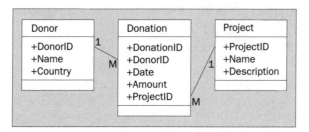

Sometimes relationships are one-to-one. Suppose that each of a manufacturer's products comes with one (and only one) user manual, and each manual only describes the product it accompanies:

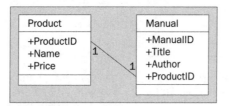

One-to-one relationships are somewhat rare, since one of the entities can often be represented simply as attributes of the other. Some database designers may choose to collapse the schema above into one entity:

Such a design decision would depend on several factors, such as the performance or significance of the individual entities within the application. For example, if other entities (like an `Author` table) in the schema also have relationships with the manual, then it is probably best to keep the `Manual` entity separate from the `Product` entity.

Many-to-many relationships are usually represented with the use of mediating one-to-many tables. Returning to our charity example, we can see that there is essentially a many-to-many relationship between donors and projects. Each donor may contribute to many projects, and each project may benefit from multiple donors. If we were to try to include the `ProjectIDs` in the `Donor` table, and the `DonorIDs` in the `Project` table, we would end up with a denormalized mess on our hands. The introduction of the `Donation` table deconstructs the many-to-many relationship into two very manageable one-to-many relationships.

A **recursive** relationship occurs when a column in a table refers to the primary key in the same table. This is very useful when describing hierarchical data structures in a table. In the following table of categories for an encyclopedia web site, the `ParentID` field refers to the `CategoryID` field:

CategoryID	Name	ParentID
1	Home	0
2	History	1
3	Mathematics	1
4	Asian History	2
5	Age of Exploration	2
6	Ancient India	4
7	Trigonometry	3
8	Algebra	3

The `History` category parents the `Asian History` category, which in turn parents the `Ancient India` category, and so on. Each record has a relationship with at least one other record in the same table. The following entity relationship diagram demonstrates the relationship:

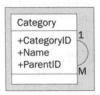

Summary

In this chapter, we have discussed the principles behind relational database design. Let us skim through them here.

Data is stored in two-dimensional tables consisting of columns (fields) and rows (records). Multi-dimensional data is represented by a system of relationships among two-dimensional tables. This usually leads to data storage becoming redundant, and also difficult to maintain on account of addition and deletion anomalies. This is only the case if we do not normalize the data.

Normalization is a process by which redundancy and inconsistency are reduced or eliminated from a database's schema. Denormalization is generally undesirable but sometimes necessary for performance reasons. Keys are fields or combinations of fields used to identify records. We also saw how entity relationship diagrams are used to map out the design of a database before it is built.

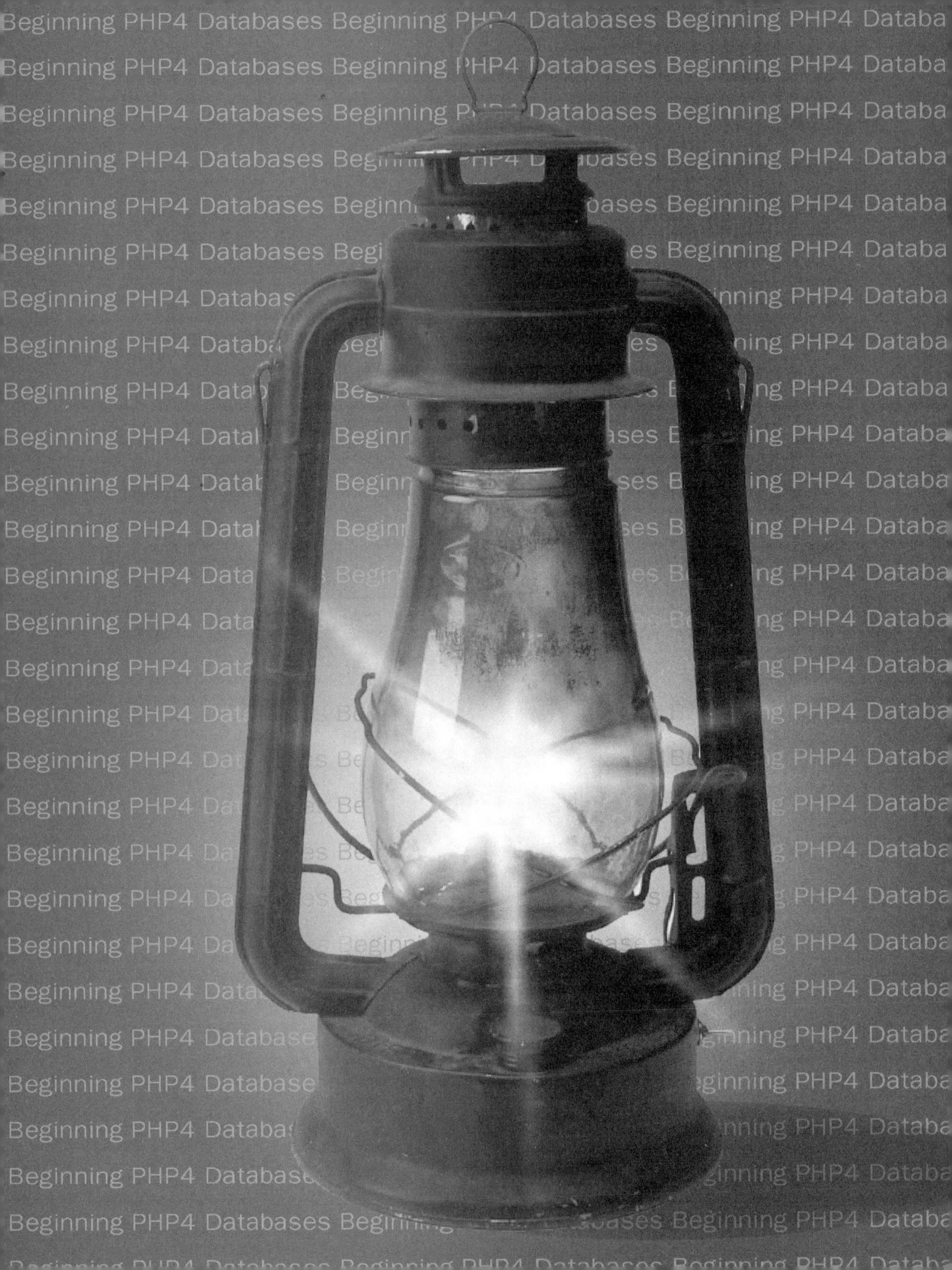
Beginning PHP4 Databases

The Structured Query Language

Chapter 2 introduced us to the relational database model as it evolved from some of the other database models, and Chapter 3 gave us a basic understanding on how to organize data in tables including the importance of normalization.

As we first saw in Chapter 2, **SQL (Structured Query Language)** is used to manipulate sets of data in RDBMS. This chapter will take the concept of databases and tables further and explain how to create and modify structures within our databases used to organize our data in the relational model. The next chapter will cover entering, deleting, changing, and manipulating the data in our relational tables.

This chapter should also familiarize you with the different ways to classify and structure data within a database for the benefit of efficient storage and rapid retrieval. We will conclude by looking at some database design considerations concerning application programming and database structure.

Upon completion of this chapter, you should have a thorough understanding of the following topics:

- ❑ History of the Structured Query Language
- ❑ Different specifications of SQL used by popular database vendors
- ❑ How SQL and relational databases work together
- ❑ An introduction to transactions
- ❑ SQL data types
- ❑ Backus-Naur Form notation of SQL syntax
- ❑ Practical use of SQL Data Definition Language statements

The Evolution of SQL

SQL has had a long and varied existence both academically and in the enterprise. So an understanding of the major participants in SQL development as well as the different flavors that relational database vendors will have implemented should help a programmer to be aware of the issues faced when developing the PHP applications.

Codd and Crew

Dr. E. F. Codd first published his paper on the Relational Model in 1970, while working at the San Jose IBM research laboratory. It was titled "A Relational Model of Data for Large Shared Data Banks".

The impact of Codd's first paper and the research at IBM can be seen by the flurry of subsequent activity undertaken to produce real software to harness the power of these relational concepts. IBM had the jump on the competition and produced an initial database implementation of Codd's research called System R. This had a data manipulation language dubbed SEQUEL, or the Structured English Query Language. During revisions the SEQUEL name was shortened to SQL, recursively defined in good UNIX fashion as the SQL Query Language. This evolution might be why SQL is often pronounced "See-Kwell", but it's arguably more proper to pronounce the SQL acronym as its component letters "Ess-Cue-Elle".

With the success of the System R implementation, IBM and other vendors rushed to produce commercial products that would become what we know today as Relational Database Management Systems. A company by the name Relational Software Incorporated brought the first RDBMS to market in 1979, and named it **Oracle**. The company later changed its name to Oracle Corporation. Two years later, IBM released its first RDBMS, SQL/DS, and then later released DB2 in 1983.

Throughout the 1980's, many other vendors released products that implemented SQL and the relational model but it wasn't until 1986 that a technical committee within **ANSI**, the American National Standards Institute, codified the SQL standard as ANSI SQL-86.

SQL-86, SQL-92, and SQL:1999

ANSI's X3H2 committee formalized the SQL-86 standard, and then **ISO**, the International Standards Organization, published the Database Language SQL specification in 1987 as a strict, vendor-neutral subset of the SQL-86 standard. Several shortcomings in the SQL-86 specification, including lack of referential integrity and vague determination on how to embed SQL in other programming languages (such as C, Ada, and COBOL) were addressed in a revision of the SQL specification published in 1992 called SQL-92.

There are at least two other groups that had an impact on how SQL-92 was implemented, the X/Open group and SAG(SQL Access Group). X/Open is a group comprised mostly of UNIX vendors that publish portability guides for different platforms. With regard to SQL, X/Open published guides for the application developer encouraging practices that allowed cross-platform functionality. SAG was another consortium including IBM and Microsoft that developed the **SQL/CLI**, or the SQL Call Level Interface, so that the new SQL-92 could be used in remote, client-server fashion. As a final note on these organizations, the **ODBC (Open Database Connectivity)** standard, was developed by X/Open and SAG as an implementation of SQL/CLI according to their recommendations.

SQL:1999 is the latest iteration of the SQL standard. Originally named SQL3 while in a working stage, it was named SQL:1999 upon publication (note that it was not named "SQL-99"). The four-digit date use is perhaps a nod to Y2K concerns that were prevalent in 1999. The use of a colon instead of a hyphen reflects the increased international use of SQL from 1992 to 1999 and conformance with the ISO instead of ANSI naming conventions. The SQL:1999 standard is contained in the joint committee article entitled: ISO/IEC 9075:1999(E) Information technology – Database languages – SQL.

It's also important to note here that vendors will provide RDBMs that comply to the standard at the entry (or transitional), intermediate, or full level.

Further Specification Partitioning

The SQL standard has grown in size throughout its evolution, as new features and core functional areas were added. Between 1992 and 1999 additional work was done to improve the specification and add new functional areas. The interim publishing of SQL/CLI was in 1995, followed by SQL/PSM (covering the use of stored procedures, or Persistent Stored Modules) in 1996, and SQL/OLB (covering Object Language Bindings in SQL for use in languages such as Java) in 1998. With this there was a clear separation between different areas of the SQL standard. When SQL:1999 was finally published, it included these components as well as changes made to SQL-92.

To keep things clear, the SQL standard was broken up in eight parts by ISO and ANSI in 1993. As a summary of the above section, here is a chart describing the different areas of the SQL multi-part standard:

Part	Name	Description
1	Framework	Information about how the SQL specification is documented
2	Core (or Foundation)	Core SQL Standard – what we will be mostly seeing in this book
3	SQL/CLI	The CLI-95 standard: Call Level Interface
4	SQL/PSM	The PSM-96 standard: Persistent Stored Modules
5	SQL/Bindings	Programming language bindings, between SQL data types, objects, and programming language variables
6	Removed	Formerly SQL/XA – dealing with transaction managers (the dedicated section was removed from the standard)
7	SQL/Temporal	Time-series data types and how to manipulate them
8	Removed	The dedicated section was removed from the standard as the partitioning solidified
9	SQL/MED	Management of External Data – manipulating non-SQL data using SQL
10	SQL/OLB	Object programming language bindings

Several items in this table are still in the revision process. A Part 11 called SQL/Schemata (merging Part 2 and Part 5) has been proposed to the standard. However, the Core, CLI, and PSM are all in wide use and relevant to our tasks as programmers. As mentioned earlier, ODBC is an implementation of CLI used in external SQL, PSM is the specification for how databases handle stored SQL (more on this in Chapter 7) and of course, the main "body" of SQL commands that we deal with directly is in the *Core* section of the multi-part specification.

SQL Concepts in Relational Databases

Going back to Chapter 2 and our coverage of Codd's Rules and the Relational Model, it would be tempting to assume that a RDBMS is a true implementation of the Relational Model. While this is not far off, there are some differences between the academic model and a practical application. For instance, that between the concepts of a **relation** in the model as equated to a **table** in RDBMS. They are nearly identical, except that a table can have duplicate rows. This is a simple example to point out that while vendor implementations of database systems provide the power of the Relational Model to our programming tasks, they might not hold to the theories as tightly as we may expect. This having been said, RDBMS implementations are targeted at real-world management of data, so will often implement features to supplement a pure Relational Model.

One area of practical implementation at the vendor level that is extremely important, is that of **transactions**. A transaction is a set of operations on data that must occur either all together or not at all.

Take for example the real-world example of a financial transaction – withdrawing money from an Automated Teller Machine. Let us postulate that several things might have to occur for the financial transaction to happen properly:

1. Specifying the amount you wish to receive at the ATM terminal

2. Checking the account balance to determine if funds are available

3. Deducting the withdrawal from your bank account

4. Delivering the cash to you at the ATM so you can go buy a pizza

Viewing these four simple steps as a single transaction shows us how important it is that they occur together and in order. Transactions in the context of RDBMS also are concerned with the operations of **commit** and **rollback**. What this means is, if all four steps occur successfully, the transaction is committed or finalized. If one of the component steps of the transaction fails, then it is "rolled back". This resets the system to a state before the first step of the transaction.

A rollback's usefulness becomes clear when you consider a system failure interrupting the transaction between steps 3 and 4. The above section should give you an idea of the issues involved when designing your application to use transactions. While an ATM financial transaction is not really a database transaction in the strictest sense, it is analogous and serves to illustrate the concept.

Transactions and ACIDity

In the context of database systems, transactions are primarily concerned with four criteria. An RDBMS treatment of transactions needs to meet the ACID criteria that are listed below:

❑ Atomicity

❑ Consistency

❑ Isolation

❑ Durability

Turn to Chapter 6 for an in-depth coverage on ACID criteria and transactions in PHP.

SQL Data Types

A **data type** specifies the type of information a field in our database rows will hold. This will have wide impact on the development process, including affecting the application logic used to manipulate the data, storage space, and performance considerations of the data within our database, and conversion between data of different types providing portability of the application across RDBMSs.

Adherence to a data type also controls what kind of information a database is willing to accept. As we will see, trying to insert the word ONE in an field of type INTEGER will produce errors or otherwise cause something to happen in lieu of storing the word ONE in the database.

The next section will go through the data types laid out by the SQL standard. Keep in mind that there will be some differences in vendor implementations, both in naming of and in adherence to data types, which are controlled by the database engine.

Numeric Data Types

These are a class of numbers. Specifying that a field is one of the numeric types means that it will only contain numeric data. This numerical data can be of either exact or approximate value.

If exact, the numeric data types will specify a **precision** and **scale**. Precision specifies how many significant digits the specific data has, and scale specifies how many decimal places the data has.

If approximate, numeric data types specify a precision, and have a **mantissa** and an **exponent**. A mantissa is the main signed (positive or negative) integer in the data, and the exponent is a signed integer that indicates the magnitude of the mantissa. In addition, the numeric data types can often be created as signed or unsigned, with a signed data type possessing twice the possible values.

We will now look at the different numeric data types.

INTEGER and SMALLINT

These two types specify numeric data of an exact value. Integer values, often abbreviated as INT and SMALLINT, are not specified with any parameters since their precision and scale are handled by the underlying vendor database implementation. An example of an INT or SMALLINT value would be 1.

Choices about which one to use when specifying a field definition should be based on the size of the numbers needed to populate the field. If larger numbers aren't going to be needed by the application, SMALLINT may save some storage space or provide minor speed gains depending on the database implementation. Also, some RDBMSs may implement TINYINT, a data type with a single digit of precision that can be used in place of the Boolean type that we will discuss in a moment.

NUMERIC and DECIMAL

These data types allow specification of precision (P) and scale (S). In the case of NUMERIC, the resulting field is controlled completely by your definition. With DECIMAL, also written as DEC, the scale is controlled by your definition but the precision might be implemented larger than you specify if the database implementation is written to do so. A point on optimization here – specifying a larger precision than required, when creating a schema, will have negative impacts on performance and storage efficiency, as the RDBMS must account for the possibility of additional digits. This also means that data types with a greater range, or list of possible values, will often be less efficient.

As an example of defining fields with these data types, DEC(5,3) or NUMERIC(5,3) could hold the number 12.345 where the 5 specifies the precision, or number of digits in the data, and 3 specifies the scale, or number of decimal places. Also, NUMERIC is often used to represent money when defined with a scale of 2.

REAL

This is the first one of the approximate numeric types, and defines a single precision floating point number. Examples of a REAL type might be .5 or 5.

DOUBLE

DOUBLE is also an approximate like REAL, but constitutes a double precision number, such as .05 or 5.0 or 50.

FLOAT

FLOAT is the third approximate numeric type, and can be annotated FLOAT(P), indicating that the precision is specified in the field definition. An example of FLOAT(5) could be 123.45 or 1.2345. Regarding the mantissa and exponent, FLOAT as well as REAL and DOUBLE will actually be split into exponential notation and stored by the database implementation in that fashion.

Character Data Types

Character types include words, letters, and other text-based data (like PHP code, XML), and specify the size of the data type. The types of characters that can be stored in your database are going to be determined by the character sets that your database supports. This should include the western character set Latin-1 and ASCII at the minimum. The character sets in use in our schema will also determine sorting of character type results. In addition, different implementations handle over-filling of character data types differently. Many databases will simply accept the text and truncate it to fit, while others will store it but require special parameters passed to retrieve the complete data.

The take-away lesson here is – develop good habits and know your data types.

We will now look at the character data types.

CHAR

CHAR is an abbreviation for CHARACTER. Either type-specifier is correct when defining a field. CHAR takes a parameter of length, so CHAR(20) defines a character field that will store a string of twenty characters. Note that defining a CHAR type causes the field to fill up to that amount of characters. For example, if you entered the word aardvark into a CHAR(20) field, the string would be stored with twelve blanks after the text.

Defining a field simply as CHAR is the same as specifying CHAR(1).

VARCHAR

VARCHAR stands for Varying Character (or Character Varying, depending on the publication). It is just like CHAR, with the exception that it does not pad out the field with blanks. Inserting aardvark into a VARCHAR(20) field would only result in eight characters stored. This of course has positive benefits on storage, but it may decrease performance, as the RDBMS now needs to take into account different amounts of memory for values across a single column.

VARCHAR's length must be defined; there is no default of 1 like CHAR.

CLOB

CLOB stands for Character Large Object, and it's used for storage of very large strings of characters such as document pages, code in text (such as XML, HTML, or PHP) or other large pages of text data. CLOB was added in SQL:1999 and may not be supported in your database so check your documentation. Some RDBMS's may also have TEXT or MEMO fields to serve this purpose.

As well as specifying a number of characters in the definition, for example CLOB(50), the size can also be specified with K, M, and G, which stand for kilo, mega, and giga indicating 1024, 1024^2, and 1024^3 respectively. For example, CLOB(100K) would define a CLOB of up to 102,400 characters.

NCHAR, NVARCHAR, and NCLOB

The N-Character types were added in SQL-92 as well. N stands for National. These three types are identical to the previous three character types, with the exception that they are defined to use foreign language character sets, such as Arabic, Japanese, or Chinese. This is again database vendor-specific, and while the SQL standard specifies the data type, most database products have not implemented these types.

Binary Data Types

Binary refers to information coded in a series of ones and zeros. Binary data types can store data in these encodings, or in strings of any arbitrary characters. Character data is reduced to its binary value when used in these types. Again, choosing a data type closely defined to the type of data that will be stored is very important for performance and storage efficiency.

The binary data types BIT and VARBIT were added in SQL-92, and BLOB was added in SQL-1999.

BIT

BIT was added to allow databases to store arbitrary strings of bits. Like CHAR, specifying simply BIT in a field definition implies BIT(1). Similar to CHAR, BIT(x) definitions pad storage of data with empty spaces.

VARBIT

VARBIT (or more properly BIT VARYING) has a form like VARCHAR, allowing storage of varying length bit strings and requiring specification of the maximum length in the field definition. For example, VARBIT(10) allows binary data up to ten places.

BLOB

BLOB is a new type in SQL:1999, and stands for **Binary Large Objects**. Like CLOB, BLOB types are used for storing large strings of bytes. Also like CLOB, the BLOB data type may be specified with the K, M, and G – short for kilo, mega, and giga. BLOB(10G) would define a binary object of up to 10,073,741,842 bytes.

Temporal Data Types

Temporal refers to time, so temporal data types deal with different semantic categories of capturing time data.

The SQL-92 specification has an extremely complex handling of temporal data types. The standard calls for a special system table for conversion of temporal data types that handles global time zone information, synchronizing country and commerce time zones, and handling translation of Daylight Savings Time (for the United States). Not only does the standard specify ways to translate these against **UTC** (Universal Coordinated Time, which is Greenwich Mean Time), but it also handles differences in the global format.

This mapping system is very complex, and is supported only partially in database products, if at all; so check your documentation thoroughly.

Let us now look at temporal data types.

DATE

The DATE type stores information on year, month, and day.

Dates are normally stored in SQL according to the ISO 8601:1988 standard, which specifies yyyy-mm-dd format, although vendors will sometimes override this format. Unless they do, it's important to convert to this format before storing the dates in your database. Additionally, yyyy-mmm-dd is sometimes used in applications, where mmm is the three-letter month abbreviation, to allow easier reading in reports or hand sorting of printed records. For example, a set containing Jun and Jul is much easier to sort than any containing say Ju and Ju or even Jn and Jl.

Regardless of the format you choose to display in your application, standardizing and converting the date format before database storage is important and may be assisted by language, or database-specific functions.

Defining a field with data type of DATE is straightforward and takes no parameters. The DATE type is assumed to have ten positions, filled by yyyy-mm-dd.

TIME

The TIME data type is used for storing hours, minutes, and seconds, in the format hh-mm-ss[.ssssss].

What are the extra seconds for? While hh is based on military hours of 0-23, and mm is obviously 00-59, the extra seconds allow for an optional fractional component and range from 0-61.999999. The extra 2.999999 seconds (everything above 59) allow for corrections occasionally made by global time references, as well as the possibility to store precisions greater than a single second. For the most part you can safely ignore the fractional seconds unless you have a specific need for them.

Like DATE, TIME doesn't require any parameters. It is assumed to have eight positions with no fractional digits, or a minimum of ten positions if there are any fractional digits. The two additional digits are arrived at by counting the decimal point, and any digits to the right of the decimal. The SQL standard calls for support of six fractional digits, or 15 total positions, but this can be greater if a vendor chooses to support additional fractional digits in a specific implementation. A greater number of positions can optionally be added to a field declared as type TIME with a non-negative integer like: TIME(20), annotated as TIME(p).

> **Your database implementation may support TIME WITH TIME ZONE, requiring an additional 6 positions to capture the offset from UTC, ranging from −12:59 to +13:00.**

TIMESTAMP

The third temporal type is used for storing year, month, day, hour, minute, and second, in the format yyyy-mm-dd-hh-mm-ss[.ssssss], assumed to be 19 positions, or 21 minimum with fractional digits. Again, a minimum of six fractional digits should be supported by SQL-92-compliant database systems.

TIMESTAMP can be considered a combination of DATE and TIME, so it should not be surprising that the number of positions can optionally be specified with TIMESTAMP(p).

> **Your database implementation may also support TIMESTAMP WITH TIME ZONE, requiring an additional 6 positions to capture the offset from UTC, ranging from −12:59 to +13:00.**

INTERVAL

An INTERVAL type is used to describe the **difference** between two temporal values. Two INTERVAL types are commonly used, with **year-month** and **day-time** intervals being allowed by SQL:1999. Year-month simply contains yyyy-mm, and day-time contains the fields dd and any other temporal values besides year or month, for example hours, minutes, or seconds.

> **INTERVAL data types only mandate that the first temporal value be specified, so it's perfectly valid to only use a year value in an INTERVAL type.**

While vendor implementations may vary widely here, for completeness some appropriate definitions of INTERVAL types using the different ranges include:

- ❑ INTERVAL YEAR
- ❑ INTERVAL MONTH
- ❑ INTERVAL YEAR TO MONTH
- ❑ INTERVAL DAY
- ❑ INTERVAL SECOND
- ❑ INTERVAL HOUR
- ❑ INTERVAL DAY TO SECOND
- ❑ INTERVAL DAY TO MINUTE
- ❑ INTERVAL DAY TO HOUR

> It's also important to note that the number of positions can be specified, and if they are not, the temporal value defaults to two positions. For example INTERVAL YEAR(4) is appropriate to address Y2K concerns.

Other Data Types

Aside from the data types already covered, there are several other types you may come across when working with RDBMS's that implement the SQL:1999 standard more completely. Most database vendors will not support many of these types, so familiarity with your database environment is essential. That being said, there are some very powerful additional types specified in SQL:1999 and utilizing them in your applications can offload some of the application logic burden to the database in a simple fashion. Be aware, however, that using features that are not adequately supported in most RDBMSs may have the drawback of making your application implementation-specific.

Let us now look at these additional data types.

BOOLEAN

A True/False programming logic structure is handled by the BOOLEAN data type, first introduced in SQL:1999. Depending on the RDBMS implementation, you can store one or a combination of True, False, T, F, 1, and 0. Since the BOOLEAN type is optimized for the three-value logic of Yes/No/Unknown, it is often more efficient than using a 1 and 0 in an INT or TINYINT.

LOCATOR

As mentioned earlier in the chapter, it is sometimes useful to store Binary and Character Large Objects using the BLOB and CLOB types. One programming concern here is that manipulating data in these fields from your PHP application might require transferring the large object type column to the client application environment. To reduce the overhead associated with bringing the entire BLOB data across the wire, SQL:1999 introduced the LOCATOR type.

Like ARRAY, LOCATOR is declared in the context of another data type: <datatype> AS LOCATOR. For example: BLOB(10M) AS LOCATOR.

The LOCATOR is used in SQL statements as a parameter to manipulating LOB types.

> Tables actually never have a field of type LOCATOR; instead of a declaration on a field, LOCATOR can instead be thought of as a virtual record handle created to point to the LOB-typed fields.

ROW

Also new in SQL:1999, there is now a dedicated ROW data type. While SQL has of course always handled rows, you as the programmer can now create rows explicitly. As you will see in the next section, creating tables with specific row definitions does not require use of this type, but the ROW data type allows complex structures to be created using the declaration syntax ROW(field_1, field_2, field_n). Here each field_n is expanded as NAME, DATATYPE, and OPTIONS. For example:

```
ROW( foo VARCHAR(100), bar BLOB(2M) )
```

It's also possible to create more complex structures, as shown in the following example:

```
ROW( first ROW( foo VARCHAR(100), bar BLOB(2M) ), second ROW( foo2 VARCHAR(20),
bar2 BLOB(1M) ) )
```

This can be useful to simplify your schema creation scripts, or to allow your application to create tables itself with syntax that is more concise. As always, explore your database documentation to determine how the explicit ROW type (often called Anonymous ROW) is implemented by your RDBMS.

User-Defined

During the long gap between the codification of SQL-92 and SQL:1999 publication, developers and database vendors added on to SQL implementations in proprietary ways. Among these were ways of handling impending object technology, which resulted in SQL:1999 allowing for user-defined data types.

When the user defines a data type, its name and properties (meta data) are stored in the RDBMS's system tables and the new type is treated with similar rules as the existing native types.

There are two categories of user-defined data types in SQL:1999 – DISTINCT and STRUCTURED.

DISTINCT

The DISTINCT type is a persistent named type, derived from a single other data type. As an example, an application used to track baseball statistics could declare a field name BATTING_AVG as NUMERIC(3,3), which would give us a sample data of, say, .115.

So why is this more useful than using the underlying data type and attributes?

Simply put, DISTINCT types enable the programmer to ensure that only data defined as that new type is added to the database. It should be apparent that the definition of a DISTINCT type is usually narrower than the parent type, giving the programmer finer control over the data types in the application and providing a mechanism for flexibly extending the RDBMS data types. Also, SQL:1999 does not allow mathematical functions against the DISTINCT types, or between the DISTINCT types and the underlying type unless explicit conversion back to the underlying type is performed first, and computations functions are supported against the underlying type. That being said, you will see in Chapter 7 that PSM-96 supports a very wide range of function declaration, and these can be created for DISTINCT data types as well as native types.

STRUCTURED

The second user-defined type is STRUCTURED type, which may be considered as a complex type defined as a combination of other types. A STRUCTURED type can have attributes that form any of the other types.

Conversion of Types: Casting

We have spent the bulk of the past few pages discussing how the SQL standard specifies data typing. For example, dividing the data storage metaphors into conceptual buckets used to keep data of different types separate from each other. This is of extreme value to the application developer, but what if we encounter a case where we need to compare data of one type to data of another type?

This is where CASTing comes in. A CAST expression selects data from one data type and converts it into another. In conditions where the two types are similar, all this does is allow us to do comparisons between them in our SQL statements.

We will see more SQL statements later on in the book, but the typical CAST syntax could be expressed as such:

```
<SQL statement>…
CAST (table.column AS <new_datatype>);
```

In addition, the syntax below is valid:

```
CAST NULL AS <new datatype>;
```

This allows us to perform comparisons in SQL across tables of different structure. Note that you will get an error if you attempt to convert data across internal data type constraints. For example, attempting to convert a BLOB into an INT will not work due to size constraints.

Nulls

As mentioned earlier in the book, allowing data types to have a Null value infers the possibility of missing data. Simply put, a Null value in a field implies that the value is unkown. This is different from a zero value, and may be considered undefined. By default, fields are allowed this state, although specifying NOT NULL in a field definition forces values to be entered for each field.

Be careful not to use NOT NULL indiscrimately. It might make sense for some of the fields of your database table, but only if every row of that table has a value for all of those fields. For fields that might have empty rows, do not use the NOT NULL declaration. Allowing Nulls is quite common, and is not terribly bad database design. Note that it is also possible to specify the default values for a field at definition time to ensure that some value is inserted by the database.

Also, with regards to BOOLEAN types, allowing Nulls provides the programmer to use a 3-value logic structure, essentially adding Unknown to True or False.

Data Definition Language

So far in the chapter, we have covered the different types of data that SQL-compliant RDBMS's may understand, as well as the basic syntax for declaring new fields of each type. The declarations will actually be used in SQL's Data Definition Language, abbreviated SQL DDL or simply DDL, which is a subset of SQL that deals with creation and manipulation of SQL objects in the database.

It's important to note that DDL is actually an SQL-92 term, where SQL statements are delineated into three **classes** of statements, comprised of DDL, **DML (Data Manipulation Language)**, and **DCL (Data Control Language)**. We will cover DML and DCL in the next chapter, but in short they handle acting on data in a database and changing permissions of a database user over these data structures.

With the advent of SQL:1999, the divisions of Core SQL have changed a bit, revising the divisions into seven core categories as shown below:

Core Class Statements	Use
SQL Connection Statements	Opening and closing client connections
SQL Control Statements	Controlling execution of SQL statements
SQL Data Statements	Creating and manipulating field data in the database
SQL Diagnostic Statements	Retrieving, debugging, and error information
SQL Schema Statements	Creating and manipulating the database structural objects
SQL Session Statements	Altering parameters of the SQL connection
SQL Transaction Statements	Controlling the start and end of transactions

With this in mind, it could be argued that SQL DDL is no longer a proper recourse for describing creation and control of higher-level database objects. However, for practical purposes the SQL DDL and the SQL Schema statements are equivalent and both terms are in common use across SQL:1999 implementations.

Moving forward, we shall discuss some of the common higher-level structures that will contain the fields, or rows of data. After we have a better understanding of the database objects that we can create, we will pull it all together and create database structures that contain the higher-level structures as well as the field data types discussed earlier.

We have learnt about **meta data** being data about other data. Taking this definition into the context of how a database controls the shape and structure of its container objects, meta data may be seen as information that a RDBMS uses to keep track of its own current state. This includes not only information about the data types of fields, but all of the other database objects used to manipulate the structure and storage of this data. A list of table names in the database catalog, and user privileges on tables are examples of meta data that can be queried.

SQL DDL Keywords

Before we begin coverage on the database objects that we may wish to create to structure our application data, there are several keywords that can be used in combination with the data types and SQL data objects to actually do the work of instantiating, modifying, and deleting database structure.

Among these keywords, the following three are the most commonly used:

❑   CREATE

❑   DROP

❑   ALTER

CREATE

As its name implies, the CREATE keyword instantiates an instance of a database object with all required database object parameters within the RDBMS:

```
CREATE SCHEMA [name of schema] [AUTHORIZATION schema_owner]
[DEFAULT CHARACTER SET name_of_character_set];
```

This example is fairly self-explanatory. A CREATE SCHEMA command takes the name of the schema and assigns ownership to a user in the database and sets the default character set used in the schema.

DROP

The DROP keyword is, of course, the converse of CREATE. It deletes the resources associated with a table and removing its definition from the meta data stored in the database:

```
DROP TABLE [databasename.] [owner_name.] tablename;
```

This can be generalized as:

```
DROP database_object_type [owner_name.] database_object_name
```

Again, this is fairly self-explanatory. The DROP statement takes optional parameters to uniquely identify the database object we wish to remove.

ALTER

ALTER is a keyword used to modify the structure of data objects by changing their meta data definition as presented in the schema tables. It can be used against most of the database objects we have covered in this section:

```
ALTER TABLE table_name [ADD [COLUMN] column_name datatype datatype_attributes];
```

The ALTER statement can have ADD, DROP, or ALTER lines associated with it, depending on the type of database object we wish to alter. It is also important to note that an ALTER statement for a table could include another ALTER statement on a column as well as the ADD syntax shown in the above syntax.

As we cover database objects, we will see more examples of CREATE, DROP, and ALTER used to manipulate the structure of our databases.

Database Objects

While there is some debate over the appropriate list of database objects, and certainly some variation across vendor-specific implementations of these objects, the following list is fairly complete and adheres to the SQL:1999 standard. As always, familiarity with your database documentation will save you a great deal of pain, and allow you to quote the specifications with the exact features and syntax that your database products implement.

Schemas

A schema is a uniquely named set of database objects owned by a specific user. The term database, as used in common parlance, would actually be more accurately termed a schema:

```
CREATE SCHEMA taskforward AUTHORIZATION admin;
```

While this example is syntactically correct, many RDBMS vendors implement a CREATE DATABASE command instead.

Catalogs

A catalog is a uniquely named set of schemas. Catalogs will contain not only user schemas, but an INFORMATION_SCHEMA, which holds meta data information on all of the other database objects contained within that catalog. There is another concept, the **Cluster**, which is a catalog of catalogs, containing meta data on all of the catalogs available to an SQL session. Most RDBMSs don't implement true clusters, but instead manage meta data specific to a cluster concept, such as database-wide permissions, in a master catalog. Also, not all RDBMSs implement catalogs, as is seen by the lack of this feature in MySQL.

Tables

We have mentioned tables several times in this book thus far. It should be clear to the reader that a table (based on the Relational Model concept of a relation) is a series of uniquely identifiable rows of data. Drilling down, there are actually two distinct types of table objects supported by the SQL:1999 standard – **Base** and **Derived** tables.

Base Table Types

Base tables are the ones that are stored in the database; for example, their data actually resides in columns and rows within the table.

Among the Base table types are:

- ❑ Persistent Base tables
- ❑ Global Temporary tables
- ❑ Local Temporary tables

Persistent Base tables are what we might think of as standard tables. For example, they are created, exist unless removed, and are accessible to SQL across the entire schema.

Global Temporary tables are temporary. Their meta data definitions are stored in the schema permanently, but the actual table structure isn't manifested until referenced in an SQL statement. One ramification of this is that temporary tables cannot be shared across different SQL connection sessions, as each one will cause a materialization of the data.

Local Temporary tables may be created or declared. A created Local Temporary table acts like a Global Temporary with differences in user rights. A declared Local Temporary is accessed only by a stored SQL program within the database – a PSM, or Persistent Stored Module, as clarified further in the section on PSMs further down the page.

Base tables are created as inherently read-write, by specifying the table name, data types, and parameters:

```
CREATE TABLE table_name (
column_name data_type [parameters]
);
```

Derived Table Types

The Derived table types refer to those tables that are created using data and rows from one or more Base tables from an SQL query. We will get more into queries in the next chapter, but suffice it to say that Derived tables can be supersets of other tables or canned queries called **Views**, which aid in mapping an application-specific view of data to a virtual table from the underlying database structure. Views will be covered in detail in Chapter 7, but it is important to understand how they can benefit the application programmer with alternative perspectives on data.

Derived tables are created as either read-write or read-only:

```
CREATE VIEW view_name (
column_list
AS (Select statement)
);
```

Columns

A column is a component of a table, with a unique name describing a single attribute of the table object. Alternative names for this object include `Attribute` and `Field`.

Domains

A domain is a range of allowable values for a specific column.

Triggers

A trigger falls under the category of an SQL rule as well. While rules generally specify the range of values that a database column may contain, triggers are definitions on columns that can act on values within columns based on specific criteria. As an example, a Human Resources database application might specify a trigger to update a field in a benefits table when a promotion causes a job code to change in another table. Triggers are a great way to off load application logic 'weight' from the application layer to the database system.

We will cover this in more depth in Chapter 7, but as we can see from this syntax example, triggers often work with procedures, defined next:

```
CREATE TRIGGER trigger_name
BEFORE UPDATE OF column_list
ON table_name
FOR EACH ROW
CALL PROCEDURE procedure_name();
```

Procedures

As discussed previously in the chapter, procedures are governed by the SQL/PSM partition of the SQL:1999 specification, originally designated as PSM-96. Procedures are functions comprised of SQL statements embedded directly within the database. They are another great way to offload application logic to the database server (Chapter 7 will cover Procedures in greater depth). In addition, Persistent Stored Modules can be extended and used by other applications – we will see examples of this in Chapter 14 where the Virtuoso database wraps PSMs from other databases in web services logic.

Basic syntax for PSM creation would be as follows:

```
CREATE PROCEDURE procedure_name()
(column_name datatype, column_name2 datatype)
AS 'SELECT statement…'
END PROCEDURE procedure_name;
```

As we can see, the PSM simply names and stored an SQL statement in the RDBMS.

Indexes

Indexes are schema objects built against a specific table to enhance performance of SELECT, UPDATE, and DELETE statements. For example, the positioned action on a database table.

The performance enhancements come about due to the fact that RDBMS systems do not store rows in an particular order. For example, adding and updating rows doesn't change the physical order of their storage in the underlying tables.

We will cover indexes in detail in Chapter 7. For now, it should suffice to see the generic syntax:

```
CREATE INDEX index_name ON tablename (column_to_index);
```

and:

```
DROP INDEX index_name;
```

Nested Relationship of Database Objects

Now that we have seen the different types of database schema objects that might be supported by a vendor implementation of SQL:1999, it would be helpful to view them in relation to each other visually. The diagram overleaf is a representation of the various database objects shown as nested concepts.

Even though we have named the outermost layer the Database, it's important to note that SQL:1999 avoids using this term as it has many different connotations across vendors and no real clear meaning:

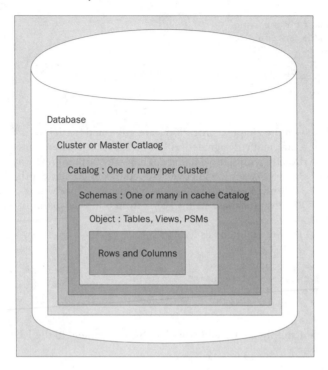

BNF: Backus-Naur Form

Let us divert a bit from the description of database objects to discuss notation commonly used to specify SQL syntax.

Always check the database documentation for your specific database to determine the manner in which the vendor has implemented certain SQL standard features.

Upon perusing the relevant documentation, however, you may simply find rather cryptic statements in **BNF** that convey the syntax that the vendor supports. Let us look at BNF for a moment to give you some tools to comprehend this notation when you come across it.

What Is BNF?

BNF is an acronym for Backus Naur Form – a way of providing shorthand notation for any language. John Backus introduced it in 1963, with the name **Backus Normal Form**. Subsequent additions by Peter Naur brought it to a practical form. Naur first used it to describe the syntax for the Algol 60 programming language to clarify a syntax form definition that Backus had made for an earlier version of the language, Algol 58.

BNF notation has become the de facto standard on describing programming languages. Aside from your database vendor documentation, it has been used in countless books on countless programming languages to clearly specify the syntax rules of the language without relying on possibly confusing semantics of conversational language. BNF is also typically used to arrive on the agreed-upon features of a compiled language (such as C) when designing it, to ensure that compilers produce code that does what the programmer expects.

BNF uses a series of symbols in combination with the keywords of a language to indicate syntax rules. The common symbols used for these "meta commands" are:

Symbol	Meaning
: : =	Used to mean "is defined as"
|	Used to mean "or"
< >	Used to define a category name
" "	Used to surround keywords that are literal words, also called terminals
[]	Used to surround optional items
{ }	Used to surround items that can be repeated one or more times

A BNF rule defining a syntax rule (a keyword that is also called a nonterminal) could be written in the following form:

```
nonterminal ::= alternative_1 | alternative_2 | alternative_N;
```

This simply means that the rule is defined as having one of the stated alternative conditions.

Example: DDL BNF

Here is an example of the BNF definition of one part of our DDL coverage, the syntax used to describe the SQL schema statement:

```
<SQL schema statement> ::=
  <SQL schema definition statement>
  <SQL schema manipulation statement>
```

This can be translated, as the SQL schema statement consists of an SQL schema definition statement or an SQL schema manipulation statement.

Of course, the BNF notation would then define the constituent parts as:

```
<SQL schema definition statement> ::=
  <schema definition>
  <table definition>
  <view definition>
```

125

```
<grant statement>
<domain statement>
<character set definition>
<collation definition>
<translation definition>
<assertion definition>
<schema definition> ::=
CREATE SCHEMA <schema name clause>
[ <schema character set specification> ]
[ <schema element … ]
```

And so on. This example, if expanded to cover all the BNF parts of this single SQL Schema statement, would take several pages to show completely.

Note, that single character terminals to the right of the : : =, such as the semicolon, should always be in quotes so they stand out from meta commands.

Here is an example of the zero-or-many meta command indicated by the curly brackets { }:

```
CREATE FUNCTION function_name
RETURNS datatype
LANGUAGE {ADA | C | SQL }]
...;
```

As we can see, the curly brackets indicate that we may use one of the options given, but are not required to.

Vendor Compliance To SQL:1999

Throughout the chapter, we have referred to the fact that some features of SQL:1999 might not be supported fully by your particular database. It's common for RDBMSs to now support a full set of the SQL-92 standard, at least at the entry compliance level, if not intermediate or full, but the SQL:1999 standard still has a long way to go with regard to acceptance.

Let us now see what a database vendor has to do to claim compliance with the SQL:1999 standard.

Core SQL Compliance

Core compliance to SQL:1999 essentially means that a database vendor has full support of the SQL-92 standard. This is not to say that vendors do not support comparable features as laid out in SQL:1999. However, they have chosen to do this in a way that leaves some gaps between how SQL:1999 specifies features and how the database vendor chooses to implement syntax. This can take the form of unsupported features, alternative syntax implementations, or even extensions beyond SQL:1999 that provide additional functionality, although the last option is rare.

Compliance to a standard has, of course, two imperatives – functional and marketing. Claiming SQL:1999 compliance garners a database vendor additional notice in the market. The sheer size of the SQL:1999 standard means that a vendor has to be committed to the standard in its own right to reach a high degree of feature implementation. Additionally, database vendors thrive on differences.

Supporting proprietary features and excluding standard features reduces the **commoditization** of the database. For example, it makes that specific database less interchangeable with other products and creates vendor lock-in. SQL:1999 was not created in a vacuum, however. The standard covers useful and necessary features of SQL that RDBMS's should possess. However, it's entirely possible that a lack of complete support for the entire SQL:1999 standard will still provide the developer with a rich and functionally adequate set of SQL features. To this end, compliance with the SQL:1999 standard is awarded if a database vendor implements the Core SQL:1999 features as well as one of nine possible packages.

Package-Level Compliance

The additional features packages have been broken down as follows:

Package Number	Package Feature Set
PKG001	Datetime: additional enhanced date-time functionality
PKG002	Data Integrity: additional data integrity and security
PKG003	OLAP: support for On-Line Analytical Processing functionality
PKG004	PSM: full support for Procedures (Persistent Stored Modules) in PSM-96
PKG005	CLI: full support for the Call Level Interface features in CLI-95
PKG006	Objects: at least basic object support
PKG007	Objects II: advanced object support
PKG008	Active Database support
PKG009	SQL/MM: support for the SQL Multi-Media content features

Implementation of a single package along with Core SQL:1999 constitutes compliance, but most major RDBMS vendors support at least two of these additional packages at this point of evolution in the RDBMS market.

Bringing It All Together: DDL and Our Task Example

Throughout the chapter we've discussed SQL data types, structuring databases with DDL, and some of the concerns with regard to differing vendor implementations. Let us integrate the information gained so far by designing a sample application and creating the database tables for use in later chapters.

The Problem

All good application design starts by asking what we want this application to do. From there, we should generate a set of requirements that can be translated in deliverable bits of code representing different features, GUI items, and the like.

As we have mentioned some examples on managing tasks in Chapter 2, let us look at a slightly more fully-fledged task and project management application. For the sake of clarity, let us give it a name – TaskFoward.

So, what do we want this application to do? As a concise statement, this application should move tasks forward by managing overall task and project associations.

The functional specifications listed below will help us move on to initial database design:

❑ Manage individual tasks, including status, task duration estimate, priority, completion dates, assignment and ownership issues, and hierarchies

❑ Manage projects as a collection of tasks, with completion dates dependent on task status

❑ Group task into categories

❑ Intelligently display sets of tasks based on categories

❑ Manage multiple users

❑ Allow tasks to be assigned to other users

❑ Allow tasks views to be shared with other users

❑ Manage privilege levels for viewing, assigning, changing, and sharing tasks

❑ Notify user of missed tasks or important deadlines

❑ Display a calendar or To-Do list

Entity Relationship Diagram

As we have seen in Chapter 3, breaking down the elements of our problem into entities, attributes, and relationships is important to designing our schema. With some consideration we can pick the attributes, or nouns, and relationships, or verbs of our application as follows:

❑ Projects contain tasks

❑ Users assign, create, or are assigned tasks

❑ Users create or own projects

Looking at the relationships between entities, we see the following:

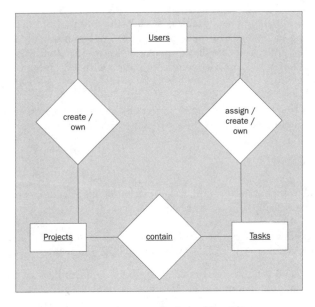

Adding in the attributes for the entities, we get something like this:

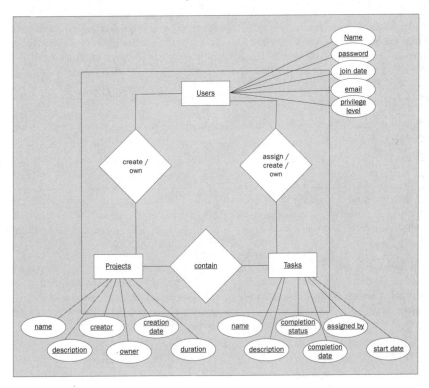

Schema Design

Designing the database schema, or set of tables, is really the first part of the development process where we move from modeling the features of the application to implementing the underlying data structures. Seen from a high level, applications are about managing knowledge, but what is knowledge? Well, information is data in context, so knowledge is information with a unifying context that enables decision-making and action.

In this case, we are putting task data into the context of users and projects, enabling action by users of our application. The schema we create is the set of tables and their columns used to store the data for our application and users.

Considerations

When designing database schemas for application modeling, it's very important that we don't lose sight of the following criteria. Ideally, our schema must:

❑ Provide coherent and efficient relational structuring of data including normalization, limiting of data redundancy, and providing for efficient SQL queries.

❑ Capture data as information. For instance, provide in a simple way for applying context to stored data with table names and column names.

❑ Provide flexibility in application design by allowing muliple ways of managing data based on the structure of the relations.

❑ Scale. The database structure should not have to be changed as information increases, say, when the number of users and tasks increases, and shouldn't become less efficient or slow as the amount of data grows (or at least not quickly – the amount of data stored will always have some acceptable effect on the database system).

Data To Capture

From the bulleted specification listed earlier, let us reshuffle the order and devise the bits of data that we want to capture:

Feature	Relevant Data
Manage individual tasks, including status, duration estimate, priority, completion dates, assignment and ownership issue	Task data: name, description, creation date, due date, assigned by, assigned to, parent project, estimated duration, estimated completion date
Manage projects as a collection of tasks, with completion dates dependent on task status. Intelligently display sets of tasks based on details such as assignment and project categories	Project data: name, description, creation date, owner, assigned by, assigned to, estimated completion date, estimated duration, child tasks in project, category of project

Feature	Relevant Data
Manage multiple users	User data: username, user identification, user privilege level, join date for application, tasks for user, user's superiors, user's subordinates, users that have access to task of other users
Manage privilege levels for viewing, assigning, changing tasks. Allow tasks to be assigned to other users	Privilege data: administrative level of user, users that can assign tasks
Notify users of important events	User contact info

Table Creation

Now let us break down the items we want to capture into a table structure, extending our initial simple entity relationship diagram into a table format based on the features we want to provide. It's often useful to simply list the table names and intended rows initially to get a sense of where we are going. We will then create the DDL statements to do the actual work of creating the tables and schema. The section below will list the proposed table structure as well as the data types and notes on what the fields may contain.

A Note on Table Naming

As you read the coming sections you will see that the tables are all named as singular, while the data is typically plural. For example, tf_user contains users. This is standard practice in that a single instance of a table is a row, and tables should be named in some meaningful way based on the rows of data they represent. That having been said, it is entirely possible for a table to only contain one row, and since it is referring to the entity, keeping names in the singular is appropriate.

User Table

This of course uniquely identifies our users, provides contact information, privilege level (meaning admin or regular user), and stores the user password. We have called this tf_user (an abbreviation for TaskForward user) as some databases disallow tables with the name user, and reserve this word for their own use:

```
tf_user
----------------------
PK_user(integer, or vendor-specific auto-incrementing identity)
fname (varchar(50), first name of the user)
priv_level (integer, 1 = senior exec, 2 = department manager, > 3 = user
password (varchar(20), we may wish to encrypt this as well using crypt())
email (varchar(100), contact email for user event notification)
join_date (date, not strictly necessary but it might be nice to have)
last_modified (timestamp, tracking any alteration of this table)
```

Project Table

This table will track project details:

```
tf_project
-------------------------
PK_proj (integer, or vendor-specific auto-incrementing identity)
name (varchar(30), simple name for project)
description (varchar(255), longer summary text describing the project)

FK_user_owner (integer, inserted from user_id in tf_user table when assigned. This
assumes that a Project can have only one owner.)
create_date (dat, track beginning of project)
duration (interval, number of days from summary of all task duration within
project, inserted from trigger on task table)

last_modified (timestamp, tracking change of date on projects)
```

Task Table

This table will hold all the details for each individual task:

```
tf_task
-------------------------
PK_task (integer, or vendor-specific auto-incrementing identity)
name (varchar(30), short descriptive name for task)
description (varchar(255), longer summary text for task)
completed (Boolean, T/F)
complete_date (date, inserted from trigger when set to true)
assigned_by (integer, from user_id)
duration (interval, number of days for completion)
start_date(date, when task is assigned)
end_date (date, inserted by trigger, from start date and duration)
FK_project (integer, foreign key on project table)
```

User and Tasks Table

While we could include an assigned-to field in the above task table, there is a potential many-to-many relationship of users to tasks. With normalization in mind, we have created a mapping table that associates users and tasks:

```
tf_user_task
-------------------------
PK_user_task (integer, or vendor-specific auto-incrementing identity)
FK_user (integer, foreign key from tf_user table)
FK_task (integer, foreign key from task table)
timestmp (timestamp, tracks assigned date)
```

DDL Statement

Now let us bring it all together. Based on the outline of our database needs in the previous section, a final DDL would look something like the sections opposite. The trailing semicolon is not really part of the DDL, but many client interfaces require it for statement execution, so it's a good idea to get in the habit of including it.

> The IDENTITY keyword we have used here is not actually valid SQL:1999. What it
> means is "create the column as an automatically incrementing field". Most relational
> databases have some facility to do this, so we shall use the IDENTITY keyword below
> to show this. There are different arguments for and against auto-incrementing
> columns and their use, but we will show it here, as at the very least it's useful to create
> a unique column regardless of other keys.

*SQL:1999 does not provide any specification on auto-incrementing fields. So, different vendors have
handled this in different ways. Some use the keyword* Auto Increment *when creating a data
type, some use* Identity, *etc. Either way, this field cannot be used to count the number of records
in your table, since it will develop holes as data is added and deleted.*

Schema or Database

The database can be created as:

```
CREATE DATABASE taskforward AUTHORIZATION taskadmin;
```

User Table

The user table, tf_user, can be constructed as follows:

```
CREATE TABLE tf_user (
 PK_user INTEGER NOT NULL,
 fname VARCHAR(50),
 priv_level INTEGER NOT NULL,
 password VARCHAR(20) NOT NULL,
 email VARCHAR (100) NOT NULL,
 join_date DATETIME,
 last_modified TIMESTAMP,

 CONSTRAINT PK_user PRIMARY KEY (PK_user)
);
```

As you can see, using the keyword PRIMARY KEY indicates a primary key on the table, enforcing NOT
NULL and unique status as well as auto-indexing in most RDBMSs.

Project Table

For the project table, tf_project, the SQL statement could read as:

```
CREATE TABLE tf_project (
PK_proj INTEGER NOT NULL,
name VARCHAR (30) NOT NULL,
description VARCHAR (255),
FK_user_owner INTEGER NOT NULL,
create_date DATETIME,
duration INTERVAL,
last_modified TIMESTAMP,
```

```
CONSTRAINT PK_proj PRIMARY KEY (PK_proj),
CONSTRAINT FK_user_owner FOREIGN KEY (FK_user_owner) REFERENCES tf_user (PK_user)
);
```

Task Table

Next, we build the task table:

```
CREATE TABLE tf_task (
PK_task INTEGER NOT NULL,
name VARCHAR (30) NOT NULL,
description VARCHAR (255),
completed BOOLEAN NOT NULL,
complete_date DATE,
assigned_by INTEGER,
duration INTERVAL,
start_date DATE,
end_date DATE,
FK_proj INTEGER,

CONSTRAINT PK_task PRIMARY KEY (PK_task),
CONSTRAINT FK_proj FOREIGN KEY (FK_proj) REFERENCES project (PK_proj)
);
```

User and Tasks Mapping Table

Lastly, the mapping table is structured as follows:

```
CREATE TABLE tf_user_task (
PK_user_task INTEGER NOT NULL,
FK_user INTEGER NOT NULL,
FK_task INTEGER NOT NULL,
last_modified TIMESTAMP,
CONSTRAINT PK_user_task PRIMARY KEY (PK_user_task),
CONSTRAINT FK_user FOREIGN KEY (FK_user) REFERENCES tf_user (PK_user),
CONSTRAINT FK_task FOREIGN KEY (FK_task) REFERENCES task (PK_task)
);
```

Let us now take the DDL statement explained above and show the slightly different syntax required for a couple of the DBMSs that we will be working with in this book. We start with MySQL, as it has some clear differences from the standard SQL:1999 syntax.

MySQL

Connecting to the MySQL database will go something like this:

```
# mysql -u root -p
Enter password:
Welcome to the MySQL monitor. Commands end with ; or \g.
Your MySQL connection id is 3 to server version: 3.23.49-entropy.ch

Type help; or \h for help. Type \c to clear the buffer.
mysql>
```

The DDL for MySQL includes a few changes. Among them are using AUTO_INCREMENT on the keys and TINYINT for Boolean (using 0 and 1). Data integrity across keys in different tables will also have to be handled programmatically.

The DDL may be either entered manually, cut and pasted, or saved to a text file and then run with some variation of this command.

For UNIX:

```
/usr/local/data/mysql < ddl_statement.txt
```

For Windows:

```
c:\data\mysql < ddl_statement.txt
```

Note that the syntax for reading in files will require username and password depending on how your environment is set up.

You may also use a GUI client such as PHPMyAdmin (http://phpmyadmin.sourceforge.net/) to create the database and tables. The ddl_statement.txt contains the statements below:

```
CREATE DATABASE taskforward;

USE taskforward;

CREATE TABLE tf_user
(
PK_user INTEGER NOT NULL AUTO_INCREMENT,
fname VARCHAR(50),
priv_level INTEGER,
password VARCHAR(20),
email VARCHAR (100),
join_date DATETIME,
last_modified TIMESTAMP,
KEY PK_user (PK_user)
);

CREATE TABLE tf_project
(
PK_proj INTEGER NOT NULL AUTO_INCREMENT,
name VARCHAR (30),
description VARCHAR (255),
owner INTEGER,
create_date DATE,
duration INTERVAL,
last_modified TIMESTAMP,

KEY PK_proj (PK_proj)
);
```

```
CREATE TABLE tf_task
(
PK_task INTEGER NOT NULL AUTO_INCREMENT,
name VARCHAR (30),
description VARCHAR (255),
completed TINYINT,
complete_date DATE,
FK_assigned_by INTEGER,
duration INTERVAL,
start_date DATE,
end_date DATE,
FK_proj INTEGER,
KEY PK_task (PK_task)
);

CREATE TABLE tf_user_task
(
PK_user_task INTEGER NOT NULL AUTO_INCREMENT,
PK_user INTEGER,
PK_task INTEGER,
last_modified TIMESTAMP,
KEY PK_user_task (PK_user_task)
);
```

To verify the table creation, you can use the following command (remember to add the terminating semicolon, which tells MySQL where each SQL command ends):

```
mysql> SHOW TABLES;
+-----------------------+
| Tables_in_taskforward |
+-----------------------+
| tf_project            |
| tf_task               |
| tf_user               |
| tf_user_task          |
+-----------------------+
4 rows in set (0.00 sec)

mysql>
```

PostgreSQL

Another common database has greater support for SQL:1999 features; for our schema we will use the database, used by PHP developers and the Open Source community at large, PostgreSQL. You will see that PostgreSQL supports foreign keys and data types such as Boolean.

We will use the createdb and the psql application to create and connect to our new database:

```
postgres% /usr/local/bin/createdb taskforward
CREATE DATABASE
```

```
postgres% psql taskforward
Welcome to psql, the PostgreSQL interactive terminal.

Type: \copyright for distribution terms
      \h for help with SQL commands
      \? for help on internal slash commands
      \g or terminate with semicolon to execute query
      \q to quit


taskforward=#
```

The PostgreSQL variation on the DDL described in the earlier section is as follows, and may be saved in a file called taskforward_ddl.sql and loaded using a variation of the following:

```
postgres% /usr/local/bin/psql -d taskforward -f taskforward_ddl.sql
```

The contents of the DDL statement are as follows:

```
CREATE TABLE tf_user (
pk_user INTEGER,
fname VARCHAR(50),
priv_level INTEGER NOT NULL,
password VARCHAR(20) NOT NULL,
email VARCHAR (100) NOT NULL,
join_date DATETIME,
last_modified TIMESTAMP,
CONSTRAINT pk_user PRIMARY KEY (pk_user)
);
CREATE TABLE tf_project (
pk_proj INTEGER NOT NULL,
name VARCHAR (30) NOT NULL,
description VARCHAR (255),

fk_user_owner INTEGER NOT NULL,
create_date DATETIME,
duration INTERVAL,
last_modified TIMESTAMP,
CONSTRAINT pk_proj PRIMARY KEY (pk_proj),
CONSTRAINT fk_user_owner FOREIGN KEY (fk_user_owner) REFERENCES tf_user (pk_user)
);
CREATE TABLE tf_task (
pk_task INTEGER NOT NULL,
name VARCHAR (30) NOT NULL,
description VARCHAR (255),
completed BOOLEAN NOT NULL,
complete_date DATE,
fk_assigned_by INTEGER,
duration INTERVAL,
start_date DATE,
end_date DATE,
fk_proj INTEGER,
```

```
CONSTRAINT pk_task PRIMARY KEY (pk_task),
CONSTRAINT fk_proj FOREIGN KEY (fk_proj) REFERENCES tf_project (pk_proj),
CONSTRAINT fk_assigned_by FOREIGN KEY (fk_assigned_by) REFERENCES tf_user
(pk_user)
);

CREATE TABLE user_task (
pk_user_task INTEGER NOT NULL,
fk_user INTEGER NOT NULL,
fk_task INTEGER NOT NULL,
last_modified TIMESTAMP,
CONSTRAINT pk_user_task PRIMARY KEY (pk_user_task),
CONSTRAINT fk_user FOREIGN KEY (fk_user) REFERENCES tf_user (pk_user),
CONSTRAINT fk_task FOREIGN KEY (fk_task) REFERENCES tf_task (pk_task)
);
```

Instead of using an auto-incrementing column type, PostgreSQL creates a column on each table called **OID (Object Identification Numbers)**. This is usually hidden from the user but may be used if explicitly referenced, and serves the purpose of uniquely identifying rows. As an alternative, PostgreSQL can also use SEQUENCEs, which are database objects created by the user, that act as counters. While sequences can be shared by tables, you can also create a separate sequence for each table requiring uniquely numbered rows.

Here is an example of our tf_user table with a SEQUENCE created and used:

```
CREATE SEQUENCE tf_seq;
CREATE TABLE tf_user (
pk_user INTEGER DEFAULT NEXTVAL('tf_seq')
fname VARCHAR(50),
priv_level INTEGER NOT NULL,
password VARCHAR(20) NOT NULL,
email VARCHAR (100) NOT NULL,
join_date DATETIME,
timestmp TIMESTAMP,
CONSTRAINT pk_user PRIMARY KEY (pk_user)
);
```

Alternatively, see the next chapter for examples of how the PEAR::DB libraries handle auto-incrementing for you.

We will explain the syntax in the next chapter, but to get a list of tables in PostgreSQL, you can issue the following command:

```
taskforward=# select * from pg_tables;
```

The output will be:

```
   tablename      | tableowner | hasindexes | hasrules | hastriggers
------------------+------------+------------+----------+-------------
 pg_type          | postgres   | t          | f        | f
 pg_attribute     | postgres   | t          | f        | f
 pg_class         | postgres   | t          | f        | f
 pg_group         | postgres   | t          | f        | f
 pg_database      | postgres   | t          | f        | f
 pg_xactlock      | postgres   | f          | f        | f
 pg_inherits      | postgres   | t          | f        | f
 pg_index         | postgres   | t          | f        | f
 pg_operator      | postgres   | t          | f        | f
 pg_opclass       | postgres   | t          | f        | f
 pg_am            | postgres   | t          | f        | f
 pg_amop          | postgres   | t          | f        | f
 pg_amproc        | postgres   | t          | f        | f
 pg_language      | postgres   | t          | f        | f
 pg_largeobject   | postgres   | t          | f        | f
 pg_aggregate     | postgres   | t          | f        | f
 pg_trigger       | postgres   | t          | f        | f
 pg_listener      | postgres   | f          | f        | f
 pg_shadow        | postgres   | t          | f        | t
 pg_attrdef       | postgres   | t          | f        | f
 pg_description   | postgres   | t          | f        | f
 pg_proc          | postgres   | t          | f        | f
 pg_relcheck      | postgres   | t          | f        | f
 pg_rewrite       | postgres   | t          | f        | f
 pg_statistic     | postgres   | t          | f        | f
 tf_project       | postgres   | t          | f        | t
 tf_user_task     | postgres   | t          | f        | t
 tf_task          | postgres   | t          | f        | t
 tf_user          | postgres   | t          | f        | t
(29 rows)

taskforward=#
```

You will notice that there are both tables we created, and schema tables created by the RDBMS directly.

Other RDBMSs that you may come across should be some variation of the above two examples. For additional syntax change, please refer to the documentation for your database and database client access, as well as the default SQL:1999 standard.

Summary

In this chapter, we have dealt primarily with how SQL represents data and how it is used to define a database schema. We touched on design issues that databases present and built some basic database schemas to model and build applications upon.

The next chapter will take our sample application further, and begin programming PHP against our sample schema to create database-driven events, as well as cover the Data Manipulation Language. Take time to study this chapter with respect to the RDBMS of your choice, and examine any differences between the SQL:1999 DDL and your implementation.

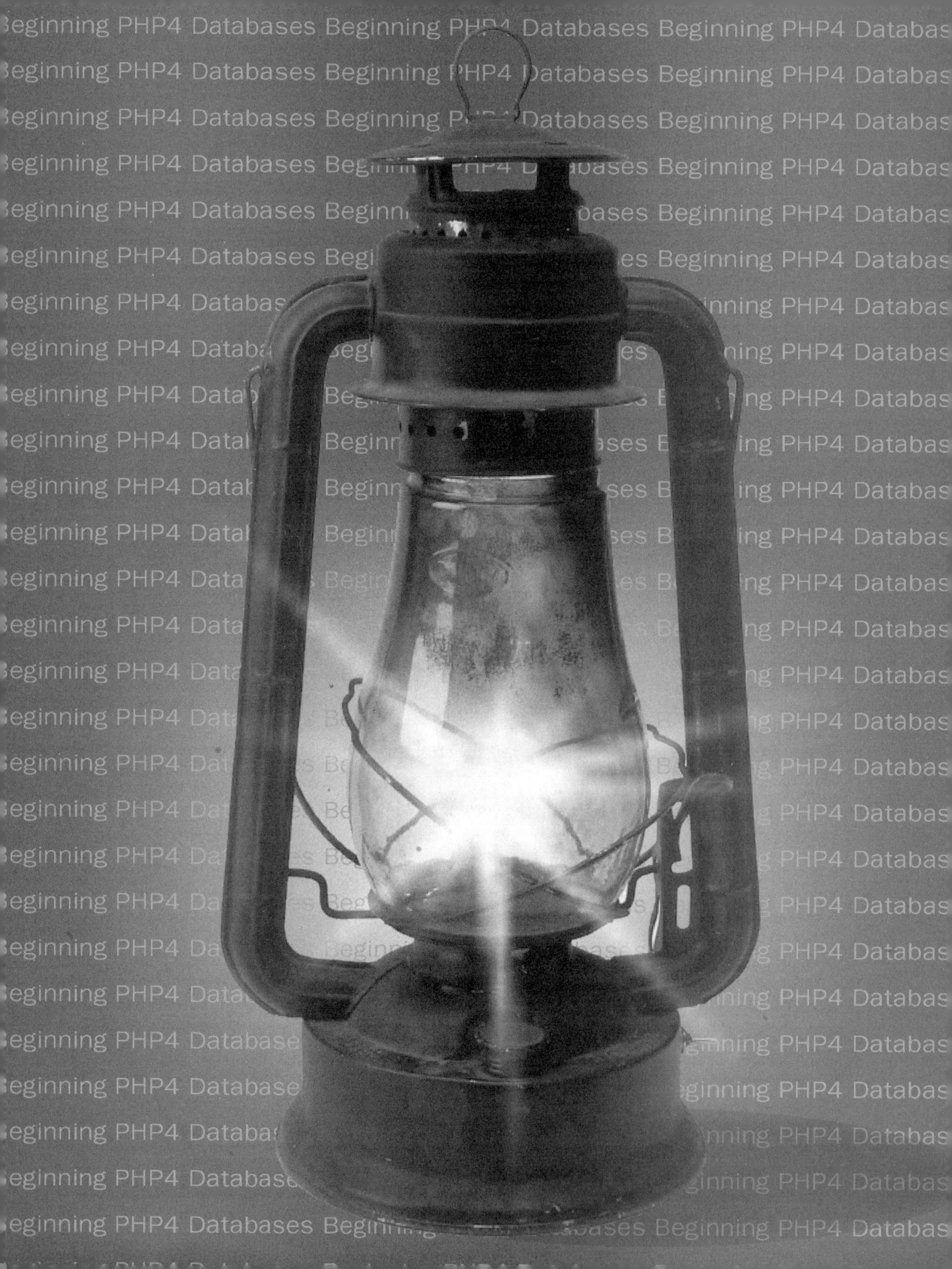
Beginning PHP4 Databases

SQL: Data Manipulation and Retrieval

In the last chapter we mainly dealt with how the Structured Query Language (SQL) is used to control tables and other database objects maintained by a Relational Database Management System (RDBMS). In this chapter, we will focus on how an application interacts with the database via SQL to manipulate information in the database. We will revisit the sample application schema presented in the last chapter, and model data on it for our sample application.

After reading this chapter, you should have a thorough understanding, both in concept and practice, of the following topics:

- ❑ Syntax and construction used in adding, changing, and removing data from database tables
- ❑ Embedding SQL in PHP scripts
- ❑ Retrieving data and displaying it in web pages
- ❑ Sorting and grouping data when retrieving it
- ❑ Using joins and other advanced methods of retrieving data from single and multiple tables

Now that we have an understanding of database structure, it's important to highlight that when we retrieve the data in our tables using SQL, we do so by isolating **sets** of rows in our tables. These sets are not true mathematical sets, but merely rows of data. We will get into the syntax and variations of SQL statements in just a moment, but looked at conceptually, a SQL statement is constructed by first specifying a list of tables to act on and then specifying rows within the tables for specific operations.

So what does this all mean? Well, as we saw in the last chapter, metadata in our databases and the Data Definition Language (DDL) are both about storage structure without semantics, or simply providing a container regardless of the meaning of the data. Manipulating table data with SQL is about applying a semantic, or a context, on the data, thus creating specific information from rows of data. In this chapter, we will look at ways of applying context and getting information. This is done by asking the RDBMS engine to carry out statistical analysis by specifying a set of conditional statements using SQL, which returns specific rows based on the conditions that define this shared context, or specifying conditions where we wish to remove or change rows.

Setting Up Our Example

OK, to get away from the theoretical and into the practical side. We need some data to work with throughout the rest of the chapter. We are going to use the `project` table, `tf_user` table, and `tf_task` table from the `taskforward` schema in the previous chapter.

Let's look at our PostgreSQL example. Assuming you are using a Unix variant, open up your terminal and access the `psql` interface to PostgreSQL:

```
[localhost:~] postgres% psql taskforward
Welcome to psql, the PostgreSQL interactive terminal.

Type:   \copyright for distribution terms
        \h for help with SQL commands
        \? for help on internal slash commands
        \g or terminate with semicolon to execute query
        \q to quit
```

To refresh your memory, we can look at the tables in the database with the following statement:

```
taskforward=# SELECT * FROM pg_tables;
```

You should see the same tables we used in the previous chapter.

We can also issue a PostgreSQL specific command, \dt, to show just the user-created tables:

```
taskforward=# \dt
          List of relations
     Name       | Type  |  Owner
----------------+-------+----------
 tf_project     | table | postgres
 tf_task        | table | postgres
 tf_user        | table | postgres
 user_task      | table | postgres
(4 rows)
```

Let's use the same syntax as seen in the last chapter (we shall discuss this in detail below) and retrieve all the rows in the following table:

```
taskforward=# SELECT * FROM tf_user;
 pk_user | fname | priv_level | password | email | join_date | modified
---------+-------+------------+----------+-------+-----------+----------
(0 rows)
```

We are only showing the results from this table, as all the tables are empty at the moment. Let's specify a basic set of data to begin working with.

The sample data in the `tf_user` table is as follows:

pk_user	fname	priv_level	password	email
1	Larry	1	imtheboss	larry@taskforward.org
5	Sue	2	sue1pass	sue@taskforward.org
100	Joe	3	tempjoe	joe@taskforward.org

Don't worry about the values right now; we will use discuss the `priv_level` in more detail later in the chapter. For clarity, understand that a `priv_level` of 1 indicates an executive, 2 indicates a department manager, and 3 indicates a regular department employee. For now, let's suppose Larry is the CEO, Sue runs a support department, and Joe is a newly hired employee in Sue's department. This means that each user is represented by a unique row within the `tf_user` table.

The sample data in the `tf_project` table is as follows:

name	description	Creator	owner	duration (in days)
Support Q4	Summary of support department quarterly performance	1	5	90

This is fairly self-explanatory; we have one project created by Larry and assigned to Sue to track performance metrics of the support department for the fourth quarter of the fiscal year.

Finally, the sample data in the `tf_task` table is:

pk_task	name	description	completed	complete_date	assigned_by	duration
1	Activity report	summary of what Joe has done this week	False		5	5
2	Month plan	goals for next month based on Larry's strategic focus	False		5	5

Here we have two tasks, both assigned by Sue, to track Joe's activity for the week and to prepare a department goals report for the next month. We can see the duration for both is 5, indicating five days.

Of course, these tasks haven't been assigned to anyone; we will look at adding task and user correlations in our `user_task` table later on. First let's look at how we put this data into our tables.

Where to Use SQL

As we mentioned above, SQL statements act on sets of rows. It's also important to point out that they can be used in a few different places. The type of SELECT action we just saw, where we passed an SQL statement in the RDBMS native client interface, can be called direct invocation. After explaining a bit more of the syntax, we will show how to invoke SQL embedded within a "host" language, in this case PHP. In Chapter 7, we will look at stored invocation, where we build SQL language structures directly inside the database and call them from PHP.

SQL statements can be invoked from a host language, like PHP, but the actual SQL syntax involves constructing a series of operators, clauses, and conditionals. The SQL statements can return or change data in our tables, or retrieve information about our data, both by querying the DDL or asking the RDBMS to return information about tables.

Moving forward, we will look at the different components of SQL that can be combined to build up our statements.

Operators and Clauses in SQL Statements

We are going to get into a lot of different SQL language constructs, but remember – it's all about sets of data. The parts of SQL that we are going to be dealing with revolve around specifying those sets, in the manner highlighted below (it shows the abstract sense of the information supplied to the DBMS):

> **Statement Operation → Tablename → Clause → Conditional Predicate**

Clauses and predicates are optional, but an SQL statement requires pointers to the table and an initial operation to tell the database what kind of action we are taking.

Seen another way, a statement can be broken down as follows:

❑ Operators are the first part of the statement and indicate the statement type

❑ Clauses add conditional logic

❑ Predicates further condition the result sets reduced by clauses

Also, clauses and predicates can be chained together using AND and OR, as well as NOT.

While the following list is in no way exhaustive, it's a fairly complete list of the SQL statement components that most RDBMS flavors support:

Primary Operations	Additional Clauses	Some Predicates
Insert	Where	Between
Update	From	Having

Primary Operations	Additional Clauses	Some Predicates
Delete	Case	Like
Select	Set	Similar
		In
		Exists
		Distinct
		Is Null

Let's drill down into the operations, using our sample data to assist in the examples. We will introduce clauses and predicates later in the chapter.

INSERT

INSERT is used to add rows to a table. Expanding this with conditionals, we see the INSERT operator indicates to a statement to add some data to some columns in some rows in a table.

A VALUES INSERT specifies a table row and a list of values for that row. Here is a pseudocode example:

```
// Values Insertion:
INSERT INTO table (comma separated list of columns)
  VALUES (comma separated list of values);
```

The number and order of the columns must match the number and order of the values; in this case the order of the values is constrained by matching data types to the column list. It is possible to omit the list of columns if the list of values matches the number of columns and has the correct data types, but this makes the SQL more difficult to read and is generally considered bad form.

Operators and Table Constraints

When columns are specified in the SELECT statement, they do not have to be named identically to the columns in the INSERT, but they should be of the same data types. If they are not, we will violate the DDL constraints specified when creating the tables, and probably get an error. This is true for many database integrity constraints including data types, violation of Primary Key uniqueness, nulls, updatablility of a table, and so forth.

It is possible to alter types using CAST and some RDBMS implementations possess functions to either convert properly or allow sloppy type handling. However, it is important to know what our RDBMS vendor has done, as it is possible to lose track of the data in an application quite easily if we don't know the details. This can be done by reading the docs on the database and testing that types act the way we expect them to for specific inserts in the applications we design.

Try It Out – Insert Statement

In practice, INSERT statements are often used as INSERT INTO with the remaining parameters following. Let's look at an example using our sample data and psql terminal:

```
taskforward=# INSERT INTO tf_user
taskforward-# (pk_user, fname, priv_level, password, email)
taskforward-# VALUES (1, 'Larry', 1, 'imtheboss', 'larry@taskforward.org');
```

Upon successful completion, PostgreSQL returns an INSERT ID:

```
INSERT 32941 1
```

This is the INSERT ID from my computer; don't worry if yours is not the same.

Many database systems will report things like 1 row affected – PostgreSQL does this for SELECTs, for instance:

```
taskforward=# SELECT * FROM tf_user;
pk_user|fname|priv_level|password |          email         |join_date|modified
-------+-----+----------+---------+------------------------+---------+--------
    1  |Larry|    1     |imtheboss|larry@taskforward.org|         |
(1 row)
```

We will not go into a *How It Works* section here, as it is self-explanatory.

Try It Out – Using INSERT with PHP

In the real world, we often have tools to move data into our database. Batch updates can take place using a variety of methods. The simplest way would be to create a file containing a set of DDL and INSERT statements that can be consumed by the database. An example of this is the backup functions of PHPMyAdmin (http://www.phpmyadmin.org).

It's also entirely possible to sequentially access data using PHP and embed this in a SQL INSERT statement, for example, a text file exported from another application.

Let's put our tf_user data in a comma-separated text file called users.txt and save it in our htdocs directory. Note, we still put the strings in single quotes, as this data will be processed by SQL:

```
1,'Larry',1,'imtheboss','larry@taskforward.org'
5,'Sue',2,'sue1pass','sue@taskforward.org'
100,'Joe',3,'tempjoe','joe@taskforward'
```

We will cover the DELETE statement in detail in a moment, but for now run this statement against your psql interface to clear all the rows of data from the tf_user table:

```
taskforward=# DELETE FROM tf_user;
```

Now let's look at a simple PHP example to load the user.txt file into our PostgreSQL database. In practice something similar could be done with the PosgreSQL \copy command, but for the sake of database independence this is a good example.

First, let's create our database connection environment file. Fire up your text editor and save the following code in a file called `database.env.php`. You may need to alter the values for your specific environment, depending on how you setup your database authentication:

```php
<?php
$username = "postgres";
$password = "";
$hostname = "localhost";
$dbname = "taskforward";
?>
```

Starting with the PEAR DB example from Chapter 2, let's modify it to pull our sample data from the text file `users.txt`, by opening a PEAR DB connection to our database, inputting the location of the text file, and exploding each line in the text file to create our INSERT statements. Save the following in a file called `text_insert.php`:

```php
<?php
/*
The $_POST["submit"] variable will not be equal to Insert until we send the form.
Depending on if we are waiting for form submission or not
either show the form or the results
*/

if( $_POST["submit"]=="Insert") {

//PEAR::DB and required variables
require_once "DB.php";
require_once "database.env.php";

//create the PEAR::DB DSN and output notification to the screen.
$dsn = "pgsql://$username:$password@$hostname/$dbname";
echo "defining dsn<br>";

//connect to the database and output notification to the screen
$db = DB::connect($dsn);
echo "connecting to database<br>";

//always check for errors
if (DB::isError($db)) {
  die ($db->getMessage());
}

//open file for tf_user, search in include_path
$lines=file("$datafile");

echo "data file being used: $datafile<br>";

/*
We will read text file into an array and read each line out of the array
then we will split the line into insert values and perform the inserts
*/

while (list ($key, $value) = each ($lines))
{
  $insert_value=explode(",", $value);
```

```
    //create SQL statement, based on $lines array
    $sql="insert into tf_user (pk_user, fname, priv_level, password, email)
      values ($insert_value[0], $insert_value[1], $insert_value[2],
      $insert_value[3], $insert_value[4])";

    //perform the insert
    $result = $db->query($sql);

    //output a comment to the screen for each line inserted
    echo "SQL executed: $sql<br>";

    //always check for errors
    if (DB::isError($result)) {
      die ($result->getMessage());
    }
}

//provide some acknowledgement of the process
echo "inserts loop completed<br>";

//disconnect   - free up those resources
$db->disconnect();

}
/*
This is the end of the "if" everything past here will be shown only if the form
has not been submitted
*/
?>

<h2>Enter Datafile Name</h2>
<FORM ACTION="<?php echo $PHP_SELF; ?>" METHOD="POST">

<INPUT TYPE=TEXT NAME="datafile"></textarea>
<BR>
<INPUT TYPE="SUBMIT" NAME="submit" VALUE="Insert">
</FORM>
```

Examining the page in our browser results in a page that looks like this:

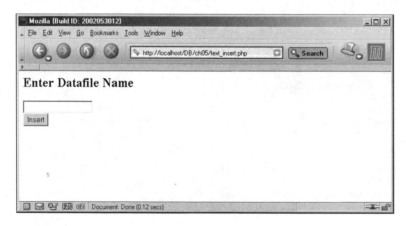

If we type `users.txt` into the form and hit the Insert button, we get a verbose report of the insert process:

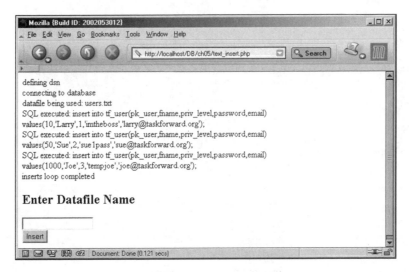

Let's jump over to our psql client for a second and double check the results (we will get into the SELECT statement in a moment):

```
taskforward=# SELECT * FROM tf_user;
user_id|fname|priv_level|password |        email        |join_date|timestamp
-------+-----+----------+--------+---------------------+---------+---------
      1|Larry|         1|imtheboss|larry@taskforward.org|         |
      5|Sue  |         2|sue1pass |sue@taskforward.org  |         |
    100|Joe  |         3|tempjoe  |joe@taskforward.org  |         |
(3 rows)
```

As you can see, we developed a pretty simple script to enter the contents of a text file in our tf_user database.

Try It Out – Another Example of INSERT with PHP

Let's also show an alternative method based on the previous one – a simple HTML form to take an INSERT statement and run it against our PostgreSQL database. Open your text editor up and create a document called pg_insert.php with the following contents:

```php
<?php

if( $_POST["submit"]=="Insert"){
require_once "DB.php";
  require_once "database.env.php";

  $dsn = "pgsql://$username:$password@$hostname/$dbname";
  echo "defining dsn<br>";

  $db = DB::connect($dsn);
```

```
    echo "connecting to database<br>";

    if (DB::isError($db)) {
      die ($db->getMessage());
    }

    $query=stripslashes($sql_query);
    echo "SQL Query to be sent is: $query<br>";

    $result = $db->query($query);
    echo "creating db query object<br><br>";

    if (DB::isError($result)) {
      die ($result->getMessage());
    }

    $db->disconnect();

}

?>

<h2>Enter Insert/Update Query</h2>
<FORM ACTION="<?php echo $PHP_SELF?>" METHOD="POST">
<TEXTAREA rows="5" cols="100" name="sql_query"></textarea>
<BR>
<INPUT TYPE="SUBMIT" NAME="submit" VALUE="Insert">
</FORM>
```

The output of our `pg_insert.php` page in a browser will be as follows:

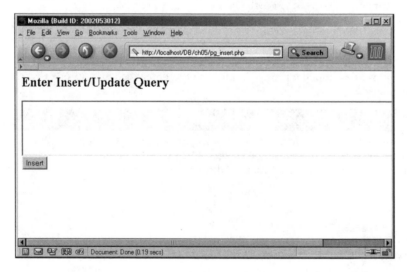

We can add an INSERT statement to the page (don't forget to run the DELETE statement first if you are going to use data that is identical to the earlier example).

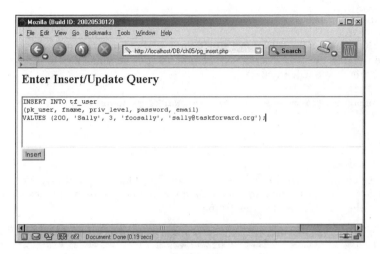

Click the INSERT button and we should receive a verbose report back from the script. If we run into any errors, the verbose report on that stage will fail, which provides a good starting point for debugging:

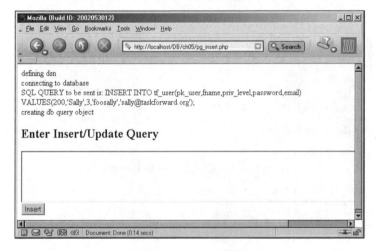

Now, let's look at how to view the information we just inserted.

SELECT

The SELECT operator is used to select data from columns in our tables. More generally, this operator indicates a clause to retrieve some data from some columns in some rows in some tables.

As we have seen earlier in the chapter, a SELECT * FROM TABLE statement can be used to return all of the rows of data in a table. A more general overview of the syntax might be as follows:

```
SELECT (list of columns) FROM (list of tables)
   [WHERE some search criteria are true]
```

Note that the WHERE clause is optional.

We can show this in action, by selecting a single fname from our tf_user table based on a specific pk_user value against our psql interface (remember to add the semicolon to indicate the psql that we have finished typing). We will have:

```
taskforward=# SELECT fname FROM tf_user WHERE pk_user = 1;
 fname
-------
 Larry
(1 row)
```

Here we also see our first use of the WHERE predicate. It can be though of as a comparison predicate. What this means is that it sets up an initial condition, and then compares our search term, in this case the integer 1, to the possible rows in the database.

Try It Out – Select Statement with PHP

Now let's create a PHP script to perform a SELECT * statement against a table. We will first query the system tables for a list of tables and then build an SQL statement to perform the SELECT. Lastly we will create an associative array of column names to data items for each row and output the summary results to the screen.

Fire up your text editor again, and save the following in a file called pg_selectstar.php. You will note that we are outputting fewer messages to the browser to indicate steps in our application – feel free to add this in if you like:

```php
<?php
//PEAR:DB library and required connection parameters
require "DB.php";
require "database.env.php";

//define the connect string
$dsn = "pgsql://$username:$password@$hostname/$dbname";

//connect to the database
$db = DB::connect($dsn);

//always check for errors!
if (DB::isError($result)) {
    die ($db->getMessage());
}

/* show the results only if form has been submitted
Checking for a value this time, alternate method from earlier example
Don't forget to use "==" to compare, versus "=" to assign!
*/
if ($submit =="Query"){

//echo back the query -  very useful in debugging.
echo "Results of Select * From $table<br><br>";

// define the database query - $table from our select form element below
$query = "SELECT * FROM $table";

//perform the query
```

```
$result = $db->query($query);

//always check for errors
if (DB::isError($result)) {
    die ($result->getMessage());
}

/*
get an associative row of the database column names -> values
print them out, keeping the association for ease of understanding
*/

while($row = $result->fetchRow(DB_FETCHMODE_ASSOC)){
        while (list ($key, $val) = each ($row)) {
        echo "$key => $val<br>";
        }
        echo "<br>";
}

//free those resources
$db->disconnect();

//if the form has not been submitted, show the form instead of results
}else{
echo "<h2>Select a table to dump to the screen</h2>";

//get list of tables in database
$query = "SELECT tablename FROM pg_tables";

$result = $db->query($query);

/*
in the form below, get is okay to use although it is not really secure. It is
useful
to look at the URL after form submission so we can see the actual values
of our script submission

also an alternative way of handling form submission checking
looking for value of "VALUE" -  peek at your URL after submission,
e.g."submit=query"
matching the test earlier.  Note that this will only work for
register_globals=on, something that is turned off by default in PHP
now. Instead it's preferable to use if( $_POST[ 'submit' ] == "Query") {}
*/

?>

<FORM ACTION="pg_selectstar.php" METHOD=get>
<select name="table">
        <?php
        while($row = $result->fetchRow()){
        echo "<option> $row[0]</option>";
        }
}
        ?>
</select>
<INPUT TYPE="submit" NAME="submit" VALUE="Query">
</FORM>
```

So what does this look like? Open your browser and point it to the file we just created:

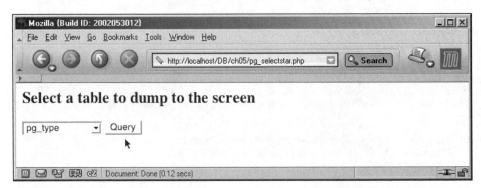

Selecting the drop-down, we see a list of the tables in our PostgreSQL database:

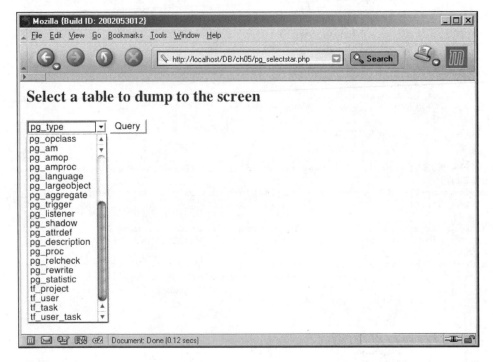

If we select `tf_user` from the drop-down and submit the form, we get a simple formatted column output of this table:

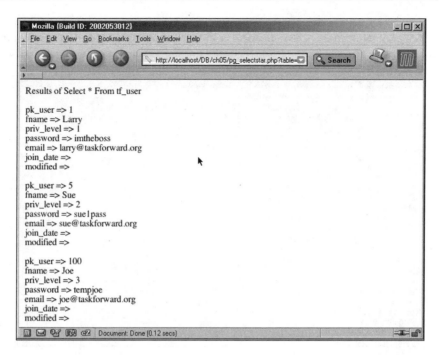

How It Works

This example is pretty straightforward. We are simply using the PEAR::DB connection, that we are already familiar with, and the `fetchRow()` method, provided by the `DB.php` library, with the `DB_FETCHMODE_ASSOC` parameter to return an associative array of results. In this case, our associative array pairs have keys corresponding to the column names of the table and values corresponding to that column's field in a specific result row.

Then we simply use the PHP functions `list()` and `each()` in combination to populate a result set with the key / value pairs in our associative array:

```
while($row = $result->fetchRow(DB_FETCHMODE_ASSOC)){
        while (list ($key, $val) = each ($row)) {
        echo "$key => $val<br>";
        }
        echo "<br>";
}
```

While our form occurs later in the code, it will be shown first if our `submit` value isn't returned. We use a `while` statement to iterate over the result set of the `SELECT *` on `pg_tables` with a `fetchRow` to populate the drop-down listbox in our HTML form:

```
<select name="table">
        <?php
        while($row = $result->fetchRow()){
        echo "<option> $row[0]</option>";
        }
```

While not related to the `taskforward` schema, since we have pulled up all the tables listed in the `pg_tables` relation, we can use this same form to query system tables. Here is a result of the `pg_type` table, which holds metadata definitions for the data types that this instance of PosgreSQL supports:

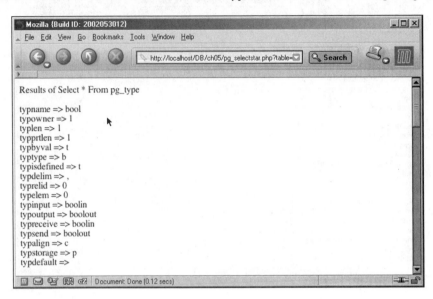

SELECT *

It's perhaps important to note that using the wildcard * in SELECT statements is potentially hazardous to the health of our statements. A SELECT * requests all the columns and returns all the rows, as we mentioned earlier, but it does so blindly. While this is not problematic for simple ad hoc direct execution, using this kind of statement in an application is much more expensive than specifying all the columns we want.

Using SELECT * can also cause problems in cases where the table definition has been changed. Take for example a stored procedure, otherwise known as a **P**ersistent **S**tored **M**odule, or PSM. We will go into PSM's in depth in Chapter 8, but for now we can simply think of a PSM as an SQL statement that has been stored within the database. Such stored SQL, as well as other persistent database objects that include columns, are created with an understanding of the specific table structure. Attempting to use a SELECT * from a PSM once the target table has been altered may throw errors if some of the columns in the target table have changed, even if the statement does not reference these changed columns directly. Getting into the habit of specifying a list of columns explicitly in our SQL statements will ensure that we maintain better performance and reduce the possibility of other problems.

Comparison Operators

It's worth an aside to point out that SQL, just like PHP, has a series of operators in the language for the comparison of values. These will look familiar to most developers with any experience, but for clarity, the syntax of the operators is as follows:

Operator	Meaning
<	less than
=	equal to
>	greater than
<=	less than or equal to
<>	not equal to Note: some RDBMS implementations also support the non-SQL standard syntax: "!="
>=	greater than or equal to

These comparison operators may be used throughout our SQL statements to compare character data types, numerics, and datetime types. Also, as we will see a bit later in the chapter, the words LIKE, BETWEEN, IS NULL, and NOT can be used directly.

Try It Out – Using Additional Predicates

Some other predicates that we will commonly use with WHERE in our SQL SELECT statements are BETWEEN and LIKE. BETWEEN specifies a range for the results while LIKE specifies a match that uses wildcards.

Here is an example of each one, using our sample data and psql inteface beginning with BETWEEN:

```
taskforward=# SELECT fname FROM tf_user WHERE priv_level BETWEEN 0 and 2;
 fname
-------
 Larry
 Sue
(2 rows)
```

Let's have a quick look at LIKE now. Note, wildcards of % and _ may be used, where _ specifies a single character and % allows for the possibility of multiple characters.

```
taskforward=# SELECT fname FROM tf_user WHERE email LIKE '%taskforward%';
 fname
-------
 Larry
 Sue
 Joe
(3 rows)
```

The IS NULL Predicate

As we mentioned in the last chapter, a NULL value for a data type indicates an empty value. This is different from a zero value and instead means that the value is unknown. Using IS NULL or NOT NULL in an SQL statement can be quite useful when setting up logic operators in our code. As an example, we discussed that Booleans can contain True/False values. With Nulls allowed, a Boolean can now be said to have **Third Value Logic**, equating to the values of True/False/Maybe.

157

In our example below, we see that NULL is used in the comparison part of an SQL statement, or more simply, used after the IS. This example might be useful for setting a default password for users who have not signed up in our database, for instance if a partial data file was loaded:

```
UPDATE tf_user SET password to 'temp' WHERE  password IS NULL;
```

We should also take into account the use of empty strings, as PHP will insert an empty string if the NULL keyword is not used in the DDL:

```
UPDATE tf_user SET  password to 'temp' WHERE  password IS NULL
  OR password == "";
```

UPDATE

So far we have seen operations that enable us to add data to tables and retrieve data. It's also necessary to be able to change data and SQL provides the UPDATE operator for this. Simply put, an UPDATE statement is used to update or change rows of one table. In practice, programmers will often have to execute a series of UPDATE statements within a transaction to achieve the result desired by the application.

UPDATE statements are used with SET, in the following manner:

```
UPDATE  some_table SET columns equal to new values
   [WHERE  some search criteria must be true]
```

Like the operators thus far, we see that UPDATE is also used with the WHERE predicate.

Try It Out – The UPDATE Statement

Let's assume that initially Joe had an improper value for priv_level. Here is how we could change the value to 5:

```
taskforward=# UPDATE tf_user SET priv_level = 5 WHERE fname = 'Joe';
UPDATE 1


taskforward=# SELECT  * FROM tf_user;
pk_user|fname|priv_level|password |      email      |join_date|timestamp
-------+-----+----------+---------+---------------------+---------+---------
     1 |Larry|        1 |imtheboss|larry@taskforward.org|         |
     5 |Sue  |        2 |sue1pass |sue@taskforward.org  |         |
   100 |Joe  |        5 |tempjoe  |joe@taskforward.org  |         |
(3 rows)
```

DELETE

DELETE is pretty straightforward and covers the last condition for acting on data – removing it. To keep in line with our other explanations of operators, a DELETE statement simply removes one or more rows from one table.

In practice, DELETE statements are often used with FROM, in the following manner:

```
DELETE FROM some_table WHERE some search criteria are true
```

The WHERE part of this clause is used to set up a condition with all matching rows in the table deleted.

Try It Out – The DELETE Statement

As we saw in the last chapter, a priv_level in our tf_user table greater than or equal to 3 indicates employees who are not concerned with management. Let's assume that this division of the company is transferring all non-management users out, requiring that they be removed from the tf_user table:

```
taskforward=# DELETE FROM tf_user WHERE priv_level > 2;
DELETE 1


taskforward=# SELECT * FROM tf_user;
pk_user|fname|priv_level|password |        email         |join_date|timestamp
-------+-----+----------+---------+----------------------+---------+---------
      1 |Larry|         1 |imtheboss|larry@taskforward.org|         |
      5 |Sue  |         2 |sue1pass |sue@taskforward.org  |         |
(2 rows)
```

How It Works

As you may have noticed earlier, the WHERE clause is optional, so:

```
DELETE FROM tablename;
```

would have just removed all the records from a table, so we used the WHERE clause, and then simply performed a SELECT for proof. If we hadn't used the WHERE clause, as shown, our results would have been quite different.

```
taskforward=# DELETE FROM tf_user;
DELETE 2


taskforward=# SELECT * FROM tf_user;
user_id|fname|priv_level|password|email|join_date|timestamp
-------+-----+----------+--------+-----+---------+-----------
(0 rows)
```

As you can see, PostgreSQL has reported DELETE 2, indicating how many records the DELETE statement affected.

While this type of statement may not be useful in many cases, be aware that if you are building SQL statements up conditionally in PHP and you drop the WHERE clause for some reason, you will empty your table. We will talk a bit more about building up statements conditionally later on in the chapter.

Go ahead and run your insert.php or manually load the data into the tf_user table again, as we will need it for later examples.

Commit and Rollback

When an SQL query is run against the database engine resulting in a change of the values in the database tables that change is not necessarily permanent. It's possible for a database system to hold the changes in a temporary state until the database session is ended, at which point it will **commit** the changes, or make them permanent.

A **rollback** command simply instructs the database to reverse all the changes since the last checkpoint, or commit statement, and begin a new transaction.

It's also important to mention transactions again here. As we saw in Chapter 4, a transaction is a set of SQL statements that are intended to be run as a coherent group. It's also true that a single SQL statement is executed within a transaction in most databases. This means that if your database server is powered down while halfway through deletion of 1000 rows, upon recovery you will find that none of the rows have been deleted.

Some databases will not allow rollbacks unless you explicitly alter the **autocommit** behavior of the connection or if you explicitly begin a transaction. As you may remember, the autocommit mode of a connection causes the RDBMS to end the transaction and commit all changes at the end of each SQL statement. This mode is also called implicit transaction or chained mode. You should check the default setup of your database to determine how it handles default statement execution. Some databases commit each SQL statement by default and some do not. It's also likely that the database driver you are using can be configured to set the autocommit behavior, either in a DSN or as a special configuration parameter.

If the autocommit state has been turned off, you can either explicitly issue a commit command, a rollback command, or finish a transaction. We will get into transactions in much greater detail in Chapter 7, but again, read your database documentation carefully. You will be in for some unpleasant surprises if you try to use transactions in a default MySQL instance or against other databases whose autocommit default is on.

As an example, with some popular RDBMS, issuing a `BEGIN WORK` turns off the default autocommit mode in PostgreSQL while Sybase uses `SET CHAINED`, and MS SQL Server uses SET `IMPLICIT_TRANSACTIONS`.

Sorting and Aggregating

I bet you thought we were finished with SQL statement components? Not quite, this section covers the predicates that deal with how data is returned from our database our `SELECT` statements. So, what's the difference between sorting and aggregating? Simply put, sorting changes the order of the data that is returned to us, while aggregating creates new data based on something selected by our query. It's important to note that sorting and aggregating may not be used together in the same SQL statement.

Let's look at each of these categories and some specific predicates to achieve each.

Sorting

The sorting predicates include ORDER BY and GROUP BY. While they sound similar they can return vastly different types of result sets, so experiment with them as you become familiar with the definitions below.

ORDER BY

An ORDER BY might be thought of as a simple sorting mechanism, like sorting a list of addresses by the first name or country. It returns the result set to us sorted by whichever column(s) we specify, according to the following syntax:

```
SELECT some columns
FROM a table
ORDER BY a column or comma-separated list of columns.
```

Try It Out – ORDER BY

```
taskforward=# SELECT fname FROM tf_user ORDER BY pk_user;
 fname
-------
 Larry
 Sue
 Joe
(3 rows)
```

It's also useful to use the qualifiers ASC and DESC, for ascending and descending, to control how the results come back. This can save a lot of processing power and increase performance in our PHP applications if we are pulling arrays from our database already sorted.

```
taskforward=# SELECT fname
taskforward-# FROM tf_user ORDER BY pk_user DESC;
 fname
-------
 Joe
 Sue
 Larry
(3 rows)
```

As mentioned in the definition, it's possible to sort by more than one column using ORDER BY, simply by specifying a list of columns in the ORDER BY section of the statement. To show this, we need to first insert another user into our table with some of the same values – let's suppose that a second "Joe" was hired.

Using our pg_insert.php script, we can run the following statement:

```
INSERT INTO tf_user (pk_user, fname, priv_level, password, email) VALUES
   (10, 'Joe', 3, 'newjoe', 'joe2@taskforward.org' );
```

161

Try It Out – Multiple Columns in ORDER BY

Now we can use more than one column in an ORDER BY:

```
taskforward=# SELECT fname, password FROM tf_user ORDER BY fname, password;
 fname | password
-------+-----------
 Joe   | newjoe
 Joe   | tempjoe
 Larry | imtheboss
 Sue   | sue1pass
(4 rows)
```

Here we can see that the SELECT has returned values ordered alphabetically, first by fname and then by the password. Let's reverse the ORDER BY columns, and see what happens:

```
taskforward=# SELECT fname, password FROM tf_user ORDER BY password, fname;
 fname | password
-------+-----------
 Larry | imtheboss
 Joe   | newjoe
 Sue   | sue1pass
 Joe   | tempjoe
(4 rows)
```

As you can see, the latter example is ordering first by the password and secondly by the fname.

GROUP BY

Like ORDER BY, a GROUP BY specifies a column to sort the result set on, but instead it returns rows grouped together where there are identical items in the results.

Try It Out – GROUP BY

Let's look at a couple of quick examples, which demonstrate the effects of the GROUP BY statement:

```
taskforward=# SELECT password, fname FROM tf_user GROUP BY password, fname;
 password  | fname
-----------+-------
 imtheboss | Larry
 newjoe    | Joe
 sue1pass  | Sue
 tempjoe   | Joe
(4 rows)
```

Not terribly exciting – this looks just like a SELECT * right? But let's see the example if we reverse the GROUP BY items:

```
taskforward=# SELECT password, fname FROM tf_user GROUP BY fname, password;
 password  | fname
-----------+-------
 newjoe    | Joe
 tempjoe   | Joe
 imtheboss | Larry
 suelpass  | Sue
(4 rows)
```

Now we can see that GROUP BY is acting like ORDER BY. But how are they different? Let's see what happens when we query only for fname:

```
taskforward=# SELECT fname FROM tf_user GROUP BY fname;
 fname
-------
 Joe
 Larry
 Sue
(3 rows)
```

When comparing this to a query without the GROUP BY we see that the database eliminated the duplicates and returned a set of unique values for fname. This is acting like a DISTINCT predicate, which we will explore in a moment.

One important restriction of the GROUP BY predicate is that it is creating a new table for us, so we cannot specify columns in the SELECT that are not used in an aggregate function (including GROUP BY) or we will get an error.

PostgreSQL provides a friendly reminder, but other databases may not, so be careful when using GROUP BY:

```
taskforward=# SELECT password FROM tf_user GROUP BY fname;
ERROR:  Attribute tf_user.password must be GROUPed or used in an aggregate
function
```

Sets and Aggregate Functions

Unlike the sorting features of SQL, there are several keywords that can be used in our SQL statements to return a set of data generated by an underlying result set.

COUNT

The COUNT function is used to, not surprisingly, count the rows in a result set. It can be used against a specific column, such as:

```
SELECT COUNT(column) FROM table
```

Let's have a look at an example of its use.

Try It Out – Count

Go back into the psql interface and try the following:

```
taskforward=# SELECT COUNT(fname) FROM tf_user;
 count
-------
     4
(1 row)
```

Alternatively, it's often very useful to use the wildcard option:

```
SELECT COUNT(*) FROM table
```

Or:

```
taskforward=# SELECT COUNT(*) FROM tf_user;
 count
-------
     4
(1 row)
```

This latter example returns the number of rows in a table. It's important to note here that NULL will be counted by a COUNT (*), as it queries the metadata about the table, so has no interest in the actual values of the table columns.

You will notice the 1 row returned by psql – this is an indicator of the number of rows in our result set, not in the database. Since we performed a COUNT, then we have generated a result table with only one row, although that row contains the information that the target table consisted of four rows. This is especially important to remember when using any of the num_rows functions in PHP, for example pg_num_rows, mysql_num_row, odbc_num_rows – they will all return the result of the statement, so you must look for the value of the query result instead of the num_rows result.

DISTINCT

DISTINCT is used to qualify the columns in an SQL query, and eliminates any duplicates in the column before returning the final result set. A DISTINCT keyword would look something like this:

```
SELECT DISTINCT column FROM table WHERE conditional clause
```

You may also chain these two keywords together in a complex expression, such as:

```
SELECT COUNT(DISTINCT column) FROM table
```

Using `DISTINCT` in this way is possible in many places in SQL statements and will remove both the `NULL` values and duplicates to ensure we have a clean result set. Of course, `DISTINCT` does require that our database engine perform a query on an initial result set, so be aware of possible performance concerns as this may become expensive if overused.

The results obtained through an example of `DISTINCT` will look like our `GROUP BY` on `fname`.

SUM

The `SUM` function returns an additive result on the columns specified by the `SELECT` statement, using the syntax:

```
SELECT SUM (column) FROM table
```

This works for data types where addition makes sense, such as the numeric and interval types.

Try It Out – SUM

Let's look at an example of `SUM` in action:

```
taskforward=# SELECT SUM (priv_level) FROM tf_user WHERE pk_user > 1;
 sum
-----
   8
(1 row)
```

It's also important to note that `SUM` will return `NULL` if the result set is empty:

```
taskforward=# SELECT SUM (priv_level) FROM tf_user WHERE pk_user > 200;
 sum
-----

(1 row)
```

MIN

The `MIN` function is used to return the smallest value in a column, using the syntax:

```
SELECT MIN (column) FROM table
```

Try It Out – MIN

Back in our psql interface, we can say something like this:

```
taskforward=# SELECT MIN (priv_level) FROM tf_user;
 min
-----
   1
(1 row)
```

165

It's important to note that the return value for MIN is just that – a value. Using MIN doesn't tell us about the shape of the data, such as if several rows contain the minimum value. Unlike SUM and AVG (discussed shortly), MIN can be used against non-numeric data types, such as character types:

```
taskforward=# SELECT MIN (password) FROM tf_user;
    min
-----------
 imtheboss
(1 row)
```

In this case imtheboss has been returned as it starts with i, which has a lower number associated with it when compared to the other passwords (sue1pass, tempjoe, and newjoe).

MAX

As the converse of MIN, MAX simply returns the largest value in a column, using the syntax:

```
SELECT MAX (column) FROM table
```

Try It Out – MAX

Like MIN, MAX may also be used against the non-numeric as well as numeric data types:

```
taskforward=# SELECT MAX (password) FROM tf_user;
   max
---------
 tempjoe
(1 row)
```

Try It Out – Min with Max

It's also sometimes useful to use MIN and MAX in the same statement, such as:

```
SELECT MIN (column), MAX (column) FROM table.
```

This of course returns two values as shown here:

```
taskforward=# SELECT MIN (pk_user), MAX (priv_level) FROM tf_user;
 min | max
-----+-----
   1 |   3
(1 row)
```

AVG

The AVG function returns an average of the values in the specified column, using the syntax:

```
SELECT AVG (column) FROM table
```

Try It Out – AVG

Again, use of `AVG` must be restricted to numeric and interval types:

```
taskforward=# SELECT AVG (priv_level) FROM tf_user;
      avg
---------------
 2.2500000000
(1 row)
```

More SQL Syntax

Let's discuss some of the other SQL syntax we can use with PHP and within our client interface to the RDBMS.

Building Dynamic Queries in PHP

Just as we bound the SQL statement to the variable `$sql_query` in our web-based database client created by `pg_insert.php`, we can also assemble our statements piecemeal by building up each component of the SQL statement. While this restricts the range of our SQL statements to what is planned for ahead of time, this type of logic allows us to condense our code to a single location where we have similar types of statements in use.

Conditionally

As we mentioned earlier, we can use `AND`, `OR`, `NOT`, and so forth, in our SQL statements, to chain together multiple logic clauses and create fairly complex statements. While these types of statements are often exceptionally useful, remember that increases in length and complexity of statements may be potentially costly with regards to execution time. That being said, an SQL statement that returns more specific information, like fewer rows, can allow for better performance in our application by limiting the amount of data that must be carried over the network. Consider both implications when writing statements.

Bound Parameters

In many cases, we also might not know the value of a conditional clause in our SQL statement at design time, either due to user-supplied criteria or to dynamic PHP scripts that use similar SQL statements. To assist here, SQL provides the concept of a bound parameter. Simply put, this allows us to generate an SQL statement with a placeholder for the conditional criteria.

To improve performance, we can prepare an SQL statement once and then execute it multiple times against the database. This concept of statement preparation may be thought of as instructing the database engine to develop the execution plan for a specific SQL statement ahead of time and then executing the statement later without incurring the costs of preparing the statement.

The PHP ODBC functions `odbc_prepare()` and `odbc_execute()` are good examples of this, used as an alternative to `odbc_exec()` or `odbc_do()`. The `odbc_exec/odbc_do()` functions are synonymous and directly execute our SQL statement, or prepare and execute it all in one go. While using `odbc_prepare()` and `odbc_execute()` requires a couple more lines of code, we can prepare and then execute it again and again.

167

Try It Out – Prepare and Execute

As an example, let's take one of the ODBC examples from Chapter 2 and amend it to use
`odbc_prepare()` and `odbc_execute()`:

```php
<?php
//location of libiodbc
putenv("LD_LIBRARY_PATH=/usr/openlink/odbcsdk/lib");
//driver setup info
putenv("ODBCINSTINI=/usr/openlink/bin/odbcinst.ini");
//DSN information
putenv("ODBCINI=/etc/odbc.ini");

$dsn="OpenLink";
$usr="db2";
$pwd="";

//assign the SQL statement to a variable
$sql="SELECT * FROM account where branch = 6";

//create a connection handle
$connection = odbc_connect($dsn, $usr, $pwd) or die (odbc_error());

//prepare the SQL statement
$result=odbc_prepare($connection, $sql);

//execute the results
odbc_execute($result);

//display the results, autoformat in an html table
odbc_result_all($result);

//close the connection - always good form
odbc_close($result);
?>
```

How It Works

The `odbc_prepare()` causes the RDBMS to create an execution plan for the SQL statement,
essentially precompiling it for execution. The `odbc_execute()` then calls for the result of the
previously prepared statement. While this could have been combined into one step using
`odbc_exec()` or `odbc_do()`, like so:

```php
$result = odbc_exec($connection, $sql)
```

We have the benefit of being able to call `odbc_execute($result)` repeatedly if we do not close our
script and it will return the results much faster than forcing the RDBMS to prepare and execute all at
once with an `odbc_exec()` or `odbc_do()`.

Complex SQL Statements

Now that we have covered the building blocks of SQL syntax we can use to create simple statements, let's talk a bit about statements that work with multiple tables or nest SQL statements within others. For this section, even more than the others in this chapter, please carefully review your database system documentation as we are getting into SQL:1999 features that may be implemented with different syntax across database vendors or may not be implemented at all. Also it may be a good idea to check the website of your database vendor, as SQL compliance information should be readily available.

Temporary Table

What is a temporary table? We mentioned temp tables a couple of times in Chapter 4. To review, temp tables are metadata definitions stored in the schema with the actual table manifested when referenced in an SQL statement. This is true from a user standpoint, but it's also important to consider that much of the SQL we have encountered in this chapter is actually executed by the database system through creation of new temporary tables.

Take for example our DISTINCT keyword. The database engine will typically create a temporary table that contains all of the columns in a result set before eliminating duplicates and generating a result set from the remaining columns. The RDBMS does this for performance reasons, as it's much cheaper to remove the duplicates from the smaller set based on the distinct rows than to remove them from the final and potentially larger result set.

With this in mind, the next few concepts dealing with SQL statements should be thought of as generating temporary result sets in table form under the covers before returning the result sets that we ask for. Keep this in mind as you design your SQL, as the processing required to generate all of these temp tables may cause your SQL to incur not insignificant performance penalties.

Joins

So far in this chapter the majority of SQL statements that we have constructed focus on returning data from a single table or modifying data in a single table. While this is useful, if we have followed the normalization principles covered in Chapter 3 then our database schema will consist of data in tables that is semantically unrelated – normalization has removed any association of meaning between tables. To provide appropriate context and generate information from our data, it is necessary to create the relationships between multiple tables and update or return information based on new relationships. SQL statements that create these relationships are called joins.

Since we have only been dealing with one main table so far, let's add some rows to our tf_task table, as it is currently empty. We can use either our pg_insert.php script or our psql client to add the following rows to the tf_task table, pulled from the listing at the beginning of the chapter:

```
INSERT into tf_task (pk_task, name, description, completed, fk_assigned_by,
    duration) VALUES (1, 'activity_report', 'summary of what Joe has done this
    week','F',5,'5');
```

```
INSERT into tf_task (pk_task, name, description, completed, fk_assigned_by,
    duration) VALUES (2, 'month_plan', 'goals for next month based on
    strategic focus','F',5,'5');
```

Before we get into the syntax of different join types, let's talk about how we specify a column name in our SQL statements. Up to this point we have used a simple, or unqualified, column name like so:

```
SELECT column FROM table
```

With this sort of statement we can assume that the specified column exists in the specified table and in fact, we will get an error if this is not the case. SQL does, however, provide for explicitly qualified column names. Qualifying our columns in a statement would look something like this:

```
SELECT table.column FROM table
```

This isn't terribly useful with a single table, but we will see in a moment that it is necessary when writing SQL statements against more than one table.

Perhaps the simplest form of a join is that of a **Cartesian Product**, or a cross product of each table. While this doesn't provide us with a useful subset of data, it shows the general join syntax that we can build on. In addition, errors in joins will often result in a Cartesian Product, so it's good to know what one looks like, although they should be avoided:

```
SELECT, one_table.*, another_table.* FROM one_table, another_table
```

Try It Out – Cartesian Product

Looking at our `taskforward` schema, a simple Cartesian product on the `tf_user` and `tf_task` table would be:

```
taskforward=# SELECT tf_user.*, tf_task.* FROM tf_user, tf_task;
```

How It Works

As you will see, this evaluates every row in one table against every possible row in a second table, creating a monster table (that doesn't have a whole lot of relevant information).

If we add in a conditional WHERE to our SQL statement, we can equate the `tf_task.fk_assigned_by` field to the `tf_user.pk_user` field, and produce some meaningful results, in this case a list of tasks assigned by each user.

Try It Out – Joins

```
taskforward=# SELECT tf_user.*, tf_task.*
taskforward-# FROM tf_user, tf_task
taskforward-# WHERE tf_user.pk_user = tf_task.fk_assigned_by;
```

How It Works

By specifying a conditional statement that narrows down the result set, the WHERE clause, we have eliminated the Cartesian Product and produced something useful.

This is perhaps the most straightforward style of join and is often called an **equi-join**.

Let's digress for just a bit to discuss an easier way to write our SQL statements that is commonly supported by SQL:92 and other databases.

Just like our table name qualifier, it's also syntactically legal to specify an alias for each table qualifier and then define the alias in the FROM clause after it has been used. This can dramatically shorten SQL statements when there are many fully qualified columns specified. Here is our previous example with the correlated aliases:

```
taskforward=# SELECT u.fname, t.description
taskforward-# FROM tf_user u, tf_task t
taskforward-# WHERE u.pk_user = t.fk_assigned_by;
 fname  |                 description
--------+---------------------------------------------
 Sue    | summary of what Joe has done this week
 Sue    | goals for next month based on strategic focus
 (2 rows)
```

How It Works

As can be seen, we have a meaningful equi-join, returning a list of tasks that Sue has assigned.

Other Joins in SQL:1999

Moving forward, there are many types of joins that SQL:1999 databases support. While support and syntax will vary across different database implementations, here are the most common ones you may come across with a pseudocode example of each.

CROSS JOIN

The CROSS JOIN is simply a Cartesian product, specified with alternate syntax:

```
SELECT * FROM one_table CROSS JOIN another_table
```

While this is the same as our simple Cartesian Product, it's important to note that WHERE clauses typically cannot be used with a CROSS JOIN.

NATURAL JOIN

A NATURAL JOIN is similar to the Cartesian Product or CROSS JOIN, but it only evaluates the rows in tables where the columns have the same name.

```
SELECT * FROM one_table NATURAL JOIN another table
```

Joins on Specific Columns

There are two ways to specify that we wish to return a result set where a column from one table is semantically meaningful with a column in another table, even if the columns are named differently. Examples of the differing syntax are as follows:

```
SELECT * FROM one_table JOIN another_table ON
   one_table.column = another_table.column
```

And

```
SELECT * FROM one_table JOIN another_table
   USING (column, column)
```

Both syntaxes are functionally equivalent, but notice that the USING version doesn't use a table qualifier and instead relies on matching the order of the specified columns with the order of the target tables.

Using the ON syntax here may remind you of the WHERE clause covered earlier, and indeed it may be thought of as similar. We can further extend these statements and limit our result sets by adding in WHERE clauses as well as chaining keywords. For example:

```
SELECT * FROM one_table JOIN another_table ON
   one_table.column = another_table.column AND
   one_table.column_two = another_table.column_four WHERE
   one_table.column > some_value
```

INNER and OUTER Joins

So far we have seen that the result sets from our joins are comprised of results only where there is data in both tables. These are INNER joins, and for the most part will serve just fine to return the majority of our data.

Instead, if we want to mandate that all the rows from one of the join target tables is returned, we can perform an OUTER JOIN. In practice, OUTER JOINs are performed with the keywords LEFT and RIGHT, such as:

```
SELECT * FROM one_table LEFT OUTER JOIN another_table ON
   one_table.column = another_table.column
```

And:

```
SELECT * FROM one_table RIGHT OUTER JOIN another_table ON
   one_table.column = another_table.column
```

So what is the difference between the LEFT and RIGHT keywords used here? You may have guessed already, or if ambitious you may have experimented, but the keyword simply tells the SQL parser which table to preserve the rows from. LEFT indicates the result set must preserve the rows from the table on the "left" side of the JOIN expression, the first target table specified and, naturally, RIGHT specifies that rows must be preserved from the "right" or second table.

Lastly, it's possible to preserve rows from both tables (and introduce lots of empty values) in our result set by using the keyword FULL instead:

```
SELECT * FROM one_table FULL OUTER JOIN another_table ON
   one_table.column = another_table.column
```

Try It Out – Full Outer Join

As seen, the FULL OUTER JOIN syntax against our taskforward tables looks like this:

```
taskforward=# SELECT * FROM tf_user FULL OUTER JOIN tf_task
taskforward-# ON tf_user.pk_user = tf_task.fk_assigned_by;
```

This statement returns all the rows from both the tf_user and tf_task table, as they are both preserved by the FULL OUTER JOIN.

Unions

So what if we want to return all the rows involved in a multiple table query, without regards to the equality of row values in columns across tables? Enter the UNION statement. UNION was introduced in SQL:86, although it's implementation remained scarce until database vendors had strong SQL:92 and some SQL:1999 support. Simply put, a UNION returns all the columns in the first target table as well as all the columns in the second target table, wherever the WHERE clause is satisfied:

```
SELECT * FROM one_table UNION SELECT * FROM another_table
```

Be aware, however, that a UNION query is often very expensive in terms of performance and there are not many situations where a thoughtful use of joins is not sufficient.

Sub-selects and Correlated Subqueries

A subquery or sub-select is essentially a nested query, where the keywords, clauses, and predicates in the main query are predicated on the results of a secondary query. We can use this to develop SQL statements that act on one table based on data in another table.

The pseuducode for this type of query would be:

```
SELECT column FROM table WHERE column IN (SELECT column FROM another table)
```

Of course, the primary operator may be INSERT, DELETE, or UPDATE as well as SELECT.

We can also use this approach to specify multiple comparison columns:

```
SELECT * FROM table WHERE column1, column2 IN
    (SELECT column1, column2 FROM another table)
```

Using IN

While not a true subquery, there is an alternate way to use the IN predicate that bears mentioning. In fact, it's much simpler and allows us to simply specify a list of acceptable comparison values for use in our statement:

```
SELECT * FROM table WHERE column IN ('value1', 'value2', 'value3')
```

The IN can be used for multiple column comparisons.

You will notice that this use of IN has the same effect as chaining together multiple values with an OR statement, as in:

```
SELECT * FROM table WHERE column = 'value1'OR column = 'value2'
  OR column = 'value3'
```

One benefit of using IN instead of OR to accomplish this comparison is that the execution time for the IN version of this statement is potentially much less, since the database engine makes fewer passes through the temporary table it creates during comparison evaluation.

It is of course valid to use NOT IN to create a negative comparison as well.

The CASE Statement

Just like PHP, SQL provides a CASE statement. Like PHP, the syntax requires we specify an initial value and then compare possible values against it, with target results depending on evaluation of the CASE condition.

Here is a pseudocode example, shown with an UPDATE statement:

```
UPDATE table SET column =
  CASE
    WHEN column = 'value1'
    THEN column = 'value2'
    WHEN column2 = 'value1'
    THEN column2 = 'value3'
  ELSE NULL
  END
```

One note on CASE – the ELSE NULL is optional. If it's not included then it will be assumed and other ELSE values may be specified. ELSE NULL is simply a way of setting the default return value to NULL if none of our case conditions are met.

You may see how there are many benefits to this sort of SQL statement, including optimization, as this allows us to send a single SQL statement to the database instead of multiple statements. It's also possible to do some very powerful application modeling with a CASE statement. Take for example, the priv_level field in our tf_user table. We have the boss table as a lookup resource to control the different priv_levels, but what if we simply wanted to specify this in the application instead of the database?

Try It Out – A CASE Statement

Using a SELECT operator with CASE can return text values to our application instead of the integers actually in the priv_level column. Let's show an example of this and also specify a value instead of ELSE NULL:

```
taskforward=# SELECT fname, priv_level, CASE
taskforward-# WHEN priv_level = 1 THEN 'executive'
taskforward-# WHEN priv_level = 2 THEN 'manager'
taskforward-# WHEN priv_level = 3 THEN 'staff'
```

```
taskforward-# ELSE 'no privs_defined'
taskforward-# END FROM tf_user;
 fname | priv_level |    case
-------+------------+-----------
 Larry |          1 | executive
 Sue   |          2 | manager
 Joe   |          3 | staff
 Joe   |          3 | staff
 (4 rows)
```

Subqueries as a Work-Around?

Now that we understand how temp tables work in joins and nested SQL queries, it's worth mentioning briefly how to use temp table features of databases to get around other limitations. Take for example a database without Foreign Key support. Up until this point, we would be forced to perform two deletes or inserts when changing data in two tables that we wished to enforce rudimentary referential integrity on. With temp tables we have another option, first by creating a temp table containing the common values and then executing SQL against both tables by specifying a subquery against the values in our temp table.

A pseudocode example would be as follows – experiment with this syntax in your database implementation to see what works for your environment:

```
CREATE LOCAL TEMPORY TABLE delete_me (column_name datatype)

INSERT INTO delete_me SELECT column_name from table1

DELETE FROM table1 WHERE column_name IN
  (SELECT column_name FROM delete_me)

DELETE FROM table2 WHERE column_name IN
  (SELECT column_name FROM delete_me)
```

Summary

As we finish this chapter, we should have an understanding of how PHP can embed SQL statements in our scripts to manipulate data in the RDBMS. We should be comfortable opening, closing, and working with database sessions natively and with PHP as well as syntax components of SQL:1999 as supported by various database server implementations, including SQL statement operators, clauses, predicates, conditional evaluation, and combining statements.

Also, we have covered multi-table SQL statements including joins and unions, as well as complex SQL features such as the CASE statement. Diving beneath the covers, we now understand a bit of how databases actually construct result sets using temporary tables and execution plans, and how we may use this to our benefit in join planning and working around some referential integrity feature deficits.

Moving into the next chapters, we will be able to build on these concepts with more advanced SQL and RDBMS concepts such as referential integrity, cursors, views, Persistent Stored Modules, and a more advanced treatment of PEAR DB.

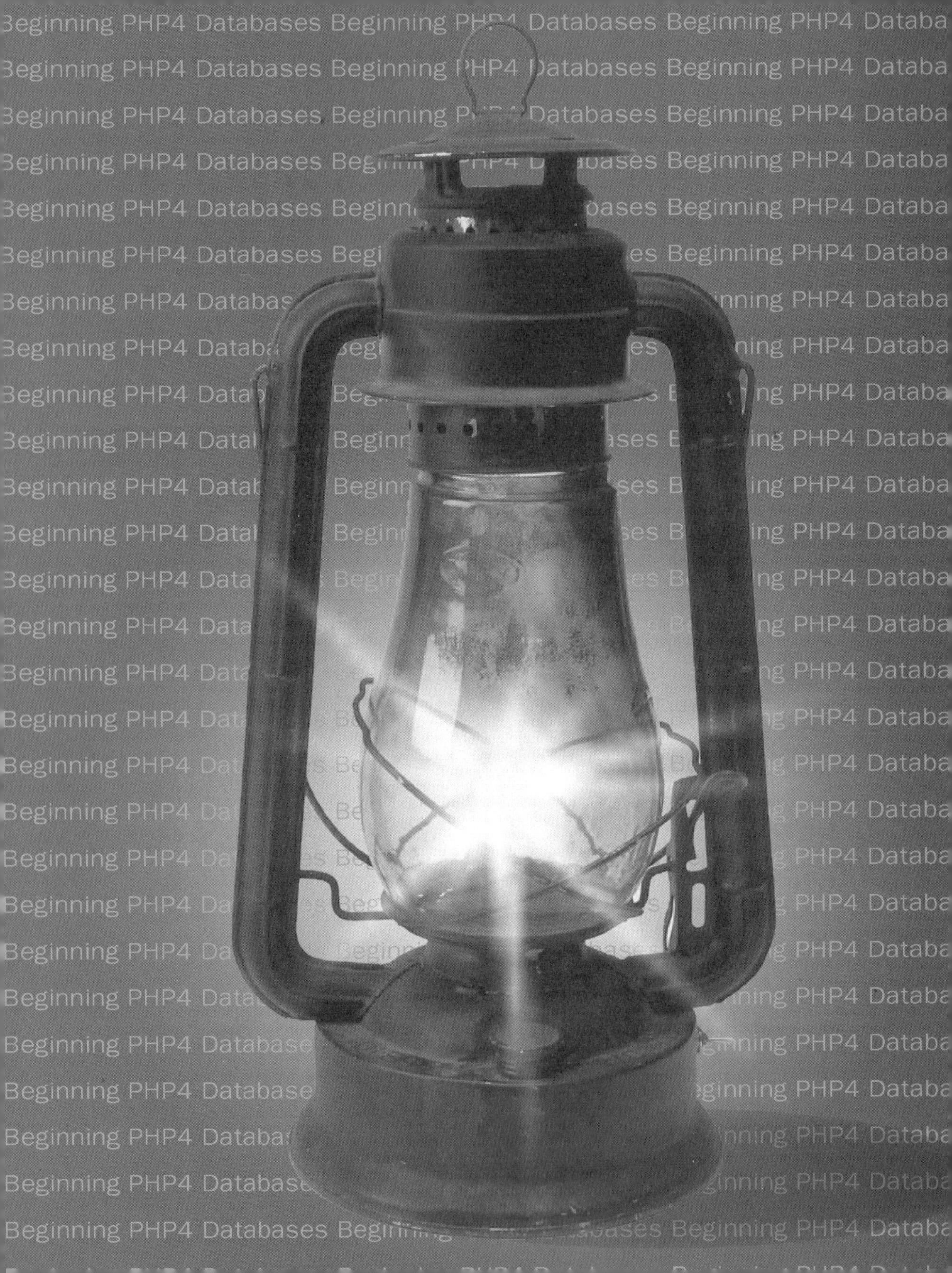
Beginning PHP4 Databases

Data Consistency

When talking about data consistency in terms of a relational database, we are actually referring to a fairly wide array of interrelated topics. Therefore, it's difficult to precisely define data consistency. In a broad sense, it could be said that achieving data consistency in our database applications means that the data stored is accurate, robust, and behaves reliably.

Obviously, when we write our application we assume that our database will do what we expect. But there are some common issues that can easily arise that might throw off our results, meaning that the database will not provide the correct data to our application. This is particularly true in multi-user applications. As this is a book on PHP and databases, and there is a good chance that you are developing a web-based application that is inherently multi-user with PHP, these are problems that you need to be aware of. Some of the situations you may well enounter might include:

- ❑ Gathering user input for some kind of analysis or processing
- ❑ Collecting and storing contact information
- ❑ Displaying or mailing information submitted by an HTML form

The two faces of good development that will promote your success are:

- ❑ Well-designed database tables
- ❑ Effective usage of the consistency features of your RDBMS

Data Consistency Handling By an RDBMS

An RDBMS almost certainly provides functionality that help us ensure consistent data. A solid understanding of how to implement this functionality will go a long way towards making our applications work correctly.

Locking

Locking provides a mechanism that can help solve one of the most basic potential problems in a multi-user database environment. There is a story that illustrates the problem, which is so ubiquitous it actually has a name, the "lost-update problem". It goes something like this.

Evan and Nate both live in Los Angeles, and want to get on the same plane to Hawaii. They call their travel agents at the same time and it turns out that there is only one seat left on the plane. The following sequence of events then happens:

1. Nate's travel agent is faster, and gets the order in first. Nate is happy he has the ticket and starts packing.

2. Evan's travel agent gets his order unaware that the last ticket has already been sold.

3. This new data for Evan overwrites the original data for Nate, and Evan now has the ticket.

4. When Nate, who actually got the ticket first, gets to the airport, nobody knows him.

This is a typical example of a mutual-exclusion problem in programming, often referred to as a **MUTEX**. Clearly, there is a danger zone where it's possible for data to be overwritten. What needs to happen in the software is that when it tries to actually book the ticket, the relevant information needs to be frozen long enough to make sure that the seat is still available and then actually assign the seat to the passenger.

Simultaneous operations interfering with each other cause what is known as **concurrency**. Locks provide a mechanism for the RDBMS to prevent this.

A lock does more or less what its name implies. When a user selects some piece of data, a lock is placed on that data. As long as the lock is in place, no other user can update that data.

There are different kinds of locks, but the most important distinction between **exclusive** and **shared** locks is:

Exclusive locks	**Shared locks**
An exclusive lock is applied by the RDBMS during a WRITE operation such as INSERT, UPDATE, and DELETE. No other operation can acquire any type of lock on the data until the original lock is released.	A shared lock is applied by the RDBMS during a READ operation such as SELECT. When other operations attempt to perform a READ operation on that data, they too acquire shared locks on it. However, no WRITE operation may acquire an exclusive lock on the data while any shared lock is in place.

Let's try and put this more clearly. If we are doing an operation which will actually change the data in the database, then we acquire an exclusive lock on that piece of data. This means that until we are done, no other process can do anything with that piece of data, including reading it. On the other hand, if we are doing something that does not actually change the data such as reading it, then all we do is make sure that nobody else can change the data before we have read what we want.

Now, what happens when we try and do something and can't because the data is locked? The operation we are performing gets queued up by the RDBMS and waits until it is allowed to execute. This can potentially cause problems. For example, if we are performing a huge INSERT operation that takes thirty seconds to finish, then nobody can read that data for those thirty seconds. If our application is a web site and people are trying to look at that data and can't for such a long time, this is clearly a problem.

Table-, Row-, and Record-Level Locking

For the most part, the RDBMS will take care of most of the locking operations for us, without our having to worry about them. In fact, most of the locks that happen in our database will occur without us ever knowing about them. However, many systems also allow the user to explicitly control some types of locking. There are basically three "levels" of locking that can occur: table, row, and record.

In the case of a table-level lock, all of the data in the table in question is locked for the duration of our procedure. This means that until we are done, no updates can be made to any of the data anywhere in the table. Accordingly, these are typically used when we are making updates to several rows in the same table sequentially, and we don't want any other procedures interfering with our queries.

A row-level lock affects all of the data in a specific row. This is useful when we are updating several records within a specific row and we need to ensure that they are all done sequentially. In this case, other rows in the table are still available to be updated by other processes while we are updating the row we have locked.

The most fine-grained type of lock is a record-level lock. As you might have guessed, this simply locks a single element of a particular row so that nobody else can use it until it is unlocked. To be honest, this is something that the database takes care of by itself in almost every case. It's entirely possible that we will never have to actively deal with a record-level lock ourself. We've mentioned it here mostly for completeness.

The syntax for performing locks is database-specific. For example, the popular MySQL RDBMS only provides table-level locking in its 3.x series, while MySQL 4.x and PostgreSQL provide both table- and row-level locks. We'll talk a little more about how to use locks in practice later in the chapter.

Constraints – Pre-Entry Check On Data

A vital part of data consistency is making sure that all the data that goes into our database necessarily obeys certain rules.

This is a step beyond simply indicating that a certain record is of a particular type, like say char(10) for example. A constraint actually looks at the data attempting to get saved in a database, and checks it to make sure that it satisfies a pre-laid condition.

The SQL standard defines the following keywords for constraints:

Constraint	Usage
PRIMARY KEY	This keyword is necessarily unique, and cannot be Null. Else, it is rejected. It is defined at the table level if more than one column is included.
UNIQUE	This keyword guarantees that each value in the column is unique, but allows Nulls. Keep in mind though that only one value can be Null.
DEFAULT	This keyword forces the database to always insert the specified default value for a field in a record if one is not provided by a given INSERT query.
CHECK	This keyword allows you to examine the format of data being entered based on validation rules that you supply. If the data in question does not adhere to the validation rules, then the query is rejected. Rules are defined using the SQL syntax for your database.
REFERENCES and FOREIGN KEY	These keywords are used together to bind primary and foreign keys. If data is inserted into a FOREIGN KEY column that was created using REFERENCES, then that data entry should be present in the table and column referenced. Otherwise, the data is rejected.

The last two entries may look a little confusing, so let's look at quick examples that may help clear things up. Assume that one of the columns in your database is going to contain Social Security Numbers. In the United States, these are generally written in the following format:

```
XXX-XX-XXXX
```

Where X represents any digit. We can use CHECK (the current versions of MySQL do not support CHECK) to make sure that the incoming data does in fact look like this with a statement like the following:

```
CREATE TABLE tablename (
(ssn char(11)
NOT NULL
CHECK (ssn LIKE '[0-9][0-9][0-9]-[0-9][0-9]-[0-9][0-9][0-9][0-9]')
));
```

With this statement, we guarantee two things about the ssn field. First, it cannot be Null. Second, it has the aforementioned format. So, if an application tries to make the following query:

```
INSERT INTO tablename (ssn) VALUES ('111223333');
```

it would fail. A valid query would be like:

```
INSERT INTO tablename (ssn) VALUES ('111-22-3333');
```

This would succeed since it uses the correct format.

Understanding how to use CHECK can be a powerful tool in maintaining your data consistency since it allows you to look at data using any of the tools provided by SQL. So, for example, we could ensure that a certain field can be modified only on Tuesday, or we can disallow entry to any data value that is not from a pre-approved list of possibilities.

Using REFERENCES is generally a simpler operation. It is used to tie a foreign key in a particular table to a primary key in another table. Let's assume we want a table of book titles that includes a certain publisher ID number as a foreign key. This would, in theory, reference the primary publisher ID number in a separate table. Using REFERENCES allows us to force this condition, as we shall see below. If we have a publishers table created like so:

```
CREATE TABLE publishers (
pub_id char(10) NOT NULL PRIMARY KEY,
pub_name varchar(100) NOT NULL
);
```

then we can tie the pub_id field to a corresponding books table to the pub_id in the publishers table with the following CREATE statement:

```
CREATE TABLE books (
title_id char(10) NOT NULL PRIMARY KEY,
title varchar(100) NOT NULL,
pub_id char(10) REFERENCES publishers (pub_id)
);
```

If an application tries to enter a value for pub_id that does not correspond to one of the pub_id values in the table publishers, the query would be rejected. But there are some further effects that are caused by REFERENCES. You cannot delete a row from the publishers table if the pub_id for that row is referenced somewhere in the books table. Furthermore, you cannot modify the pub_id in the table books if the modification you attempt breaks the relationship with the table publishers. If you try to do this then the "offending" query or queries will fail. These are two examples of the way in which data integrity is maintained by the system.

Referential Integrity

In a nutshell, the idea of referential integrity is that if you change a particular data value in a table, then that change must be reflected in every table that makes use of that piece of data. In practice, this ensures that a given primary key value always matches the values of any foreign keys that reference it. Hence the formal definition from E. F. Codd:

> **"For each distinct non-null foreign key value in a relational database, there must exist a matching primary key value from the same domain."**

Conceptually, using our previous idea of a small book table that references a publisher ID, the idea of proper referential integrity looks like this:

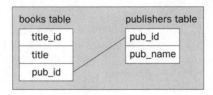

The idea being that the foreign key `pub_id` in the `books` table matches the primary key `pub_id` in the `publishers` table. If, however, you alter the value of either of these fields but fail to update the other, you break the referential integrity as shown in the diagram below:

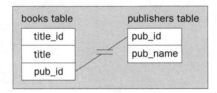

Use of the REFERENCES keyword when defining our tables can help us out somewhat, since it ensures us that foreign keys cannot be added unless they match an existing primary key. The tricky part comes about when you wish to modify one of the values in question.

Again, REFERENCES effectively gives us one solution to this problem. If it is used, then it is not possible to change any of the references values in a way that would break the relationship. So the basic tactic in that case is "do not allow the modification of primary keys."

However, there may be occasions when we will want to change these keys. In such instances, the general resort is making sure that when a primary key is changed in the table `publishers`, the corresponding foreign key in the table `books` is changed to the same value. This can be accomplished from within the database by using **triggers** or by your application using **transactions**. We'll talk about these issues next.

We should point out that not every database supports triggers and/or transactions. In these situations, it is more critical that you pay extra attention to issues of referential integrity in your code so that you don't do anything to break it. A first good practice is to be very aware of where your foreign keys are in your schema. A second one is to make sure that you use columns like the `pub_id` field we used above that are not likely to change very often.

Triggers

A trigger is a named collection of SQL statements, which automatically execute when a particular operation is carried out on a column or table. It may be thought of as similar to a trained watchdog that sits in your database and waits for a situation – in our case, say an attempt to modify a particular piece of data. Whenever it senses this, it jumps into action; a trigger, in analogy, carries out a SQL procedure that is predefined. This procedure might stop the attempt based on some condition, or it might execute additional SQL statements alongside the one initially attempted. The syntax for a typical trigger looks like this:

```
CREATE TRIGGER trigger_name
ON table_name
FOR [ INSERT | UPDATE | DELETE ]
      [, { INSERT | UPDATE | DELETE } ]...
AS sql_statements
  [IF UPDATE (column_name)
  [{AND | OR} UPDATE (column_name)] ...]
```

This may look a little intimidating. So, we shall now create an example that would take care of our potential referential integrity problem from before. Before we do that, there is one more thing about triggers that we will have to understand.

There are two conceptual tables that are automatically created when using triggers – deleted and inserted. These tables can be used in a trigger just like normal tables. These are used in conjunction with the trigger table (the one to which the trigger is assigned) to make decisions. It is important to understand how the inserted, deleted, and trigger tables manifest when implementing INSERT, DELETE, and UPDATE statements. Here's how:

❑   INSERT
    The newly created rows go into both the trigger and inserted tables.

❑   DELETE
    The deleted rows go into the deleted table and are removed from the trigger table.

❑   UPDATE
    Is is basically like doing a DELETE followed by an INSERT. The data in the old rows is stored in the deleted table. The data in the new rows is available in both the inserted and trigger tables.

With all of this in mind, let us create a trigger that will automatically update the pub_id of the table books if the pub_id of the table publishers is changed via an UPDATE command. Here, we'll use syntax compatible with MS-SQL, which supports this operation:

```
CREATE TRIGGER fix_books
ON publishers
FOR UPDATE
AS
DECLARE @pub_id char(10),
        @old_pub_id char(10)

IF UPDATE (pub_id)
  BEGIN
    SELECT @pub_id = pub_id FROM inserted
    SELECT @old_pub_id = pub_id FROM deleted
    UPDATE books
    SET pub_id = @pub_id
    FROM books
    WHERE books.pub_id = @old_pub_id
  END
```

The first few lines declare the trigger on the table publishers for UPDATE-type commands. Next, we declare a few variables. Then, if the UPDATE command affects the pub_id field on the table publishers, we get copies of the old and new pub_id. With those obtained, we perform an UPDATE on the table books to update the pub_id field(s) to the appropriate new values.

You'll notice that BEGIN and END keywords are being used. This defines a transaction. We'll talk about this in the next section. In fact, we'll return to this very example to see exactly what's happening.

If we've done our job correctly, then this will ensure that we don't compromise our referential integrity between these two tables. However, it should be noted that there is an important flaw in this example. The UPDATE statement to the table publishers could have affected more than one pub_id, in which case this trigger wouldn't update everything it needed to. In production, we would want to check and make sure that only one row was affected by the UPDATE command. If more than one row had been affected, we would have stopped the command from executing, since we couldn't effectively affect the table targeted.

Transactions

A transaction is a way of grouping a set of SQL statements so that they execute in the exact sequence entered, regardless of other system operations. Basically, they are a way of ensuring that a group of statements are executed as a group.

In a typical situation, an RDBMS might be getting many queries from different processes (such as a web server) at essentially the same time. Part of what your database does is queueing up these queries and then executing them in some order. Transactions give you some control over this process.

Why Use Transactions?

Of course, one might ask the question "why do I need any control over this?" After all, the database is optimized already, and at first glance it might seem best to let it do its job. Let us take an example of how one can get into problems fairly easily.

Imagine that you have two bank accounts, a checking account and a savings account, and that you have $2000 in your checking account. You electronically wire your cousin $1000 from your checking account. Then, right away, you transfer $1000 from your savings into your checking to get the balance back up to $2000.

However, right in between these two operations, your checking account is billed $1500 to cover your rent payment for that month. Since at that instant you only have $1000 dollars in that account, the bill doesn't get paid and your landlord gets angry with you. This is despite the fact that you actually should have had enough money to cover your rent.

What you needed was to have the first two operations in a transaction, meaning that they would have been executed together and no other operations would have been allowed until both operations had succeeded. Then, it wouldn't have mattered whether the bill for your rent came before or after the transaction. Things would have worked out either way.

This is one way in which transactions are useful. They allow you to maintain the consistency of your data when there are many queries being submitted to your database.

The ACID Properties

Touched upon in the beginning chapters treating concepts of DBMS, this defines a criterion whose fulfilment is essential for any transaction. **ACID** is an acronym for Atomicity, Consistency, Isolation, and Durability. Let's look at each of these in detail:

- **Atomicity**
  In a transaction affecting more than one instance of data, either all of the changes are committed or none are.

- **Consistency**
  A transaction may only leave the system in one of two states. Either there is a new, valid state of data or all data is returned to the state that it was in before the transaction was attempted.

- **Isolation**
  A transaction that is underway but is not yet fully committed must be completely isolated from any other transaction.

- **Durability**
  Data is saved to the system in such a way that even if the system is shut down and restarted, the data will remain available in the correct state.

The basic idea as you can certainly see is that the database should automatically preserve the data in a useful state regardless of any other issues that might come about when making modifications. In fact, some very high-powered databases such as Oracle go to very extreme measures to ensure that no matter what happens, the database can restore itself to the state it was in before the catastrophe.

We should make note of something implied in the Consistency part of the ACID definition. It says that a transaction should either be fully successful, or should return the data to its original state. When the database returns to its original state, it is called a **rollback**. Rollbacks can occur automatically in some cases or can be forced by the programmer.

Let's take our example about the money moving from and to bank accounts. Assume that the database operation had been done properly as a transaction, so that the query that moved the money out of your checking account was immediately followed by the query that moved money into your checking account from your savings account. Finally, imagine that for some reason, the second query, meaning the one that was supposed to put money into your checking account, had failed. The database would then have automatically reversed the first query, so your checking account would still have $2000 in it.

Now that we understand this conceptually, we should look at a more concrete example. As indicated in the section on triggers, we actually used a transaction defined by the BEGIN and END keywords. The specific keywords used are database-dependent, although there is a formal definition defined in the SQL:1999 standard. You should refer to your database vendor's documentation for the exact details, but the logical flow is effectively the same. Typically, the syntax looks like this:

```
BEGIN
   SQL STATEMENT 1
   SQL STATEMENT 2

COMMIT
```

It's also possible to use ROLLBACK to put everything back how it was if some problem encountered is:

```
BEGIN
   IF(some_condition)
     BEGIN
        SQL STATEMENT 1
        SQL STATEMENT 2
        ...
     END
   ELSE
        ROLLBACK
END
```

The trigger example we saw before worked, but we really should have checked to make sure that only one row had been affected by the update. Let's add on to the example to make sure this is the case. And if it's not, we'll do a rollback to get our data back to the state it started in.

The code for the new and improved trigger is this:

```
CREATE TRIGGER fix_books
ON publishers
FOR UPDATE
AS
DECLARE @pub_id char(10),
        @old_pub_id char(10),
        @affected_rows int
SET @affected_rows = @@ROWCOUNT
IF (@affected_rows = 0)
   RETURN
IF UPDATE(pub_id)
   BEGIN
   IF (@affected_rows = 1)
     BEGIN
        SELECT @pub_id = pub_id FROM inserted
        SELECT @old_pub_id = pub_id FROM deleted
        UPDATE books
        SET pub_id = @pub_id
        FROM books
        WHERE books.pub_id = @old_pub_id
     END
   ELSE
     BEGIN
        RAISERROR('You cannot update multiple rows because we have
                   a cascading trigger in place.')
        ROLLBACK TRANSACTION
     END
   END
```

Let's walk through this. The first few lines through the DECLARE statement just define the trigger on the publishers table for updates. Next, we define the @affected_rows variable to see how many rows were affected by the UPDATE statement that fired the trigger. If this is zero, then nothing goes affected and we can just leave.

Assuming that the UPDATE affected the pub_id field we care about, we see if there was just one affected row. If so, then we do a transaction to make sure that the pub_id in the books field gets changed to the correct value. If there was more than one affected row, however, we put out an error message and use ROLLBACK to get everything the way it was before the UPDATE statement that fired the trigger.

Transactions in PHP

We should certainly look at a bit of real PHP code that we could use to define a transaction. Let's define a transaction to handle our problem with the checking and savings accounts. We'll assume that we're using a MySQL database, with InnoDB or BDB tables, which support these transactions.

Try It Out – Transactions in PHP

Let's assume that we just have two very simple tables, checking and savings, with the following data:

Table	cust_id	funds
checking	1234	2000.00
savings	1234	5000.00

We'll use the unified PEAR database access classes here. For more information on why we're using these classes, refer to Chapter 9. Keep in mind that the PEAR libraries have to be in your include_path, locatable in the php.ini file, for this to work properly.

1. We'll start out by defining our DSN (Data Source Name), which is the universal connection string:

```php
<?php
require_once('DB.php');

// define our DSN
$dbtype   = "mysql";
$username = "dbuser";
$password = "dbpassword";
$host     = "localhost";
$dbname   = "bankaccounts";

$dsn = "$dbtype://$username:$password@$host/$dbname";
```

2. Substitute variable names as appropriate for your system. Next, we will get our PEAR::DB object to use:

```php
$db = DB::connect($dsn);
// ALWAYS CHECK FOR ERRORS!
// DB::isError is used to differentiate between an error and a valid
//connection
if (DB::isError($db)) {
    die ($db->getMessage());
}
```

3. Now we'll define a SQL statement which defines the transaction. The first UPDATE represents money going from your checking account to your cousin. The second UPDATE represents money getting taken out of your savings account. The last UPDATE represents the money going back into your checking account so that you can pay your rent. As you can see in the code below, what we're doing is putting each of the query strings into an array called $sql:

```
// Now that we have our $db object to use
// get our SQL queries. We'll put them in
// an array so we can just loop through and
// execute them sequentially.
$sql[] = "BEGIN";
$sql[] = "UPDATE checking SET funds = funds - 1000 WHERE cust_id = '1234'";
$sql[] = "UPDATE savings SET funds = funds - 1000 WHERE cust_id = '1234'";
$sql[] = "UPDATE checking SET funds = funds + 1000 WHERE cust_id = '1234'";
$sql[] = "COMMIT";
```

4. Finally, perform the queries and make sure that we get a valid result for each of them. We do this by looping through the $sql array using a foreach() statement:

```
// Loop through the $sql array and actually
// execute the queries. Note that we still
// check for errors every time.
foreach( $sql as $thisquery ) {
    $rs = $db->query($thisquery);
    // ALWAYS CHECK $rs FOR ERRORS!
  if (DB::isError($rs)) {
    die ($rs->getMessage());
  }
}


// disconnect from database
$db->disconnect();

// Print out a short confirmation message to make sure
// we see that everything worked
print "Funds Moved Successfully";

?>
```

Now, the important thing to keep in mind here again is that if part of the transaction had failed, then everything would have been reset to the original values. This is one of the most powerful ways in which transactions can enforce your data consistency.

How It Works

The important part to understand here is the queries that we put in the $sql array. We immediately define a transaction with the BEGIN keyword. We then use three sequential queries that simulate the money moving around. Finally, the COMMIT keyword is sent which ends the transaction.

Everything else can be understood in terms of the standard steps that you will generally go through when performing database queries. You connect to the database system, pick the specific database you are interested in, perform queries (possibly getting results back), and finally disconnect. As you can see, this is exactly what we've done here.

Let's now look at consistency handling and checks in PHP applications.

Data Entry

We have looked at some of the things that a modern RDBMS system can do to help us maintain consistent data. However, we cannot put all of the responsibility on the database software. A good PHP programmer always does everything possible to ensure that the proper data is getting put into the database before it actually gets to a database query. One of the golden rules of database programming is that it's almost always harder to get data than it is to display it once you have it.

Controlling What Goes in

It is always necessary to guard yourself and your application against bad data. This is especially true in any web-based application, where data is typically submitted using a form. Ordinary users can make mistakes while entering data, and malicious users can intentionally try to break your applications.

Also, it is critical that we use PHP to perform some sanity checks to make sure that the data entered by the user actually looks like we expect it to. Now, you might point out that it's possible to avoid entering bad data through the clever use of CHECK constraints that we covered earlier. If these constraints are available on our system, then we can and should use them. However, we should also check the data with PHP for several reasons.

First, not all database systems support CHECK constraints. If you want your PHP application to be safely portable across different databases you should not rely on that feature. Second, if you do get bad data and a CHECK constraint keeps it from being entered into the database, the only information you have about the problem is the error message you get when the query fails. Using PHP to check the data gives you much more control over how you handle it. By using PHP to identify bad data, creating a database connection and attempting a query when you don't need to can be conveniently avoided, thus saving system resources.

Let's now look at an example of a simple PHP validation application.

Try It Out – A Simple PHP Validation Application

Let's build a simple PHP application that records people's names, phone numbers, and e-mail addresses into a simple database. Along the way, we'll use good techniques to make sure that we're looking at the correct data and that the data is formatted correctly. We'll use a MySQL database containing one table called contact_data.

1. For this example, first create a database contactbook in MySQL using the command:

```
mysql> CREATE database contactbook;
```

2. In this database, create the contact_data table with the following CREATE statement:

```
CREATE TABLE contact_data
(
```

```
    ID int(11) NOT NULL auto_increment,
    NAME char(64) NOT NULL default '',
    PHONE char(12) NOT NULL default '',
    EMAIL char(32) NOT NULL default '',
    PRIMARY KEY  (ID)
) TYPE=MyISAM;
```

3. Create a file called `contact_data.php` in your web server's root directory. We'll start by putting in the HTML for a simple form. There's just a tiny bit of PHP used in the `action` attribute of the `<form>` element, as we will see:

```html
<html>
  <head>
    <title>Simple Contact Data Collector</title>
    <style type="text/css">

  body {
    margin-top: 50px;
    margin-left: 50px;
    font: 11pt verdana, helvetica, arial, sans-serif;
}

    </style>
  </head>
  <body>

<form name="contact_data" action="<?php echo $_SERVER["PHP_SELF"] ?>"
method="post">
<table border="0" cellpadding="3" cellspacing="4">
<tr>
  <td>Name:</td>
  <td><input type="text" name="name"></td>
</tr>
<tr>
  <td>Phone Number (XXX-XXX-XXXX):</td>
  <td><input type="text" name="phone"></td>
</tr>
<tr>
  <td>Email Address:</td>
  <td><input type="text" name="email"></td>
</tr>
<tr>
  <td><input type="submit" name="submit" value="Submit"></td>
  <td> </td>
</tr>
</table>
</form>

</body>
</html>
```

The page should initially look as follows:

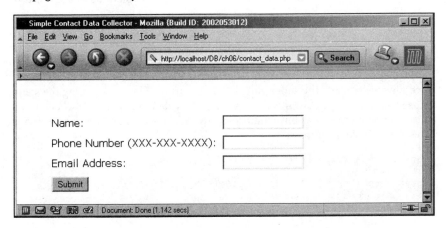

Let's identify the things that we should check for to make sure that we're getting good data. We need to make sure that:

❑ The user actually enters something in the name field

❑ The phone number entered has the format XXX-XXX-XXXX

❑ The e-mail address entered is formatted correctly

4. With this in mind, let's start coding the PHP we'll need to accept the page when it is submitted. This should go at the very top of the page, before the initial <html> tag:

```php
<?php
require_once("DB.php");

// database variables for our dsn
$dbtype = "mysql";
$dbuser = "root";
$dbpass = "";
$dbhost = "localhost";
$dbname = "contactbook";

// DB::connect will return a Pear DB object on success, or a Pear DB Error
// object on error
$dsn = "$dbtype://$dbuser:$dbpass@$dbhost/$dbname";
```

Here, we've just defined our DSN variable in case we need it.

5. Next, we'll check to make sure that the form was actually submitted, since when we first go to the page it hasn't been and we shouldn't do anything:

```php
if( !strcmp($_POST["submit"],"Submit") ) {
```

6. Now, we'll define a variable called $err to track any problems that come up:

```php
$err = "";
```

7. The first check we'll do is to make sure that they entered something in the name field:

```
// check to make sure they entered a name
if( !strlen(trim($_POST["name"])) ) {
  $err .= "You must enter a name.<br>\n";
}
```

8. Notice how we're using the super global $_POST array. This is becoming the standard practice because register_globals is now set to Off by default. Next we'll check to make sure that the phone number was formatted correctly. We'll use a Perl-compatible regular expression to make it simpler:

```
// check to make sure the phone number is in the
// correct format
if( !preg_match( "/^(\d{3}-\d{3}-\d{4})$/" , $_POST["phone"] ) ) {
  $err .= "You must enter a valid phone number.<br>
    You entered " . $_POST["phone"] . "<br><br>\n";
}
```

If you are new to Perl regular expressions then you should definitely spend some time reading about them, as they are incredibly powerful tools. What the above says is that the $_POST["phone"] variable should look like "three digits, a hyphen, three digits, a hyphen, and finally four digits." Which is exactly the format we want for our phone number. The full documentation for the Perl regular expression functions can be found at http://www.php.net/manual/en/ref.pcre.php.

9. Finally, we'll look at the format of the e-mail address. Again, preg_match() will be used:

```
// check to make sure it's a valid e-mail address
if( !preg_match( "/[a-z0-9|_|-|\.]+\@[a-z0-9|\.|-]+\.[a-z]{2,3}$/i" ,
$_POST["email"] ) ) {
  $err .= "You must enter a valid email address.<br> You entered " .
$_POST["email"] . "<br><br>\n";
}
```

10. Now, if there are no errors, we'll enter the data into the database. This highlights another good reason to check your data with PHP. If there are any errors, then we never make the machine create a database connection and query, which enhances the performance of the system:

```
// if no errors, enter into database
if( !strlen($err) ) {
  // create DB object
  $db = DB::connect($dsn);
  if( DB::isError($db) ) {
    die ($db->getMessage());
  }
```

11. We'll use the DB class method quote() to get our variables ready for insertion:

```
// Eliminate 'quote-conflicts' for error-free insertion
$phone = $db->quote($_POST["phone"]);
$email = $db->quote($_POST["email"]);
$name = $db->quote($_POST["name"]);
```

12. The last steps are to define our SQL query, do the insert, and disconnect from the database:

```
// define our INSERT query
$sql = "INSERT INTO contact_data (NAME , PHONE , EMAIL)
VALUES ($name , $phone , $email)";

// do the query
$result = $db->query($sql);
if( DB::isError($result) ) {
   die ($result->getMessage());
}

// disconnect
$db->disconnect();
  }
}
?>
```

13. The only thing left to do is to put a little bit of PHP output on the page to let the user know what happened. The following code should go immediately after the <body> tag, and before the <form> tag:

```
<?php
if( strlen($err) > 0 ) {
  echo $err;
}
else
  if ( !strcmp($_POST["submit"],"Submit") ) {
    echo "<b>Data stored successfully!</b><br><br>\n";
}
?>
```

14. If the user makes any mistakes, they will get a useful error message. For example, if we put in a faulty e-mail address and phone number, and submit the form, the output is shown as follows:

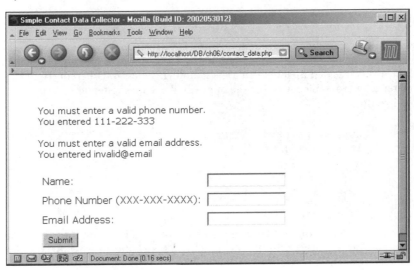

15. However, if everything is inserted correctly, the output is shown as follows:

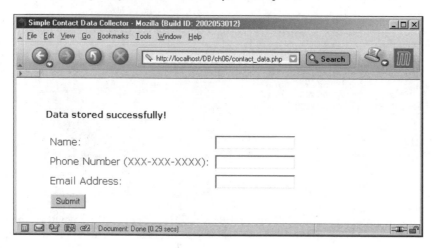

How It Works

We just need one web page to accomplish our task. This page contains a form that the user will enter values into for the fields we want to collect. We also write a small script on this page that would inspect this data to make sure that it looks correct. If it is correct, the script puts it into the database. If not, the script generates a useful error message.

Controlling Consistency with SQL Locks

As we mentioned before, most of the time the RDBMS system that you are using takes care of issues like locking for you, without your explicit intervention. However, on occasion, it can be desirable to force the system to lock some bit of data while you are looking at it or manipulating it.

Table Locks

Some database systems give the programmer control over table locks and row locks. This allows explicit control of concurrency issues. The most common way to do this is with a table-level lock. As stated earlier, this means that the entire table you are examining is locked. Different RDBMS implementations provide different kinds of table locks, but the ones you'll use most often are READ and WRITE. The basic syntax looks like this:

```
LOCK TABLES table_name { READ | WRITE }
    [, table_name { READ | WRITE } ... ]

... SQL CODE ...

UNLOCK TABLES
```

If a process gets a READ lock on a table, then it and any other connection thread can only read from that table until the lock is released. In the case of a WRITE lock, the process that acquires it is the only one that can read or write from the table until the table is unlocked.

A point of interest that is specific to the MySQL database is the availability of low priority WRITE locks. The syntax for this is just a slight modification of the above syntax:

```
LOCK TABLES table_name { READ | [LOW PRIORITY] WRITE }
    [, table_name { READ | [LOW PRIORITY] WRITE } ... ]

... SQL CODE ...

UNLOCK TABLES
```

A low priority WRITE lock will wait to lock the table until there are no connection threads attempting to acquire a READ lock. This can be useful if your application is reading from a table a great deal and you don't want to interrupt things any more than you have to when you modify data in some way.

There are basically two reasons that we might want to use a table lock. The first is when we are going to run a large number of operations on a table or a group of tables. If we lock the table(s) in question then typically the operations will finish up much faster than if we don't lock the tables. Of course, the downside is that if we are executing any INSERT queries, then other processes won't even be able to see the data in the locked table(s) until the lock is released.

The second reason to use table locks is to emulate transactions on databases that don't support them natively. Look at the following example using MySQL syntax:

```
LOCK TABLES customers READ, profits WRITE;
SELECT @total:=SUM(sales) FROM customers WHERE cust_id = some_id;
UPDATE profits SET total_profits = @total WHERE cust_id = some_id;
UNLOCK TABLES;
```

Without locking the tables, it is conceivable that another process could have changed the values of the cust_id field in the tables between the two statements. This would have resulted in inconsistent data and the results would have been incorrect. With the table locks in place, this sequence emulates a transaction and you don't have to worry.

Let's see how we would do this using actual PHP commands. We'll assume that you already have a PEAR database object called $db created, which we did in the previous examples. Also, we'll assume that you have a $some_id variable defined properly to match with the cust_id field in the table. Just to keep things easy to read, we won't do the usual error checking that we did before, though you would want to do that in any kind of production environment. The code above would translate into PHP like this:

```
$db->query("LOCK TABLES customers READ, profits WRITE");
$total = $db->getOne("SELECT SUM(sales) FROM customers WHERE cust_id = $some_id");
$db->query("UPDATE profits SET total_profits = $total WHERE cust_id = $some_id");
$db->query("UNLOCK TABLES");
```

Row Locks

Some relational databases, such as PostgreSQL, support row-level locking. This is basically on the same lines as table-level locking. Only, it affects just specific rows. Other rows in the table are still available to be read and modified by other processes, thus improving system performance.

There is, however, an important difference that distinguishes row locks from table locks. Row locks are attained using the SELECT FOR UPDATE syntax, which is used inside transactions. A typical example might look like this:

```
BEGIN WORK;
SELECT value FROM some_table WHERE ID = some_id FOR UPDATE;
UPDATE some_table SET value = value + 3 WHERE ID = some_id;
COMMIT;
```

Within this transaction, all of the rows identified in the SELECT statement are locked until the COMMIT occurs, and no other process is able to read from or write to them.

There has long been debate about the usefulness of row-level versus table-level locks. Table locks are faster and require less memory than row locks, although the latter do provide for more granularity in your control over what is happening. The most important thing is to make sure that you are keeping your data consistent and that you are writing clean and well-thought-out code.

The State of Current RDBMS Systems

Unfortunately, not all RDBMS systems support the same syntax. Therefore, to really take advantage of the features of a particular system there is typically some overhead required getting used to the specific nuances. Also, not all systems support the same feature set. The table below outlines some of the important features supported by four of the systems that you are likely to encounter – MS SQL Server, MySQL (with InnoDB tables enabled), Oracle, and PostgreSQL:

Feature	MS SQL Server	MySQL	Oracle	PostgreSQL
Stored Procedures	Supported	Not Supported	Supported	Supported
Check Syntax	Supported	Not Supported	Supported	Supported
Triggers	Supported	Not Supported	Supported	Supported
Transactions	Supported	Supported	Supported	Supported
Indexes	Supported	Supported	Supported	Supported
Joins	Supported	Supported	Supported	Supported
Views	Supported	Not Supported	Supported	Supported
Grant	Supported	Supported	Supported	Supported
Revoke	Supported	Supported	Supported	Supported

Summary

Maintaining data consistency is absolutely critical in good application development. Without careful attention to the consistency issues, your applications will be unscalable and prone to producing incorrect results.

Different RDBMS systems support different sets of functionality that you can employ to help you get a handle on your data consistency. You should carefully read the documentation for the system you intend to use, to understand the features available, and how you may use them. Also, you should think about your data consistency issues at the beginning of your database design process. These are problems that can be very hard to go back and fix.

Do not rely fully on your database functionality to maintain consistent data. As you are writing your applications, use PHP's built-in functionality to examine the data you intend to store in the RDBMS. This can help save system resources and give you more control over the feedback submitted for entry into your database.

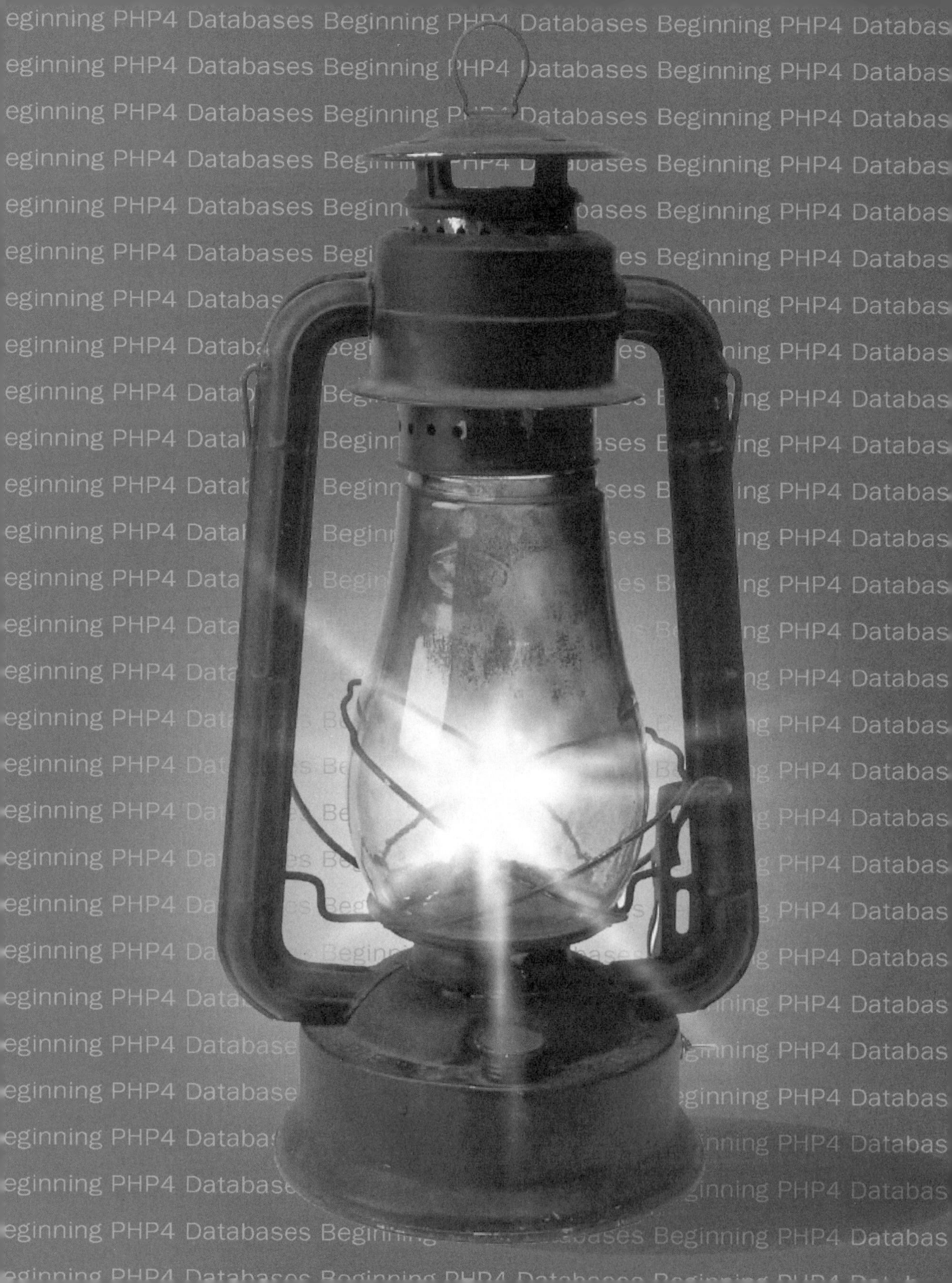
Beginning PHP4 Databases

Advanced SQL and PHP

So far, we have been looking at how PHP interacts with SQL statements embedded in our scripts when passing data between applications and databases. It is also possible to store SQL directly in the database and use more advanced database features to manipulate server-side data.

Some of these more advanced features are not present in all databases and many SQL features are not implemented in MySQL. PostgreSQL, along with other commercial databases like Oracle, MS SQL Server, Sybase ASE, and OpenLink Virtuoso, have excellent support for these features. As always, it's a good idea to check implementation details and supported features with the specific vendor.

So, why do we need to store SQL within a database when we have shown in earlier chapters that data can be manipulated quite conveniently with SQL embedded in PHP scripts? The ability to act on data without crossing over to the client layer for each step allows us to offload application functionality onto database systems. This not only enables some additional power and ease of data handling in our applications, but can also be used to enforce dynamic data changes without user interaction. Also, like we saw in the Joins section in Chapter 5, we can store custom utilities modules to view data in different ways.

In this chapter, we will gain a functional understanding of the following topics:

- ❑ Stored Procedures / Persistent Stored Modules
- ❑ Cursors
- ❑ Triggers
- ❑ Views
- ❑ Indexes

A note of caution – this is a wide area to squeeze into a single chapter, and the caveats about RDBMS vendor-specific implementations hold here perhaps more than in other chapters. Also, since some of the PHP database API sets are still playing catch-up with these advanced features, we are going to focus on a conceptually complete overview of each area and provide some concrete PHP usage examples with our sample `taskforward` application. As you work through the chapter try these examples in your RDBMS of choice.

Stored SQL

Restricting SQL use to PHP scripts is not always the best way to utilize the features of SQL. Ideally, we want to balance SQL usage and minimize network traffic by offloading some of the processing of our data to the database. This can provide additional power as stored SQL procedures can work with parameters that other database APIs cannot within PHP. In addition, this allows the same SQL to be used by multiple applications, even those that are written using disparate languages. Let us start the chapter by taking an in-depth look at the different ways SQL can actually be stored within the database to extend the power and speed of our PHP applications.

Persistent Stored Modules

In this chapter, we are going to look at Stored SQL Procedures, or more correctly named Persistent Stored Modules. In 1996, SQL/PSM (Structured Query Language/ Persistent Stored Modules) was added to the main SQL:92 specification to define how SQL functions can be created and persisted in the RDBMS space and executed in the RDBMS environment, instead of in the host language environment (in this case PHP). This partitioning is often referred to as PSM96, but was actually included in the SQL Foundation (Core) partition in SQL:1999.

The ability to create PSM code in our database systems enables the application developer to write significant portions of the data-processing functions required by the applications directly in the database. This can be done directly in SQL – without the need to mix in another language.

It is important to highlight that PSM are created and remain in the database beyond any transient state such as a transaction. PSM functions and procedures can act on changes in table data without any interaction with the host data. They do not incur any network traffic to define a database object, populate it with data, or make changes to the database.

As always, vendor-specific implementations have some variability of syntax and feature support. PSM96 is implemented in slightly different flavors, with examples being Oracle's PL/SQL, SQL Server's Transact-SQL, Virtuoso's VSP, and PostgreSQL's PL/PGSQL.

It is also important to note that many RDBMS implementations allow creation of stored modules in the database environment using languages other than SQL. For example, PostgreSQL allows TCL, Perl, and C modules; Oracle allows Java; and OpenLink Virtuoso allows C, Java, .NET assemblies, and even PHP directly.

SQL / PSM Features

Moving through the rest of this section, we will cover the major features of the SQL/PSM spec as implemented in SQL:1999 as it's used in our RDBMS, including:

- ❏ CREATE and DROP for stored modules and routines

- ❏ Input and Output parameters of PSM code

- ❏ CALL statements for interacting with PSM

- ❏ Variables in PSM

- ❏ LOOP statements in PSM, including WHILE, FOR and BEGIN/END blocks, CREATE, and DROP

Depending on the specific vendor implementation, you will create functions, modules, or procedures, and assign an SQL statement to them. The actual name for the stored SQL depends on the database, for example, you create functions in PostgreSQL, while Oracle and most of the major RDBMS work with procedures.

In PostgreSQL:

```
CREATE FUNCTION function_name()
(column_name1  datatype,
 column_name2  datatype
...
 )
AS 'SQL statement-body';
LANGUAGE 'sql';
```

As can be seen above, the function definition has no parameters within the parentheses, and also requires a language declaration at the end, as PostgreSQL supports functions in several languages including SQL, TCL, and pl/pgsql – a PostgreSQL specific implementation of a stored procedure language.

PosgreSQL requires the full list of datatypes for the function arguments to drop a PSM:

```
DROP FUNCTION function_name(datatype1, datatype2, ...);
```

In other RDBMS:

```
CREATE PROCEDURE procedure_name()
(column_name1  datatype,
 column_name2  datatype
 )
AS 'SQL statement-body'
END PROCEDURE procedure_name
```

Dropping these objects is often as straightforward as:

```
DROP procedure_name;
```

Or in some cases:

```
DROP module_name CASCADE;
```

As we will see in a moment, the CREATE syntax will be used when we create other database objects for use within procedures.

The CASCADE keyword will cause other database objects that depend on the PSM to also be dropped. Omitting this keyword will produce errors if the database system identifies any dependent objects.

Input and Output Params

Stored modules, which we will look at later, are much more useful with parameters that can be passed to and from SQL.

In PostgreSQL:

```
CREATE FUNCTION function_name(input_param1, input_param2,...)
RETURNS datatype
AS 'SQL statement-body';
LANGUAGE 'sql';
```

In MS SQL Server or Sybase ASE:

```
USE database_name;
CREATE PROCEDURE procedure_name
@input_variable [datatype] (,
@output_variable [datatype] OUTPUT
AS 'SQL statement-body'
);
```

To use these procedures with input and output values, we call the procedure with the appropriate variable passed to it and will receive a return value equal to the results of the SELECT statement.

Calling Procedures

Depending on the RDBMS implementation, calling the procedure or function will usually take one of the following formats, embedded in (for example) a PHP query:

PostgreSQL:

```
SELECT function_name(input_variable, output_variable);
```

Oracle and most other RDBMS:

```
EXECUTE paramer_name(@input_variable, @output_variable);
```

Also valid with Oracle:

```
CALL procedure_name(input_variable, ouput_variable);
```

Combining Multiple Statements

Since PSM are indended to be functionally complete above and beyond Core SQL, we can combine multiple SQL statements in our PSM. For example, in logic processing structures, we can use BEGIN or FOR to initiate a loop to perform additional actions within our stored module and then END to close.

Here is a pseudocode example of a PSM acting on a Cursor – don't worry, we will get to Cursors in a moment.

```
CREATE PROCEDURE procedure_name (:input_variable datatype)
BEGIN
   OPEN cursor_name;
   FETCH cursor_name INTO :output_variable;
END;
```

Try It Out: Using PSM with PHP

Let's look at some examples of using Persistent Stored Modules with our PHP scripts. For simplicity's sake, we will create and manipulate PostgreSQL functions.

The following examples will show how to use stored SQL to add a new user to our tf_user table. Since the creation of a function is based on the schema of a table, we first ask PostgreSQL to recall the structure of this table using the \d command that describes a table:

```
taskforward=# \d tf_user

   Table "tf_user"
   Column    |            Type            | Modifiers
-------------+----------------------------+-----------
 pk_user     | integer                    | not null
 fname       | character varying(50)      |
 priv_level  | integer                    |
 password    | character varying(20)      |
 email       | character varying(100)     |
 join_date   | timestamp without time zone |
 timestamp   | timestamp with time zone   |
Primary key: user_id
```

With this information, we can now create a stored function that adds a pk_user, fname, priv_level, password, and email to the td_user table:

```
CREATE FUNCTION add_tf_user(int, varchar(50), int, varchar(20), varchar(100))
RETURNS varchar
AS
'
INSERT INTO tf_user (pk_user, fname, priv_level, password, email)
VALUES ($1,$2, $3, $4, $5);
SELECT ''added the user ''|| $2::VARCHAR
'
LANGUAGE 'sql';
```

How It Works

The SELECT line is necessary for two reasons: first, in PostgreSQL, all functions that can be called interactively need to return data, and secondly, by using the $2::VARCHAR we are telling PostgreSQL to assign the fname we passed into the output variable. The || symbol, created with a double pipe, is used to concatenate strings, so we are telling the SQL engine to combine the text added the user with the variable indicated by $2.

The numbered variables in the VALUES section could be anything – they are simply placeholders for data elements that will be passed in later.

Entering this query into a PSQL interface looks something like this:

```
taskforward=#
taskforward=# CREATE FUNCTION add_tf_user(int, varchar(50), int, varchar(20),
varchar(100))
taskforward-# RETURNS varchar
taskforward-# AS '
taskforward'# INSERT INTO tf_user (pk_user, fname, priv_level, password, email)
taskforward'# VALUES($1,$2, $3, $4, $5);
taskforward'# SELECT ''added the user''|| $2::VARCHAR
taskforward'# '
taskforward-# LANGUAGE 'sql';

CREATE
```

PostgreSQL indicates a successful CREATE statement by returning a CREATE message, as shown here.

As mentioned earlier, the corresponding DROP FUNCTION statement in PostgreSQL requires the input parameters to be specified:

```
taskforward=# DROP FUNCTION add_tf_user(int, varchar(50), int, varchar(20),
varchar(100));
```

This function will result in the following being displayed by PostgreSQL:

```
DROP
```

Luckily, you can also ask the PostgreSQL database to describe the function for you if you forget, using \df to describe the functions:

```
taskforward=# \df add_tf_user;

  List of functions
 Result data type  |    Name     |            Argument data types
-------------------+-------------+--------------------------------------------
 character varying | add_tf_user | integer, character varying, integer, character
                                   varying, character varying
 (1 row)
```

> Simply specifying \df in a PSQL interface without any arguments will return all of the functions in the database.

Try It Out: Using PSM with PHP

Now let's look at how to apply this to PHP.

First, let's create our database connection environment file as shown in earlier chapters. If you haven't done it before, fire up your text editor and save the following in a file named datatbase.env.php. You will need to alter the values for your specific environment, depending on how you set your database authentication up.

```php
<?php

$username = "postgres";
$password = "";
$hostname = "localhost";
$dbname = "taskforward";

?>
```

Starting with the PEAR:DB example from Chapter 2, let's modify it to pull our sample data from the text file users.txt. Save the following in a file called tf_useradd.php:

```php
<?php

/*
the submit variable will not be defined until we send the form
so depending on if we are waiting for form submission or not
either show the form or the results
*/
if ($_POST["submit"]=="Add User"){

echo "Adding a user to the TaskFoward database<br />";

//PEAR:DB and required variables
require_once "DB.php";
require_once "database.env.php";

//create the PEAR:DB DSN and output notification to the screen.
$dsn = "pgsql://$username:$password@$hostname/$dbname";
echo "defining dsn<br />";

//connect to the database and output notification to the screen
$db = DB::connect($dsn);
echo "connecting to database<br />";
```

```
//always check for errors
if (DB::isError($db)) {
  die ($db->getMessage());
}

//here PosgreSQL uses "SELECT" to call a stored procedure
$query="SELECT add_tf_user($pk_user, '$fname', $priv_level, '$password',
'$email')";
echo "query being sent to the database is: $query<br />";

$result = $db->query($query);
echo "creating db query object<br /><br />";
//execute query and output notification

//always check for errors
if (DB::isError($result)) {
  die ($result->getMessage());
}

//return the new username to the PHP script
while($row = $result -> fetchrow()){
list ($key, $val) = each ($row);
echo "$val<br />";
}

//disconnect free up those resources
$db->disconnect();

exit();
}
//this is end of the "if"
//everything past here will be shown only if the form has not been submitted
?>

<h2>Add User</h2>
<FORM ACTION="<?php echo "$PHP_SELF"; ?>" METHOD="POST">

<h3>Enter New User Information</h3>

<INPUT TYPE="TEXT" name="pk_user"></textarea>User ID
<BR /><BR />
<INPUT TYPE="TEXT" name="fname"></textarea>First Name
<BR /><BR />
<INPUT TYPE="TEXT" name="priv_level"></textarea>Priv Level
<BR /><BR />
<INPUT TYPE="TEXT" name="password"></textarea>Password
<BR /><BR />
<INPUT TYPE="TEXT" name="email"></textarea>Email Address
<BR /><BR />
<INPUT TYPE="SUBMIT" NAME="submit" VALUE="Add User">
</FORM>
```

Open up your browser and pull up `tf_adduser.php`:

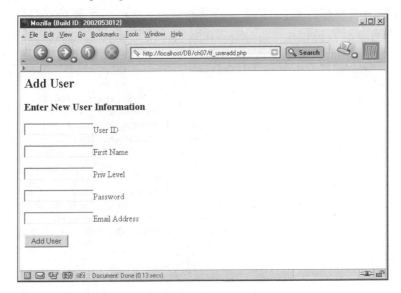

Submitting this form gives us a verbose output and a success message:

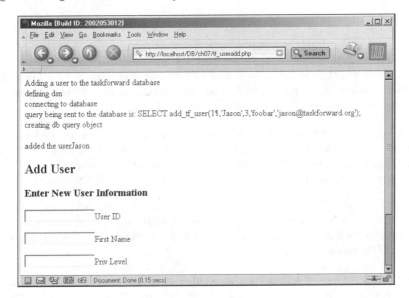

How It Works

As you can see, the result page echos out information on each stage of our script. The verbose output is purely for learning purposes only. You would not want to echo all this information back normally and would in fact probably use an encryption method like md5 (http://www.php.net/md5) to encrypt the password in a real-world situation.

Go ahead and add some users to your `tf_user table` with this form – you will need to use unique User ID's if you have not set up an autoincrement field for this value as mentioned in Chapter 4.

Looking at a `SELECT * FROM tf_user` after this might show you data like this:

```
 pk_user |  fname   | priv_level | password  |           email           | join_date
---------+----------+------------+-----------+---------------------------+---------
       1 | Larry    |     1      | imtheboss | larry@taskforward.org     |
       5 | Sue      |     2      | sue1pass  | sue@taskforward.org       |
     100 | Joe      |     3      | tempjoe   | joe@taskforward.org       |
      10 | Joe      |     3      | newjoe    | joe2@taskforward.org      |
       4 | Phillip  |     2      | foo       | phillip@taskforward.org   |
       6 | Ellen    |     3      | foobar    | ellen@taskforward.org     |
       7 | Sally    |     3      | foo       | sally@taskforward.org     |
       8 | James    |     3      | foo       | james@taskforward.org     |
       9 | Emily    |     3      | foobar    | emily@taskforward.org     |
      11 | Jason    |     3      | foobar    | jason@taskforward.org     |
      12 | Michael  |     3      | foobar    | michael@taskforward.org   |
(11 rows)
```

For table clarity, we have removed the `modified` *field from the display above.*

Cursors

Throughout the book, we have been dealing with returning result sets to our PHP applications or updating data, using SQL queries. It bears emphasizing, however, that while SQL deals with data in sets, PHP does not. PHP can retrieve sets of data into the application space by using an array as one example, but it needs to act on individual data by first selecting a specific row of a result set. This is the reason that we need to iterate over result arrays when returning data from a query.

The differences in how PHP and SQL handle data illustrate a mismatch in the underlying data representation mechanisms of the two languages. (You may remember that the Core SQL features were developed to make SQL a portable database interface to enable other languages to use SQL bindings.) **Cursors** are one feature that helps alleviate this mismatch with regards to result set handling.

Essentially, a cursor lets you deal with all the data in a result set, in the database space one row at a time. Without this option, all data must be pulled into the PHP space one row at a time – something that can become very expensive with regards to network traffic between the database and webserver, as well as requiring additional coding in your PHP scripts.

Cursors occur within database transactions, so require an open transaction. Some RDBMS require you to begin a transaction explicitly, while others will assume a transaction when data is selected into a cursor, although it's better form to explicitly open the transaction.

The actual use of a cursor within the database space is quite similar to iterating over an array in the PHP application space and can be conceptualized as including the following parts:

- ❑ **declaring** the cursor as a database object for a `SELECT` statement
- ❑ **opening** the cursor
- ❑ **fetching** a row of data in the cursor into a variable
- ❑ **moving** a pointer around a multi-row result set and looping over the data
- ❑ **closing** the cursor

A syntactical example would be as follows:

```
DECLARE cursor_name CURSOR FOR
SELECT statement
OPEN cursor_name;
FETCH cursor_name INTO :variable;
CLOSE cursor_name;
```

This overview breaks down into the SQL commands of `declare`, `open`, `fetch`, and `close`. We will go into each of these statements in depth in just a moment.

Also, regardless of the RDBMS behavior in opening the transaction for you, commiting a transaction with an open cursur implies closing the cursor, unless the cursor has been specially delared as holdable – a new cursor declaration option in SQL:1999 that allows for cursors to be semi-persistent, or remain resident in the database space outside of a transaction.

Cursor Models

As we explain the different cursor actions, let's delve into the different types of cursors and how they can be used to deal with result sets.

Forward-Only Cursors

A static and forward-only cursor is the default and basic type supported by RDBMS. Think of this as a "napkin dispenser" you might find at a restaurant. The napkins are the individual data rows, loaded into the cursor and then processed sequentially as you pull each "napkin" out of the cursor. We simply run down the results, process them one row at a time, and move to the next row.

But, why is it called static? This refers to the fact that the result set fetched into the cursor is detached from the underlying database rows and is not sensitive to changes in the underlying data. If another SQL statement updates a row fetched into a static cursor, it is not detected until the transaction surrounding the cursor is closed. Alternatively, some RDBMS support dynamic cursors, which regenerate the result set as the cursor's pointer is moved along the rows and is thus able to capture changes.

Scrollable Cursors

You may want to traverse data differently than in a single-direction sequential fashion as above; this is where a scrollable cursor comes in. Typical scrollable cursors allow you to jump ahead to a later row, and then back to a row. Some implementations may also support bi-directional scrollable cursors, allowing total freedom in positioning.

As a side note, even when a RDBMS implementation doesn't support bi-directional scrollable cursors, a sophisticated database driver implementation will provide this functionality. A good example of this is OpenLink Software's ODBC Drivers (http://www.openlinksw.com).

Holdable Cursors

A holdable cursor, as hinted above, is one that is not implicitly closed when the surrounding transaction is committed. By default, a cursor will be created 'without hold'. If you specify 'with hold', it may be persisted beyond the end of the transaction, and may therefore be used across different parts of your application logic. Note: support for holdable cursors is still very limited in RDBMS implementations.

Keyset and Rowset Cursors

So far we have been discussing cursors that can be considered **rowset**-driven. Think back to the static cursor, and its counterpart, the dynamic cursor. While there is a difference in sensitivity to change, both static and dynamic cursors function with the concept of a rowset, or a set or rows comprising the result of a SELECT and read into the cursor. Essentially, the rowset can be correlated to what the fetch has returned, although it is actually a smaller number of rows. If a result set consists of say 1000 rows, a rowset might consist of 10 rows. Then the 10 rows constitute the sliding window that is shuttled down the result set. One last clarification between a result set and rowset is that the rowset data is in the active application space of the RDBMS, while the result set is still effectively "in" the table and not taking up any additional temporary memory.

Alternatively, a **keyset**-driven cursor generates a set of keys, or row identifiers, for the result set, instead of generating the full rows as found in the rowset. The keyset-driven cursor generates the result rows when the key for a specific row is accessed, which allows better performance when dealing with larger sets of data. Also, like a dynamic cursor, a keyset cursor maintains sensitivity to deletions in the underlying data, but unlike a dynamic cursor, which creates the results as needed, the keyset cursor will display blanks in the result set if rows are deleted by another SQL statement, since it has generated a static keyset. In addition, a keyset-driven cursor will never be aware of insertions by another SQL statement, as it has no keys for that new item.

The following diagram shows how a keyset-driven cursor is used:

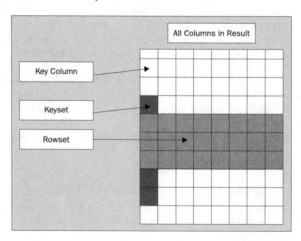

Mixed Cursors

The last, and arguably most sophisticated type of cursor is the mixed cursor. A mixed cursor can be thought of as combination of the dynamic rowset cursor and the keyset cursor. Not only is it sensitive to changes in underlying data by generating the result rows when a specific key is referenced, but it generates keysets that are smaller than rowsets, generating new keysets as it reaches the end of each one. As you might imagine, this is slightly less sensitive to change than a full dynamic cursor, but it is substantially cheaper in terms of database resources to implement.

Cursor Syntax

Now that we have a basic understanding of the Cursor models, let's go back into the SQL clauses used to create and manage cursors.

Declare

As we saw previously, the DECLARE syntax creates the cursor. The options in this syntax include parameters for sensitivity, scrollability, holdability, returnability, and updatability. The meaning of these terms quickly becomes apparent as we consider the cursor models.

Broken down, the DECLARE clause looks something like this:

```
DECLARE cursor_name [sensitivity]
[scrollability] CURSOR
[holdabililty] [returnability]
FOR
query_expression [updatability];
```

Options for sensitivity are: Sensitive, Insensitive, and Asensitive. Scrollability can be set to Scroll and No Scroll. To persist cursors past a transaction we would set holdabiltiy to With Hold, otherwise the default of Without Hold will apply.

The query expression would typically be any standard SQL and could also include a parameterized query, for instance, passing in the evaluation value for the WHERE clause at execution time. To do this in a cursor, you can set the value as :variable_name. The colon tells the database engine that the variable is to be passed in from PHP and evaluated when the cursor is opened.

Fetch

Fetch is used to pull the current row of data from a cursor into a variable and can take the form of FETCH NEXT, FETCH PRIOR, FETCH FIRST, FETCH LAST, or FETCH RELATIVE. Seen in an example, FETCH looks something like this:

```
FETCH NEXT
FROM cursor_name
INTO :variable_list;
```

The variable_list is a comma-separated list of variables that corresponds to the number of items in the row returned by FETCH. The colon before the variable indicates that the database should treat the variable or variables as being passed in from the application space instead of being drawn from a stored module in the database space.

FETCH RELATIVE requires an integer to specify which row relative to the current one should be returned. For example:

- ❏ FETCH RELATIVE 0 returns the same row again
- ❏ FETCH RELATIVE 1 returns the same as FETCH NEXT
- ❏ FETCH RELATIVE -1 returns the same as FETCH PRIOR
- ❏ FETCH RELATIVE 2 skips a row

Open and Close

These two calls are fairly straightforward and are simply passed to the database like so:

```
OPEN cursor_name;
```

And:

```
CLOSE cursor_name;
```

A cursor can be closed before the end of a transaction to free up resources, as this releases the result set held within the cursor. Also, in many cases, such as MS SQL Server, Sybase, and Informix, DEALLOCATE needs to be used to free up the resources associated with the cursor even after the cursor is closed:

```
DEALLOCATE cursor_name;
```

Cursor Positioning

When we issue the OPEN cursor statement, or are working within a cursor, so we must assume that the movable pointer points to a position in the result set. Depending on the RDBMS implementation, or any movement we have caused after opening the cursor, this position has to be either before some row of the result set, on some row of the result set, or after the last row of the result set.

The CURRENT OF clause can be used with WHERE, to help act on a specific row in the result set contained by your cursor:

```
UPDATE table_name
SET column = "new value"
WHERE CURRENT OF cursor_name
```

Keep this in mind as you manipulate data with cursors.

Move

The MOVE statement is not true SQL:1999 but some database implementations, including PostgreSQL, support it so it's worth a mention. Essentially, MOVE works like FETCH to set the position of the cursor, but does not return a row, so it's used only for positioning. MOVE requires qualifiers of direction including FORWARD and RELATIVE, as well as an integer. MOVE also uses IN instead of FROM.

With this in mind, it should be apparent that for RDBMS' that support MOVE, the following are equivalent:

```
MOVE FORWARD 2
IN cursor_name;
FETCH NEXT INTO :variable;
```

And:

```
FETCH RELATIVE 3
FROM cursor_name INTO :variable;
```

Triggers

Like PSM, triggers are set up on the server side, or database space, but unlike PSM, which are typically called from a host language like PHP, triggers typically engage when particular changes occur in the database. They can be thought of as special stored procedures that get automatically invoked, or triggered, by changes in the data in the database and are based on a set of pre-specfied criteria.

Most major RDBMS vendors support triggers to some extent. Although the Trigger specification was kept out of the SQL:92 spec and deferred to SQL:1999, they have been in wide use for over 10 years.

What are Triggers

Triggers are schema objects defined on a table. They wait for a certain sequence of statements, for example, insert, update, or delete, to execute on the data in the table. It's important to clarify that triggers are tied to a single table and cannot be defined for multiple tables. Triggers may be fired once per statement or once per each row of data affected by said insert, update, and delete statements.

Triggers can be used for a wide variety of tasks where it's useful to respond to database changes. Examples include creating logs of data changes, cleaning up 'leftover' data that an application doesn't deal with fully, and enforcing referential integrity where the underlying RDBMS doesn't provide for this, or where the constraint is too complex to express as a referential integrity statement.

Creating Triggers

Typically, a trigger takes into account the table it's being defined for, a criteria action to be watched for, a time value, which helps the trigger act on the data in the table when the trigger criteria is met, and the resulting trigger action, or SQL statement. Since criteria are based on changes in the data, the trigger can act on the state of the data before or after the trigger criteria is met.

With this in mind, trigger actions can be INSERTs, UPDATEs, and DELETEs, and can be qualified with BEFORE or AFTER.

Let's look at an example of a trigger that calls a procedure when specific columns are altered. In this case the procedure would be able to use the data in the changed rows *before* it is actually changed. This is often useful when using a trigger to create a record or log of changed data.

```
CREATE TRIGGER trigger_name
BEFORE UPDATE OF column_list
ON table_name
FOR EACH ROW
CALL PROCEDURE procedure_name();
```

Now, let's examine the syntax and alternatives. The statement clearly captures updates in the database. A subsequent procedure may be to record the fact of the change, in a log table. BEFORE is the time value here, also called a Temporal Dependency, specifying that the trigger is to act on the state of the data before the UPDATE. AFTER would also be a valid qualifier. The UPDATE could have as easily been INSERT or DELETE. You will also notice the OF column_list clause. This could have been omitted – it's purely optional depending on how granular you require your trigger to be, and would be omitted if the trigger is on an entire table.

Lastly, the FOR EACH clause can also specify STATEMENT instead of ROW. This would be used if you wanted to perform the triggerd SQL statement once based on the triggering SQL statement, regardless of how many rows were affected,

The CALL statement might be an EXECUTE instead, as we saw above.

In addition, the definition of the PSM can be embedded within the trigger definition, to make it more readable or to tie a specific procedure definition to one trigger:

```
CREATE TRIGGER trigger_name
BEFORE UPDATE OF column_list
ON table_name
FOR EACH ROW
BEGIN
<procedure-definition>
END;
```

Triggers can be removed from the schema with simple DROP statements:

```
DROP TRIGGER trigger_name;
```

Try It Out: Triggers

Triggers are, of course, most useful when they don't require any user intervention. Let's create an example in our taskfoward schema to use triggers in the event that a user record is removed from the database. The first thing we should ask is what would happen in the real world to the tasks of an ex-employee. We assign the tasks to that user's boss. To implement the same logic in our system, let us modify our taskforward schema. We have not been using the priv_level column so far, but have been adding users with levels equal to 1, 2, or 3. Recollect that 1 and 2 indicate senior executive and department manager respectively, while 3 (and below) indicate department employee roles.

We can see from our tf_user table that there are two users who have a priv_level of less than 3, indicating they possess managerial positions.

```
taskforward=# SELECT pk_user, fname, priv_level
taskforward-# FROM tf_user;

 pk_user | fname | priv_level
---------+-------+------------
       1 | Larry |          1
       5 | Sue   |          2
     100 | Joe   |          3
(3 rows)
```

And we can see from our `user_task` table that Joe (with `fk_user` = 100) has a task assigned to him:

```
taskforward=# SELECT * FROM user_task;

 pk_user_task | fk_user | fk_task | last_modified
--------------+---------+---------+----------
            1 |       5 |       2 |
            2 |     100 |       3 |
(2 rows)
```

Let's assume that Joe, who is a subordinate of Larry, leaves. When the row for Joe is deleted in `tf_user`, the corresponding row in `user_task` will also be deleted since the `pk_user` from `tf_user` is tied via a constraint to `fk_user` in `user_task`. Ideally, we want our database to automatically designate his tasks to Larry, who is his boss. We shall tackle this situation in two stages.

First, we will create a function to update the `fk_user` field for a row in the `user_task` table:

```
taskforward=# CREATE FUNCTION trigger_orphaned_task()
taskforward-# RETURNS opaque
taskforward-# AS 'BEGIN
taskforward'# old.fk_user = 1;
taskforward'# RETURN new;
taskforward'# END;'
taskforward-# LANGUAGE 'plpgsql';
```

From our trigger syntax earlier, we know that something like this would also work:

```
taskforward=# CREATE TRIGGER deleted_user
taskforward-# BEFORE DELETE
taskforward-# ON user_task
taskforward-# FOR EACH ROW
taskforward-# EXECUTE PROCEDURE trigger_orphaned_task();
```

After creating this we can see any deletions in the `tf_user` table cause the `fk_user` column in the `user_task` table to be changed to 1.

```
taskforward=# DELETE FROM user_task
taskforward-# WHERE fk_user = 100;

DELETE 0
```

```
taskforward=# SELECT pk_user_task, fk_user, fk_task
taskforward-# FROM user_task;

 pk_user_task | fk_user | fk_task
--------------+---------+---------
            1 |       5 |       2
            2 |       1 |       3
(2 rows)
```

How It Works

So, what's going on here? To begin with, we have used LANGUAGE 'plpgsql', which is a database-specific stored procedure language, in this case for PostgreSQL. To use this language in your own PostgreSQL instance, run the createlang plpgsql taskforward command from the operating system command prompt as the PostgreSQL user (whichever user you usually run psql as). Notice that you need to specify the database you wish to install this language for, in our case, taskforward.

While similar to SQL, one big difference we see is the use of old and new keywords in our SQL statement. Since the function trigger_orphaned_task is meant to be used in the case of rows being deleted from the tf_user table, we want to be able to reference the pk_user values that existed before the DELETE and before we make any changes via UPDATE to the user_task table. In this instance, old.fk_user in the user_task table is the employee that leaves, and new.fk_user is the new value, or 1, that we are setting this to.

Most RDBMS flavors will have some way of referencing rows based on the state of the data before and after the trigger action. Check with your RDBMS for specifics. In the case of PostgreSQL, old represents the row being deleted in DELETE triggers and new represents a row in INSERT triggers, while both old and new can be used for UPDATE triggers.

Views

A **view** is another type of schema object that provides a great deal of power and flexibility to the database application developer. Unlike the other utilities that deal with the manipulation of data with SQL, views enable us to look at data in different ways. These virtual tables created by views can be used to limit access to full tables for security reasons or to present a simple table that represents a complex combination of multiple tables.

In other chapters, it has been mentioned that an SQL statement provides a contextual relationship to data, as it selected it from tables. Views allow us to build a context in a persistent manner without executing SQL statements each time by creating a persisted virtual table. These virtual tables act like regular tables, allowing us to perform SQL statements on data already aggregated into table relationships. Views essentially contain the non-persisted results of another SELECT statement, so performing a SELECT against a view can be thought of as compounding SELECTs.

The following diagram shows how a view presents a virtual table comprised of data from underlying base tables:

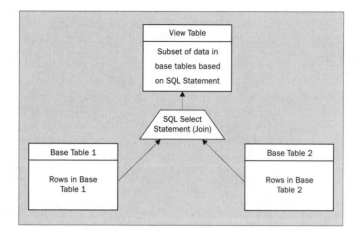

Creating Views

Creating a view in a table is straightforward. The syntax needs to specify a name, a list of columns to use in the view, which is optional, and the SELECT query to be used to populate the view.

```
CREATE VIEW view_name
column_list
AS SELECT statement...
```

An important note to mention again is that the SELECT statements in views can include a single table or multiple tables, effectively creating unique data structures.

Views and CHECK OPTION

There is a special constraint that can be used when creating views that ensures that any SQL run against a view is within the parameters of the initial creation. Take the following pseudocode for example:

```
CREATE VIEW view_name
AS SELECT column_list
FROM table_name
WHERE condition_is_true
WITH CHECK OPTION;
```

The CHECK OPTION clause is used only in views where data is updated or inserted. It ensures that the SQL statement executed in the view does not violate the integrity constraints set on the data.

Benefits and Limits of Views

Since we are dealing with a schema object based on other tables, it should not come as a surprise that views can only be dropped, not altered. Also, views can only receive UPDATE statements if they are qualified as updatable on creation. This is however an optional feature, and may not be supported by your RDBMS. Updating a view, if legal in your RDBMS and included in the CREATE statement, will alter the base table data.

You may now be wondering if views are worth it? It may seem like a lot of extra work to create and maintain additional table-like schema objects, especially since a properly constructed SELECT statement would provide the same data. There are two factors arguing in favor of views; speed and simplicity.

First, let's look at simplicity. While it is entirely possible that we could arrive at the same data by using SQL statements, think about the fact that we would have to use a more complex JOIN statement to achieve what a simple SELECT against a view from multiple tables can achieve directly. Also, subqueries might have to be used in complex cases.

Now let's look at speed. We actually should have a pretty good idea of how the above complexity can introduce speed issues, but consider SQL execution for a moment. When a RDBMS receives an SQL statement it must parse the statement for validity, as well as generate an execution plan that is efficient for the data involved. With that in mind, it becomes apparent that both JOINs and subqueries are more complex than simple SELECTs, and require construction of a comparatively complex execution plan by the RDBMS engine. In contrast, a view will have at least part of that execution plan precompiled, hastening the execution time of the query.

An additional benefit of views occurs when we don't want an application to see all of the columns in a given table. What if we wish to give an application developer access to an employee table, but prefer to hide certain information that is either irrelevant or raises security concerns? With views we can create a virtual schema that maps closely to the application modules being created for a specific purpose.

Limitations of stored SQL should also be mentioned. Firstly, triggers cannot be created on views in most RDBMS implementations. While some RDBMS might support this, the SQL:1999 specification prohibits this for reasons of database integrity. Secondly, cursors can typically not be created on views either, as they lack the primary key essential to the creation of one. This invalidates any attempt to create a keyset for the cursor. In addition, creating additional database objects always takes up space and can adversely affect performance.

Inspite of these limitations, carefully planned views are a powerful and often under-utilized feature of enterprise RDBMS. Experiment with them in your own environment for elegant solutions to your programming problems.

Using Views in PHP

Views in PHP are treated just like tables, with the constraints discussed above on updatability.

Let us add some additional data to our task table with the pg_insert.php script so we have something to show the benefit of views with.

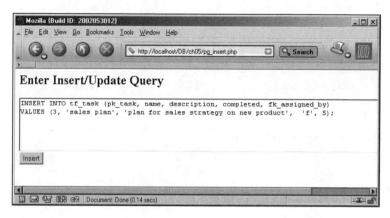

Adding additional rows to our tasks table gives us with something like this:

```
taskforward=# SELECT pk_task, name, description, completed, fk_assigned_by
taskforward-# FROM tf_task;
```

The result of this query would be a listing of these five field values corresponding to all records in the tf_task table.

Now let's update the user_task table to make some assignments, using out pg_insert.php script.

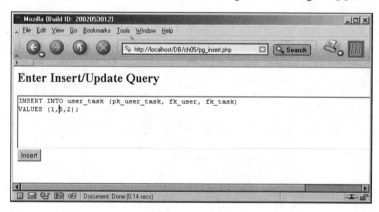

Remember, if you try to insert a fk_user or fk_task that doesn't exists as a pk_user in the tf_user table or a pk_task in the tf_task table, you will get a referential constraint error.

For example, this:

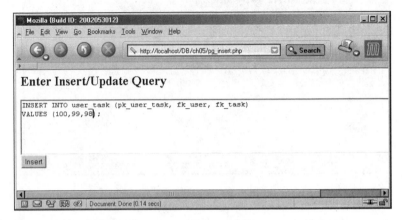

Results in this:

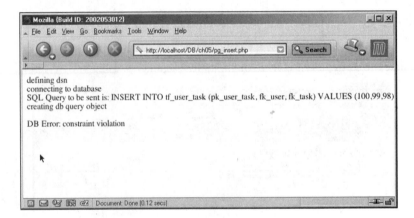

Adding another row correctly can give us this data:

```
taskforward=# SELECT pk_user_task as key, fk_user as userif, fk_task as taskid
taskforward-# FROM user_task;

 key | userid | taskid
-----+--------+--------
   1 |      5 |      2
   2 |    100 |      3
(2 rows)
```

Here you will also notice we snuck in some aliasing in our SQL statement by using the syntax SELECT column as alias. What this does is return the results to us with different column names. In this example, we have renamed the pk_user_task column to key.

Try It Out: Views

Let's write a view to show us all the unassigned tasks in the database. We can determine what tasks are left unassigned by comparing the pk_task values found in the tf_task table with the fk_task values found in the user_task table:

```
taskforward=# SELECT DISTINCT pk_task
taskforward-# FROM tf_task;

 pk_task
---------
       1
       2
       3
       4
       5
       6
(6 rows)


taskforward=# SELECT DISTINCT fk_task
taskforward-# FROM user_task;

 fk_task
---------
       2
       4
(2 rows)
```

Now that we know which values are in each table so we can go on to construct a complex SQL statement using a subqery to return the unique values:

```
SELECT pk_task
FROM tf_task
WHERE pk_task NOT IN (
SELECT DISTINCT fk_task
FROM user_task
);
```

And shown against our database client:

```
taskforward=# SELECT DISTINCT pk_task
taskforward-# FROM tf_task
taskforward-# WHERE pk_task NOT IN (
taskforward(# SELECT fk_task
taskforward(# FROM user_task
taskforward(# );
```

```
    pk_task
 ---------
        1
        3
        5
        6
(4 rows)
```

This is a fairly simple looking SQL statement. But, you may want to frequently use it, singly or in combination with others. This brings to mind two problems. First, a long and convoluted SQL statement can be tricky to debug, and second, the RDBMS is required to parse and execute two SQL statements to return our required data. If we include this SQL statement liberally, then we would require parsing very frequently.

It can greatly simplify things and provide some performance enhancements if we offload this query into a view:

```
taskforward=# CREATE VIEW tf_unassigned_tasks AS
taskforward-# SELECT pk_task
taskforward-# FROM tf_task
taskforward-# WHERE pk_task NOT IN (
taskforward(# SELECT fk_task
taskforward(# FROM user_task
taskforward(# );
```

Now, we can get this information with a simple SELECT:

```
taskforward=# SELECT *
taskforward-# FROM tf_unassigned_tasks;
```

```
    pk_task
 ---------
        1
        3
        5
        6
(4 rows)
```

How It Works

As we can see, views are often used to create "real world" tables that contain only the records we want, as a single normalized table will typically not map well to application logic. We can also use the power of views further and use the data in this view to produce additional results:

```
taskforward=# SELECT t.pk_task, t.name, t.description
taskforward-# FROM tf_unassigned_tasks u, tf_task t
taskforward-# WHERE u.pk_task = t.pk_task;
```

```
  pk_task |         name            |               description
----------+-------------------------+-----------------------------------------
        1 | activity report         | summary of what Joe has done this week
        3 | sales plan              | plan for sales strategy on new product
        5 | bug summary             | generate bug list as reported this week
        6 | organize sales meeting  | schedule meeting with sales team
(4 rows)
```

You will notice that we are using a Join as well as table aliases: unassigned_tasks u means that we can use u.column_name to reference unassigned_tasks.column_name.

Indexes

While not within the SQL:1999 specification, indexes are implemented by most vendors to optimize SQL statements. Simply put, indexes are schema objects built against a specific table on the values in a column. Indexes are primarily used to enhance performance of SELECT, UPDATE, and DELETE statements, all of which have to look through records to act on data.

The performance enhancements come about because RDBMS systems do not store rows in any particular order. Adding and updating rows doesn't change the physical order of their storage in the underlying tables. Thus, to execute an SQL statement that targets specific rows, the database engine must search through a potentially large number of rows to identify the rows that satisfy the query. Explicitly creating an index on a column causes the RDBMS to record information about the position and placement of the values in the indexed column(s). Such a record of rows for a column enables rapid seeking along that column(s), especially since indexes are created according to the file structure, with the actual records being listed sequentially one after the other in the index, which often requires a complicated pointing structure to the records in the table.

With that in mind, it makes sense to create indexes on columns frequently used in SELECT statements, as opposed to ones that are not.

Index Creation

Indexes may be created on a single column or a combination of columns during table creation, or later. For instance, by appending the following to a CREATE TABLE statement:

```
CREATE INDEX index_name ON tablename (column_to_index);
```

Or by executing SQL to add an index to an existing table:

```
ALTER TABLE table_name ADD INDEX index_name (column_to_index);
```

And of course we can always:

```
DROP INDEX index_name;
```

And in many cases we can append DROP EXISTING after the CREATE INDEX statement to force a rebuilding of an existing index.

Index Types

Let's discuss some of the different types of indexes supported in various RDBMS. Please note that syntax and features vary greatly across vendor implementations.

Unique Indexes

This is an easily understood index type – a Unique Index mandates that no duplicate values exist in the column. Good candidates for these indexes include key columns, primary or foreign, and in fact some RDBMS create indexes on key columns automatically.

Compound Indexes

A Compound Index is often called a multi-column index, which is fairly self-explanatory. These indexes are created to include more than one column. This can be used to optimize performance where the SQL statement's WHERE clause uses all the columns in the compound index.

Clustered and Nonclustered

If a specific RDBMS supports the CLUSTERED keyword, the RDBMS will choose to execute queries based on what it knows about the physical ordering of underlying disk storage.

Nonclustered indexes are optimized to a logical ordering of the table structure and are the default state where these options are supported.

Using Indexes

Given the varied nature of indexes, you might be thinking that it makes sense to determine implementation specifics for your database and create many indexes to optimize performance. While indexes *are* oriented towards performance enhancement, creation of too many indexes on a table will drastically drag down performance, as the RDBMS requires significant processing power to maintain statistics on the indexed column. Even though indexes do increase performance for retrieving data, they can often impair performance for inserting data.

It's important to point out that ideal columns for index creation should be fixed length data types, so an INT(10) type would result in faster retreival than a VARCHAR(10) typed column. It must also be considered that using indexes increases the physical storage footprint of the database, as space is required to hold the index keys and pointers to data.

Summary

This chapter has covered a number of the more advanced features that can be carried out using SQL with PHP. We looked at how to use **Stored Procedures / Persistent Stored Modules** (PSM) to enable complex business rules and move application logic into the RDBMS. After that we then moved on to calling **Cursors** from PHP to get single rows of data from a result set. We also discussed how **Triggers** can be implemented with SQL statements and PSM to allow our RDBMS to act on our behalf without intervention. From there we moved onto using **Views** to encapsulate complex queries and to offload frequently used queries to the RDBMS. Finally, we rounded off the chapter with the performance benefits and concerns of using **Indexes**.

In the next chapter, we are going to take these advanced ideas further and look at how PHP is used in conjunction with relational databases.

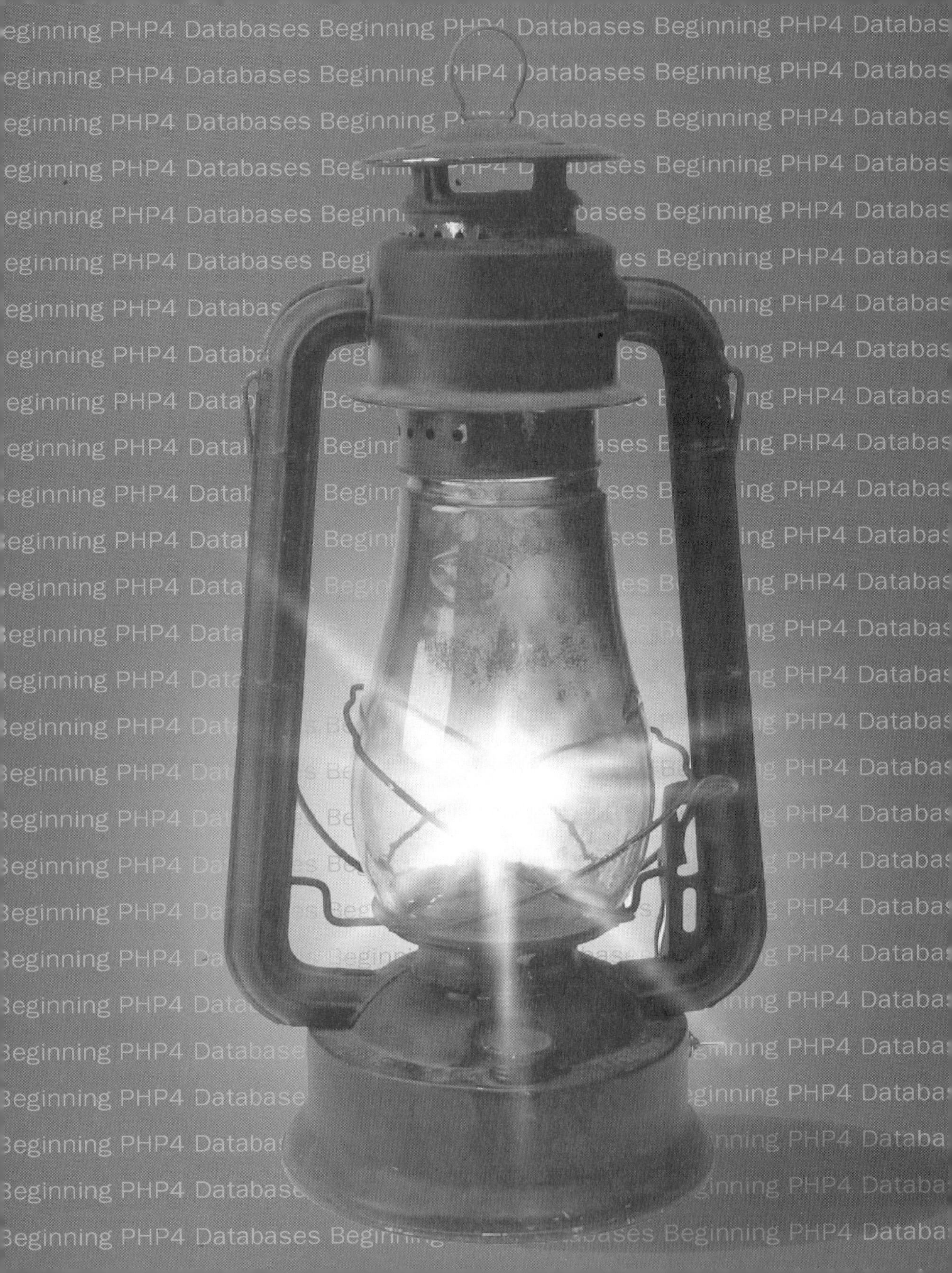
Beginning PHP4 Databases

PHP and Relational Databases

When developing database-driven applications in PHP, there are a great many choices that are left to developers. Due to PHP's wide breadth of use, there are a large number of different RDBMS systems that could be used on many different platforms. But making the best choice of the database system for a project is only the tip of the iceberg in terms of planning out how we attack the problem.

Here are the issues we need to figure out before starting our development project:

- ❑   What database will we use?
- ❑   Will we use native PHP functions or an abstraction layer to interact with the database?
- ❑   If we are using an abstraction layer, which one?
- ❑   Will the code be mostly procedural or object oriented?
- ❑   How can the code be modularized?
- ❑   Will we be using a multi-tier development model?

This chapter will introduce you to the parts of PHP that you will need to understand to make informed decisions about these sorts of questions. We will look at topics such as the built-in functions, the databases supported, and will try and clear up a little of the mystery surrounding buzzwords like "n-tier development" and "modular code." Along the way, we will also talk about how to use abstraction layers that help us to handle different kinds of databases easily while still writing code that's simple to use.

We will start off by talking about the development model conceptually, so that we can understand the separation of tasks that will help to organize our application into easily understood pieces.

Multi-Tier Development

Multi-tier development is one of the many catch phrases that is often encountered. In this section, we are going to explain what is usually meant by the term, and why it's important to us as developers.

Three-Tier Development

The most common development model that you'll see is called Three Tier. In fact, when people use the term Multi Tier, it is often Three Tier that they are really talking about. The basic idea behind it is to try and think of a web application as being composed of three different parts. These parts will be separate, but will all work together to create a functional product. Briefly, the three parts are:

❑ Presentation Layer (data display)

❑ Application Logic (data manipulation)

❑ Back-end Database (data storage)

The client computer only interacts with the presentation layer, though what gets presented gets generated by the application logic and database layers:

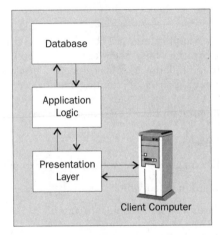

The Presentation Layer

The presentation part of an application is, quite simply, whatever the user is going to see. In a web-based project, there will generally be a few components to this.

First, there will mostly be HTML or XHTML that is coded to give structure to the pages in the browser. Additionally, there will be CSS stylesheets to define presentation issues such as fonts, colors, and layout. Also, this will include any graphics being used.

If possible, it is always a good idea to create the presentation layer by itself first. When done correctly, you should be able to create a complete "mock up" of your application with no live data or PHP code. A complete mock up is one where you can click on everything that the user will be able to click on, and the site will do the appropriate thing with static dummy data.

This may seem like a lot of extra work, especially if you are eager to jump in and start with your PHP coding. However, it is actually time well spent. On the web, nobody will use your application if it does not have a good user interface. No matter how well-written your PHP is, it will all be for naught if nobody ever uses it.

The Application Logic Layer

This is where our PHP code lives. All of the functions, classes, global variables, if/then statements, and so on should reside in files distinct from the HTML or XHTML pages.

Again, this may seem like a needless amount of extra work. After all, if we're going to use a function on a certain page, why not just define it on that page? The problem is that in practice, we often use functions which are written in many different places. So if we defined that function on every page that it was used on, we would end up with a great deal of code duplication which is undesirable from a maintenance standpoint.

The most common practice for small to medium-sized applications is to have one file in which we define any global variables the application will need, and another file where we define any custom functions being used. We then simply include these files on the web pages where they are needed using the require_once() function.

If the application is larger, then we typically group the custom functions into several files. For example, if we create a bunch of functions to manipulate strings in some way, and another bunch to handle network operations, then we might put these into files such as string_funcs.php and network_funcs.php respectively. Then, we could use require_once() to load just the functionality we need for a particular page. This avoids the overhead of potentially loading code that we don't actually need.

In the case of custom-written classes, the general practice is one class per file, with the name of the file being the same as the name of the class. So, if we create a class called SuperCool then we would want to store that class, by itself, in a file called SuperCool.php and include it when needed in the application.

Conceptually, the purpose of the application logic layer is to process any information that gets sent from the presentation layer (such as data from a submitted form), process it, and return the correct information back to the presentation layer for display. It's possible that this can be done entirely within the application logic layer. For example, if the needed response is to answer the question, "what is the date three days from right now?" then everything can be handled with a few PHP functions. However, often in database-driven applications, the request will require that the application logic layer interface with the database layer to gather some kind of information.

The Database Layer

The database layer (often referred to as the back-end layer) is possibly the most simple to understand conceptually. This layer is used to store information for later use plus any rules or logic that are defined within the database. Once the information has been stored, it can be retrieved, updated, or deleted. However, those are operations that typically get handled from the application layer.

The only real point to make about the database layer is that we should never design our back-end setup to be PHP-specific in some way. A well-designed database is just that, a database. You never know when the data may be needed by some other application separate from the one we are working on. Crafting the schemas carefully and following the principles of good database design covered earlier in the book will always be the best bet.

N-Tier Development

Beyond the concept of Three Tier development lies the idea of "n-tier" development. This is also something of a catch phrase, and often an "n-tier" model can be thought of as a three tier model with some extra things added.

For example, the presentation layer is often physically handled by a web server such as Apache. But in a larger production environment, we might have several such servers and a load balancer in front of them to distribute the client requests. So the clients are really connecting to the load balancer first. This balancer effectively adds another network layer.

Also, in a larger environment, we would rarely just have a single database server. More often we would have a master server that would replicate itself to a number of slave servers. Any write operations such as INSERT or UPDATE queries would go to the master server, and any read operations such as SELECT queries would be directed to the slaves. This assumes that the application has many more read queries than write queries, which is typical of web-based applications. In this case, the database part of the application actually has two layers.

It is easy to see that this sort of model can be extended basically indefinitely, hence the "n-tier" label. The important thing to understand is that we want to conceptually isolate the parts of our application as best we can. The reason for this is twofold. First, if the parts of the system are relatively isolated, then it is generally much easier to locate problems when something breaks. Equally important is that it allows a number of people to work on projects each doing what they do best. You can have user interface people working on the presentation layer, PHP coders working on the application layer, and DBAs working on the database layer. Each of these subsystems can then be performance tuned to generate the best possible efficiency.

Now that we've looked at the pieces that we would use to put an application together, it's time to start thinking in more specific terms. Obviously, this is going to require knowing and understanding how PHP interacts with database systems. The most basic starting point for this discussion is the native database functions available in the language.

The Built-In Database Functions

If you have ever looked at the online documentation for the PHP language, then you have certainly noticed that there are a lot of functions available to the aspiring programmer. Some of these, such as the string handling functions, are available in any version of PHP. Others, such as the mhash functions, require that we have certain libraries on our system and that the PHP module was built to recognize those libraries.

The PHP database functions mostly fall into the latter category, meaning that for a specific supported database, we must have that database installed on our system and that our module must have the functionality it needs built into it.

For example, if we have the PostgreSQL system installed on our machine and if (on UNIX) the PHP installation was built with the --with-pgsql configure option, then a wealth of functions will be available, which allow us to interact with a PostgreSQL database. These PHP functions are typically just thin wrappers around the native C API provided by the database vendor.

The pseudo exception is the case of the MySQL system. The client code needed by PHP is actually included in the PHP distribution, so we don't even need to have MySQL installed to get the PHP support functions to be available. Of course, they won't do much good if we don't have MySQL running on the machine or don't want to use MySQL. Also, MySQL is available for just about every platform, and is included with many Linux and Unix systems.

As mentioned earlier, each database system can provide PHP with its own suite of functions. These typically have the name format – `dbtype_function()`.

Here `dbtype` represents the kind of RDBMS and `function()` tells us what the function does. Each of the databases has slightly different functions since each database has variances in regard to the features it supplies. However, there are a fair number of functions for common tasks that are uniform across almost all of the vendors. These include:

- `dbtype_connect()`
- `dbtype_close()`
- `dbtype_select_db()`
- `dbtype_query()`
- `dbtype_fetch_row()`
- `dbtype_num_rows()`
- `dbtype_num_fields()`

A notable exception is Oracle databases. These PHP functions interact with the database using something called the Oracle Call Interface that is supplied by the Oracle-provided client library. Although these functions have a different naming scheme, it is easy enough to see that they do basically the same things as the functions for the other database systems.

PHP-Supported Databases

PHP has native support for a wide array of different RDBMS systems. These include:

- FrontBase, http://www.frontbase.com
- Informix, http://www-3.ibm.com/software/data/informix/
- InterBase, http://www.borland.com/interbase/
- Microsoft SQL Server, http://www.microsoft.com/sql/default.asp
- MSQL, http://www.hughes.com.au/
- MySQL, http://www.mysql.com
- ODBC
- Oracle, http://www.oracle.com
- PostgreSQL, http://www.postgresql.org
- Sybase, http://www.sybase.com

We should note that ODBC is not actually a database. It's a way of accessing other databases, but we're including it in this list because PHP does provide specific ODBC functions. We'll talk more about ODBC in an upcoming section.

Now, there's an important point that you may quickly be realizing. Each of these different databases listed above has its own suite of functions, and all of those suites are slightly different. And that means that at the end of the day, there are a ton of different database functions in the PHP language. However, although there are a lot of functions, and their syntaxes can be slightly different, you will find that they all do more or less the same things.

Later in the chapter, we're going to talk about ways to lessen the headache of potentially having so many functions to keep track of by using an abstraction layer.

Examples of Connections

Let's pause for a moment and look at some pseudo-code to understand this better. As noted, basically all of the native database APIs have some similar functions. Let's look at how we might connect to a few different RDBMS systems:

```
// some variables we'll commonly need
// to connect

$dbhost = "localhost";
$dbname = "db_name";
$dbuser = "username";
$dbpass = "password";
```

```
// connect to an Informix database
$connection = ifx_connect("$dbname@$dbhost" , $dbuser , $dbpass);
if( !$connection ) {
   die("Couldn't establish connection to Informix!");
}
```

```
// connect to an Interbase database
$connection = ibase_connect($dbhost , $dbuser , $dbpass);
if( !$connection ) {
   die("Couldn't establish connection to Interbase!");
}
```

```
// connect to a MS SQL Server database
$connection = mssql_connect($dbhost , $dbuser , $dbpass);
if( !$connection ) {
   die("Couldn't establish connection to MS SQL Server!");
}
```

```
// connect to a MySQL database
$connection = mysql_connect($dbhost , $dbuser , $dbpass);
if( !$connection ) {
   die("Couldn't establish connection to MySQL!");
}
```

```
// connect to a PostgreSQL database
$connection = pg_connect("dbname=$dbname host=$dbhost user=$dbuser
password=$dbpass");
if( !$connection ) {
  die("Couldn't establish connection to PostgreSQL!");
}
```

There are several things to notice here. First, in every case, we get the return value of the connection function and check it to make sure that we did in fact connect to the database. If we didn't, we call the die() function to end the script execution, and print out a useful error message. This is a bit tedious to do, but it is an essential part of the process. The small amount of extra time it takes to check for errors now could save a great deal of debugging time later if something stops working.

Also, you may have noticed that the signatures for the functions mentioned are not necessarily identical. Some are, as in the cases of mssql_connect() and mysql_connect(). However, mysql_connect() and pg_connect() take slightly different arguments, though it is easy to see that they are essentially equivalent and contain the same information.

Again, you are probably thinking now that this can really be a lot to keep track of because there are so many different database functions, and those may be very similar or only somewhat similar depending on the database in question. In the upcoming sections, we will talk more about abstraction layers that take a lot of this burden away from you.

First, however, we will look at a more real-world example of database interaction using the native PHP functions.

A Closer Look At MySQL

Here, we will use the built-in MySQL PHP functions to query a database and display the results. Although we are using MySQL for this example, the basic program flow could be used for any of the databases supported by PHP. We are choosing MySQL here for a few reasons. First, as a PHP developer, it is quite likely that sooner or later we will be using a MySQL database. Second, it's very easy to get started with because the MySQL functions are always built into PHP.

Try It Out – A Simple Query

Let's assume that you have a MySQL database called simple_db that contains one table called simple_table. Let's further assume that you have the following structure:

```
+------------+--------------+------+-----+------------+----------------+
| Field      | Type         | Null | Key | Default    | Extra          |
+------------+--------------+------+-----+------------+----------------+
| id         | tinyint(4)   |      | PRI | NULL       | auto_increment |
| first_name | varchar(255) |      |     |            |                |
| last_name  | varchar(255) |      |     |            |                |
| birth_date | date         |      |     | 0000-00-00 |                |
+------------+--------------+------+-----+------------+----------------+
```

1. This can be created with the following SQL statement:

```
CREATE TABLE simple_table (
  id tinyint(4) NOT NULL auto_increment,
  first_name varchar(255) NOT NULL default '',
  last_name varchar(255) NOT NULL default '',
  birth_date date NOT NULL default '0000-00-00',
  PRIMARY KEY (id)
)
```

If you haven't already discovered it, there's an excellent web-based MySQL administration tool called phpMyAdmin that makes the creation of such tables very simple. It's available for free at http://phpmyadmin.sourceforge.net.

2. Populate simple_table with the following data:

```
+----+------------+-----------+------------+
| id | first_name | last_name | birth_date |
+----+------------+-----------+------------+
|  1 | Chris      | Lea       | 1975-03-08 |
|  2 | Christian  | Thompson  | 1978-03-12 |
|  3 | Erik       | Robison   | 1975-04-22 |
|  4 | Mary       | Lee       | 1975-07-09 |
|  5 | Sylvia     | Easbey    | 1984-02-25 |
|  6 | Claire     | Vignoles  | 1979-12-06 |
|  7 | Ann        | Moreno    | 1979-12-17 |
+----+------------+-----------+------------+
```

Of course, we use the INSERT command to do this. For example, the first record above could be created with the following:

```
INSERT INTO (first_name , last_name , birth_date)
VALUES ('Chris' , 'Lea' , '1975-03-08')
```

Now, for the following exercise, we'll need just a few of the native PHP MySQL functions. The ones we will make use of are:

Function	Usage
resource mysql_connect ([string server [, string username [, string password]]])	Establishes a connection to the MySQL server. All of the arguments are optional as they may assume default values from the php.ini file. The strings for server, username, and password correspond to the values needed to connect to your database server.
bool mysql_select_db (string dbname)	Selects the database to use, referenced by dbname. Returns true on success, false on failure.
resource mysql_query (string query)	Returns a resource identifier for the data selected by the string query if the query was a SELECT, SHOW, EXPLAIN, or DESCRIBE SQL statement. If it was a different kind of statement, then the function returns true on success and false on failure.

Funtion	Usage
`array mysql_fetch_assoc (resource result)`	Returns an associative array for the row fetched from `result`. The keys for the array will correspond to the fetched column names.

3. With these in mind, let's do a few queries on our database. Let's assume that our goal is to split the people in our database into two groups. Specifically, we want to know who amongst them was alive for at least one full year of the glorious era of the 1970's, and who was not. We'll accomplish our task with two queries to the database. Open up a new file called `query_simple.php` and put it in the root directory of your web server. The following code should go into it:

```php
<?php

// establish variables for the database
$dbhost = "localhost";
$dbname = "simple_db";
$dbuser = "root";
$dbpass = "";

// connect to the database server
if( !($conn = mysql_connect($dbhost , $dbuser , $dbpass) ) ) {
  die("Couldn't establish connection to MySQL database!");
}

// select database to use
if( !mysql_select_db($dbname) ){
  die("Couldn't connect to database $dbname!");
}

// set up first SQL query
$sql = "SELECT first_name,last_name FROM simple_table WHERE YEAR(birth_date)
  < 1979 ORDER BY last_name";
// get result
if( !($below_date = mysql_query($sql) ) ) {
  die("Invalid result for $sql");
}

// set up second SQL query
$sql = "SELECT first_name,last_name FROM simple_table WHERE YEAR(birth_date)
  >= 1979 ORDER BY last_name";
// get result
if( !($above_date = mysql_query($sql) ) ) {
  die("Invalid result for $sql");
}

?>
<html>
  <head>
    <title>Simple DB Query</title>
    <style type="text/css">
      body {
        margin: 30px 0px 0px 30px;
        font-family: verdana, helvetica, sans-serif;
```

```
      }
    </style>
  </head>
  <body>

    <h2>Born before Jan 01, 1979</h2>

    <ul>

      <?php
        // get the results for the $below_date result resource
        while($name = mysql_fetch_assoc($below_date)) {
      ?>

      <li><?php echo $name["first_name"] . " " . $name["last_name"]; ?></li>

      <? } ?>

    </ul>

    <h2>Born on or after Jan 01, 1979</h2>

    <ul>
      <?php
        // get the results for the $above_date result resource
        while($name = mysql_fetch_assoc($above_date)) {
      ?>

      <li><?php echo $name["first_name"] . " " . $name["last_name"]; ?></li>

      <?php } ?>
    </ul>
  </body>
</html>
```

4. If everything has gone as planned, the result will look like this:

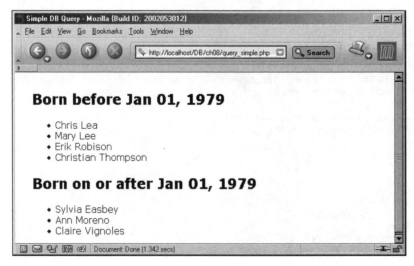

How It Works

The first thing we do is define some variables that are needed to connect to our database. This is the section that starts with:

```
// establish variables for the database
$dbhost = "localhost";
```

It's likely that you may have to change some of the values to correspond to your MySQL installation.

We then use the `mysql_connect()` and `mysql_select_db()` functions to establish a connection and tell the database server which database we are interested in making queries on. The `mysql_connect()` function returns a resource variable that corresponds to this connection. In both cases, we wrapped the function calls in conditional `if()` statements to check and make sure they executed successfully. If they didn't, we exited the script using `die()`.

Now that we have a database connection, we define an SQL query that will get us the names of the people who were born before the start of 1979. We use `mysql_query()` to actually perform the query, and again wrap the function call in a conditional statement to make sure that it was successful. We then do exactly the same thing but with a different query to get the names of people born after the start of 1979.

The `mysql_query()` function returns a result resource that we will use later when we actually want to get the data. We now have two result resources, one for each of our groups, and we are guaranteed that they are valid since we used the `if()` statements to make sure that `mysql_query()` worked properly. Note that at this point we have not actually fetched the data out of the database yet. We have created two result resources that will allow us to do so.

This ends the code block at the top of the page. There's a little HTML and CSS that defines what the output page will look like. The next interesting part is when we start back with the PHP and loop through our resultsets to actually get peoples' names and put the data into our variable $name. The $name array is an associative array since we used the `mysql_fetch_assoc()` function, and we use the values in this array to display the data on the page.

Abstraction

We have now looked at some of the native database functions available in PHP, and we have seen a few of them in actual use. As noted along the way, there are a lot of different native database utility functions in PHP because of the large number of supported databases and the associated functionality for each. This brings up some troubling problems.

If we write an application that uses a particular database, and later we want to switch to a different database, what do we do?

The first problem that we might have to deal with occurs when the new database supports different SQL syntax, or has a different feature set. In this case, we have to go through all of our SQL statements and modify them to suit the new platform. In practice, this is usually not such a problem since databases support mostly the same SQL syntax.

The second problem is that if we use the native functions, then we have to go through all of our code and change the functions for our initial database to the functions for your new database. For a larger application, this can be a very tedious process at best, and an error-prone one at worst.

Abstraction Advantages

What we need in order to avoid the problems that can potentially come up when dealing with several different data sources is some kind of abstraction layer between our PHP code and our database. When using the native database functions, our PHP application resembles a classic client-server model, where the PHP application is the client and the database is the server:

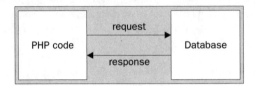

What we want is some sort of intermediate entity. We would use abstracted and transparent functions that write to this entity. In this case, abstracted means that the functions would not be database-specific, and transparent means that the API would be unified; taking the same arguments and producing the same results. The entity could then translate these to the specific database being used as shown in the diagram below:

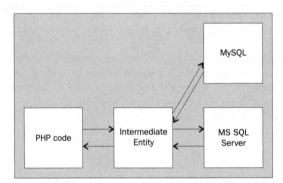

The obvious advantage here is that we can get around the problem we were thinking about earlier. As long as this intermediate entity can communicate with the database we desire, then we should have a much easier time if we ever need to switch our back-end database.

For example, if we were switching from MySQL to PostgreSQL, we would just tell the intermediate entity to start using PostgreSQL and the changes to our PHP code would be nominal.

ODBC Implementation

As you can imagine, this issue of needing a uniform way to access a variety of data sources is a common problem, and not just for PHP applications. People have been dealing with the issue of connecting to databases for quite some time, and good solutions are in place to help us out.

One of these is called ODBC, which stands for Open Database Connectivity. It is a standard that was developed by many database vendors and is designed to work on any platform. Implementations exist for Microsoft Windows, UNIX, OS/2, and other operating systems as well. Because of this, ODBC is such a ubiquitous technology that some database vendors such as IBM base their native APIs on it. It is extremely common on the Microsoft Windows platform.

The ODBC Model

There are three typical ways that an ODBC implementation might function on our machine, but we're not going to go in depth explaining all of them. The details are not typically that important to us as a PHP developer. Also, the one that we will look at, usually called a Tier 1 implementation, is the most common.

A Tier 1 model effectively adds two pieces of software to the client server chain. One is an ODBC manager and the second is an ODBC driver. Database connections are defined by the ODBC manager, based on the ODBC drivers that are available. For example, if a machine has Sybase and MySQL installed, and has the ODBC drivers for both of them, then we could define connections to both of them with the ODBC manager.

Such a connection definition is usually called DSN, which stands for Data Source Name. A DSN is nothing more than a collection of all the information that the driver needs in order to connect to the database, generally the host machine, database name, username, and password. You'll note that these are the same things that we had to provide to the connection functions of the native PHP connectivity as demonstrated earlier in this chapter. As we will see shortly, when using the ODBC functions, we actually give the DSN instead.

The communication chain in the case of ODBC database programming looks like this:

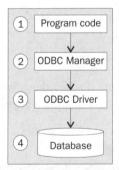

1. The program calls an ODBC function of some kind. This is sent to the ODBC manager (not the database, as in native connections).

2. The ODBC manager decides what to do as a result of the function call. Typically, it asks the driver to process the command that was issued from the program.

3. The ODBC driver translates the command into a query that the database can use and runs this query.

4. The database then produces the appropriate results.

The advantage that we get from this model is that the ODBC functions available to PHP do not change from database to database. They are always the same regardless of what the underlying RDBMS system is. This circumnavigates the problem we mentioned earlier.

Now, say we have an application that uses ODBC database functions to connect to a Sybase back-end system. At some point, we switch to an Interbase back-end. All we have to do to update our PHP application is create a new DSN for the Interbase database with our ODBC manager. Then, in our PHP application, we change the value of the DSN that we pass to the ODBC functions. If we were smart programmers this is probably a global variable defined in a configuration file, so we would only need to change it in one place. Ideally, everything would keep working as if nothing had happened. We say "ideally" because if we had used Sybase-specific SQL syntax in the original application, then this would obviously not work with the new system, and would have to be updated.

A Look At ODBC Functions

Let's revisit our earlier example. Previously, we used native MySQL functions to get the data we were interested in from our database. This of course worked well, but here we will abstract things so that we're not making use of MySQL-specific functions. Before we begin an example to demonstrate the use of ODBC, let's look at how to get it working on our machines.

Installing ODBC

Since there are many drivers for different databases, we will cover only one example here, namely how to use the MySQL ODBC driver. MySQL has an ODBC driver available called `MyODBC`, which we can compile and install for our clients if we wish. Normally our clients will be running on different machines, and possibly even a different architecture. For example, we might have the database server on UNIX or Linux and our client applications running on Windows.

Happily, if we are using Microsoft Windows as our client, we can find a precompiled ODBC driver at the MySQL site, http://www.mysql.com.

The files we need are:

❏   `myodbc-2.50.39-win95.zip` (for Windows 9x/Me), or

❏   `myodbc-2.50.39-nt.zip` (for Windows NT/2000)

Both of these files, or later versions, can be found at
http://www.mysql.com/downloads/api-myodbc.html.

Try It Out – An ODBC Query

We will assume that we have the same database name, database table, and data that we had before. The specific database is unimportant. What is important is that we have a DSN for that database defined in the ODBC manager. We'll assume it is called `sample_MySQL` for this example. This means that in the ODBC manager we'll use `sample_MySQL` as the DSN name when asked to enter it, which we'll do along with entering the information for our particular database.

1. Open up a new file called `query_odbc.php` alongside your original `query_simple.php` file. As before, the first things we will put in are variables we'll need to get a connection to our database, via ODBC this time:

```php
<?php
// establish variables for the database
$dbuser = "David";
$dbpass = "password";
$dsn = "sample_MySQL";
```

Unlike before, we don't need to define the hostname or database name. That information is already stored in the ODBC manager, and is referenced by the DSN.

2. Now, also as before, we'll make a connection:

```php
// connect to the database server
if( !($conn = odbc_connect($dsn , $dbuser , $dbpass) ) ) {
  die("Couldn't establish connection to ODBC database!");
}
```

3. Again, for comparison, you might note that before we used the `mysql_select_db()` function to pick the database being used. Again, this isn't needed here, because the DSN identifies the database to the ODBC Manager. Therefore, we'll jump right into constructing our SQL queries and getting the query results like this:

```php
// set up first SQL query
$sql = "SELECT first_name,last_name FROM simple_table WHERE YEAR(birth_date)
  < 1979 ORDER BY last_name";
// get result
if( !($below_date = odbc_exec($conn, $sql) ) ) {
  die("Invalid result for $sql");
}

// set up second SQL query
$sql = "SELECT first_name,last_name FROM simple_table WHERE YEAR(birth_date)
  >= 1979 ORDER BY last_name";

// get result
if( !($above_date = odbc_exec($conn, $sql) ) ) {
  die("Invalid result for $sql");
}

?>
```

You'll see that the `odbc_exec()` function is slightly different from the equivalent `mysql_query()` function we used before, in that we need to pass it the `$conn` variable. But effectively, these two functions are serving exactly the same purpose.

4. Display our results:

```html
<html>
  <head>
    <title>Simple ODBC DB Query</title>
```

```
<style type="text/css" media="screen">
body {
  margin: 30px 0px 0px 30px;
  font-family: verdana, helvetica, sans-serif;
}
</style>

</head>
<body>

<h2>Born before Jan 01, 1979</h2>
<ul>
  <?php
  // $name[0] will correspond to the column first_name,
  // while $name[1] will correspond to the column last_name
  while( odbc_fetch_into($below_date,$name) ) {
    echo "<li>" . $name[0] . " " . $name[1] . "</li>\n";
  }
  ?>
</ul>

<h2>Born on or after Jan 01, 1979</h2>
<ul>
<?php
  // $name[0] will correspond to the column first_name,
  // while $name[1] will correspond to the column last_name
  while( odbc_fetch_into($above_date,$name) ) {
    echo "<li>" . $name[0] . " " . $name[1] . "</li>\n";
  }
?>
  </ul>
</body>
</html>
```

Since this should display the same results as expected, we won't show the screenshot of the output again, rather, let's have a look at some of the important differences between this and our last example.

How It Works

The display code is very similar to what we used before. An unfortunate but true fact is that some of the ODBC functions have been changing in terms of how they are used and supported between early versions of PHP 4 and the current versions. The function that is easiest to use to actually get our data is `odbc_fectch_into()`.

Funtion	Usage
`resource odbc_fetch_into(resource result_id, array result_array [, int rownumber])`	This function requires two arguments. The first is the SQL query result we are interested in, and the second is an indexed array that will hold the values collected. The third, optional argument allows us to specify which row of the resultset to retrieve.

So it is functionally similar to the `mysql_fetch_assoc()` function we saw earlier. An important distinction is that it returns an indexed array starting at 0, which will be filled in with the values retrieved from the SELECT statement in the order they were requested.

Another issue with this function that is currently not very clear from the documentation is that it will automatically advance the row pointer for a resultset, again as `mysql_fetch_assoc()` did before. This makes it easy to loop through the resultset with a `while()` loop, as we did.

There are advantages and disadvantages to most technologies, and ODBC is no different. When we decide to make use of the `odbc_*` set of PHP functions, there are certain things that we gain and certain problems that we may induce as a result.

Advantages of ODBC

On the side of the advantages, the largest win we get is that we are not tying ourselves to a specific database vendor. The same ODBC functions can be used to interact with lots of different RDBMS systems.

> *Bear in mind that they don't help if we are using vendor-specific SQL syntax in the queries. If we do, these queries will need to get rewritten appropriately if we ever choose to switch back-end solutions.*

If we are using any vendor-specific SQL, then it's best to wrap those queries into a function of some sort. That way, we can just make changes in the function definition and it will take effect everywhere it's used.

Another gain that we might not think of immediately is this: ODBC allows us to interact with databases that do not have native PHP functions. For example, we can work with a MySQL database using the native functions, or using the ODBC functions (assuming that we have the ODBC drivers for MySQL installed and working on our system).

However, there are no native PHP functions for interacting with, for example, the Pervasive SQL database. Fortunately, if we needed to use this system we still could because there are ODBC drivers for Pervasive SQL. Basically, as long as one can get the drivers installed and working for the ODBC implementation, PHP's ODBC functions should work.

Disadvantages of ODBC

There is, of course, a flip side to the coin. The first thing to notice with the ODBC model is that ultimately, we are adding software to the system that didn't exist in the model when we were using the native PHP functions. In this case, we're adding the ODBC manager and the ODBC drivers. Since any new software we add must at some level require system overhead to run, there is an increase in the load on the machine. This in turn can decrease the performance of an application, since the more work the machine has to do managing ODBC, the less it can do executing our scripts.

Of course, it is only fair to note that this requirement of extra overhead is not specific to ODBC abstraction. Any abstraction layer we add over the native database functions will ultimately cause more code to be executed somewhere.

Another disadvantage with ODBC systems is in the implementation setup. You may have noticed that several times we mentioned that we needed to have the ODBC manager and drivers "set up and working." This is not always a simple thing to do in practice, particularly on Linux or other UNIX-type systems. In fact, most medium to large scale production environments will have skilled database administrators on hand full-time to take care of this sort of thing.

PHP Abstraction Layers

In the previous section, we talked about abstracting the PHP database functions so as to avoid tying ourselves to a specific database during development. The ODBC functions provided give us a good way to do this in a generalized way. However, it is possible to abstract the database interface even more with the use of a PHP-based layer of code.

A Higher Level of Abstraction

The basic idea here is to create a system in PHP that wraps the native functions into a uniform interface. At first glance, this seems both reasonable and fairly simple to implement. We could define a global variable somewhere that tells our wrapper functions what the underlying database is, and then calls the appropriate native function based on this global variable.

For example, here's a quick connection function that wraps the native connection functions for MySQL and Sybase databases:

```
// $dbtype can be "mysql" or "sybase"
$dbtype = "mysql";

function db_connect($server = '' , $user = '' , $password = '') {
  global $dbtype;
  if( 0 == strcmp($dbtype , "mysql") ) {
    return mysql_connect($server, $user, $password);
  }
  elseif( 0 == strcmp($dbtype , "sybase") ) {
    return sybase_connect($server, $user, $password);
  }
  else {
    return FALSE;
  }
}
```

As you can imagine, it wouldn't be too hard to include other databases in our db_connect() function. For example, if we wanted to add support for mSQL, it would effectively just take one extra elseif() statement to wrap the appropriate connection function.

In practice though, it actually makes more sense to define classes representing database objects than to create a bunch of wrapper functions. Typically this will make the code easier to write and work with. This is because it's fairly natural to think of a "database object" when building applications. Things such as the connection identifier and the current resultset are naturally mapped to things like member variables. Also, functions such as queries are easily thought of as object methods. This is in fact the general course of direction in modern PHP development.

Now, the heading of this section refers to the fact that a PHP layer is in most ways more abstract than the ODBC functions we looked at earlier. There is an obvious reason for this. With a PHP abstraction layer, you can wrap the ODBC functions just as you would wrap the native functions. This effectively gives you the best of both worlds.

If we are using a database that has native PHP functions, our PHP abstraction layer could use those native functions thus avoiding the added overhead of ODBC drivers and associated software. If we do need to connect to a database using ODBC though, that would be perfectly acceptable as well. In both cases we could have a common set of functions or methods to use, which again solves the original problem of being tied to a particular RDBMS system.

A Survey of Available Layers

If desired, we could develop our own PHP abstraction layer. However, it is likely that this would be a wasted effort. A valuable lesson of application development is learning not to reinvent the wheel, especially when there are many excellent options to choose from. In this section, we are going to look at some of the PHP database abstraction layers that are available on the Internet and are widely in use.

As with almost any piece of software, these were designed with slightly different goals in mind and therefore have somewhat differing features. All, however, are well-written and can significantly speed up our development time.

ADOdb

ADOdb stands for Active Data Objects Data Base. It is an object-oriented interface to databases in PHP, available for download from http://php.weblogs.com/ADODB.

It currently has support for the following databases:

- ❑ MySQL
- ❑ PostgreSQL
- ❑ Interbase
- ❑ Informix
- ❑ Oracle
- ❑ MS SQL 7
- ❑ Foxpro
- ❑ Access
- ❑ ADO
- ❑ Sybase
- ❑ DB2
- ❑ Generic ODBC

Using ADOdb allows us to create database connection objects, which can then be used to execute queries resulting in recordset objects. Methods are provided as well for fetching data from these recordsets. Also, there are built-in error-handling methods.

ADOdb also has several features that are somewhat unique to the library. First, it is designed to closely resemble Microsoft's ADO. Therefore, developers comfortable with coding things such as ASP pages in Windows should have an easy time getting started with ADOdb. Second, this library has a substantial amount of support methods that help developers deal with the differences encountered when using `INSERT` statement. Specifically, things like date manipulation and quoting can require different implementations with different RDBMS vendors. Third, there is a built-in Metatype system. This helps developers know that things such as `CHAR` and `STRING` are or are not the same across different databases.

On top of all of this, there are methods for things such as generating HTML select boxes and tables directly from SQL queries. Also, ADOdb makes it easy to create Next and Previous pager links, and to cache result data in local files.

Metabase

This is a library developed principally by Manuel Lemos (who has written quite a great deal of excellent PHP code). It is available for free download at http://phpclasses.UpperDesign.com/browse.html/package/20 although there is a free registration required. Like all of the libraries we are looking at in this section, Metabase supports many databases with a common API. Specifically:

- ❑ Interbase
- ❑ Informix
- ❑ Microsoft SQL Server
- ❑ Mini-SQL
- ❑ MySQL
- ❑ ODBC
- ❑ Oracle using Oracle Call Interface (OCI)
- ❑ PostgreSQL

The library gives us all the functionality one would expect for a uniform database API. Creating connections, performing queries, and fetching results are all covered in a standard way.

One of the distinguishing features of Metabase is that it effectively gives the programmer common procedural (function-based) and object-oriented interfaces. Depending on our needs we can either connect to the database using a Metabase connection function and then interact with it by calling other defined functions, or we can create a Metabase database object and call methods on this object.

Another noteworthy point is that Metabase has a real focus on the ability to create databases easily. Using a custom XML format defined in the documentation, we can define database schemas. Then, using supplied functions, we can create these databases and tables with little effort. Metabase itself takes care of the nuances involved with this kind of creation on different kinds of RDBMS systems.

Finally, this library supports sequences natively. Sequences are a programmatic way of figuring out what the next unique ID is for a row when performing an `INSERT` query, and can be very useful. If you are familiar with `auto_increment` fields in MySQL databases, you will see that sequences give us basically the same functionality.

Currently, efforts are underway to merge the Metabase functionality with PEAR::DB, which we are going to talk about next.

PEAR DB

PEAR stands for the **PHP Extension and Application Repository**. It is a fast growing collection of classes that aims to give PHP something equivalent to Perl's CPAN archive. PEAR DB provides a uniform API for accessing databases. It currently supports the following databases (for more information refer to http://pear.php.net/):

- ❑ MySQL
- ❑ PostgreSQL
- ❑ InterBase
- ❑ Mini SQL
- ❑ Microsoft SQL Server
- ❑ Oracle 7/8/8i
- ❑ ODBC
- ❑ Sybase
- ❑ Informix
- ❑ FrontBase

Like the other abstraction layers we've talked about here, it provides all the methods we might need for connecting to databases, running SQL queries, and fetching data from these queries. Like Metabase, it also provides native support for sequences allowing us to easily generate unique identifiers for our `INSERT` statements.

An interesting point is that unlike the previous abstraction layers, there is really nothing in PEAR::DB that is not directly related to some sort of database function. For example, there's nothing like the automatic select box generation of ADOdb. The interface is also completely object-oriented. There are no functions that are not object methods, and there are also no variables introduced into the global namespace.

Another useful feature is that since this layer is built on top of the standard PEAR classes, we have instant access to the uniform PEAR error handling.

Finally, this code is included by default in the PHP source distribution, as are the rest of the production PEAR classes.

Why We Choose PEAR DB

In this book, we will consistently make use of PEAR::DB as our database abstraction layer. In fact, the next chapter will give you an exhaustive introduction into the use of PEAR::DB, including the standard methods you'll use and the basic steps you'll always take when handling databases.

There are a few reasons that we use PEAR::DB instead of one of the other excellent layers listed here. The most important of these is, simply, that PEAR::DB is part of PHP itself now. As noted, it is included with the source PHP distribution along with the many other excellent PEAR classes that are available. This matters because the PHP development community is increasingly pushing for increased use of PEAR in all applicable facets of development, from XML processing to mail handling. By the time that PHP 5 is released, there is hope that PEAR will be the de facto standard for many PHP development tasks.

Also, PEAR::DB offers the most modern object-oriented interface available. As you will see in the next chapter, it uses standard DSN-style string for establishing connections, and all the member variables and methods are fully encapsulated into the objects.

Finally, as mentioned, it allows us to make use of the PEAR error-handling class. This is the most general error-handling class available today, and it is really very easy to use.

Summary

The PHP language has matured a great deal over the last few years. The current release has a plethora of capabilities for interacting with databases. In fact, many supporters of the language point to this as one of its most outstanding features in comparison with other languages.

We talked about what is meant by the phrase Multi-Tier development. The idea of splitting our application into distinct systems working together allows faster development, more modular and maintainable designs, and ultimately more efficient applications.

PHP natively supports a large number of RDBMS systems, both free and commercial. This means that there are functions that may be built into the language that interact with the database in question. However, there is not a common API that covers all of the supported databases, so all the functions are slightly different.

One way around this inconsistency is to use ODBC functions. These provide a uniform API that allows us to access many different databases, and little code modification is needed to switch between them.

A more advanced way to get a uniform API is to make use of a PHP abstraction layer. We talked about several of these, and highlighted some of the features offered. We also talked about why we are going to make use of the PEAR::DB abstraction layer in this book.

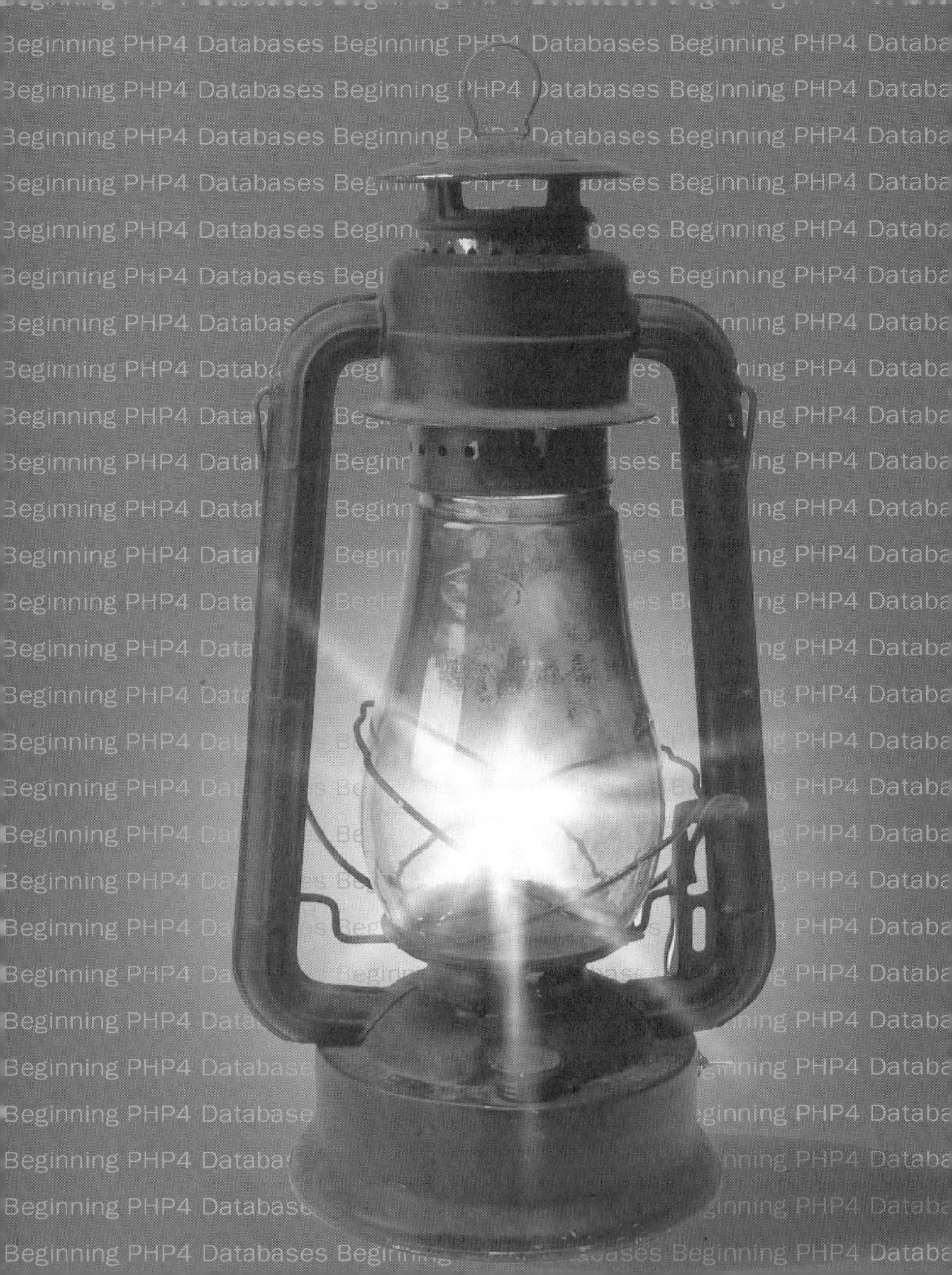
Beginning PHP4 Databases

Dissecting PEAR::DB

PEAR's importance to PHP continues to grow with the development of each new package. One of the oldest and most used components of PEAR is `PEAR::DB`, which has emerged as PHP's standard database abstraction layer.

Often the best way to understand how something works is to open it up and look inside. In this chapter, we'll put `PEAR::DB` under the microscope to obtain a better understanding of its functionality, and to see some code written by very smart people.

Specifically, in this chapter, we will look at the following:

- ❑ The basics of PEAR
- ❑ The `DB`, `DB_common`, and `DB_result` classes
- ❑ The implementation classes

In this chapter, we shall see the code of the implementation classes in `PEAR::DB`. Some would argue that doing so defeats one of the purposes of having an abstraction layer. After all, `PEAR::DB` presents a consistent interface so that you, as the developer, do not have to know how it works internally. However, as we shall see throughout this chapter, the code gives new insights into how best to use it, as well as the many benefits that come with reading expertly designed code.

For those in a hurry, the good news is that the online PEAR documentation (http://pear.php.net/manual/en/) provides enough detail about how PEAR is used in applications, if you want to jump straight in and try it out. The detailed examination in this chapter is intended to deepen our understanding of PEAR and its abstraction layer, but like any good set of classes, a summary of PEAR's interface is all that is needed to use it effectively.

PEAR is automatically installed with PHP, unless you include the --without-pear option at the time that PHP is installed. For the most up-to-date version, PEAR can be downloaded from http://pear.php.net/manual/en/installation.php, or individual packages can be found at http://pear.php.net/packages.php.

If you prefer an automatic installation process, you can use the following command from your UNIX term window to download the PEAR package manager:

```
$ lynx -source http://pear.php.net/go-pear | sh
```

Then you can list and fetch the packages:

```
$ pear list-remote-packages
$ pear install http://pear.php.net/get/<package>
```

You may want to adjust your php.ini file to make sure that the include_path setting includes the proper directory for your PEAR installation. As you include PEAR files in your application, note that all paths are relative to the PEAR root path.

Reviewing the Basics of PEAR

PEAR is a sophisticated set of professionally designed classes. PEAR classes tend to be elaborate and well conceived, and using them can drastically reduce the time it takes to develop an application. One drawback, however, is that they are not usually the speediest when it comes to code execution. This performance hit from using PEAR is often exaggerated. On most modern equipment, as with tools for caching script binaries and the like, the difference is negligible. Nevertheless, if execution speed is your top priority, then PEAR might not be your best choice. If quality, robustness, and maintainability of code are your top priorities, then PEAR is the code base for you.

PEAR classes must conform to strict coding standards that can be found at http://pear.php.net/manual/en/standards.php. This includes the use of PHPDoc-style comments that allow for automatic code documentation by the PHPDoc utility. For more information, see http://www.phpdoc.de/.

The most important file in PEAR is PEAR.php, located in the PEAR root directory. In this file we find:

❑   Declarations of the constants and global variables that are used throughout PEAR

❑   The PEAR base class

❑   The PEAR_Error class

The PEAR base class is almost never directly instantiated. We should never really have a reason to create a PEAR base object like this:

```
$my_pear = new PEAR();
```

The resulting object would have no independently useful functionality. Instead, the PEAR class is meant only as a base class from which other classes inherit, and as a class for holding static methods. For example, the PEAR::isError() static method is a convenient way to determine whether a variable contains a PEAR_Error object (or a subclass thereof). In the example below, we call an imaginary PEAR method, and then use isError() to check the result for errors:

```
$result = $obj->go();
if (PEAR::isError ($result)) {
  echo ($result->getMessage());
}
```

Remember that we use the :: operator instead of the -> operator to access a static member of a class.

Destructor Simulation

When a subclass extends the PEAR class, it automatically gains a convenient feature. Unlike Java, PHP4 does not natively support destructors, methods that execute when an object is destroyed. Destructors are often used for clean-up work: closing open connections, saving output to a file, and the like. The PEAR class uses the built-in register_shutdown() PHP function to emulate destructors for all objects which inherit from PEAR. In order for a subclass to take advantage of the destructor simulation, three conditions must be met:

1. The subclass must call the PEAR() constructor in its own constructor:

```
class Widget extends PEAR {

  /**
  * Constructor
  */
  function Widget() {
  $this->PEAR();
  ...
  }
}
```

2. The subclass must name its destructor method in a standard way. The method's name must be the name of the class preceded by an underscore:

```
/**
* Destructor
*/
function _Widget() {
..
}
```

3. The subclass must be instantiated by reference rather than by value:

```
$widg =& new Widget(); // Not $widg = new Widget();
```

In the above example, the method _Widget() can be defined to handle any operations that we wish to perform when the script finishes execution.

PEAR_Error

The PEAR_Error class brings sophisticated error handling to applications. Rather than simply returning an error code or an error message when something goes wrong, methods throughout the PEAR universe produce objects that may contain this data and more, including user information, details for debugging, and an error level.

PEAR_Error's properties are accessed via get() methods, like this:

```
if (PEAR::isError ($var)) {
  echo ($var->getUserInfo());
}
```

If all of this error checking seems tedious, it is also possible to set up an error-handling CALLBACK function that handles the errors automatically:

```
// set an error handler
PEAR::setErrorHandling (PEAR_ERROR_CALLBACK, "logError");
```

Now whenever an error object is instantiated, PEAR_Error's constructor passes the new error to the logError() function, which we can create ourselves:

```
function logError (&$error) {
  // uncomment next line to see object properties
  // print_r ($error);

  // Create a string to hold the error (with a timestamp)
  // Access object properties to get different
  // bits of information about the error.

  $entry =
  '[' . date("Ymd H:i:s") . '] ' .
  'Error: ' . $error->code . ': ' . $error->message . "\n"
  // uncomment next line for debug info:
  // . "\t Debug string: " . $error->userinfo . "\n"
  ;

  // Append error entry to a log file.
  $fp = @fopen("error.log", "a+");
  @fwrite ($fp, $entry);
  @fclose ($fp);
  }
```

PEAR_Error is also intended as a base class from which other more specific error classes can inherit, as we shall see in the next section.

The PEAR::DB Object Model and Code Files

PEAR is a hierarchy of classes. Most of the classes in PEAR ultimately inherit from the PEAR base class. The following diagram depicts the relationship of inheritance among the base class, the PEAR_Error class, and the PEAR::DB abstraction layer classes:

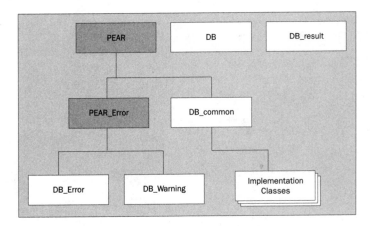

Most of the PEAR::DB classes are located in the file DB.php in the PEAR root directory. The DB_common class and the various implementation classes are each located in separate files in the DB subdirectory. Each implementation class pertains to a specific DBMS. For example, the file pgsql.php contains the class for PostgreSQL and the file ifx.php contains the class for Informix. It is only in these classes that we find the actual built-in PHP database functions such as pg_pconnect() or ifx_query().

In the file DB.php, the comments on license and authors' references appears first, as in version 1.2 of PEAR::DB. Finally comes the PHP code that makes PEAR::DB work. Let's examine the subclasses individually and see what they do. PEAR is a vast ocean of code, so it is not feasible to examine every line of it here. Instead, we shall focus on the juicier bits that will help us understand the basic mechanisms.

The DB_Error and DB_Warning Classes

Peeking inside the file DB.php, we find several classes, including DB_Error and DB_Warning. These two classes have identical behavior and nearly identical code, since they are used for almost the same purpose: both are containers for messages from the database system. Typically, a database system will return an error code when an operation fails, or a warning for less-severe abnormalities. Due to their similarity, an examination of any one of them is sufficient for understanding both classes. We shall study the DB_Error class here:

```
/**
 * DB_Error implements a class for reporting portable database error
 * messages.
 *
 * @package DB
 * @author Stig Bakken <ssb@fast.no>
 */
class DB_Error extends PEAR_Error
{
    /**
     * DB_Error constructor.
     *
     * @param mixed DB error code, or string with error message.
     * @param integer what "error mode" to operate in
```

```
 * @param integer what error level to use for $mode & AR_ERROR_TRIGGER
 * @param mixed additional debug info, such as the last query
 *
 * @access public
 *
 * @see PEAR_Error
 */

function DB_Error($code = DB_ERROR, $mode = PEAR_ERROR_RETURN,
$level = E_USER_NOTICE, $debuginfo = null)
{
  if (is_int($code)) {
    $this->PEAR_Error('DB Error: ' . DB::errorMessage($code), $code,
    $mode, $level, $debuginfo);
  } else {
      $this->PEAR_Error("DB Error: $code", DB_ERROR, $mode, $level,
      $debuginfo);
  }
}
}
```

Since this class extends PEAR_Error, we know that it has access to the methods of the parent class, such as getMessage(). The only method unique to the subclass is its constructor, which calls the constructor of the parent class, as we can see in the if() statement shown in the previous code snippet.

Notice that the DB_Error() method receives four arguments, while the PEAR_Error() method receives five. DB_Error() does not receive a message string. Instead, it attempts to create the message based on a numeric error code. The static method DB::errorMessage() returns a generic error message that does not vary from one DBMS to another. Remember that the goal of a good database abstraction layer is to exhibit the exact same behavior to the application regardless of the back-end systems it connects to. If the constructor receives a text message instead of a numeric code, then it has no choice but to use the message it receives. This condition triggers the else block of code.

When debugging a complex problem, it usually helps to know the native error message returned by the database system rather than an abstracted, generic message. For this reason, many of the implementation classes will also include the native error details in the $debuginfo parameter.

The DB Class

The DB class is also located in the file DB.php. It is a utility class containing static methods that are used throughout PEAR::DB. As such, the DB class is not instantiated, and it does not extend the PEAR base class.

More On Errors

We have already seen that the method DB::errorMessage() returns the text message for a given numeric error code. It maintains a static array of error codes and the corresponding messages. DB::errorMessage() is meant to be a private method. While it is used by other PEAR methods, we should not need to call it in our PEAR applications.

`DB::isError()` and `DB::isWarning()` on the other hand, are public methods used extensively both within PEAR and in end-user applications:

```
/**
 * Tell whether a result code from a DB method is an error
 *
 * @param int result code
 *
 * @return bool whether $value is an error
 *
 * @access public
 */
function isError($value) {
   return (is_object($value) &&
   (get_class($value) == 'db_error' ||
   is_subclass_of($value, 'db_error')));
}
```

`DB::isError()` uses the built-in PHP object functions to return `true` only if `$value` is an instance of `DB_Error()` or a subclass thereof. Instances of `DB_Warning()` or other `PEAR_Error` classes will not be detected by the method. Similarly, `DB::isWarning()` will return `true` only for warnings, not `DB_Error()` objects. If we want hyper-sensitive error handling that detects any kind of error (including warnings), we can use `PEAR::isError()` instead, but in the case of testing for a valid database connection or query result, `DB::isError()` should suffice. Since warnings are non-fatal, they usually are handled differently from errors.

DB::connect()

Besides the error handling methods, DB's next most familiar method to `PEAR::DB` users is `connect()`. This function returns an object that represents the database connection. More precisely, it returns an instance of the appropriate implementation class. If we are attempting to connect to a Sybase database, it returns an instance of `DB_Sybase` if successful or `DB_Error()` in case of failure. The method `connect()`, as we shall see below, accepts parameters containing information necessary to establish the connection and any options for initializing the connection object:

```
/**
 * Create a new DB connection object and connect to the specified
 * database
 *
 * @param mixed "data source name", see the DB::parseDSN
 * method for a description of the dsn format. Can also be
 * specified as an array of the format returned by DB::parseDSN.
 *
 * @param mixed An associative array of option names and
 * their values. For backwards compatibility, this parameter may
 * also be a Boolean that tells whether the connection should be
 * persistent. See DB_common::setOption for more information on
 * connection options.
 *
 * @return mixed a newly created DB connection object, or a DB
```

```
* error object on error
*
* @see DB::parseDSN
* @see DB::isError
* @see DB_common::setOption
*/
```

The $options parameter we see below is usually either for debugging or for indicating whether a connection should be persistent. The variable dsn has been explained later, immediately after the code section below:

```
function &connect($dsn, $options = false)
{
  if (is_array($dsn)) {
    $dsninfo = $dsn;
  } else {
      $dsninfo = DB::parseDSN($dsn);
    }
  $type = $dsninfo["phptype"];

  if (is_array($options) && isset($options["debug"]) &&
    $options["debug"] >= 2) {
    // expose php errors with sufficient debug level
    include_once "DB/${type}.php";
  } else {
      @include_once "DB/${type}.php";
    }

  $classname = "DB_${type}";
  if (!class_exists($classname)) {
    return PEAR::raiseError(null, DB_ERROR_NOT_FOUND,
    null, null, null, 'DB_Error', true);
  }

  @$obj =& new $classname;

  if (is_array($options)) {
    foreach ($options as $option => $value) {
      $test = $obj->setOption($option, $value);
      if (DB::isError($test)) {
        return $test;
      }
    }
  } else {
      $obj->setOption('persistent', $options);
    }
  $err = $obj->connect($dsninfo, $obj->getOption('persistent'));
  if (DB::isError($err)) {
    $err->addUserInfo($dsn);
    return $err;
  }

  return $obj;
}
```

As indicated in the method's documentation comment, the first parameter $dsn (data source name) may be either a string or an array. The string may take any of the following formats, depending on the configuration of your database server:

```
phptype://username:password@protocol+hostspec:110//usr/db_file.db
phptype://username:password@hostspec/database_name
phptype://username:password@hostspec
phptype://username@hostspec
phptype://hostspec/database
phptype://hostspec
phptype(dbsyntax)
phptype
```

Here is an example:

```
$dsn = 'mysql://admin:e5jm400@kablooey.com/kablooey';
```

The array version of this dsn is:

```
$dsn = array (
    'phptype' => 'mysql',
    'hostspec' => 'kablooey.com',
    'database' => 'kablooey',
    'username' => 'admin',
    'password' => 'e5jm400'
);
```

It is a bit more efficient to pass the array than the string, since the method ultimately needs it in the array format. If we do pass the string, connect() passes it to DB::parseDSN() in order to obtain the array. DB::parseDSN() is a very large method, and since it is not so critical to our understanding of PEAR::DB, we will not analyze it in this book.

Once DB::connect() has the connection info in its $dsninfo array, it includes the appropriate implementation file:

```
$type = $dsninfo["phptype"];

if (is_array($options) && isset($options["debug"]) &&
    $options["debug"] >= 2) {
    // expose php errors with sufficient debug level
    include_once "DB/${type}.php";
} else {
    @include_once "DB/${type}.php";
    }
```

The purpose of the if() statement is to determine whether include_once() should be called with or without error suppression. If the information in the $options array indicates that we are currently debugging our application, then it does not suppress the errors. Using our sample $dsn, this code would include the file mysql.php.

In the next section of code, we test for the class and instantiate it:

```
$classname = "DB_${type}";
if (!class_exists($classname)) {
  return PEAR::raiseError(null, DB_ERROR_NOT_FOUND,
  null, null, null, 'DB_Error', true);
}

@$obj =& new $classname;
```

The PEAR::raiseError() static method is the preferred way to create error objects in PEAR (as opposed to simply creating an instance of an error class). DB_ERROR_NOT_FOUND is a constant that represents an error code for "not found" conditions. In this case, it is passed as the error code when the needed class is not found. The sixth parameter of PEAR::raiseError() is the class of the error to be returned. We specifically want a DB_Error() in this instance, as opposed to a PEAR_Error() or a DB_Warning().

The object is created by reference using =&, in order to take advantage of the destructor simulation described previously in this chapter. Now that we have an object representing the database connection, it is time to set any options that the application requires:

```
if (is_array($options)) {
  foreach ($options as $option => $value) {
    $test = $obj->setOption($option, $value);
    if (DB::isError($test)) {
      return $test;
    }
  }
} else {
    $obj->setOption('persistent', $options);
  }
```

For each option passed, it attempts to call the implementation class' setOption() method. As the name implies, this method is simply used to set the values of options within the implementation objects. If no option is specified, the persistent option is set by default, resulting in a persistent database connection. If the setOption() method returns a DB_Error object for any of the other options, the connect() method returns the error object. For this reason, when we call DB::connect() it is important to check whether we receive the database object we are expecting, or an error object instead. The error object may not even originate in connect(). In this case, it can occur in setOption() and "trickle" through connect() to our application.

Lastly comes the attempt to connect to the database:

```
$err = $obj->connect($dsninfo, $obj->getOption('persistent'));
if (DB::isError($err)) {
  $err->addUserInfo($dsn);
  return $err;
}

return $obj;
```

Here the static DB::connect() method calls the connect() method of the implementation class (DB_mysql), passing it the DSN information and whether the connection should be persistent or not. If DB_mysql::connect() fails, it returns a DB_Error object which is captured in the variable $err. In the regrettable event of such an error, we include the DSN information for debugging purposes (DB_Error inherits addUserInfo() from the PEAR_Error class).

If there is no error, then we return the fully connected DB object (say DB_mysql, DB_pgsql).

Other DB Methods

The DB class contains a few other static methods. We will just mention a couple of them here:

❏ DB::isManip()
This receives a query statement and returns true if it is a data definition query (involving say CREATE, ALTER, or DROP) or a data manipulation query (with INSERT, UPDATE, LOCK, and the like).

❏ DB::isConnection()
This returns true if the value passed to it is a valid database connection object, such as an instance of DB_mysql or DB_ifx.

The DB_common Class

Located in common.php, DB_common is the base class for all of the implementation classes. Some of the methods in it are merely abstract methods, place-holders meant to be overridden by methods in the subclasses (somewhat similar to abstract methods in Java, but not as formalized). One example is modifyLimitQuery():

```
/**
 * This method is used by back ends to alter limited queries
 *
 * @param string $query query to modify
 * @param integer $from the row to start to fetching
 * @param integer $count the numbers of rows to fetch
 *
 * @return the new (modified) query
 *
 * @access private
 */

function modifyLimitQuery($query, $from, $count)
{
    return $query;
}
```

On its own, this is not the most useful method. But when overridden in the Oracle implementation class for example, it has more than a dozen lines of code.

This method is used by the limitQuery() method, whose purpose is to process "limit" queries (queries for which a restriction is placed on the number of rows to return or affect). Each DBMS handles this functionality very differently. Remember that the primary goal of a database abstraction layer is to mask back-end differences behind a unified interface. That is why we define modifyLimitQuery() here in DB_common, so that it is called the same way for all database implementations; but we let the separate implementation classes handle the actual DBMS-specific work.

The abstract methods are designed to behave gracefully if the subclass does not override them. For example, the Informix implementation class does not override DB_common's rollback() method. Therefore if rollback() is called, DB_common's rollback() method executes, and returns an error informing the application that the feature is not supported:

```
/**
 * starts a rollback
 *
 * @return mixed DB_Error
 *
 * @access public
 */
function rollback()
{
    return $this->raiseError(DB_ERROR_NOT_CAPABLE);
}
```

Not all of DB_common's methods are abstract; however with nearly forty methods, it would be rather overwhelming to describe all of them in detail here. Instead we will showcase the most important methods for the new user. You are strongly encouraged to look through the code to read and dissect the other methods. Perusing PEAR code is one of the best ways to improve PHP and object-oriented design skills. PEAR is a work of collaboration by some of the world's best PHP programmers, and they want you to join their ranks.

DB_common::query()

This is perhaps the most familiar DB_common method to users of PEAR::DB. As the name implies, it is used to execute a query in the database. Here is an example of its use in an application:

```
$sql = 'SELECT name, age FROM person';
// Execute the query with the database handler object:
$result = $dbh->query ($sql);
// Check for errors:
if (DB::isError ($result)) return $result;
```

In the example above, query() returns a resultset object, or an error if we are having a bad day. For data manipulation queries, such as an UPDATE query, it may simply return true (or an error). Here is the function declaration:

```
/**
 * Send a query to the database and return any results with a
 * DB_result object.
 *
```

```
 *  @access public
 *
 *  @param string $query the SQL query or the statement to prepare
 *  @param string $params the data to be added to the query
 *  @return mixed a DB_result object or DB_OK on success, a DB
 *   error on failure
 *
 *  @see DB::isError
 *  @see DB_common::prepare
 *  @see DB_common::execute
 */

function &query($query, $params = array()) {
  if (sizeof($params) > 0) {
    sth = $this->prepare($query);
    if (DB::isError($sth)) {
      return $sth;
    }
    return $this->execute($sth, $params);
  } else {
      $result = $this->simpleQuery($query);
      if (DB::isError($result) || $result === DB_OK) {
        return $result;
      } else {
          return new DB_result($this, $result);
      }
  }
}
```

This method can handle two different types of queries:

❑   In simple queries, the statement contains both the SQL code (or stored procedure name) and the data. The SELECT statement in the previous example is a simple query.

❑   In a prepared query, the statement contains only a generic template of the SQL code. The data is provided separately in an array. This is useful if the same query needs to be executed repeatedly with different data each time.

The $params variable lets the query() method know which type of query to process. If it contains a non-empty array, it passes the array to the prepare() method and then passes the resulting prepared statement to the execute() method. Most developers just use simple queries and place them in loops if they need repetition, so we will not dwell on how prepared queries work.

If the $params array is empty, the query() method passes the query statement to the simpleQuery() method and stores the result in the $result variable. If we look in the file common.php however, you may be surprised to find that class DB_common does not have a simpleQuery() method. Recall that the DB_common class is never instantiated; it serves only as a parent to the implementation class. When the variable $this appears in DB_common, it actually refers to an instance of one of DB_common's subclasses. It is the responsibility of each implementation class to define a simpleQuery() method, which contains the DBMS-specific functions for handling the query. For example, DB_mysql::simpleQuery() invokes the PHP function mysql_query().

Every `simpleQuery()` method returns one of three things. If an error is encountered, it returns a `DB_Error` object, which `query()` then returns. For successful manipulation queries, `simpleQuery()` returns the value for `DB_OK`. Again, `query()` simply returns this value as well. For other successful queries (such as `SELECT` queries or stored procedure calls), `simpleQuery()` returns the result-set resource that the built-in PHP function produces. In this case the `query()` method creates a `DB_result` object, passing the database object (`$this`) and the result set to `DB_result`'s constructor.

Later in the chapter we'll look inside the `DB_result` class to see what makes it tick. For now, we can just take a quick look at some of its behavior. The `DB_result` object returned by `query()` contains the requested data, or the result of the query manipulation. To access the actual data, we must then call a `fetchRow()` method of the result object, often in a loop, if there is more than one record:

```
$sql = 'SELECT name, age FROM person';
// Execute the query with the database handler object:
$result = $dbh->query ($sql);
// Check for errors:
if (DB::isError ($result)) return $result;
while ($row = $result->fetchRow()) {
  // Check for errors:
  if (DB::isError ($row)) return $row;
    echo ($row[0]) ;
 //
}
```

Or just once if only one record is expected:

```
$sql = 'SELECT COUNT(1) FROM person';
// Execute the query with the database handler object:
$result = $dbh->query ($sql);
// Check for errors:
if (DB::isError ($result)) return $result;
  $row = $result->fetchRow();
// Check for errors:
if (DB::isError ($row)) return $row;
  $num_person = $row[0];
```

One of the advantages of using an abstraction layer like `PEAR::DB` is the presence of quick methods that save us from having to do all of the work shown in these examples. Methods such as `getRow()`, `getOne()`, and `getAll()` provide quick and easy ways to execute methods without sacrificing the robust error handling of `query()` and `fetchRow()`.

Other Useful DB_common Methods

Following is a summary of a few of the additional methods of DB_common (for a full list, visit http://pear.php.net):

❑ `DB_common::getOne()`

This receives a query statement and returns only the first column of the first row of the result set, or a `DB_Error` object in case of error. Normally, we would only use this method with a statement that is expected to return a single value:

```
$sql = 'SELECT COUNT(1) FROM person';
$num_person = $dbh->getOne ($sql);
// Check for errors:
if (DB::isError ($num_person))
  return $num_person;
```

❑ DB_common::getAll()

This is similar to getOne(), except it returns the entire result set as a two-dimensional array:

```
$sql = 'SELECT name, age FROM person';
$result = $dbh->getAll ($sql);
// Check for errors:
if (DB::isError ($result))
  return $result;
  foreach ($result as $row) {
    echo ("Name: $row[0], Age: $row[1]<br />");
  }
```

❑ getRow()

This returns only the first row of the result set as an array.

❑ getCol()

This returns the first column of the result set as an array.

❑ getAssoc()

This is like getAll(), except it uses the first column as the index of the outer array.

❑ DB_common::numRows()

This is an abstract method, which receives a DB_result object and returns the number of rows, or a DB_Error.

❑ DB_common::affectedRows()

This abstract method returns the number of rows affected by the previous query, if the previous query was a manipulation query. In case of error, it returns a DB_Error.

❑ DB_common::nextId()

This returns the next free ID of a sequence.

As with limit queries, each DBMS has a different way of handling record IDs, or surrogate keys, when new records are inserted. Instead of using built-in PHP functions such as mysql_insert_id() after a query has executed, PEAR::DB uses **sequences** to determine the next available ID in advance. Sequences are created with the createSequence() method, and the nextId() method returns the next ID for that sequence.

Note that sequences may not work for all situations. If the same database is used by more than one application, such as a PHP application using PEAR::DB and a Java program, then conflicts may occur with sequences (with MySQL's auto_increment, for instance). In such situations, a work-around may be needed to bypass the abstraction layer. For more information about key incrementation with sequences, please see the PEAR documentation at
http://pear.php.net/manual/en/core.db.tut_sequences.php.

The DB_result Class

By now we know that the DB_result class is used to represent query results. It has the following properties:

❑ The database handle $dbh

❑ A reference to the database implementation object

❑ $result – the result set resource returned by the native PHP function, such as ifx_query()

❑ $row_counter, which is used to keep track of the currently referenced record in the set

Here is the implementation of the DB_result class:

```
/**
 * This class implements a wrapper for a DB result set.
 * A new instance of this class will be returned by the DB implementation
 * after processing a query that returns data.
 *
 * @package DB
 * @author Stig Bakken <ssb@fast.no>
 */

class DB_result
{
  var $dbh;
  var $result;
  var $row_counter = null;
  /**
   * for limit queries, the row to start fetching
   * @var integer
   */
  var $limit_from = null;

  /**
   * for limit queries, the number of rows to fetch
   * @var integer
   */
  var $limit_count = null;
```

The properties $limit_from and $limit_count are used to handle limit queries. The DB_common::limitQuery() method sets these properties explicitly, immediately after creating the DB_result object. If the application calls query() instead of limitQuery(), the two properties would contain Null values.

DB_result::fetchRow()

We have already seen the fetchRow() method in action. Here is its complete code:

```
/**
 * Fetch and return a row of data (it uses driver->fetchInto for that)
 * @param int format of fetched row
 * @param int the row number to fetch
 *
```

```
 * @return array a row of data, Null on no more rows or PEAR_Error on error
 *
 * @access public
 */
function fetchRow($fetchmode = DB_FETCHMODE_DEFAULT, $rownum=null)
{
  if ($fetchmode === DB_FETCHMODE_DEFAULT) {
    $fetchmode = $this->dbh->fetchmode;
  }
  if ($fetchmode === DB_FETCHMODE_OBJECT) {
    $fetchmode = DB_FETCHMODE_ASSOC;
    $object_class = $this->dbh->fetchmode_object_class;
  }
  if ($this->limit_from !== null) {
    if ($this->row_counter === null) {
      $this->row_counter = $this->limit_from;
      // For Interbase
      if ($this->dbh->features['limit'] == false) {
        $i = 0;
        while ($i++ < $this->limit_from) {
          $this->dbh->fetchInto($this->result, $arr, $fetchmode);
        }
      }
    }
    if ($this->row_counter >= ($this->limit_from + $this->limit_count)) {
      return null;
    }
    if ($this->dbh->features['limit'] == 'emulate') {
      $rownum = $this->row_counter;
    }
    $this->row_counter++;
  }
  $res = $this->dbh->fetchInto($this->result, $arr, $fetchmode, $rownum);
  if ($res !== DB_OK) {
    return $res;
  }
  if (isset($object_class)) {
    // default mode specified in DB_common::fetchmode_object_class property
    if ($object_class == 'stdClass') {
      $ret = (object) $arr;
    } else {
        $ret =& new $object_class($arr);
    }
    return $ret;
  }
  return $arr;
}
```

This first section of code is concerned with whether the rows of the result set should be associative arrays using the table field names as indices, numerically indexed arrays, or objects. By default, rows are indexed numerically, beginning with zero, as in the previous example:

```
$row = $result->fetchRow();
// Check for errors:
if (DB::isError ($row)) return $row;
  $num_person = $row[0];
```

To preserve the field names, pass DB_FETCHMODE_ASSOC as the first argument to fetchRow():

```
$sql = 'SELECT name, age FROM person';
// Execute the query with the database handler object:
$result = $dbh->query ($sql);
// Check for errors:
if (DB::isError ($result)) return $result;
  while ($row = $result->fetchRow (DB_FETCHMODE_ASSOC)) {
    // Check for errors:
    if (DB::isError ($row)) return $row;
      echo ($row['name']);
    //
  }
```

The middle section of the function deals with details of limit queries. We shall skip ahead to the part where the row is fetched:

```
$res = $this->dbh->fetchInto($this->result, $arr,
$fetchmode, $rownum);
if ($res !== DB_OK) {
  return $res;
}
```

Here we see why it is sometimes so difficult to track down exactly how PEAR works.
DB_result::fetchRow() relies on the fetchInto() method of the implementation classes, such as DB_mysql::fetchInto(). This is because the actual functionality of fetching a row from a result set resource is DBMS-dependent. For MySQL, the PHP function mysql_fetch_row() (or one like it) is needed.

DB_mysql::fetchInto() does not return a row. Instead, an array is passed to it by reference, and fetchInto() fills the array with the row data. Therefore the variable $res will only indicate whether the operation was successful or not. It is the variable $arr that holds the precious data.
DB_result::fetchRow() then does a little more "mode" checking to determine whether the array should be returned as an object. This occurs only if the method was called with the DB_FETCHMODE_OBJECT option, which results in the $object_class variable being set:

```
    if (isset($object_class)) {
      // default mode specified in DB_common::fetchmode_object_class property
      if ($object_class == 'stdClass') {
        $ret = (object) $arr;
      } else {
          $ret =& new $object_class($arr);
        }
      return $ret;
    }
    return $arr;
  }
```

If no object conversion is necessary, we simply return the row array.

Other DB_result Methods

Here are a few other methods that you may want to dissect on your own:

❑ free()
This is used to release the resources (memory) allocated for the result set, which can make a significant difference for large applications or over-taxed servers. Note that DB_common methods such as getOne() and getAll() handle this automatically for us. free() invokes the freeResult() method of the implementation classes.

❑ numCols() and numRows()
These use the implementation classes' methods of the same names to determine the number of columns and rows of a result set respectively.

❑ fetchInto()
This is similar to fetchRow() except that it does not return the row data. Instead, it receives an array parameter by reference. It populates the array with the row data, and returns DB_OK or an error.

The Implementation Classes

The implementation classes are the only place in PEAR::DB where one will find the built-in PHP database functions. This is what we are trying to abstract.

As mentioned in the previous section, when DB_result::fetchRow() or DB_result::fetchInto() is called, it is really DB_mysql::fetchInto() that does the work (in this case, assuming our back-end database to be MySQL). Let us see what's really going on:

```
/**
 * Fetch a row and insert the data into an existing array.
 *
 * @param $result MySQL result identifier
 * @param $arr (reference) array where data from the row is stored
 * @param $fetchmode how the array data should be indexed
 * @param $rownum the row number to fetch
 * @access public
 *
 * @return int DB_OK on success, a DB error on failure
 */
function fetchInto($result, &$arr, $fetchmode, $rownum=null)
{
  if ($rownum !== null) {
    if (!@mysql_data_seek($result, $rownum)) {
      return null;
    }
  }
  if ($fetchmode & DB_FETCHMODE_ASSOC) {
    $arr = @mysql_fetch_array($result, MYSQL_ASSOC);
  } else {
    $arr = @mysql_fetch_row($result);
```

```
      }
   if (!$arr) {
    $errno = @mysql_errno($this->connection);
    if (!$errno) {
      return NULL;
    }
    return $this->mysqlRaiseError($errno);
   }
   return DB_OK;
}
```

We already know that the method receives an array $arr by reference. It can also receive an optional parameter $rownum to request a specific row. If this is set, fetchInto() uses mysql_data_seek() to move the result set's pointer to the desired row:

```
if ($rownum !== null) {
  if (!@mysql_data_seek($result, $rownum)) {
    return null;
  }
}
```

The inner if() statement returns null if the requested row does not exist. Next, we fetch the row. The built-in function we use depends on the specified fetch mode:

```
if ($fetchmode & DB_FETCHMODE_ASSOC) {
  $arr = @mysql_fetch_array($result, MYSQL_ASSOC);
} else {
  $arr = @mysql_fetch_row($result);
}
```

All that is left now is to check for errors and respond appropriately. If $arr does not contain data, we need to call mysql_errno() to determine whether an error occurred (in which case a DB_Error should be returned), or whether there were simply no more rows to return (in which case fetchInto() returns Null):

```
if (!$arr) {
  $errno = @mysql_errno($this->connection);
    if (!$errno) {
      return NULL;
    }
    return $this->mysqlRaiseError($errno);
  }
  return DB_OK;
```

To demonstrate the necessity of separate implementation classes, let's compare DB_mysql::fetchInto() to its counterpart in the Oracle implementation class, DB_oci8::fetchInto():

```
/**
 * Fetch a row and insert the data into an existing array.
 *
 * @param $result oci8 result identifier
 * @param $arr (reference) array where data from the row is stored
 * @param $fetchmode how the array data should be indexed
 * @param $rownum the row number to fetch (not yet supported)
 *
 * @return int DB_OK on success, a DB error code on failure
 */
function fetchInto($result, &$arr, $fetchmode = DB_FETCHMODE_DEFAULT,
$rownum=NULL)
{
  if ($rownum !== NULL) {
    return $this->raiseError(DB_ERROR_NOT_CAPABLE);
  }
  if ($fetchmode & DB_FETCHMODE_ASSOC) {
    $moredata = @OCIFetchInto($result,$arr,
    OCI_ASSOC+OCI_RETURN_NULLS+OCI_RETURN_LOBS);
    if ($moredata && $this->options['optimize'] == 'portability') {
      $arr = array_change_key_case($arr, CASE_LOWER);
    }
  } else {
      $moredata = @OCIFetchInto($result,$arr,
      OCI_RETURN_NULLS+OCI_RETURN_LOBS);
  }
  if (!$moredata) {
    return NULL;
  }
  return DB_OK;
}
```

Or to the same method in the Informix implementation class:

```
/**
 * Fetch a row and return as array.
 *
 * @param $result Informix result identifier
 * @param $row (reference) array where data from the row is stored
 * @param $fetchmode how the resulting array should be indexed
 * @param $rownum the row number to fetch
 *
 * @return int an array on success, a DB error code on failure, NULL
 *   if there is no more data
 */
function fetchInto($result, &$row, $fetchmode, $rownum=null)
{
  if (($rownum !== null) && ($rownum < 0)) {
    return null;
  }
  // if $rownum is null, fetch row will return the next row
  if (!$row = @ifx_fetch_row($result, $rownum)) {
```

```
      return null;
   }
   if ($fetchmode !== DB_FETCHMODE_ASSOC) {
     $i=0;
     $order = array();
     foreach ($row as $key => $val) {
       $order[$i++] = $val;
     }
     $row = $order;
   }
   return DB_OK;
}
```

These methods differ so greatly because the built-in PHP API functions differ greatly across DBMSs.

The implementation classes also demonstrate one of the inherent qualities of PEAR::DB. Many developers often dismiss the idea of using PEAR::DB, concluding that they can build their own abstraction layers rather easily. So they build simple wrapper functions, for example a query() function which is a wrapper for pg_query(). Then, to migrate an application to Oracle, only the wrapper functions need to be changed. However, this could still mean significantly wasteful effort. While the application for the most part does not require any major changes, the abstraction layer itself practically has to be rewritten.

With PEAR::DB on the other hand, thanks to the sophistication of the implementation classes, migrating from one database to another is simply a matter of including the correct PEAR file and changing the phptype in the DSN from pgsql to oci8. If you correctly use only standard SQL and avoid proprietary database functions, your application would be highly portable.

The Future of PEAR::DB

Even with its widespread popularity and stellar design, PEAR::DB is surprisingly changing. The short-term changes include minor bug fixes and improvements, and some added functionality and new implementation classes. But it is the long-term plans for the abstraction layer that really deserve notice. PEAR::DB will someday give way to PEAR::MDB. Still under development at the time of this writing, MDB is a merger of DB and Metabases. For now, it suffices to know that Metabases provide a unified database API.

In addition to the now familiar functionality of DB such as query(), MDB will offer many specific database methods, such as createIndex() and alterTable() for data definition language operations. It will also sport advanced features that bridge the gap between relational databases and XML schemata. Its design is aimed to make it compatible with applications written for PEAR::DB. In fact, when the two projects finally merge, the resulting project will retain the name PEAR::DB. It is highly likely that the original PEAR::DB will also be supported for years to come, due to its large installed user base. For more information about PEAR::MDB, see the online documentation at http://pear.php.net.

PHP's improvements that will arrive with version 5 are likely to bring other changes to the code of PEAR::DB, although probably not to the way PEAR::DB is used in applications. For example, future versions of PEAR::DB may take advantage of PHP5's built-in Java-style exception handling, and all of PEAR may switch to the newly supported object destructors.

Summary

In this chapter we analyzed key portions of the PEAR::DB code to find out how it works. We introduced abstract classes in PEAR::DB, and a hierarchy of other class objects that produce the database objects, result set objects, and error objects. We saw individual implementation classes that handle DBMS-dependent tasks. Lastly, we saw some robust error handling done by PEAR::DB.

Overall, we got a feel of the internals of the implementation of PEAR::DB, and are definitely better aware of its constructs, that you would not only be seeing often elsewhere in the book, but should also be using in projects of your own.

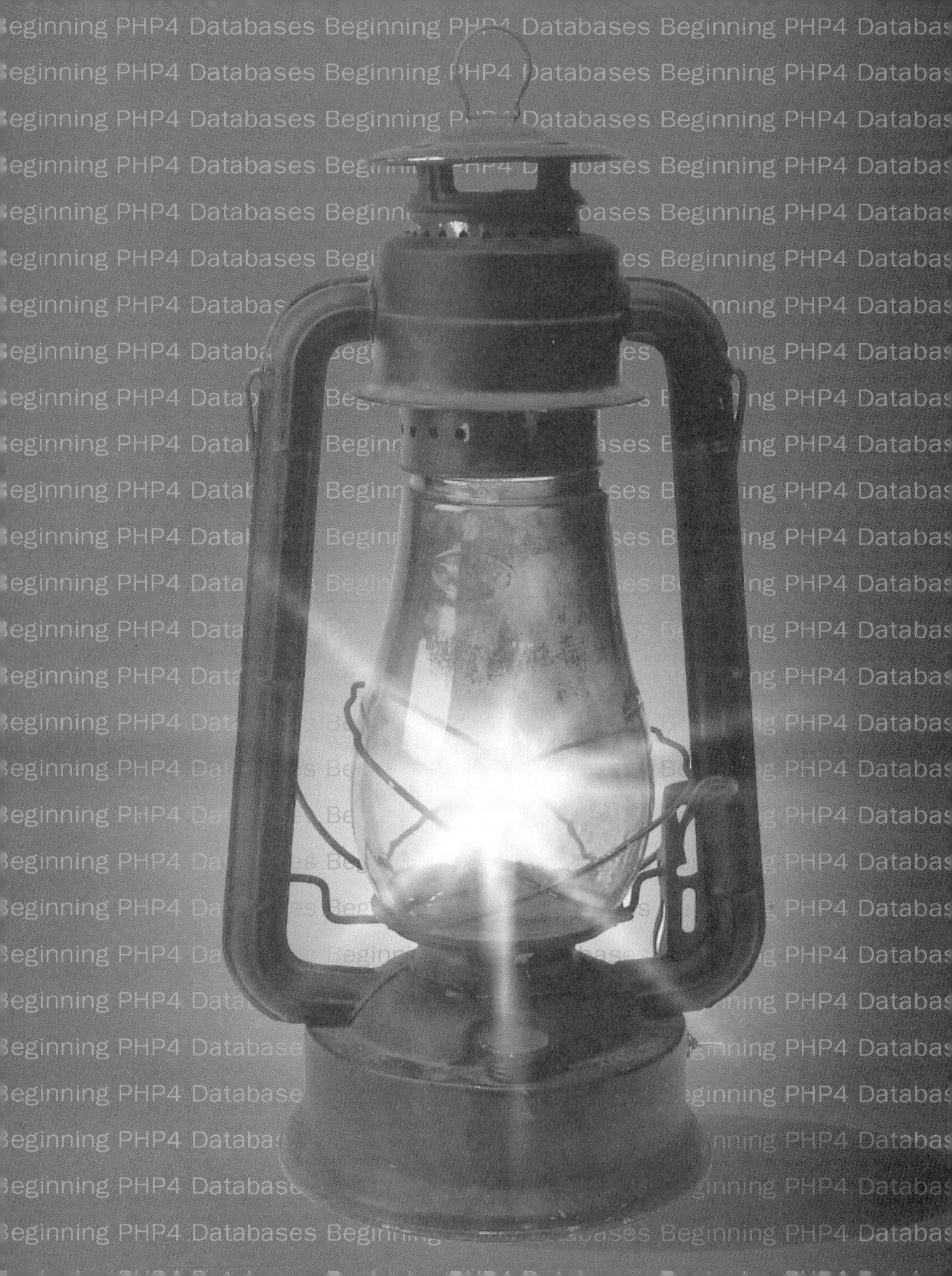
Beginning PHP4 Databases

Case Study: Using PEAR::DB – An Accounts Receivable Application

This book is focused on teaching you to understand databases, the SQL query language, and the functionality that the PHP language provides to help us interact with these databases. This is, of course, all the necessary knowledge for a PHP developer to possess. It is now, however, time to put a little of that knowledge into action. After all, writing useful applications is the end goal.

This chapter features a case study where we are going to build a simple accounts receivable application. It is going to have a database back end and we will use the built-in PEAR database access class (for more information on PEAR::DB refer to Chapter 9) to help us. Specifically in this chapter, we will:

- ❑ Define the program execution
- ❑ Design the application
- ❑ Code the application
- ❑ Review our work in detail

Along the way, we will also encounter and figure out several of the most common obstacles that we are likely run into with any database-driven application. This should give us a firm grounding for more advanced development in the future.

With any project, the first step is to define our goals, so let's do just that.

Basic Goals

Thinking about the project goals for an application is one of the most important, and often most overlooked, steps of development. But we will take some time here to think carefully about what we are trying to do as well as what we are *not* trying to do.

The first thing to understand is that we are not attempting to build a complete, production-grade accounting application. The purpose of this case study is not to write an online version of Quicken (an extremely popular accounting application for Microsoft Windows) in PHP. What we are trying to do is go through a well-defined development process for a very simple accounts receivable application that will expose us to some of the real-world issues we will face in development.

As we progress, we will point out places where we might act differently in a larger and/or production-level environment. Likewise, we will also make note of the spots where we are making deliberate simplifications to help ensure clarity of the example.

Now, with that in mind, we will start off by doing nothing more complicated than drawing up a high-level list of things that we want to accomplish.

Simplicity

Remember that this is to be only an accounts receivable application. We will not concern ourselves with bank account balances, bills, employee wages, taxes, or any other issues that one might see in a fully fledged accounting program.

We are doing an exercise in this chapter, so the most important thing for us is to understand the process.

Ease of Use

We want the user to be able to see the most important pieces of information very quickly. Also, the user should be able to navigate around the application quickly and efficiently.

The user interface is often an overlooked part of the development process, especially when developers are the people chiefly involved. We should always remember that no matter how well-programmed our application is, nobody will ever want to use it if it looks bad, or if it has a poor user interface.

Database Back End

For the application in this chapter, the data will be stored in a MySQL database. There are many database options to choose from. MySQL is an excellent choice for this application for several reasons. It is freely and widely available, the client is built into PHP automatically, and it is very fast.

Although we will use MySQL here, it should not be very difficult to move this application to a different database if desired.

Use of PEAR:DB

We will handle all database access for the application using PHP's PEAR libraries for unified database interaction. This is, after all, a book on PHP and databases, and the PEAR database classes are increasingly the way things are handled in the real world.

This pretty much covers our goals. In a nutshell, we want a simple application to create and track invoices. It needs to be easy-to-use, and we want to use PHP, MySQL, and PEAR to get the job done.

Supported Functionality

Now, we should make a list of the functionality that we intend to include. A simple list is all that's needed, but it is always nice to have this kind of list in one place so we can refer to it easily. We will build in ability to:

❑ Create invoices

❑ See a quick overview of outstanding invoices

❑ See a quick overview of paid invoices

❑ See a quick review of overdue invoices

❑ See a detailed review of any given invoice, paid or not

Defining Program Execution

The next step is to define how our program will actually run once it is completed. You can think of this part of the process as a refinement of the *Basic Goals* section. Here, we will think about how we are going to meet our goals with a little more detail involved.

Typically, a good way to start this process is to represent our application in a diagram. This can be done with standard technologies such as UML, which is a sophisticated way of pre-planning your application's execution. However, that's probably overkill for this application. The diagram shown in the section below will suffice.

Application Overview

With an accounts receivable application such as this one, there are essentially two different functions that we can do. The first is creating an invoice, and the second is reviewing invoices. Anything else we do is basically embellishing one of these two functions. The diagram given below outlines how our application will work:

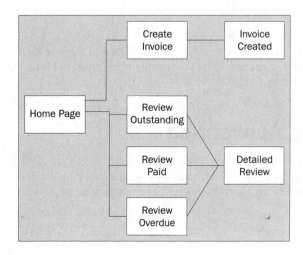

Accordingly, there are two main branches from our homepage. The top one shows a path to a page that will let us create a new invoice. This could be a form on a web page that we fill in. When we submit it, we go to a confirmation page, which shows us what we have entered.

The second branch is for reviewing invoices that we've created. Here, there are three different options relating to outstanding, paid, and overdue invoices. Each of these screens will show a number of the invoice summaries for invoices in the appropriate categories. From each of these screens, the user will be able to see a full description of any given invoice on the final screen.

Storing and Retrieving SQL Data

At this point, we may wonder why there are three choices for reviewing invoices, whereas there was only one choice for creating a new invoice. The answer to this question is twofold.

To begin with, we're not giving our user the ability to create different kinds of invoices. Creating an invoice does just that. However, the user may very well be interested in looking at the invoices he or she has made in different ways. This brings us to the second issue. One of the golden truths of web-based database application development is:

It is generally harder to get information into your database than it is to display it once you have it.

Now, granted, it is usually not all that troublesome to get your data stored, but it is a more complicated process than getting the data out once you have it. To explain further, just look at the syntax definition for INSERT statements, and compare it to the definition for SELECT statements. A SELECT query has many more options that allow us to easily see the data we are looking for and to retrieve it in an ordered fashion. Essentially, we have a lot of options when we are getting data out that will allow us to get just what we want in a format that is convenient.

Conversely, when putting data into a database system, we have to consider a few things. The first and foremost thing is making sure that the design of the database itself is sound. This can be difficult especially as the complexity of the application grows because you will be confronted with a wide array of possibilities. Another problem that we have to keep in mind is the issue of data consistency, which was covered in Chapter 6. This can be a time-consuming part of the process, but is vital in creating robust applications.

As a result, we need to take care when putting data into the database, but we have lots of options that are easy to exercise when looking at that data. This is reflected in our overview, and matches up nicely with the needs of the user. Creating an invoice is only done once, but it can be looked at in several different ways depending on what the user needs.

Designing the Application

We need to spend a little time thinking about how we are going to structure the different parts of our application. It's very important to have a clear idea of how everything will fit together before we start. This can help us to identify problems before we've already written a bunch of code.

3-Tier Approach

Our application will use a classic 3-tier approach. If you haven't encountered this term, or if you have but didn't know what it meant, have no fear. It is a fancy name for a fairly simple concept.

The basic idea is to logically split the application into three different parts: the database layer, the application code (often called the business layer), and the presentation layer as shown in the diagram below:

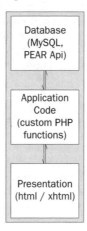

Database Layer

The database layer of an application is where the stored data resides. Also included here is the API that we can use to retrieve or manipulate that data. It is conceptually very simple. It houses data that may be expanded, modified, or deleted by code in our application code layer depending on the application's purpose. It does not store any information about what the data will look like when it's presented. Simply put, it's structured SQL data, along with the functionality needed to see it.

Application Code Layer

This part of the application is all the PHP code that we write. This will probably involve functions that we create or that we can make use of. This code will interact with both the Database layer and the Presentation layer. It will be responsible for getting data from the database, and also for getting that data onto a computer screen or to another computer.

Presentation Layer

This is the part of the application that the end user will actually see. In this case, it consists of the HTML or XHTML that gets sent to the browser. Naturally, this output will include dynamic elements that are fetched from the database by the Application Code layer.

Putting It Together

So how do these three layers come together to make a full application? Ideally, we'd like to keep them as separate as possible. This means that any modifications we make will affect the application globally, which is typically what you want. For example, if you change someone's name in a database, you want that change to be reflected immediately from anywhere in the application.

In practice, of course, it's impossible to completely separate PHP code from the web pages that make up our application. At a minimum, you'll need to use something like the `require_once()` language construct to include your classes and/or functions, and some `echo()` or `print()` statements to put dynamic content onto the page.

Generally, for large applications, it's best to keep everything as separate as possible since it makes maintenance easier. However, for smaller applications such as the one we are about to create, it tends to be overkill, and can actually make finding what you need to work on harder than it's worth. Therefore, we will adopt the following strategy. All of our functions and constants will be stored in one external file. However, any SQL that we use on a particular page will be defined on that page. This will work out well, since each page of our application does a specific job, so having the SQL statements embedded into the page in question will let us see what's going on clearly.

Database Schema

Now that we understand what our approach is, and we have an overview to follow, we can get on to some actual work. The first thing to do is define a database schema.

The database we're interested in is going to contain information about invoices. And when we create an invoice, we are of course billing someone. So it makes sense that we should have two tables, one for invoices and one for clients. We will need a third table also, that will simply be a lookup table that links a client to a particular invoice.

Let's examine the fields we'll choose to collect in our `invoices` table:

Column Name	Function
invoice_id	A unique ID for each invoice that will serve as a primary key for the table
description_short	A short string that will hold a quick description of the job we are billing for
description_full	A longer description that describes the job in full detail
amount_due	The amount we are owed
invoice_paid	A Boolean switch that will simply indicate whether or not the client has paid their bill
date_due	A date-time field that will indicate when the client is delinquent if they haven't yet paid
date_posted	A date-time field that will indicate when the invoice was added to the database

This should provide us with the information needed to see how much money we are owed, and how much we have been paid. Next is our `clients` table:

Column Name	Function
client_firstname	A short string that holds the client's first name
client_lastname	A short string that holds the client's last name
client_street	A short string with the street address for the client
client_city	A short string that holds the client's city
client_state	A short string that holds the client's state
client_zip	A short string that holds the client's Zip code
client_phone	A short string that holds the client's phone number

Obviously, the above table is set up to contain addresses and phone numbers the way that they are used in the United States. If you're not in the US, then please just play along, since it's the idea that we're trying to push here. It should be easy to modify this table to better suit your own locale if you wish.

Finally, there is our very simple lookup table that we will need to determine which invoices are attached to specific clients. It only contains two fields, the client and invoice IDs:

Column Name	Function
client_id	An integer corresponding to a specific client ID
invoice_id	An integer corresponding to an invoice linked to the client ID on the same row

The following SQL statements will create the appropriate tables for us. We're going to assume that the name of the database is billing but it should be easy for you to adjust this to your setup if need be:

```
CREATE TABLE invoices
(
    invoice_id int(11) NOT NULL auto_increment,
    description_short varchar(255) NOT NULL default '',
    description_full text NOT NULL,
    amount_due float NOT NULL default '0',
    invoice_paid tinyint(4) NOT NULL default '0',
    date_due datetime NOT NULL default '0000-00-00 00:00:00',
    date_posted datetime NOT NULL default '0000-00-00 00:00:00',
    PRIMARY KEY (invoice_id)
)
TYPE=MyISAM;

CREATE TABLE clients
(
    client_id int(11) NOT NULL auto_increment,
    client_firstname varchar(255) NOT NULL default '',
    client_lastname varchar(255) NOT NULL default '',
```

```
    client_street varchar(255) NOT NULL default '',
   ·client_city varchar(255) NOT NULL default '',
    client_state char(2) NOT NULL default '',
    client_zip varchar(10) NOT NULL default '',
    client_phone varchar(12) NOT NULL default '',
    PRIMARY KEY  (client_id)
)
TYPE=MyISAM;

CREATE TABLE client_invoices
(
    client_id int(11) NOT NULL default '0',
    invoice_id int(11) NOT NULL default '0'
)
TYPE=MyISAM;
```

Run the above SQL statements to create the table `invoices` in the database for us to use. If you put the above into a file called `billing.mysql`, then the following command-line action will create the tables on the `billing` database for you:

```
$ mysql -uusername -ppassword billing < billing.mysql
```

where `username` and `password` are your system-specific values.

> *If you haven't already discovered it, there's an excellent web-based administration tool for MySQL called phpMyAdmin. It's available for free at http://phpmyadmin.sourceforge.net/ and is highly recommended.*

Files and Uses

Now that we have our `invoices` table set up, we're almost ready to begin coding the application. Before we jump into that, let's look over a list of all the files that will make up our application and what they will do:

File	Use
`billing.css`	This file will contain CSS code that will be used on all of the web pages to define the presentation.
`billing_includes.php`	All of the functions and global variables used by the application will go into this file, which will be included on all of the pages.
`index.php`	The home page for the application. It will have links for creating and reviewing invoices, and will present some quick overview information.
`new_invoice.php`	This page will allow us to create a new invoice via a web form. When the form is submitted, it will verify that the data entered looks appropriate and either put the data into the database or generate an error message depending on what it finds.

File	Use
Invoice_review.php	Here, the user will be able to see a summary of invoices. The page will have different "modes" depending on what kind of invoice the user wishes to view.
Invoice_review_detail.php	This file allows the user to see the full data for an invoice, and to set an invoice as paid if desired.

You may want to refer back to this table as we go along, as we will be jumping back and forth between files to some extent. You should create a directory called Accounting under your web server root directory, and put all of these files there. Also, make sure that the DB class files must be in your include_path, since we'll be including them as well.

Coding the Application

We have planned everything out carefully, so now it's time to begin actually writing the application. We will start by creating some of the presentation elements.

Defining the Presentation with CSS

We shall start with the billing.css file that was mentioned in the table of files earlier. We will first define some attributes for the body, td, a, and input elements:

```
body, td {
  background: #ffffff;
  font: 0.8em verdana, helvetica, arial, sans-serif;
  color: #454545;
  line-height: 1.5em;
  margin: 0px 0px 0px 0px;
}

a {
  color: #cc0033;
  text-decoration: none;
}

a:hover {
  text-decoration: underline;
}

a:active {
  color: 4545aa;
}

input {
  font: 0.8em verdana, helvetica, arial, sans-serif;
  color: #333333;
```

```
    background-color: #d3d3dd;
    border-style: solid;
    border-width: 1px;
    border-color: #333333;
    padding: 2px;
}

input[type="submit"] {
    color: #666666;
    margin: 1px;
    border: 1px solid #333333;
}

input[type="submit"]:hover {
    color: #333333;
    margin: 1px;
    border: 1px solid #333333;
}
```

Next, we will create some css classes that will make sure our forms look consistent:

```
.textarea {
    font: 0.8em verdana, helvetica, arial, sans-serif;
    color: #333333;
    background-color: #d3d3dd;
    border-style: solid;
    border-width: 1px;
    border-color: #333333;
    padding: 2px;
}

.dateselect {
    font: 9px verdana, arial, sans-serif;
    color: #333333;
    background-color: #d3d3dd;
    border: 1px #333333;
}
```

Finally, we will define some elements and classes that will define the layout on the home page and subsequent pages:

```
/**** now some actual page elements ****/

#pageheader {
    margin-left: 50px;
    margin-top: 60px;
    border: 2px solid #222222;
    padding: 8px;
    font: 1.8em verdana, helvetica, arial, sans-serif;
    color: #444444;
    width: 600px;
```

```
    }

#pageheader a {
  text-decoration: none;
  color: inherit;
}

#pageheader a:hover {
  text-decoration: underline;
}

#pagecontent {
  margin-top: 15px;
  margin-left: 50px;
  border: 2px solid #222222;
  padding: 8px;
  width: 600px;
}

.sectionheading {
  border-bottom: 1px dashed #aaaaaa;
  width: 100%;
  margin: 0px 0px 3px 0px;
}

.darker {
  padding: 3px;
  background: #dedede;
}

.lighter {
  padding: 3px;
  background: #eeeeee;
}
```

This book is about PHP programming, not CSS. So we're not going to go into detail and explain what this file does. If you want to learn more about CSS there are many excellent books available, and the specifications are available for free download from the W3C site (http://www.w3.org/Style/CSS/). Suffice to say that this stylesheet defines the look and feel of our web pages.

The Home Page

Next, let's code up the home page. Create the file index.php and save it in the Accounting directory. The following code goes into it:

```
<html>
  <head>

    <title>Billing System</title>

    <style type="text/css">
```

```
      @import url(billing.css);
    </style>

</head>
<body>

  <div id="pageheader">
    <a href="index.php">Billing System</a> :: Main
  </div><!-- end div pageheader -->

  <div id="pagecontent">

  <div class="sectionheading">
    Select Operation
  </div><!-- end div with class sectionheading -->

  <div class="darker">
    <a href="new_invoice.php">&gt;&gt; New Invoice</a>
  </div><!-- end darker div -->

  <div class="lighter">
    <a href="invoice_review.php?type=outstanding">&gt;&gt; Outstanding
      Invoices</a>
  </div><!-- end lighter div -->

  <div class="darker">
    <a href="invoice_review.php?type=paid">&gt;&gt; Paid Invoices</a>
  </div><!-- end darker div -->

  <div class="lighter">
    <a href="invoice_review.php?type=overdue">&gt;&gt; Overdue
      Invoices</a>
  </div><!-- end lighter div -->

  <br>

  <div class="sectionheading">
    Quick Summary
  </div>

  <div class="darker">
    Total Oustanding Invoices:
  </div>

  <div class="lighter">
    Total Uncollected Funds:
  </div>

  </div><!-- end div pagecontent -->

</body>
</html>
```

As we can see, there's not yet any PHP code on this page. We'll add that later as we go along. For the time being, we want to make sure that the home page looks like it's supposed to. Getting that task out of the way now will mean that we don't have to worry about it later when working with more important things like the PHP code. Note that we imported our `billing.css` file, which makes the HTML needed for this page very simple. If everything is correct, then viewing this page in a browser will look as follows:

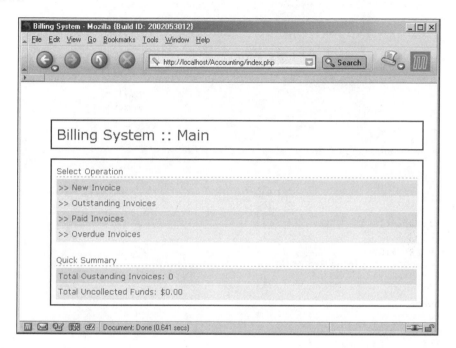

Creating an Invoice

Next, we'll move on to the `new_invoice.php` page, which again goes into the `Accounting` directory. This will be the most tedious page to complete coding in our application. The reason being the golden rule of database programming mentioned earlier. Creating an invoice ultimately involves putting data into the database. This is a harder task than getting the data out later.

Let's pause to think about the logical flow for this page. When the user first gets here, they will be presented with a form containing the invoice information to fill out and submit. Then, the page needs to check this data to make sure it's appropriate (for more information on why this is needed, read Chapter 6 on *Data Consistency*). If there are any errors in the data entered, the page should tell the user what the problem was and *not* enter the data into the database. If there were no problems, then the data goes into the database and the user should be able to see what they've entered:

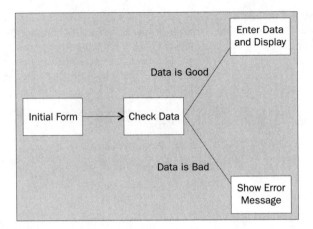

Start out with the following in the `new_invoice.php` file:

```
<html>
  <head>

    <title>Billing System</title>

    <style type="text/css">
      @import url(billing.css);
    </style>

  </head>
  <body>

    <div id="pageheader">
      <a href="index.php">Billing System</a> :: New Invoice
    </div><!-- end div pageheader -->

    <div id="pagecontent">
```

Include a conditional here. This says, "if we didn't just submit a form, show the following." The following, of course, will be the `<form>`. And in here we'll see the hidden variable that we check for in this conditional:

```
    <?php if ( $_POST["form_submitted"] != 1 ) { ?>
    <div class="sectionheading">
      Enter Invoice Information
    </div><!-- end div with class sectionheading -->

    <form name="newinvoice" action="<?php echo $_SERVER["PHP_SELF"]; ?>"
method="post">
      <input type="hidden" name="form_submitted" value="1">

      <table border="0" width="500">
```

```
         <tr>
           <td width="200">Client First Name:</td>
           <td width="300"><input type="text" size="40"
name="client_first_name"></td>
         </tr>
         <tr>
           <td width="200">Client Last Name:</td>
           <td width="300"><input type="text" size="40"
name="client_last_name"></td>
         </tr>
         <tr>
           <td>Client Street Address:</td>
           <td><input type="text" size="40" name="street_address"></td>
         </tr>
         <tr>
           <td>Client City:</td>
           <td><input type="text" size="40" name="city"></td>
         </tr>
         <tr>
           <td>Client State:</td>
           <td><input type="text" size="2" maxlength="2" name="state"></td>
         </tr>
         <tr>
           <td width="200">Client Zipcode:</td>
           <td width="300"><input type="text" size="10" maxlength="10"
name="zipcode"></td>
         </tr>
         <tr>
           <td width="200">Client Phone:</td>
           <td width="300"><input type="text" size="3" maxlength="3"
name="ph_area">
               <input type="text" size="3" maxlength="3" name="ph_pre"> -
               <input type="text" size="4" maxlength="4" name="ph_end"></td>
         </tr>
         <tr>
           <td width="200">Short Job Description:</td>
           <td width="300"><input type="text" size="40"
name="short_description"></td>
         </tr>
         <tr>
           <td width="200">Full Job Description:</td>
           <td width="300">
               <textarea name="full_description" rows="6" cols="40"
class="textarea"></textarea></td>
         </tr>
         <tr>
           <td width="200">Amount Due:</td>
           <td width="300"><input type="text" size="40" name="amount_due"></td>
         </tr>
```

The next few elements are select boxes to let the user enter a date. Since it's a pain to have to write out all of those option elements, we'll get PHP to help us out a little bit:

```
        <tr>
          <td width="200">Date Due (mm/dd/yyyy):</td>
          <td width="300">
            <select class="dateselect" name="month">
            </select> -
<?php
for( $i=1 ; $i <= 12 ; ++$i ) {
  echo "          <option value=\"" . sprintf("%02d" , $i) . "\">" . sprintf("%02d"
, $i) . "</option>\n";
}
?>
            <select class="dateselect" name="day">
<?php
for( $i=1 ; $i <= 31 ; ++$i ) {
  echo "          <option value=\"" . sprintf("%02d" , $i) . "\">" . sprintf("%02d"
, $i) . "</option>\n";
}
?>
            </select> -

            <select class="dateselect" name="year">
              <option value="<?php echo date("Y"); ?>"><?php echo date("Y");
?></option>
              <option value="<?php echo (date("Y") + 1); ?>"><?php echo (date("Y")
+ 1); ?></option>
              <option value="<?php echo (date("Y") + 2); ?>"><?php echo (date("Y")
+ 2); ?></option>
            </select>
          </td>
        </tr>
        <tr>
          <td> </td>
          <td><input type="submit" value="create invoice"></td>
        </tr>
      </table>
    </form>
```

We're assuming here that we won't set a bill to be due for more than two years away.

Now, we'll continue the conditional that we started just before the form. This means that we're at the stage where the form has just been submitted. One of two things has therefore happened: the data was good or it wasn't. Let's cover the case where there was a problem first:

```
<?php } elseif ( 0 != strcmp($err , "") ) { ?>

<?php echo $err; ?>
```

Here, $err is a variable that we haven't defined yet (but we will). If it's not empty, then that means there was some error, so we print out the $err variable which we will later set to be a useful error message.

Finally, let's look at the conditional case where the data was OK:

```php
<?php } else { ?>

<div class="sectionheading">
  The following invoice has been added to the database.
</div>

<table border="0">
  <tr>
    <td valign="top" class="darker" width="200">Client:</td>
    <td class="darker" width="300">
<?php
  echo $_POST["client_name"] . "<br />" .
  $_POST["street_address"] . "<br />" .
  $_POST["city"] . ", " . $_POST["state"] . " " . $_POST["zip"] . "<br />" .
  $_POST["ph_area"] . "-" . $_POST["ph_pre"] . "-" . $_POST["ph_end"];
?>
    </td>
  </tr>
  <tr>
    <td valign="top" class="lighter" width="200">Short Description:</td>
    <td class="lighter" width="300"><?php echo
smart_strip_slashes($_POST["short_description"]); ?></td>
  </tr>
   <tr>
    <td valign="top" class="darker" width="200">Full Description:</td>
    <td class="darker" width="300"><?php echo
smart_strip_slashes($_POST["full_description"]); ?></td>
  </tr>
  <tr>
    <td valign="top" class="lighter" width="200">Amount Due:</td>
    <td class="lighter" width="300">$<?php echo
number_format($_POST["amount_due"], 2); ?></td>
  </tr><tr>
    <td valign="top" class="darker" width="200">Date Due:</td>
    <td class="darker" width="300"><?php echo $_POST["month"] . "-" .
      $_POST["day"] . "-" . $_POST["year"]; ?></td>
  </tr>
</table>
<br />
<a href="<?php echo $_SERVER["PHP_SELF"]; ?>">Create another invoice</a>.

<?php } ?>
</div><!-- end div pagecontent -->

</body>
</html>
```

Now that we're through that, there are a few things that we should pause and take note of. First, you'll note that all along we've been making use of the super global arrays such as $_SERVER and $_POST that were recently introduced in newer versions of PHP. These were created to compensate for the decision of the PHP team to turn the php.ini register_globals setting to Off for security reasons. We should always use these arrays when accessing GET or POST data, or any available environment or server variables.

Next, we'll see the function `smart_strip_slashes()` being used in the last section of our big conditional. This is a function that we'll create just a little later; so don't worry about it for now. Basically, it will check to see if the PHP "magic quotes" feature is enabled which can cause headaches with slashes being inserted before quotes, and it will act accordingly.

You should be able to look at the page at this point to see what our layout looks like. In Mozilla 1.0, it looks like this:

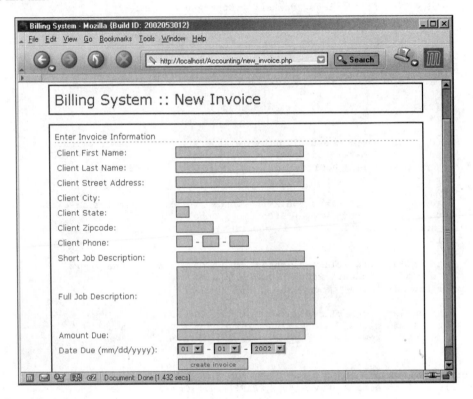

Checking the Data

Unfortunately, we're now at one of the most repetitive parts of the development. We have to examine all of the data entered into the form before we can put it into the database. This is typically not very interesting to do, which is why it often doesn't get done or gets done poorly.

Programmers are typically more interested in things like optimizing or adding new features than they are in checking over data. However, this is one of the most critical parts of the developer's job, so don't fall into that trap. If you fail to check the data properly, then you are at best inviting data which could affect your data consistency. This means that things might go into the database that have no business being there. At worse, you could potentially be opening up your application to security risks.

We will begin by putting the following PHP code at the very top of our `new_invoice.php` file, before any of the HTML:

```php
<?php
require_once("DB.php");
require_once("billing_includes.php");

// a variable to hold any error messages if the user
// didn't put things in correctly
$err = "";

?>
```

Here, we are including the PEAR database classes, and our `billing_includes.php` file. Then, we declare a variable called `$err` that will hold any error messages.

The basic strategy here is to create a set of functions that will check all the data entered into the form. These functions will return nothing (void) if the data is OK. If not, they will each return a message specific to the field that was being checked. This message will be appended to the `$err` variable which will later be checked and printed out if needed. All of the functions will live in our `billing_includes.php` file.

With this in mind, let's open up `billing_includes.php` and start creating our functions. Many of these are very similar, but we do our best to make reasonable checks wherever we can.

The function `check_client_name()` looks to make sure that the user entered a value for the client name:

```php
// {{{ check_client_name()

/**
 * Make sure the user put something in for the client name
 *
 * @access public
 * @return string if name is bad, void otherwise
 */
function check_client_name() {
  if( strlen(trim($_POST["client_name"])) == 0 ) {
    return "You must enter a Client Name.<br />\n";
  }
}

// }}}
```

You may notice the triple curly braces that are commented out around the function. These are here in case your text editor uses them for folding as many modern editors do. Folding just means that you can collapse and expand parts of your code which can make reading through things easier.

The function `check_client_street()` looks to make sure that the user put some data in for the client street address. Since this value can't be `Null` in the database, we have to make sure that the user entered something:

```php
// {{{ check_client_street()

/**
```

```
 * Make sure the user put something in for the client street
 *
 * @access public
 * @return string if street is bad, void otherwise
 */
function check_client_street() {
  if( strlen(trim($_POST["street_address"])) == 0 ) {
    return "You must enter a Client Street Address.<br />\n";
  }
}

// }}}
```

The function `check_client_city()` looks to make sure that the user entered a value for the client city:

```
// {{{ check_client_city()

/**
 * Make sure the user put something in for the client city
 *
 * @access public
 * @return string if city is bad, void otherwise
 */
function check_client_city() {
  if( strlen(trim($_POST["city"])) == 0 ) {
    return "You must enter a Client City.<br />\n";
  }
}

// }}}
```

The function `check_client_state()` makes sure that the user put in exactly two characters. Note that since we're able to make a more detailed check here, we do so using Perl-style regular expressions (if you are not familiar with these, you can find more information at http://www.php.net/manual/en/ref.pcre.php):

```
// {{{ check_client_state()

/**
 * Make sure the user put something in for the client state
 *
 * @access public
 * @return string if state is bad, void otherwise
 */
function check_client_state() {
  if( preg_match("/^[a-zA-Z]{2}$/" , $_POST["state"]) == 0 ) {
    return "You must enter a valid Client State.<br />\n";
  }
}

// }}}
```

The function `check_client_zip()` is similar to `check_client_state()`. It uses regular expressions to make sure that the zip code looks like XXXXX or XXXXX-XXXX where X is a decimal digit, since these are the two acceptable versions of Zip codes in the US:

```
// {{{ check_client_zip()

/**
 * Make sure the user put something in for the client Zip
 *
 * @access public
 * @return string if Zip is bad, void otherwise
 */
function check_client_zip() {
  if( preg_match("/^[0-9]{5}$|^[0-9]{5}-[0-9]{4}$/" , $_POST["zipcode"]) == 0 )
  {
    return "You must enter a valid Client Zipcode.<br />\n";
  }
}

// }}}
```

The function `check_client_phone()` looks to make sure that the user entered a total of ten digits for the phone number. Keep in mind that we're looking at US-style phone numbers, but it's fairly easy to change this to a different locale:

```
// {{{ check_client_phone()

/**
 * Make sure the user put something correct in for the client phone
 *
 * @access public
 * @return string if number is bad, void otherwise
 */
function check_client_phone() {
  $number = $_POST["ph_area"] . $_POST["ph_pre"] . $_POST["ph_end"];
  if( preg_match("/[0-9]{10}/" , $number) == 0) {
    return "You must enter a valid Client Phone Number.<br />\n";
  }
}

// }}}
```

The functions `check_short_description()` and `check_full_description()` just look to make sure that the user entered something in the respective fields:

```
// {{{ check_short_description()

/**
 * Make sure the user put something in for the short description
 *
 * @access public
```

```
 * @return string if description is bad, void otherwise
 */
function check_short_description() {
  if( strlen(trim($_POST["short_description"])) == 0 ) {
    return "You must enter a short job description.<br />\n";
  }
}

// }}}

// {{{ check_full_description()

/**
 * Make sure the user put something in for the short description
 *
 * @access public
 * @return string if description is bad, void otherwise
 */
function check_full_description() {
  if( strlen(trim($_POST["full_description"])) == 0 ) {
    return "You must enter a full job description.<br />\n";
  }
}

// }}}
```

The function check_amount_due() looks at the value submitted and attempts to extract a number from whatever it was. The number can be either an integer or a float that looks like 100.00, with two decimal places. So, for example, the user could type in "This client owes us $1500.00 dollars" and this function would correctly extract 1500.00 as the value to go into the database:

```
// {{{ check_amount_due()

/**
 * Make sure the user put something in for the amount due
 *
 * @access public
 * @return string if amount is bad, void otherwise
 */
function check_amount_due() {
  $amount = preg_match("/([0-9]+\.[0-9]{2})|([0-9]+)\b/" , $_POST["amount_due"] ,
$match);
  if( 0 == $amount ) {
    return "You must enter an amount due.<br />\n";
  } else { // make sure $_POST["amount_due"] is a float
    $_POST["amount_due"] = $match[0];
  }
}

// }}}
```

The function check_date_due() looks at the date entered and makes sure that it's after the current date, since we wouldn't want to try and make our clients pay earlier than the invoice was created:

```
// {{{ check_date_due()

/**
 * Make sure the user put something correct in for the date due
 *
 * @access public
 * @return string if date is bad, void otherwise
 */
function check_date_due() {
  //print (int) $_POST["month"];
  if( mktime( 0, 0, 0, (int) $_POST["month"] , (int) $_POST["day"] , (int)
    $_POST["year"] ) < time() ) {
    return "You must enter a date later than the current date.";
  }
}

// }}}
```

While we're in here, let's go ahead and write the smart_strip_slashes()function. We create this function to get around problems caused by the php.ini setting for magic_quotes_gpc. This is often a problem, because different setups have this set to different values, which can cause escaped quotes such as \ to show up where we don't want them. This function checks to see if magic_quotes_gpc is enabled, and strips slashes if necessary based on the result:

```
// {{{ smart_strip_slashes()

/**
 * Strip slashes intelligently
 *
 * @param $s the string to be (possibly) stripped
 *
 * @access public
 * @return string
 */
function smart_strip_slashes($s) {
  if( 1 == get_magic_quotes_gpc() ) {
    return stripslashes($s);
  }
  else {
    return $s;
  }
}

// }}}
```

Setting the $err Variable

Now that we've completed the tedious task of creating functions to verify our data, we can set the $err variable with their output. The following code goes in the new_invoice.php file just below where we declared the $err variable:

```
// set our error variable
$err .= check_client_first_name();
$err .= check_client_last_name();
$err .= check_client_street();
$err .= check_client_city();
$err .= check_client_state();
$err .= check_client_zip();
$err .= check_client_phone();
$err .= check_short_description();
$err .= check_full_description();
$err .= check_amount_due();
$err .= check_date_due();
```

As you can see, we're just calling each of the functions in turn and appending any output to the $err variable. Then, later in the page, we know if any errors occurred because if they did, the $err variable will have a length greater than zero. Furthermore, we can simply then print out $err to show the user what they did wrong.

With all this in place, if we hit the **create invoice** button and leave the form completely blank, we'll get the following result in the browser:

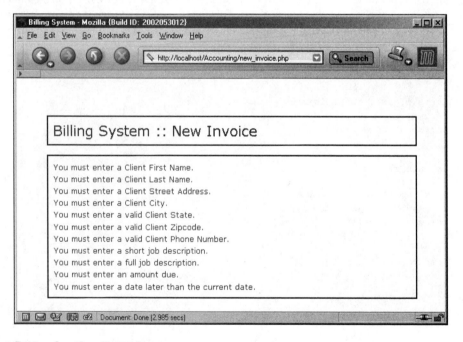

Putting Data in the Database

The final part of the invoice creation process is to put the data into the database. We'll start by putting the following code at the top of billing_includes.php. This defines some global variables that we'll need for the PEAR connection:

```
// global database variables
$dbname = "billing";
$dbhost = "localhost";
$dbuser = "username";
$dbpass = "password";
$dbtype = "mysql";

$dsn = "$dbtype://$dbuser:$dbpass@$dbhost/$dbname";
```

Obviously, you may need to change some of these variables, specifically the username and password, to suit your system.

Next, go back to the new_invoice.php file and start by creating a database connection. One nice feature of having our $err variable set is that we don't bother making a database connection, which can be resource intensive, unless we think all the data is correct and ready to be inserted. The following code goes just below where we set the $err variable:

```
// assuming that there are no errors, go ahead with SQL
if( 0 == strcmp($err , "") ) {
  // instantiate database object
  $db = DB::connect($dsn);
  if( DB::isError($db) ) {
    die ($db->getMessage());
  }
```

Next, we'll use our smart_strip_slashes() function on all of our $_POST variables to make sure everything is ready to go into MySQL:

```
// let's fix any annoying slash problems
foreach( $_POST as $k => $v ) {
  $_POST[$k] = smart_strip_slashes($_POST[$k]);
}
```

Next, we'll make liberal use of the $db object's quote() method to create variables that are ready to go into the database:

```
$client_first_name = $db->quote($_POST["client_first_name"]);
$client_last_name = $db->quote($_POST["client_last_name"]);
$client_street = $db->quote($_POST["street_address"]);
$client_city = $db->quote($_POST["city"]);
$client_state = $db->quote($_POST["state"]);
$client_zip = $db->quote($_POST["zipcode"]);
$client_phone = $db->quote($_POST["ph_area"] . "-" . $_POST["ph_pre"] .
"-" . $_POST["ph_end"]);
$short_description = $db->quote($_POST["short_description"]);
$full_description = $db->quote($_POST["full_description"]);
$amount_due = $db->quote($_POST["amount_due"]);
$date_due = $_POST["year"] . $_POST["month"] . $_POST["day"];
```

With these, we'll build our first SQL statement which will serve to put data into the `client` table in our database:

```
// first, enter the client information
$sql = "INSERT INTO clients client_firstname , client_lastname ,
client_street , client_city ,client_state , client_zip , client_phone )
        VALUES ($client_first_name , $client_last_name , $client_street ,
$client_city ,$client_state , $client_zip , $client_phone )";
```

Now, we'll execute the statement, and use the PEAR built-in error handling to check for any problems:

```
$result = $db->query($sql);
if( DB::isError($result) ) {
  die ($result->getMessage());
}
}
```

We need to grab the client ID that we just created so that we can store it later in our `client_invoices` lookup table. MySQL happens to make this very easy to do since it provides us with a `LAST_INSERT_ID()` function that will get us just what we need:

```
// get the client ID that we just created
$sql = "SELECT LAST_INSERT_ID() FROM clients";
$client_id = $db->getOne($sql);
if( DB::isError($client_id) ) {
  die ($client_id->getMessage());
}
```

Next, we will put the invoice information into our `invoices` table. This is analogous to what we did with the client data:

```
// next, enter invoice information
$sql = "INSERT INTO invoices (description_short , description_full ,
amount_due , invoice_paid , date_due , date_posted )
        VALUES ($short_description , $full_description , $amount_due ,
'0' , $date_due , NOW())";
$result = $db->query($sql);
if( DB::isError($result) ) {
  die ($result->getMessage());
}
```

Now we need the invoice ID for the same reason that we needed the client ID before, and we get it in the same way:

```
// get the invoice ID we just created
$sql = "SELECT LAST_INSERT_ID() FROM invoices";
$invoice_id = $db->getOne($sql);
if( DB::isError($invoice_id) ) {
  die ($invoice_id->getMessage());
}
```

Finally, we'll put the IDs that we've collected into our `client_invoices` table and finish off the code block:

```
// put the ids we collected into client_invoices
$sql = "INSERT INTO client_invoices (client_id , invoice_id)
        VALUES ($client_id, $invoice_id)";
$result = $db->query($sql);
if( DB::isError($result) ) {
  die ($result->getMessage());
}

}

?>
```

We're now done with the coding needed to add new invoices to our system. We have completed one of the two paths outlined on our overview earlier in the chapter, and this was arguably the harder one. The result of successfully entering a new invoice might look like this:

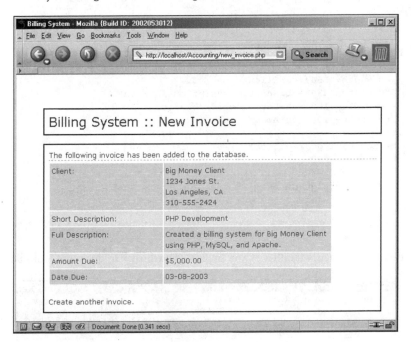

Next, we'll turn our attention to looking at the invoices we create.

Reviewing Invoice Summaries

Examining the home page, we can see that there are three different links to the page `invoice_review.php`. Each of them sets the GET variable type to something different. Our `invoice_review.php` page will generate a dynamic SQL query based partially on this variable to show the user what he or she is interested in.

Let's start by just creating the base HTML template that we'll add to later. Open up
`invoice_review.php` and put the following code into it:

```html
<html>
  <head>
    <title>Billing System</title>
    <style type="text/css" media="screen">
      @import url(billing.css);
    </style>
  </head>
  <body>

<div id="pageheader">
  <a href="index.php">Billing System</a> :: Review Invoices
</div><!-- end div pageheader -->

<div id="pagecontent">
<div class="sectionheading">
  Invoices ::
</div><!-- end div with class sectionheading -->

    <table border="0" cellpadding="3" cellspacing="0">
      <tr>
        <td width="150"><b>Client</b></td>
        <td width="250"><b>Short Description</b></td>
        <td width="100"><b>Date Posted</b></td>
        <td width="100"><b>Amount Due</b></td>
      </tr>
<!-- summaries will go right here -->
    </table>

</div><!-- end div pagecontent -->

  </body>
</html>
```

This template should look fairly familiar to you by now. The display at this point looks like the following:

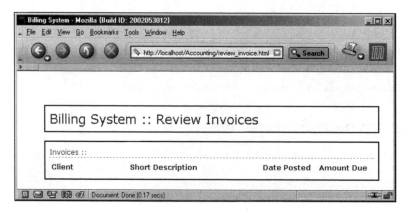

Next, we'll put in some PHP code at the very top of the page before any of the HTML. As expected, we'll include the needed files and create a database object:

```php
<?php
require_once("billing_includes.php");
require_once("DB.php");

// we're always going to connect to the database
// on this page, so let's do it now
$db = DB::connect($dsn);
if( DB::isError($db) ) {
  die ($db->getMessage());
}
```

As always, we check for any errors that might have occurred when connecting:

Now, let's take a look at the type variable that was passed. We'll set two variables based on its value. One will constitute the WHERE part of the SQL statement that we'll construct shortly. The other is simply a bit of display code that will show the user where they are:

```php
switch ($_GET["type"]) {
  case "outstanding":
    $wherestatement = "invoice_paid = 0";
    $pagetitle = "Outstanding";
    break;
  case "paid":
    $wherestatement = "invoice_paid = 1";
    $pagetitle = "Paid";
    break;
  case "overdue":
    $wherestatement = "invoice_paid = 0 AND NOW() > date_due";
    $pagetitle = "Overdue";
    break;
  default:
    $wherestatement = "invoice_paid = 0";
    $pagetitle = "Outstanding";
}
```

We'll make use of our $pagetitle variable right away. Look down in the HTML for a line that simply reads:

```
Invoices ::
```

and change it to read:

```
Invoices :: <?php echo $pagetitle; ?>
```

Now back to the task of constructing a SQL query. As we can see, the $_GET["type"] variable is used to determine what kind of invoice information to pull out of the database. So at this point we can imagine a query that looks like this:

```sql
SELECT fields FROM invoices,clients WHERE $wherestatement
```

where `fields` would indicate the things we were looking for. However, this would not be a good query from a user interface standpoint. We can probably already tell that once we execute this query, we're going to loop through the resultset and print out what we find on the page. If we have a great many invoices, then this could get very unwieldy. What we'd like to do is just show a small number of invoices on each page, and have **Next** and **Prev** links to let us look at invoice summaries not shown on the current page.

To accomplish this, we'll first need a global variable and a new function in the `billing_includes.php` page. Open it up and add the following:

```php
// global variable for the number of invoices to display
$display_invoices = 5;

// {{{ get_sql_limit()

/**
 * Get the "LIMIT" part of our SQL statement for reviewing
 *
 * @param $rowcount the number of rows to return
 *
 * @access public
 * @return string
 */

function get_sql_limit( $rowcount = 5 ) {
  // page we're on
  $curr_page = 0;

  if( isset($_GET["curr_page"]) ) {
    $curr_page = $_GET["curr_page"];
  }

    return "LIMIT $curr_page, $rowcount";
}

// }}}
```

Let's examine the `get_sql_limit()` function. It checks to see if there is a GET variable called `curr_page`. This will basically be the offset in the database table that we'll start pulling rows from. It then returns a `LIMIT` section of a SQL statement. This will allow us to just pull out a selected number of invoice records starting from some defined offset row. We should note there that not all databases support the `LIMIT` statement, though it is useful when it is supported.

Going back to the `invoice_review.php` page, we'll construct our SQL query now that we have everything ready to go. It is a little complicated since we are getting fields from both the invoices and clients tables, using a join on the `client_invoices` table to tie everything together:

```php
$sql = "SELECT i.invoice_id,description_short,date_format(date_posted, '%Y-%m-%d')
  AS date_posted, amount_due, client_firstname, client_lastname
        FROM invoices i, clients c, client_invoices ci
        WHERE i.invoice_id = ci.invoice_id
        AND c.client_id = ci.client_id
        AND ". $wherestatement . "
        ORDER BY date_posted DESC ". get_sql_limit($display_invoices);
```

We're ordering our results first by date posted. So we'll see the most recent invoices at the top of the page. We pass the global variable $display_invoices to the function. We set this to five in billing_includes.php, but if we want to change it later on, the application will automatically adjust itself to the new value.

With our query in hand, we're ready to execute the statement (and check for any problems):

```
$rs = $db->query($sql);

if( DB::isError($rs) ) {
  die ($rs->getMessage());
}
```

In order to make our nifty **Next** and **Prev** links, we'll also need to know the total number of invoices in the database of the kind we're interested in. Fortunately, the getOne() method of our $db object makes this very simple to grab:

```
// we'll need to know the total number of rows later on
$total_invoices = $db->getOne("SELECT COUNT(invoice_id) FROM invoices " .
$wherestatement);
if( DB::isError($total_invoices) ) {
  die ($total_invoices->getMessage());
}

?>
```

We're almost ready to print out the data. We'll put each record in an HTML table row. You may have noticed that elsewhere in this application, we have alternated between light and dark gray backgrounds for ease of reading. We'll do that here also, but we'll need PHP to help us out with it since the rows will be generated dynamically. This will require one more global variable and one more function in billing_includes.php:

```
// global variable for review shading CSS class
$review_shading_class = "darker";

// {{{ toggle_shading_class()

/**
 * Simple function to toggle a display parameter
 *
 * @access public
 * @return string
 */

function toggle_shading_class() {
  global $review_shading_class;

  if( 0 == strcmp($review_shading_class , "darker") ) {
    $review_shading_class = "lighter";
  }
```

```
      else {
        $review_shading_class = "darker";
      }
      return $review_shading_class;
    }

// }}}
```

Keep in mind that the `toggle_shading_class()` function is going to affect the **css** class used for display on the page. It is in no way related to PHP classes.

Now, we'll get on to the business of detailing the results. This code should go in `invoice_review.php` just below the HTML comment that conveniently says `summaries will go right here`:

```php
<?php

while( $invoice = $rs->fetchRow(DB_FETCHMODE_ASSOC) ) {
    $shading = toggle_shading_class();

?>

<tr>
    <td width="150" class="<?php echo $shading; ?>"><?php echo
$invoice["client_firstname"] . " " . $invoice["client_lastname"]; ?></td>
    <td width="250" class="<?php echo $shading; ?>">
      <a href="invoice_review_detail.php?invoice_id=<?php echo
$invoice["invoice_id"]; ?>">
      <?php echo $invoice["description_short"]; ?></a>
    </td>
    <td width="100" class="<?php echo $shading; ?>"><?php echo
      reformat_date($invoice["date_posted"]); ?></td>
    <td width="100" class="<?php echo $shading; ?>">$<?php echo
number_format($invoice["amount_due"], 2); ?></td>
</tr>

<?php } ?>
```

We're using the `fetchRow()` method of our `$rs` object, and we're passing `DB_FETCHMODE_ASSOC` to it. This means that for each record, `$invoice` will be set as an associative array with keys equal to the names of the columns in the database table. Also, for each record, we toggle the value of our `$shading` variable which sets the **css** class for the `<td>` elements. This code will print out `$display_invoices` rows in the table and will color them appropriately as in the rest of the application. Also, the short summary for each invoice will link to the `invoice_review_detail.php` page that we will create in the next section.

All that's left is to make our **Next** and **Prev** links. We'll put them right under the table with the invoice summaries. So the following code should go just after the closing `</table>` tag:

```php
<?php if( $total_invoices > $display_invoices ) { ?>
<table border="0" cellpadding="6" cellspacing="0" width="100%">
  <tr>
    <td align="left">
<?php
  if( $_GET["curr_page"] + $display_invoices < $total_invoices ) {
    echo "<a href=\"" . $_SERVER["PHP_SELF"] . "?curr_page=" .
      ($_GET["curr_page"] + $display_invoices) . "\">Prev</a>\n";
  }
?>
    </td>
    <td align="right">
<?php
  if( $_GET["curr_page"] - $display_invoices >= 0 ) {
    echo "<a href=\"" . $_SERVER["PHP_SELF"] . "?curr_page=" .
      ($_GET["curr_page"] - $display_invoices) . "\">Next</a>\n";
  }
?>
    </td>
  </tr>
</table>
<?php } ?>
```

If there are enough invoice records to warrant it, this creates a table with **Next** and **Prev** links where appropriate. These links set the GET variable curr_page which is used by the get_sql_limit() function that we wrote earlier. The result is that the user will have an easier time navigating through the results.

Detailed Invoice Review

The last new page we need to look at allows us to get a detailed review of a given invoice. Additionally, if the invoice is unpaid, there will be a form button allowing us to set the invoice as a paid one.

Before we jump into it, there is one last function we haven't yet written that we will need for this page. It does nothing more than take a date string in the MySQL storage format for a DATETIME (YYYY-MM-DD) and return a string with a US-formatted date. Put the following code into billing_includes.php:

```php
// {{{ reformat_date()

/**
 * Reformat a date from MySQL format to American format.
 *
 * @param $datestring
 *
 * @access public
 * @return string
 */

function reformat_date($datestring) {
  list($year, $month, $day) = explode("-" , $datestring);
  return "$month/$day/$year";
}

// }}}
```

Now, we will start in with the detailed review page. Open up `invoice_review_detail.php` and this time we will start directly with the PHP code. As before, we start with includes and create a `PEAR::DB` object:

```php
<?php
require_once("DB.php");
require_once("billing_includes.php");

// we'll always perform a query on this page so
// get a connection
$db = DB::connect($dsn);
if( DB::isError($db) ) {
  die ($db->getMessage());
}
```

Now, if we are coming from the `invoice_review.php` page, we can get all of the invoice information from the GET variable `invoice_id` that we passed. However, since we know that there will be a form later on in this page that will also pass such a parameter as a POST variable, we need to check for both instances:

```php
// set $invoice_id variable for the page
if( isset($_GET["invoice_id"]) ) {
  $invoice_id = $_GET["invoice_id"];
}
if( isset($_POST["invoice_id"]) ) {
  $invoice_id = $_POST["invoice_id"];
}
```

With that in hand, we can create a SQL query and get the data that we want. Again, we are selecting data from both the `clients` and `invoices` tables, using a join on the `clients_invoices` table to tie everything together:

```php
// set up sql statement and perform query
$sql = "SELECT i.invoice_id,description_short, description_full,
date_format(date_posted, '%Y-%m-%d')
        AS date_posted, date_format(date_due, '%Y-%m-%d') AS date_due,
amount_due,invoice_paid, client_firstname, client_lastname, client_street,
client_city,client_state,client_zip,client_phone
        FROM invoices i, clients c, client_invoices ci
        WHERE i.invoice_id = $invoice_id
        AND ci.invoice_id = $invoice_id
        AND c.client_id = ci.client_id";


$rs = $db->query($sql);
if( DB::isError($rs) ) {
    die ($rs->getMessage());
}

$invoice = $rs->fetchRow(DB_FETCHMODE_ASSOC);

?>
```

As before, $invoice will be an associative array with keys equal to the table column names. Continuing on, we get to the HTML:

```html
<html>
  <head>
    <title>Billing System</title>
    <style type="text/css" media="screen">
      @import url(billing.css);
    </style>
  </head>
  <body>

  <div id="pageheader">
    <a href="index.php">Billing System</a> :: Review Invoice
  </div><!-- end div pageheader -->

  <div id="pagecontent">

  <div class="sectionheading">
    Invoice ID: <?php echo $invoice["invoice_id"]; ?>
  </div>
```

Next, we'll put in a table that contains the rest of the information in the $invoice array. It's a reasonable amount of code but not very complicated:

```php
<table border="0">
<tr>
  <td valign="top" class="darker" width="200">Client:</td>
  <td class="darker" width="300">
<?php
echo $invoice["client_firstname"] . " " . $invoice["client_lastname"] . "<br />"

    $invoice["client_street"] . "<br />" .
    $invoice["client_city"] . ", " . $invoice["client_state"] . " " .
$invoice["client_zip"] . "<br />" .
    $invoice["client_phone"];
?>
  </td>
</tr>
<tr>
  <td valign="top" class="lighter" width="200">Short Description:</td>
  <td class="lighter" width="300"><?php echo
smart_strip_slashes($invoice["description_short"]); ?></td>
</tr>
<tr>
  <td valign="top" class="darker" width="200">Full Description:</td>
  <td class="darker" width="300"><?php echo
smart_strip_slashes($invoice["description_full"]); ?></td>
</tr>
<tr>
  <td valign="top" class="lighter" width="200">Amount Due:</td>
  <td class="lighter" width="300">$<?php echo
number_format($invoice["amount_due"], 2); ?></td>
</tr>
<tr>
  <td valign="top" class="darker" width="200">Date Posted:</td>
```

```
   <td class="darker" width="300"><?php echo
reformat_date($invoice["date_posted"]); ?></td>
</tr>
<tr>
  <td valign="top" class="lighter" width="200">Date Due:</td>
  <td class="lighter" width="300"><?php echo reformat_date($invoice["date_due"]);
?></td>
</tr>
```

Note that we're making use of the `reformat_date()` and `smart_strip_slashes()` functions that we've developed.

Here, at the bottom of the table, we'll insert a row that contains the **Set Invoice as Paid** button if the invoice is unpaid, or a useful message if the invoice has already been paid. Then we'll finish off the page:

```
<tr>
  <td colspan="2" align="left">
<?php
if( 0 == $invoice["invoice_paid"] ) {
?>

   <form name="updatepaid" action="<?php echo $_SERVER["PHP_SELF"]; ?>"
method="post">
     <input type="hidden" name="updatepaid" value="1">
     <input type="hidden" name="invoice_id" value="<?php echo
$invoice["invoice_id"]; ?>">
     <input type="submit" value="Set Invoice as Paid">
   </form>

<?php } else {?>
   This invoice has been paid.
<?php } ?>
  </td>
</tr>
</table>

</div>
</html>
```

We still haven't put in any code to handle the submission of the form we just coded. It's not very hard though, since we've set the hidden variable `updatepaid` in the form. The following PHP code goes at the top of the page immediately after the section where we set the variable `$invoice_id`:

```
// if we just set the invoice as paid, make that update
if( 1 == $_POST["updatepaid"] ) {
  $sql = "UPDATE invoices
    SET invoice_paid = 1
    WHERE invoice_id = " . $invoice_id;

  $rs = $db->query($sql);
  if( DB::isError($rs) ) {
    die ($rs->getMessage());
  }
}
```

It needs to come before the first query that we wrote, so that it will pick up the change if we've just set an invoice to be paid. This concludes the detailed review. A sample display of an unpaid invoice looks as follows:

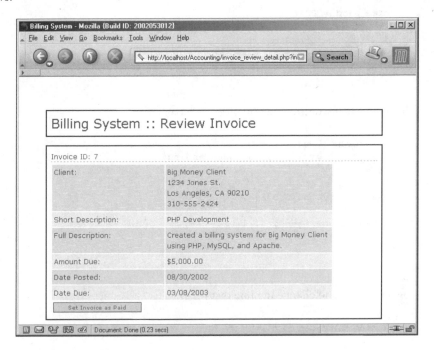

Finishing Touches

We are now inches away from being done. What could be left you ask? Well, recall that on the home page, there was a **Quick Summary** at the bottom. It allows the user to immediately see how many outstanding invoices there are, and the total amount of uncollected funds. Filling in this data requires two quick SQL queries that we shall see below.

At the top of index.php, put the following code:

```php
<?php
require_once("DB.php");
require_once("billing_includes.php");

// instantiate database object
$db = DB::connect($dsn);
if( DB::isError($db) ) {
  die ($db->getMessage());
}
```

First, we'll set up a query to see how much money we are owed and execute it. Again, we'll use that handy getOne() method:

```
// see how much we have outstanding
$sql = "SELECT SUM(amount_due) AS uncollected
  FROM invoices
  WHERE invoice_paid = 0";

$uncollected = $db->getOne($sql);
if( DB::isError($uncollected) ) {
  die ($uncollected->getMessage());
}
```

Similarly, we'll see how many outstanding invoices we have:

```
// see who is overdue
$sql = "SELECT COUNT(invoice_id) as outstanding
  FROM invoices
  WHERE invoice_paid = 0";
$outstanding = $db->getOne($sql);
if( DB::isError($outstanding) ) {
  die( $outstanding->getMessage() );
}

?>
```

Now, scroll down the page and change the line that reads:

```
Total Outstanding Invoices:
```

to:

```
Total Outstanding Invoices: <?php echo $outstanding; ?>
```

and the line:

```
Total Uncollected Funds:
```

to:

```
Total Uncollected Funds: $<?php echo number_format($uncollected , 2); ?>
```

This, finally, concludes the development of the application. The working home page now looks like this:

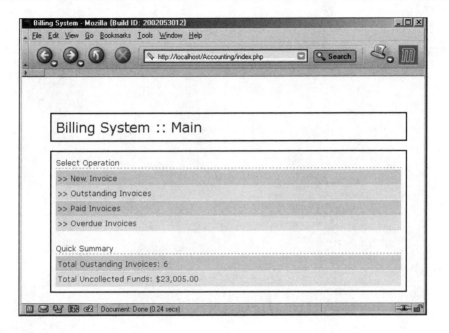

Summary

We have succeeded in finishing our example application and meeting our goals. It gave us an accounts receivable system, allowing us to enter new invoices and review them as we wish. There is a predictable interface, which users will be able to easily get around to obtain the information they are interested in.

Along the way, we created a sequence of utility functions to validate our data when we entered it into the system. Additionally, we made liberal use of the DB class, allowing us to harness the MySQL database in the back end. We employed a classic three-tier development strategy with the data, application code, and presentation code enjoying a reasonable amount of separation.

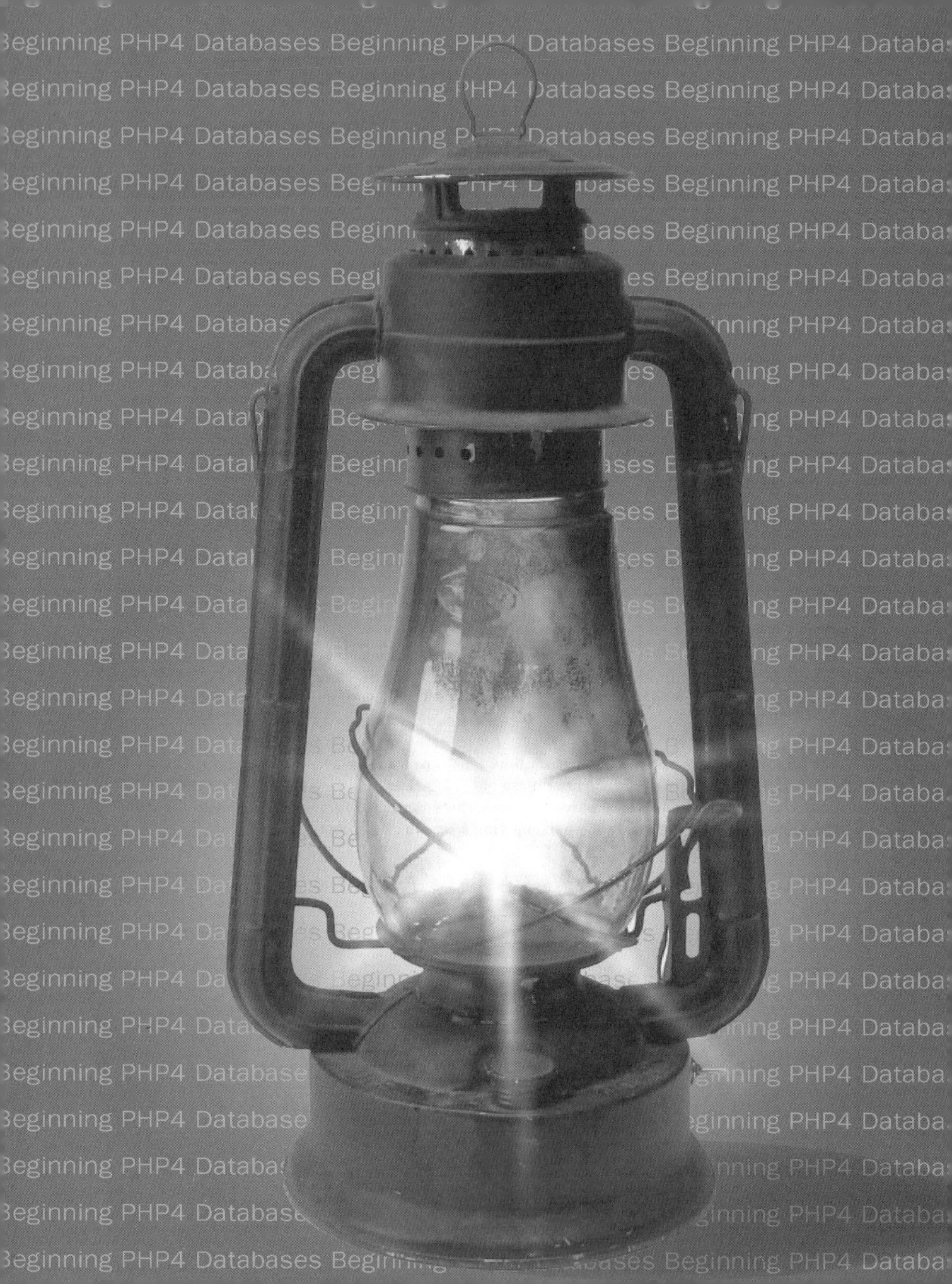
Beginning PHP4 Databases

CaseStudy: Using Object Databases – A Library Automation System

This chapter will cover how PHP can be used effectively to implement object-oriented database applications. This is illustrated using a popular object-oriented example – The Library Automation System. The library automation system is used by library administrators to issue and return items, and by library users to view their accounts and search the library catalog.

To develop this application we will go through the following steps:

- ❑   Requirement Identification
- ❑   Application Design
- ❑   Persistent Layer (database schema) Design
- ❑   Implementation

In real-world software development the above listed steps are iterative; the steps are revisited as and when problems or limitations are encountered. For example, if a limitation is found in the persistent layer design in the implementation phase, then the persistent layer design step is revisited.

Requirements

The first step in developing any application is to interview the user base to generate the list of features they would want in the application. This is important input used to define the capabilities of the application. For the library automation system, there are two categories of users: library members who use the library automation system to issue items, reissue items, and search the library catalog; and library administrators who use the library automation system to create accounts for new members, issue items to members, and to return items.

Let's assume that the following requirements were identified after interviewing our application user base:

General Requirements:

❑ The application should support book, music, and video library items, and it should be possible to extend the library system later to support additional library items.

❑ The application should be secure; unauthorized persons should not be able to access the application on a user's behalf.

Library User Requirements:

❑ Search the library catalog by title, author, or artist

❑ Issue items

❑ Reserve an already issued item

❑ View reservations made by them

❑ View items issued by them

❑ Re-issue an item (an item can be re-issued only if there are no reservations for the item)

Library Administrator Requirements:

❑ Create accounts for new library members

❑ Issue items to library members

❑ Update the library system when an item is returned

Design

Once the requirements have been identified, we will do an analysis of the requirements and come up with a class diagram for the system. From the requirements, it is clear that the system will need to have the following objects, which will have to be stored in persistent storage (database):

❑ `User`: stores details about the user. It will have attributes like first name, last name, email id, user id, and password.

❑ `Administrator`: has all the attributes of `User` and additional attributes. In object-oriented terminology – this object will inherit from the `User` object.

❑ `BookItem`: stores details of book items such as title and a list of authors

❑ `MusicItem`: stores details of music items such as title and a list of artists

❑ `VideoItem`: stores details of video items such as title and a list of artists

Additionally, the following non-real-world objects (do not represent a physical entity or attribute) will also be required:

- ❏ IssueRecord: tracks an issued item. It will store the following details:
    - ❏ Issued Item (bookitem, musicitem, videoitem)
    - ❏ Issued By user
    - ❏ Issue date
    - ❏ Return Date
    - ❏ ReservationRecord: tracks a user reservation. It will store the following details:
    - ❏ Reserved Item (bookitem, musicitem, videoitem)
    - ❏ User who made the reservation
    - ❏ Reservation Date

Now that we have listed all the objects of the system, let's build associations between these objects. The following associations exist:

- ❏ An IssueRecord object is associated with exactly one item (BookItem, MusicItem, or VideoItem)
- ❏ An Item (BookItem, MusicItem, or VideoItem) object can be associated with a maximum of one IssueRecord
- ❏ An IssueRecord object is associated with exactly one User
- ❏ A User object can be associated with any number of IssueRecord objects
- ❏ A ReservationRecord object is associated with exactly one Item
- ❏ An Item object can be associated with any number of ReservationRecord objects
- ❏ A ReservationRecord object is associated with exactly one User
- ❏ A User object can be associated with any number of ReservationRecord objects

With the current class structure we have too many associations like an IssueRecord object associated with BookItem, MusicItem, or VideoItem. To reduce the number of associations, and also complexity, let's define a class Item that is a super class of BookItem, MusicItem, and VideoItem. Now, IssueRecord and ReservationRecord objects will be associated with only the Item object instead of the BookItem, MusicItem, or VideoItem separately.

Also it is a good idea to define a common super class (PersistentObject) for all the above listed objects. This class will contain the storage related attributes.

The UML class diagram for the system will be as follows:

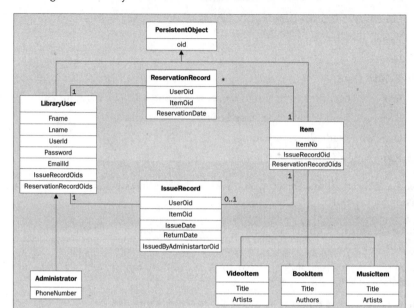

Additionally we will implement a singleton class LibrarySystem that will implement the application logic to issue items to users, search the library catalog, etc. The advantage of implementing such a class is that the **User Interface (UI)** layer will mostly interact with this single class and if interfaces of this class are preserved then the application implementation can change without affecting the UI. In design patterns terminology, this class is referred to as a Façade pattern. The LibrarySystem class is covered in more detail in the latter part of the chapter.

Finally, let's analyze the steps followed by the LibrarySystem class to implement some of the requirements:

> **Requirement**: Library Administrators should be able to issue items to members. The issueItem() method will do the following:

- ❑ Look up the LibraryUser object corresponding to the member from the persistent storage
- ❑ Look up the Item object (Book, Video, or Music) from the persistent storage.
- ❑ Create a new IssueRecord object
- ❑ Build associations between the IssueRecord, LibraryUser, and Item objects (refer to the UML diagram above)
- ❑ Save modified objects (LibraryUser, Item, IssueRecord) to the persistent storage

> **Requirement:** Library users should be able to view items issued by them. The getIssuedItems() method will do the following:

- ❑ Look up the LibraryUser object from the persistent storage
- ❑ Get IssueRecord objects associated with the LibraryUser object. An IssueRecord has details of the issued item, the issued date, return date, etc.

Requirement: Library users should be able to re-issue an item. The `reissueItem()` method will do the following:

❑ Look up the `Item` object from the persistent storage

❑ Get the `IssueRecord` object associated with the item

❑ Modify the `ReturnDate` attribute of the `IssueRecord` object

❑ Save the `IssueRecord` object to the persistent storage

Requirement: Library users should be able to reserve an issued item. The `reserveItem()` method will do the following:

❑ Look up the `LibraryUser` object corresponding to the library member from the persistent storage

❑ Look up the `Item` object from the persistent storage

❑ Create a `ReservationRecord` object

❑ Build associations between the `ReservationRecord`, `LibraryUser`, and `Item` objects (refer to the UML class diagram shown earlier)

❑ Save modified objects (`LibraryUser`, `Item`, `ReservationRecord`) to the persistent storage

Requirement: Library users should be able to view reservations made by them. The `getReservationRecords()` method will do the following:

❑ Look up the `User` object from the persistent storage

❑ Get the `ReservationRecord` objects associated with their `LibraryUser` object. A `ReservationRecord` has details of the reserved item and other information like the return date.

Choosing the Back-end Database

From the previous section, we know that the application is object-oriented in nature. It would make the application much simpler if we mapped the class structure as it is to the persistent storage (database). Unfortunately, there are no open source object-oriented databases available today and PHP doesn't have support for any of the commercial object-oriented databases. The good news is that the application depends on object features that are available in almost all the object-relational databases like PostgreSQL.

PostgreSQL

We have chosen PostgreSQL for this application for the following reasons:

❑ Stable database with transaction support

❑ Support for object features like inheritance and array data type

❑ Open source project, so it has cost advantage over other commercial databases

❑ Available on a large number of platforms

❑ Supported by the default installation of PEAR, giving PEAR DB support

PostgreSQL object-relational features used in the application are:

❑ **Inheritance**: PotgreSQL allows a table to inherit columns from another table. For example, the following table definition creates table `BookItem`, which inherits all the columns of its parent table `Item`:

```
CREATE TABLE BookItem (
   Title    VARCHAR(128)    NOT NULL,
   Authors  VARCHAR(128)[]  NOT NULL
)
INHERITS (Item);
```

❑ **Array**: PostgreSQL allows columns of a table to be defined as variable length arrays. In the above example, the `BookItem` table definition declares column `authors` to be of type array `varchar`.

❑ **Object Identifiers**: PostgreSQL, by default, assigns a unique object identifier (oid) to each row of the table. The object identifier can be used to look up any row in the PostgreSQL database.

> **For more details on PostgreSQL, refer to the PostgreSQL documentation at http://www.postgesql.org/idocs.**

Database Schema Design

In this section we will design the database schema for the application. The application data (tables and indexes) will be stored in a separate database (`lib_automation`).

The schema objects related to an application should be stored in a separate database. It helps ease the management of the application data; for example, to back up the data of this application, the administrator has to back up only one database (`lib_automation`).

Tables

The following tables are to be created in the `lib_automation` database. Notice that defined tables correspond to a class in the UML class diagram of the application:

❑ `LibraryUser`

❑ `LibraryAdministrator`

❑ `Item`

❑ `MusicItem`

❑ `BookItem`

❑ `VideoItem`

❑ `IssueRecord`

❑ `ReservationRecord`

The `LibraryUser` table contains the library user information:

Column Name	Description
Fname	First name of the user
Lname	Last name of the user
UserId	Unique user ID
Password	Clear text password of the user
EmailId	E-mail ID of the user
IssueRecordOids	Array of `IssueRecord` object identifiers (oid)
ReservationRecordOids	Array of `ReservationRecord` object identifiers (oid)

The `LibraryAdministrator` table inherits from the `LibraryUser` table:

Column Name	Description
PhoneNumber	Phone number of the administrator

The `Item` table contains the common attributes of the `BookItem`, `MusicItem`, and `VideoItem` table:

Column Name	Description
ItemNo	Unique item number of the item
IssueRecordOid	`IssueRecord` object identifier (oid)
ReservationRecordOids	Array of `ReservationRecord` object identifiers (oid)

The `BookItem` table contains the details of the book items:

Column Name	Description
Title	Title of the book item
Authors	An array of authors

The `MusicItem` table contains the details of music items:

Column Name	Description
Title	Title of the music item
Artists	An array of artists

The `VideoItem` table contains the details of video items:

Column Name	Description
Title	Title of the video item
Artists	An array of artists

The `IssueRecord` table contains the details of all the items issued by the user. For each issued item a new row is inserted in this table:

Column Name	Description
UserOid	Object identifier of the user to whom the item is issued
ItemOid	Object identifier of the issued item
IssueDate	Date the item is issued
ReturnDate	Date the item is returned
IssuedByAdministratorOid	Object identifier of the administrator who issued the item

The `ReservationRecord` table contains the details of reservations made by the user. For each reservation a new row is inserted in this table:

Column Name	Description
UserOid	Object identifier of the user who made reservation
ItemOid	Object identifier of the item on which the reservation is made
ReservationDate	Date the reservation is made

Now that we have decided on what to store in each of our tables, let's go through the SQL commands needed to create the tables:

```
CREATE TABLE LibraryUser (
  Fname                  VARCHAR(25) NOT NULL,
  Lname                  VARCHAR(25) NOT NULL,
  UserId                 VARCHAR(50),
  Password               VARCHAR(120),
  EmailId                VARCHAR(50) UNIQUE,
  IssueRecordOids        INTEGER[],
  ReservationRecordOids  INTEGER[],
  PRIMARY KEY(UserId))
WITH OIDS;

CREATE TABLE LibraryAdministrator (
  PhoneNumber            VARCHAR(32))
```

```
INHERITS (LibraryUser);

CREATE TABLE Item (
   ItemNo                    VARCHAR(25),
   IssueRecordOid            INTEGER,
   ReservationRecordOids     INTEGER[],
   PRIMARY KEY(ItemNo))
WITH OIDS;

CREATE TABLE MusicItem (
   Title                     VARCHAR(128) NOT NULL,
   Artists                   VARCHAR(50)[] NOT NULL)
INHERITS (Item);

CREATE TABLE BookItem (
   Title                     VARCHAR(128) NOT NULL,
   Authors                   VARCHAR(50)[] NOT NULL)
 INHERITS (Item);

CREATE TABLE VideoItem (
   Title                     VARCHAR(128) NOT NULL,
   Artists                   VARCHAR(50)[] NOT NULL)
INHERITS (Item);
```

An item can be issued to only one user at a time, so there can only be one entry of an item in the `IssueRecord` table:

```
CREATE TABLE IssueRecord (
   UserOid                   INTEGER NOT NULL,
   ItemOid                   INTEGER UNIQUE,
   IssueDate                 DATE NOT NULL,
   ReturnDate                DATE NOT NULL,
   IssuedByAdministratorOid  INTEGER)
WITH OIDS;
```

Also, a user cannot have two reservations on the same item:

```
CREATE TABLE ReservationRecord (
   UserOid                   INTEGER NOT NULL,
   ItemOid                   INTEGER NOT NULL,
   ReservationDate           DATE NOT NULL)
WITH OIDS;


ALTER TABLE ReservationRecord
ADD CONSTRAINT ReservationRecord_uq1 UNIQUE (UserOid, ItemOid);
```

Indexes

As discussed in Chapter 7, creating indexes will result in faster searches in the database. We are going to create indexes on the `UserId` column of `LibraryUser`, `ItemNo` column of `Item`, and `Title` column of the `BookItem`/ `MusicItem`/ `VideoItem` tables. The SQL commands for creating the indexes are:

```
create index Library_User_userid on LibraryUser(UserId);

create index Item_itemno on Item(ItemNo);

create index BookItem_title on BookItem(Title);

create index MusicItem_title on MusicItem(Title);

create index VideoItem_title on VideoItem(Title);
```

Object-Oriented Application using a Relational Database

It is possible to implement an object-oriented application using a relational database (for example, MySQL). In this section we will briefly cover how the database schema of our library automation system will change if we were to implement an object-oriented application using a relational database. To use a relational database for an object-oriented application we will have to implement mechanisms to assign unique identifiers (oid) to objects, take care of inheritance, and storing one-to-many relationships among objects.

Unique Identifiers to Objects

Relational databases do not assign unique identifiers to inserted rows automatically, so to assign unique identifiers to objects we will have to use a sequence number generator. Additionally all the tables storing objects (such as `LibraryUser`, `Item`, and `IssueRecord`) will have to define an additional column (`oid`) to store the unique oid of the object. The object creation steps will be:

1) Get the unique oid for the object from a sequence number generator. PEAR::DB API `DB::nextId()` can be used to get the value from the sequence number generator.

2) Insert the object (row) in the object table.

Readers planning to use such an approach should keep the following in mind:

❑ Once assigned, the oid column of the object table should not be changed, else the references to the object will become inconsistent.

❑ Always set a unique constraint on the oid column of object table.

❑ Objects should always be created with the scheme described above. One shouldn't directly insert rows in object tables.

❑ To create a new object from an application layer, two database round trips are required – one to get a unique number from the sequence number generator and the other to insert the row in the table. So, there is additional performance cost associated with object creation. One obvious way to avoid the cost is to use an object-relational database!

Storing One-to-Many Relationships

In the library automation system application, one user can be associated with any number of `IssueRecord` objects. In PostgreSQL databases we model this by defining a column, `issueRecordOids`, of type array of numbers, in the `LibraryUser` table. Each member of the array refers to a row in the `IssueRecord` table.

To model the same relationship in a relational database we will have to define an additional table to store the one-to-many relationship between `LibraryUser` and the `IssueRecord` objects. Note that there is no need to define the oid column for this table, as this table stores only attributes of the `LibraryUser` object. Let's call this table `UserIssueRecords` and it will have the following two columns:

- ❑ `UserOid`: This column will refer to the oid column of the `LibraryUser` table

- ❑ `IssueRecordOid`: This column will refer to the oid column of the `IssueRecord` table

A few things have to be kept in mind though:

- ❑ The application layer will have to make multiple SQL calls to load the object. For example, to load the `LibraryUser` object, the application layer will have to make a SQL call to get the attributes stored in the `LibraryUser` table, and then another SQL call to get `IssueRecordOids` corresponding to the user.

- ❑ We will have to define one such table to model each one-to-many association of the object. If an object has too many associations then the create / save operations will be very slow.

- ❑ The on delete cascade constraint should be defined on the `UserOid` column, this will result in automatic deletion of all the related rows when the user row from the `LibrayUser` table is deleted.

- ❑ The size of the association table will increase with the increase in the number of objects, so it is a good idea to create indexes on association tables. In the case of the `UserIssueRecords` table, indexes should be created on the `UserOid` column.

Inheritance

Relational databases do not inherently support mechanisms to store an inheritance hierarchy. There are several ways in which the object's class hierarchy can be stored in a relational database. One simple mechanism is to define a table with columns corresponding to all the sub-classes and an additional column to store the type of object.

For example, in our library automation example let's assume that the `BookItem` object has one author and `Video`/`MusicItem` objects have one artist, so the `Item` table will contain the following columns:

- ❑ `OID`: object identifier
- ❑ `Type`: possible values of this column will be MUSIC, BOOK, VIDEO
- ❑ `Title`
- ❑ `Artist`
- ❑ `Author`
- ❑ `ItemNo`

Now to load a `MusicItem` object, the SQL SELECT query will return the values for the `Title`, `ItemNo`, and `Artist` columns; and to load a `BookItem` object, the SQL SELECT query will return the values of the `Title`, `ItemNo`, and `Author` columns.

To search for `BookItem` objects containing "search text" in the title – the SQL query will return rows with `TYPE=BOOK` and `Title` containing "search text". The SQL query will look like:

```
SELECT oid, title, author, itemNo FROM Item WHERE title='BOOK' AND title LIKE
'%search text%';
```

You should keep the following in mind:

❏ You should be prepared to change the base table when new sub-classes are added to the system.

❏ Searches on sub-classes are expensive because the SQL operation has to search objects of all types. For example, a `BookItem` search by `Title` will have to scan rows corresponding to `MusicItem` and `VideoItem` objects as well.

❏ The table storing all the attributes will become complicated when there is an increase in the number of levels in the inheritance hierarchy.

The lib_automation Application

Before looking at the code, let's look at a few application screenshots, which will help us in understanding the code better!

This is the first page that library administrators will access when entering our application:

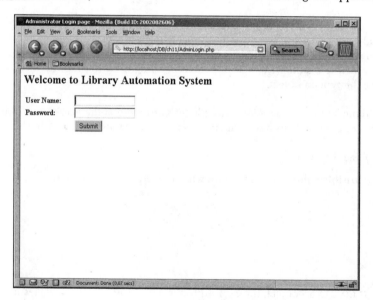

From here the administrators can authenticate themselves and access the application. For authentication, the administrator enters their `userid` and `password` in the User Name and Password input boxes and clicks on the Submit button. If authentication succeeds the administrator is taken to the main page of the application, or else the login page is displayed again with an error message.

If the authentication is successful, the following main page of the application is displayed:

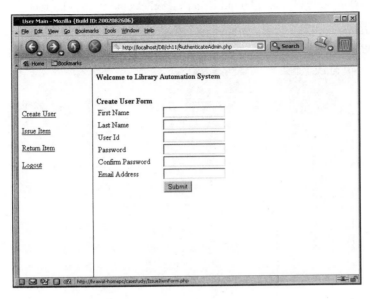

From here the administrator can create library users, issue items, or return items by clicking on the appropriate link on the left (navigation) frame. To create a new user, the administrator enters the user information in the input boxes and clicks on the Submit button.

By clicking on the Issue Item link, the Issue Item Form is then displayed:

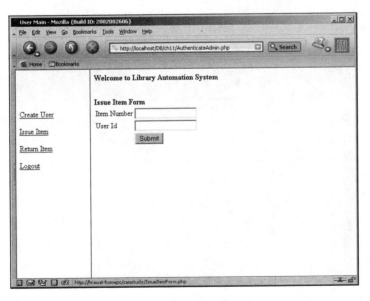

To issue an item to a user, the administrator enters the item number of the item and the `userid` of the user in the Item Number and User Id input boxes and clicks the Submit button.

If the administrator would rather log an item as being returned, the Return Item link is clicked to display the following page:

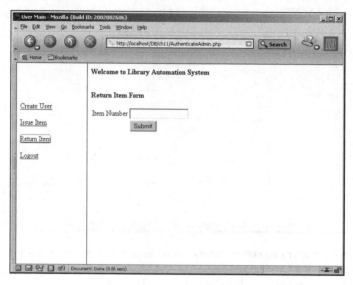

To return an item, the administrator enters the item number of the item in the Item Number text box and clicks the Submit button.

If a user logs on to the application instead of the administrator, the following page is the main page that is displayed, after the user has been sucessfully authenticated:

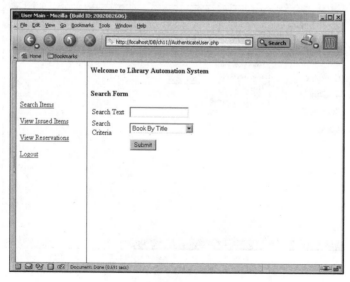

From here, the library member can search the library catalog, view items issued by him/her, or view his/her reservations by clicking on the appropriate link on the left (navigation) frame.

To search for items, the library member enters the search text in the Search Text input box, selects the search criteria from the drop-down, and clicks on the Submit button. The library member can search for keywords using the following search criteria:

- Book by Title

- Book by Author

- Music Item by Title

- Music Item by Artist

- Video Item by Title

- Video Item by Artist

The results will be displayed on a page similar to this one:

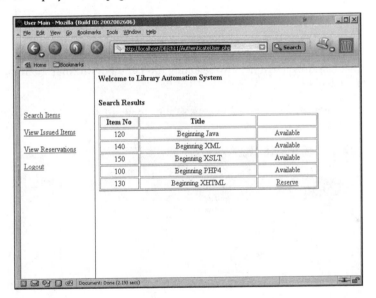

You have probably noticed that the last book in our list, Beginning XHTML, has a Reserve link in the third column. The library member can reserve issued items by clicking on this link. The value Available indicates that the item is available in the library and can be issued.

If the user is interested viewing the issued items, the following page is displayed when the View Issued Items link is clicked:

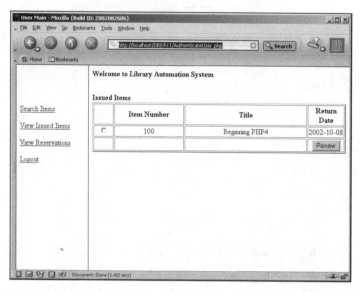

The library member can re-issue an item by selecting the radio button corresponding to the item and clicking on the Renew button.

Finally, if the user is interested in viewing all resevations made by them, the following page displays those item reservations:

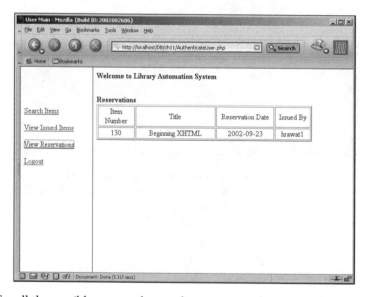

Well, that's it for all the possible screens that can be encountered in our application. Now, let's look at the code.

We are not going to go through all of the code in detail in this case study. We are going to go over what files are necessary for each part of the application generally. The actual code is provided on the www.wrox.com website to be downloaded and installed as you go through the case study.

The Application Code

The application code uses PEAR::DB APIs to access the PostgreSQL database; unfortunately the default PostgreSQL PEAR::DB driver does not provide methods to retrieve the object identifier (oid) column value of an inserted row. For this application we have added a new method, getLastOid(), to the default PostgreSQL driver. Before running this application in your setup, please copy the mypgsql.php file (which can be downloaded from www.wrox.com) to the <Location of PEAR DB installation>/DB directory.

Persistant Class Definitions

In this section we will go through the implementation of the persistent classes including the following classes:

❑ PersistentObject: This abstract class is the super class of all the persistent objects (the objects stored in the database). This class has methods to get and set the object identifiers (oid). Remember the objects stored in PostgreSQL databases are assigned a unique identifier, and the oid attribute of an object cannot be changed.

❑ User: models the library users. It inherits from the PersistentObject class and has methods to get and set the attributes of the LibraryUser object.

❑ Administrator: models library administrators.

❑ Item: This abstract class is the super class of BookItem, MusicItem, and VideoItem. This class implements common functionality applicable to its child classes.

❑ BookItem: models book items and inherits from Item class.

❑ MusicItem: models music items and inherits from Item class.

❑ VideoItem: models video items and inherits from Item class.

❑ IssueRecord: models issue records and inherits from the PersistentObject class.

❑ ReservationRecord: models reservation records and inherits from the PersistentObject class.

Utility Classes

In this section we will go through the Common and Utility classes used throughout the application. The following files are included here:

❑ Common.php: This file lists definitions of deployment-specific variables that are used in the application. These variables should be changed according to the deployment environment of your application.

❑ Utils.php: This file implements the singleton class Utils, which provides utility methods for parsing PostgreSQL array values and creating success /error messages.

❑ SessionUtils.php: This file implements the singleton class SessionUtils, which provides session management methods.

Storage Layer Implementation

Now, we will look at the implementation of the Storage layer. The Storage layer contains the following classes:

❑ UserStorage: implements methods to create new LibraryUser objects in the database, load LibraryUser objects from the database, and save modified LibraryUser objects to the database.

❑ AdministratorStorage: implements methods to load Administrator objects from the database.

❑ UserSqlStmts: declares SQL statements used by the UserStorage and AdministrtorStorage classes.

❑ ItemStorage: implements methods to load Item objects from the database and save modified Item objects to the database.

❑ BookItemStorage: implements methods to load BookItem objects from the database, search for BookItem objects by title or artist, and save modified BookItem objects to the database.

❑ MusicItemStorage: implements methods to load MusicItem objects from the database, search for MusicItem objects by title or artist, and save modified MusicItem objects to the database.

❑ VideoItemStorage: implements methods to load VideoItem objects from the database, search for VideoItem objects by title or artist, and save modified VideoItem objects to the database.

❑ ItemSqlStmts: declares SQL statements used by the ItemStorage, BookItemStorage, MusicItemStorage, and VideoItemStorage classes.

❑ IssueRecordStorage: implements methods to create new IssueRecord objects in the database, load IssueRecord objects from the database, and save modified IssueRecord objects to the database.

❑ ReservationRecordStorage: implements methods to create new ReservationRecord objects in the database, load ReservationRecord objects from the database, and save modified ReservationRecord objects to database.

❑ ReservationRecordSqlStmts: declares SQL statements used by the ReservationRecordStorage class.

Application Logic Implementation

Now, we will look at the implementation of the Application layer. The entire application logic is implemented in a singleton class, LibrarySystem. The LibrarySystem class provides methods to:

❑   Create new library users

❑   Authenticate users / administrators

❑   Issue items to a user

❑   Return an issued item to the library

❑   Reserve an issued item for a user

❑   Re-issue an item

❑   Get a list of reservation records associated with a user

❑   Get a list of issue records associated with a user

HTML Pages Implemented by the UI Layer

The UI layer implements HTML pages that are accessed by both types of users (administrators and library users). In this section we are covering only the HTML files that have PHP code embedded in them. We would recommend that you download the entire application code and look at it.

We are going to start with the Administrator pages first, as shown earlier in the chapter, and then move on to the User pages.

Administrator Pages

Logging In

This is the first page displayed to the administrator, by the `AdminLogin.php` file. The `AuthenticateAdmin.php` script is executed on the server side when the administrator submits the Login Form. If the password match succeeds, then the `AdminMain.htm` page is displayed, but if it fails, the Login page is once again displayed but with an error message this time.

Once the administrator is on the `AdminMain.htm` page, he/she can then go on to carry out the administration tasks in the following sections.

Creating a User

If the administrator wants to create a new user, the **Create User** link is followed, as shown in the Application section, to load the Create User Form page. The `CreateUser.php` script gets called when the administrator submits a Create User Form. Again, if the submit is unsuccessful, the Create User page is displayed once again with an error message.

Issuing an Item

When the administrator needs to issue an item to a user, the Issue Item Form must be displayed. Once the administrator has filled in the necessary information and clicked the **Submit** button, the `IssueItem.php` script gets called.

Returning an Item

If a user wants to return an item, the administrator needs to load the Return Item Form by clicking the Return Item link. When the administrator submits the Return Item Form, the ReturnItem.php script gets called.

Logging Out

Finally, Logout.php gets called when the administrator clicks on the Logout link from any of the pages of the application.

User Pages

Logging In

This page works in a similar manner to the login for the administrator. In this case, the AuthenticateUser.php script is called when the user enters the Login Form. If the login is successful, the UserMain.htm page is displayed and if it fails, the login page is displayed with an error message.

Once the user is on the main page, the following tasks can be carried out: searching for an item, reserving an item, viewing issued items, re-issuing items, viewing reservations, and logging out. We will look at what is involved in each of these tasks now.

Searching for an Item

If the user wants to carry out a search for an item, the search form has to be submitted. The results of the search are displayed on the Search Results page by the SearchResults.php file. On the results page, along with the item's name, a status column is also printed. If an item is not issued, then, Available is printed in the status column; otherwise a link, Reserve, is printed that points to the Reserve.php script, which we are going to look at now.

Reserving an Item

Basically, the Reserve.php script adds a user reservation to an already issued item. As stated in the last section, it gets called when the user clicks on the Reserve link on a Search Results page.

Viewing Issued Items

The user may want to view all the items that have been issued to them. To do this, the user must click the View Issued Items link from any of the pages of the application. By clicking this link, ViewIssuedItems.php is called and displays the details of any items issued by the user.

Re-Issuing Items

Once the user has determined all the items they have issued, to re-issue an item, the user must click the radio button on the results form and then click the Renew button. When this button is clicked, the RenewItem.php script is called and it opens the Print Renew Item Form as its action. The user who wants to re-issue an item submits this form.

Viewing Reservations

To view all the reservations they have made, users must click the View Reservations link. The ViewReservations.php script displays the details of all reservations made by the user.

Logging Out

The script `Logout.php` (discussed earlier) gets called when the user clicks on the Logout link. Note that the same script is used for logging out both administrators and users.

Testing

Well, that's it for the code to run our application. Now, it's time for you to experiment with our application. In order to run this code, you are going to need to insert some data into our database. In particular, you will need to create an administrator and then add some books, videos, and music items. If you cannot remember how to add information to our database, refer to the `INSERT` section in Chapter 5. Have fun.

Summary

In this chapter we have implemented a complete object-oriented application, using PHP in the middle tier. This illustrates how pure object-oriented database applications can be written in PHP. Some of the key points to remember while implementing real life object-oriented database applications are:

❑ **Precise Requirements**: Before starting design / implementation, try to get precise requirements from customers (or application users).

❑ **Good Design**: Spend sufficient time in designing the application. Before starting the implementation make sure that you have a class diagram listing all the important classes, at the very least.

❑ **Separate Storage Layer**: Implement a separate storage layer. The application layer shouldn't be aware of the persistent storage (database / file) that is used.

❑ **Separate UI and application layer**: Don't embed application logic in UI markup language code (HTML). Preferably implement entire application logic in one class that will be used by the UI layer

To keep the application simple, we implemented bare minimal features. I would encourage you to download the application code from the Wrox website and try adding features like sending e-mail to users when items reserved by them are available and adding an administrator UI for adding / removing items from the library catalog.

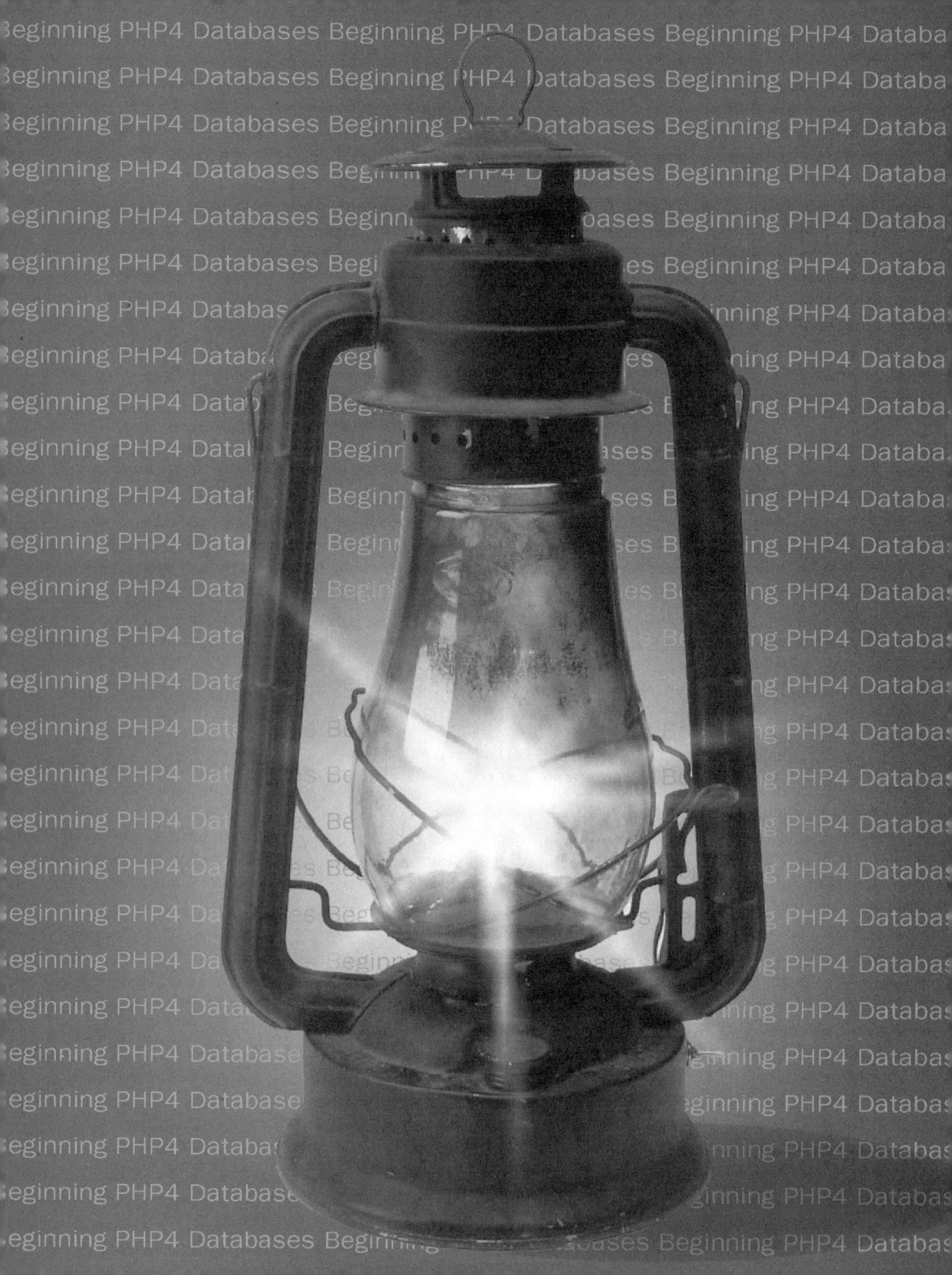
Beginning PHP4 Databases

Native XML Databases

In previous chapters, we have seen how PHP can be used to access various databases and data stores. In a technology landscape that is being increasingly dominated by XML, it is imperative that there be some solution to store data represented in XML. Native XML Databases directly address the storage of XML documents.

While several relational and object-oriented database solutions from the pre-XML days offer functionality to store XML documents, Native XML Databases are unique in that they attempt to preserve the original data of the document. In the course of this chapter, we shall do all of the following:

❑ Learn how Native XML Databases differ from traditional databases

❑ Understand how Native XML Databases work

❑ Review associated tools that we might need in the course of developing applications centered on Native XML databases

❑ Discuss the different strategies and functionality at our disposal to put Native XML Databases to work

Why Native XML Databases?

In a heterogeneous environment, such as the world wide web, the need to come up with a data storage format, that is as lightweight as it is extensible, cannot be emphasized enough. The XML standard largely meets such a requirement. Today applications are extensively written or rewritten using XML. XML is used to integrate existing legacy applications – both among themselves and to web-based interfaces. It is also being used to fuel data exchanges between corporations and as the metadata format and messaging format used in delivering web services. Aggregation and delivery of content in multiple markup languages is also done using XML. XML has evolved significantly and continues to do so. For a historical perspective please see http://www.xml.com/axml/testaxml.htm.

Like all forms of data, XML too needs a home where it can be stored and retrieved from. In its current form XML is an excellent format for exchange and representation of data.

XML documents are hierarchical in nature. Native XML preserves these hierarchical relationships in the original document, which form what is known as the document model. For instance, if an XML document were inserted into a Native XML Database system, one would be able to retrieve the document with the order of elements and attributes of the elements preserved. However, it does not mean that the Native XML Database would have to store the document in the exact text format in which it was inserted. What it means is that, as XML is being used to represent hierarchical data, we use Native XML Databases to preserve the hierarchical relationships. This means that not only do Native XML Databases preserve document level structure, but can, within a collection of XML documents, merge all documents into one hierarchical view.

Applications that deal with data that is represented in XML find it easy to maintain persistent data and manipulate it in its native form. This is because such applications do not have to implement complex code to serialize or marshal the XML data into a relational format, as is the case when using relational databases. Neither do they have to worry about having to reconstitute a semantically correct XML document from data that was stored in the traditional database. In other words, Native XML Databases work best in situations where applications need a data store that has XML-in, XML-out characteristics.

So what is a Native XML Database?

A Native XML Database is a good solution for applications dealing in XML, when it comes to persisting and retrieving data. We have seen that it preserves the ordering of elements and attributes. In this section, we shall expand on our knowledge to all the factors that define a Native XML Database.

Characteristics of a Native XML Database

XML:DB is an initiative to define Native XML Database standards and provides a reference implementation to apply the concept of Native XML Databases. Here are some of the characteristics of a Native XML Database as derived from the official definition available on the XML:DB website (http://www.xmldb.org):

1. **Fundamental storage unit is an XML document**
   This means that an XML document is the fundamental entity that can be inserted and retrieved from a Native XML Database. As an extension to this, it should also be possible to insert and retrieve multiple documents. In other words, if an application was designed to be XML-centric, it should actually benefit from using a Native XML Database.

2. **Underlying storage is not defined**
   It is easy to confuse this with the earlier description about an XML document being the fundamental unit of storage. What this characteristic means is that a vendor or developer of a Native XML Database is free to decide how the document is stored internally. The implementation may actually store the document in a relational database or in a flat file; it does not matter as long as an XML document is the fundamental unit for persistence and retrieval.

3. **Defines a logical data model**
   While the actual data model(s) supported by a Native XML Database implementation may vary from vendor to vendor (some may support the DOM model, others the Infoset model), some minimal functionality is expected from a Native XML Database. This functionality includes preservation of order of elements and ordering of attributes.

Comparison with Traditional Database Systems

So, how do Native XML Databases compare with traditional database systems that have, so far, done a fantastic job of data storage and access? Let us quickly discuss some of the traditional database systems.

Hierarchical System

One of the earliest forms of a database system was the hierarchical system, which essentially represents data as an inverted tree. In a hierarchical system, data is very easily addressed by traversing the nodes of the tree. For instance, an employee database would look something like this:

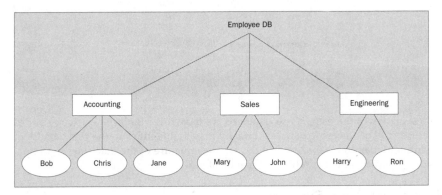

The diagram above illustrates the simplicity with which an employee record can be accessed. To look for 'Bob' working in 'Accounting', we need to drill down to the 'Accounting' node and search under this node. It is intuitive enough because data is contained under the hierarchy in which it belongs.

The hierarchical model works well when relationships are well structured and are one-to-one; in other words, where each child node has only one parent node. Here, complications have been avoided as Bob works in only Accounting, and not in Sales as well.

Relational System

Now, consider the case where another dimension is introduced, say the floor on which the employees work. All the employees of a department may not necessarily work on the same floor. To model such a situation in a hierarchical system can prove quite resource-intensive when querying for any information involving both the department and floors. In fact, there is a variant – the Network model, which is more suited for this situation. However, it is still expensive when it comes to querying for information involving multiple parents, for example, as 'select all employees in Accounting who work on the 3rd floor'.

This is where a relational database system comes into play. Let us try and represent the model we discussed using a relational database. To refresh our understanding of some basic concepts, the fundamental unit of data storage in a relational database is the field, which has a name and a value associated with it; for example, the field `EmployeeId`, which may have the value `12345`. Multiple fields comprise a record. For example, an `employee` record may consist of fields such as `Name`, `EmployeeId`, `Salary`, and so forth. A collection of such records forms a table. A field is also known as a column of the table and the record is also known by the name row.

One or more such tables constitute a schema, for instance the `employee` database schema illustrated below:

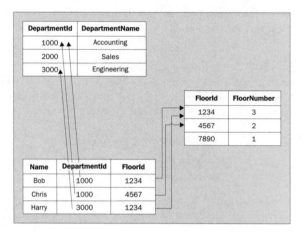

In this representation of the `employee` database, we have three tables, – `employeetable`, `floor`, and `department`. The mapping tables essentially map an identifier to the real data (department name for the department mapping). With such a model, the structure of the data does not impair the performance of queries unlike in a hierarchical database.

Object-Based Database System

Object databases constitute a more recent approach to databases, which assumes that objects have logic embedded in them to respond to queries. As a result, these objects, each of which represents a data entity, can respond to queries about department, floor, and so forth. Also, each of these objects may in turn contain data or references to other objects.

An XML database strikes a balance in that it supports containment like hierarchical databases, and supports multiple data types and references, as in object databases. However, XML by itself is not particularly well equipped to define constraints and declare types on the data it represents. This can be alleviated to a certain extent using DTDs (Document Type Definitions) or XML Schemas.

XML-Capable Databases

Several vendors offer support for storing XML data in these systems. However, we need to make the distinction between a Native XML Database, which preserves the data model of the document, and a traditional database, which is XML-capable or XML-enabled and therefore may store the XML document in it but may not guarantee the preservation of the data model. Having said that, certain applications may not be concerned with the order of attributes in an XML document. Further, XML-capable databases are an excellent solution to when the data needs to be accessed by multiple applications, some of which may not even be capable of handling data represented in XML. There are also products and solutions that act as a bridge between a pure-XML application and a relational or object database. We shall briefly examine the various vendor offerings later in the chapter.

Native XML Database Applications

Native XML Databases are not a substitute for relational or object databases. They are not even suited for all types of applications. In fact only those applications that are written to explicitly use XML as the data representation format, or use XML to a very large extent, may stand to gain at all from using a Native XML Database. Here are some of the typical applications that may benefit by using a Native XML Database:

❑ Catalogs

❑ Inventory management systems

❑ Document repositories

❑ Content management and content aggregation systems that require content to be in a standard format

❑ Queuing applications using XML as the data transport format

Typical applications unsuitable for a Native XML Database include:

❑ Invoicing systems

❑ Accounting systems

❑ Airline reservation systems

Later in the chapter, we shall be looking at some of the limitations of Native XML Databases that will clarify the scope of suitable applications further.

How Native XML Databases Works

Now that we have seen the various characteristics of Native XML Databases and how they compare with traditional database systems, we are equipped to understand how these databases work and how they semantically organize data. As we shall see, even though vendors have highly varying implementations there are some common aspects to almost all of these databases.

Storage

Perhaps the largest distinguishing factor between two vendors of Native XML Databases is how the individual implementations store their data. Certain vendors, whose area of competency has traditionally been in object databases, may choose to use an object database as the underlying data store. A relational database vendor may choose to store the data in a back-end relational database. Still another vendor may choose to simply use a file system as a data store. The original definition does allow for this, although the requirement states that the data model be preserved on retrieval.

Storing Multiple XML Documents

While it is quite useful to store an XML document in a database and query it for information, most practical applications deal with thousands, if not hundreds of thousands of documents at a time. Not all of these documents may contain the same sort of information. Therefore, grouping documents that have similar characteristics is particularly useful when querying for information. Rather than query the whole database, it is now sufficient to query just that set of documents, which logically holds the information we are seeking.

Native XML Databases support **collections**. Collections are essentially a group of documents sharing common characteristics, often organized similarly; most often these are documents that have a common DTD or XML Schema. A collection can be queried just as if it were a document. The results returned may span multiple documents in the collection, which match the query criteria. The result set also indicates the document that a particular result item corresponds to.

Schema Independence

One of the differences between a Native XML Database and traditional databases is in the schema requirements. Traditional database systems usually enforce that all data insertion only be in certain prescribed formats; in other words, it has to be in conformance with certain constraints laid out in the schema. However, the original definition does not require that documents inserted into a Native XML Database conform to a schema. It is not necessary for two documents in a collection to have the same structure or constraints, thus, Native XML Databases may be schema-independent. Several vendors still offer the capability to associate a DTD or an XML Schema to a collection and enforce schema compliance during insertion of a document to the collection.

Querying and Updating

Since the data stored is in XML format, it makes sense to have a query language that takes this aspect into consideration when querying the Native XML Database. The most popular, albeit quite limited, query mechanism is an Xpath-based query. Most vendors support XPath queries on their databases. However, as we shall soon see, XPath has certain limitations as a query language, primarily because it was not originally designed to be a query language for a Native XML Database. Due to these limitations there are new efforts afoot, such as the XQuery specification, to remedy the shortcomings of XPath as a query language.

Vendors may also offer support for other standard or proprietary query mechanisms to query the data, which was inserted as an XML document. For instance, a certain vendor may allow SQL access to the data that was initially inserted as an XML document. The underlying transport for submitting these queries may also vary. Certain products, specifically the Xindice open source project, allows XPath queries over XML-RPC, CORBA, and even HTTP (queries are sent via HTTP POST).

The most popular update mechanism currently in vogue is the XUpdate mechanism specified by the XML:DB initiative. XUpdate allows documents in the database to be updated by adding or deleting elements and attributes or modifying existing ones by sending XML documents, which contain the details of the operations.

We shall see more on querying using XPath and updating documents using XUpdate later in the chapter.

Indexing

As with traditional databases, most Native XML Database vendors offer the capability to index the contents to speedup queries. Indexes may be created on individual elements or certain attributes of an element. It is also possible to create indexes, the scope of which may encompass several attributes or just a few of them. Although aimed to improve search performance, extremely generic indexes, such as ones that such through all attributes of all elements, may deteriorate query performance. Again, with relational databases, it is common practice to add indexes for a combination of fields that are frequently used for joins. Only very few Native XML Database vendors offer the capability for specifying such indexes.

Migrating from a Relational Database

While there are certain applications that are best suited for relational databases and others that are better suited for Native XML Databases, there might exist legacy applications that perform better using a Native XML data storage mechanism, but are currently implemented to use a relational database. In this section we shall briefly see how such applications can be migrated to a Native XML Database.

Representing Data in XML

We shall consider the hypothetical relational database we discussed previously as the candidate for conversion from a relational database to an XML format, which can then be stored in a Native XML Database. Here is a typical representation of such a database:

```
<?xml version="1.0"?>
<myorg>
  <floors>
    <floor id="1234">3</floor>
    <floor id="4567">2</floor>
    <floor id="7890">1</floor>
  </floors>
  <engineering>
    <employee id="99999">
      <name>Harry</name>
      <floor>1</floor>
    </employee>
  </engineering>

  <accounting>
    <employee id="88888">
      <name>Bob</name>
      <floor>3</floor>
    </employee>
  </accounting>
</myorg>
```

So what did we do here? We created a mapping between various entities of a typical relational database and those of an XML document. In particular, we mapped a table to an element, a field or a column to an attribute or text node, and finally the database itself was encapsulated under the element myorg. We shall describe the department elements in the next section.

Containing vs. Pointing

Most of you are probably wondering about the `accounting` and `engineering` elements. This is a common dilemma when converting data from a relational database to an XML database. Should we contain or should we point? If we were to contain related data, the related elements would actually have been sub-elements of the containing element. For instance, a top-level floor element (say, first floor) could have sub-elements each of which represents employees working on that floor. If we were to point to related information, an attribute of an element may point to another element in the document. For instance, employee elements could be organized under a department element; the floor attribute of each employee element could indicate a floor element that corresponds to the floor on which the employee works.

Particularly with this example, we are left with two choices. The first choice is to represent the departments as separate elements, each of which have `employee` sub-elements under it. The second choice is to represent the departments under a `departments` element with each `department` element having an `id` attribute which is used by the `employee` element to refer to it. The latter approach may be represented as shown below:

```xml
<?xml version="1.0"?>
<myorg>
 <floors>
  <floor id="1234">3</floor>
  <floor id="4567">2</floor>
  <floor id="7890">1</floor>
 </floors>

 <departments>
  <department departmentId="1000">Accounting</department>
  <department departmentId="2000">Sales</department>
  <department departmentId="3000">Engineering</department>
 </departments>

 <employees>
  <employee id="99999">
   <name>Harry</name>
   <department>3000</department>
   <floor>1</floor>
  </employee>

  <employee id="88888">
   <name>Bob</name>
   <department>1000</department>
   <floor>3</floor>
  </employee>
 </employees>
</myorg>
```

This is represented by pointing, and is a perfectly valid way to represent the data. The initial XML representation we showed a little earlier is an example of containing. As a rule of thumb, when the relationship is one-to-one or one-to-many, it is often a good idea to use the containing strategy, as in the case where an employee belongs to a department. When the relationship is many-to-many, it is prudent to use a pointing strategy, for instance the relationship between books and authors; a book may have multiple authors while an author may have written multiple books.

Imposing Constraints

This approach works fine for simple documents. However some data sets may require constraints to be imposed on it. An XML document can be constrained to a certain extent, though not to the same extent as relational databases, using DTD (Document Type Definition) or XML Schema. Though the exact steps on how to achieve this is beyond the scope of this book, the book *Professional XML Databases* from *Wrox Press*, (ISBN 1861003587) has an excellent discussion on this topic.

> **Re-purposing an existing application may not be the only path to adoption of Native XML Database technologies. Several initiatives focus on integration rather then migration, for example, to create and hold XML within a relational database. On the other side, there could be XML native databases with well-developed ODBC interfaces. This data aggregation is desirable for common querying or data-binding mechanisms.**

Shortcomings

In its current state Native XML Databases have some limitations which can be attributed to it still being a nascent technology. In this section we shall examine some of the more significant ones.

Complex Query and Result Representation Issues

Currently, using Xpath, it is not possible to construct very complex queries; for instance one that would result in a join between two tables. Furthermore, it is not easy to specify queries that return a sorted result set. However, there are extraneous solutions to the sorting problem. For instance, if the returned results are highly structured and the structure predictable, XSLT can be used to format and sort results. Further, vendors may have their proprietary way of doing this. For instance with Xindice, it is possible to write server-side extensions with XML objects, which allow for more sophisticated sorting and formatting of query results. Lastly, in the list of query-related shortcomings, there is no standard mechanism to query metadata information about the database.

Superfluous Results

Often XPath query results may produce more information than required. A classic example is a query involving an attribute of the top-most elements of the XML document. The result returns the top element of all XML documents that match the criteria. Since the returned XML has to be well formed, all the nodes under the top element are returned. Effectively, this means that entire documents that matched the query criteria are returned.

Consider the example of a patient record database with an individual patient record represented in XML. The document may have the name and sex attributes, among others, in the top element. A query for the names of all male patients will return the entire patient records for all male patients. Designing the XML representation carefully can circumvent some of these issues.

Scalability

Several, if not most of the current offerings in the Native XML Database space do not have the same scalability properties of established database products in the traditional database arena. In terms of document size, while most of them are capable of handling a large number of documents, they may not be able to handle very large individual documents. It is common to have applications that typically handle documents several gigabytes in size.

Technology Maturity

Traditional database products have, over the years, developed enough functionality to handle voluminous data stores in the enterprise in a robust manner, supporting numerous auxiliary features. Native XML Databases, being the most recent players in this field, are yet to arrive at a level of functionality that can compare with these traditional players.

Language Binding

As mentioned earlier, applications that are the best candidates for using a Native XML Database are those that revolve around XML. However, in most real-world applications it is not sufficient to always manipulate data in XML. There may be times when the data needs to be converted into variables that can be more easily manipulated and then converted back into XML. Very few, if any, of the Native XML Database products offer a client-side data-binding model for achieving this.

> It is not always necessary to compare traditional database solutions with Native XML Database technologies. More often than not, the two play synergistic parts in a solution. In such an integrated environment, each type of technology is deployed to exploit their respective strength areas. Additionally, Native XML Databases offer much more openness and flexibility, therefore making it easier to engineer solutions integrated with traditional database technologies.

Native XML Database Products

In this section we shall take a quick look at some of the more prominent Native XML Database solutions available today.

Coherity XML Database (CXD)

This is a Native XML Database (http://www.coherity.com) that can handle large XML documents without performance degradation in queries or modifications. The database runs on several platforms and supports the following standards / interfaces:

- ❑ XPath
- ❑ XSL
- ❑ XML / HTTP
- ❑ XSQL
- ❑ DOM

XQuery will be supported in the coming versions.

To use this product with PHP there's an HTTP interface that can be used, the query can be posted to the Coherity server as an HTTP POST request and the answer will be in XML format. This method can be used to issue queries directly from the application (dynamic queries) or to execute server-side queries (queries that are stored on the CXD server).

DBDOM

DBDom (http://dbdom.sourceforge.net/) is a persistent DOM implementation. It is open source, and is written in Java. This project uses an object-relational mapping to represent XML documents as DOM trees storing the trees in a relational database. The project is in its initial stage and supports Oracle and PostgreSQL. DOM methods are implemented as stored procedures that access the relational mapping of the XML documents.

Extensible Information Server (XIS)

eXcelon Corp's eXtensible Information Server (http://www.exceloncorp.com) is a commercially licensed Native XML Database. It aggregates information from dissimilar systems and maintains a scalable, standards-based information management solution. Although high on performance and concurrency, it lags slightly in query standards support. XIS includes an XML database, an XSLT engine, and a comprehensive suite of tools for connectivity, development, and administration.

Infonyte DB

The Infonyte DB (http://www.infonyte.com/prod_db.html) is a commercially licensed Native XML Database based on a proprietary format, and can store documents of up to 1 terabyte in size. It is also optimized to handle large documents efficiently. Infonyte's product supports the following APIs:

- ❑ DOM (level 2)
- ❑ XQL'99
- ❑ XSLT
- ❑ XPath

The database can be accessed using a Java API so the PHP Java extension must be used to access the product from PHP applications.

Ipedo XML Database

The Ipedo XML database (http://www.ipedo.com/html/products_xml_dat.html) stores documents in a proprietary format and has a commercial licence. The database offers the following APIs to manipulate documents:

- ❑ XPath
- ❑ XSLT
- ❑ XQuery

The APIs can be used through COM, .NET, SOAP, and other interfaces; in particular SOAP can be used from PHP to access the database.

Tamino

Tamino (http://www.softwareag.com/tamino/architecture.htm) was one of the first native XML servers in the market and is certainly one of the most advanced products available for XML storage. It uses a proprietary format based on an ADABAS database to store XML documents.

Tamino supports the following APIs:

❑ XPath (functionality extended)

❑ XSLT

❑ DOM

❑ SAX

❑ XQuery (planned)

The Tamino database can be accessed using SOAP and several HTTP-based mechanisms. Other features include full text indexing, storing of non-XML objects, and many features related to integration between the Tamino database and other systems and architectures.

X-Hive/DB

X-Hive (http://www.x-hive.com/) is an XML database written in Java; documents are stored in an object-oriented database accessed using JDBC. Additional features include full text indexing of XML documents and version control of documents in the database. The following standards are supported in X-Hive:

❑ XPath

❑ XLink / XPointer

❑ XQuery (preview)

❑ DOM (level 2)

❑ XUpdate

❑ XSLT

❑ WebDAV

To use X-Hive from PHP we have to use the PHP Java extension to access the X-Hive Java API.

Xindice (formerly dbXML)

Xindice (http://xml.apache.org/xindice/) is a Native XML Database developed by the Apache Software Foundation, and since it is an open source and free project, we have decided to cover Xindice in more detail in this chapter.

Xindice is a Native XML Database written in Java that uses a non-standard binary format to store XML documents. Right now the database is recommended for collections of small- to mid-sized XML documents, support for large XML documents is planned for the near future. Xindice, being an open source project accords us the chance to use it as an excellent introductory tool to the world of Native XML Databases. In the next section we shall look at Xindice in further detail.

Xindice

In this section, we shall explore the Xindice database from both a conceptual standpoint and a practical one. Specifically, we shall put it to use, using both the command line interface it offers and also accessing it from PHP. We shall start with installing Xindice, proceed to review some of its features, and finally access the Xindice database from PHP in order to insert and retrieve XML documents.

Overview of Xindice

Xindice is a typical example of a Native XML Database that stores documents in a binary format on the file system. It is written entirely in Java and provides several interfaces to insert, update, and manage XML documents. The following picture should be able to provide an idea of the API structure:

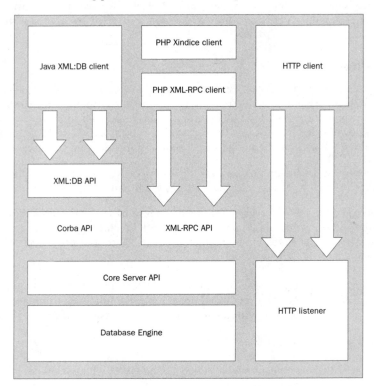

Xindice has a core server API, not exposed to developers, which is used by the database engine internally. The CORBA (Common Object Request Broker Architecture) API is built on top of this API. The core server API was intended to facilitate access to the database for non-Java clients. However, it is possible that this API will be deprecated at some point in the future in favor of RPC-like APIs, such as XML-RPC (XML Remote Procedure Call) or SOAP (Simple Object Access Protocol). Currently, the XML:DB API for accessing the database from a Java program is implemented on top of the CORBA API.

An XML-RPC API has recently been introduced with the intention of using this to replace the CORBA API at some point in the future when the former becomes more stable. Currently, the PHP API for accessing the Xindice server uses the XML-RPC API. Xindice also has an HTTP listener interface exposed. HTTP clients may 'POST' XML documents to the listener.

The figure merely illustrates how the PHP client technology stacks up over the Xindice layers. Xindice is much more flexible than that. For instance, the CORBA layer is designed such that in future other technologies that understand CORBA, such as .NET and C++, can interact at this level as well. Further, the XML-RPC API layer allows access from any other technology that can speak XML-RPC; languages such as Python, Perl, etc., are likely candidates.

Installation

Installing Xindice is quite straightforward and quick. However, we also need to install several other packages that are essential for PHP and Xindice to work together. Below are the instructions on how to go about this task.

Installing Xindice

Before anything else, we need to install Xindice, which is essentially a set of Java class files and script files to run this Java program. It is highly recommended that for version 1.0 of Xindice, the current version at the time of writing, JDK 1.3.1 be used to avoid running into some version-specific JDK bugs. Xindice may be downloaded from http://xml.apache.org/xindice. It is recommended that a binary distribution be downloaded initially, which should suffice for our purposes.

We need to uncompress the file into a directory, for example C:\Xindice (on Windows) or /usr/local/xindice (on Unix). We shall call this the install directory.

Once we have created the install directory, we need to set some environment variables. The first one to be set is XINDICE_HOME, which should point to the install directory; C:\Xindice or /usr/local/xindice. The next environment variable to be set is JAVA_HOME, which should point to the directory in which the JDK is installed.

In Windows, environment variables can be set with the DOS command prompt temporarily or set persistently from **Start Control Panel System**. For instance, the following command executed at the DOS prompt would set the PATH environment variable to the desired value.

```
set PATH=C:\xindice;%PATH%
```

We also need to set an environment variable called CLASSPATH, which is similar to the PATH environment variable of most operating systems. Java uses this environment variable to obtain a list of directories, JAR files or ZIP files, to search for when attempting to load classes. We need to add the complete path leading to the library Xindice.jar to this variable. For instance:

```
setenv CLASSPATH /usr/local/xindice/java/lib/Xindice.jar:$CLASSPATH
```

would add the `Xindice.jar` library to the `CLASSPATH` on a Unix csh shell. In Windows, it would look like this:

```
set CLASSPATH=%CLASSPATH%;C:\Xindice\java\lib\Xindice.jar
```

We can start the server by running the `start` script (Unix) or `startup` script (Windows) in the install directory. To test if the Xindice server has started successfully, we point an HTML browser, such as Netscape, to the machine running the Xindice server and port number `4080`. For example, if Xindice was installed on the machine `localhost`, then the URL to access Xindice would be http://localhost:4080. The browser should display the Xindice homepage if Xindice has been installed and started correctly.

Installing the Xindice XML-RPC Plugin

Now we need to install the XML-RPC plugin, which can be downloaded from http://xindice-xmlrpc.sourceforge.net/. This plugin is necessary for the implementation of the XML-RPC interface to Xindice. At the time of writing, this interface is in beta, though it is quite likely that this, along with a potential SOAP plugin, may be used to replace the CORBA interface.

1. After uncompressing the distribution, we need to copy the JAR files, `apache-xmlrpc.jar` and `xindice-xmlrpc-0.6.jar`, to `$XINDICE_HOME/java/lib`.

2. We need to add the XML-RPC handler (`XMLRPCHandler`) to the Xindice configuration. This can done by modifying the file `$XINDICE_HOME/config/system.xml` as shown below:

Just below the line that reads

```
<components
  class="org.apache.xindice.server.standard.StdComponentManager">
```

add the following line:

```
<component class="org.xmldatabases.xmlrpc.XMLRPCHandler"
  name="XMLRPCHandler"></component>
```

Note that this line starts with `component` and not `components`.

3. Stop and restart Xindice and the following line should show up in the list of startup messages, indicating that the plugin has been installed successfully:

```
Filter: 'XMLRPCHandler' added to filtering chain
```

Installing the XML Parser

The PHP API used to access the Xindice database requires the expat XML parser. This parser can be downloaded from http://sourceforge.net/projects/expat. Binaries for both Windows and Unix are available apart from the sources. For Windows, after installation, copy the files `libexpat.dll` and `libexpatw.dll` present under the lib sub-directory of the expat installation directory to a directory included in the Windows PATH variable from where dynamically loaded libraries are picked up. This could either be C:\Windows\system32 (Windows 95, Windows 98, Windows Me) or C:\Winnt\system32 (Windows NT, Windows 2000, Windows XP). Also, remember to uncomment the line (by removing the semi-colon (;) character) from the line shown in `php.ini`.

```
;extension=php_xslt.dll
```

needs to be changed to:

```
extension=php_xslt.dll
```

Installing the XSLT Parser

Another requirement for the aforementioned API is the Sablotron XSLT processor, which may be downloaded from http://www.gingerall.com. Sablotron is also available in both Windows and Unix binaries. For Windows, after installation, copy the file `sablot.dll` present under the bin sub-directory of the Sablotron installation directory to a directory included in the Windows PATH variable from where dynamically loaded libraries are picked up, as was the case with the expat DLLs.

Recompiling PHP

On non-Windows systems, we need to ensure that our PHP installation has been compiled with the following options:

- ❏ `--with-xml`
- ❏ `--enable-xslt`
- ❏ `--with-xslt-sablot`

We could check if these options are available in the distribution by creating a small PHP script with the following lines, and access it from a browser. This page should display the list of options PHP has been compiled with:

```php
<?php
phpinfo();
?>
```

If these options are missing, PHP needs to be recompiled with these additional options. The following steps describe compiling PHP on a Unix machine as an Apache module (Windows binary distributions pre-compiled with these options are available).

1. Download the Apache sources from http://www.apache.org and PHP sources from http://www.php.net.

2. Uncompress and un-archive the Apache and PHP distributions:

```
$ gzip -cd apache_1.3.x.tar.gz | tar xvf apache_1.3.x.tar
$ gzip -cd  php-x.y.z.tar.gz | tar xvf php-x.y.z.ta
```

x,y and z denote the actual version numbers of the distributions

3. Configure Apache:

```
$ cd apache_1.3.x
$ ./configure --prefix=/www
```

4. Configure PHP with the required options:

```
$ cd ../php-x.x.x
$ ./configure -with-mysql -with-apache=../apache_1.3.x -enable-track-vars
--with-xml -enable-xslt -with-xslt-sablot
```

5. Compile the PHP sources:

```
$ make
```

6. Install the compiled PHP distribution:

```
$ make install
```

7. Activate the new PHP module:

```
$ cd ../apache_1.3.x
$ ./configure -activate-module=src/modules/php4/libphp4.a
```

8. Compile and install Apache:

```
$ make
$ make install
```

Once this is all done, you should have PHP4 installed as an Apache module.

Installing the PHP XML-PRC Library

Now we need to install PHP's XML-RPC library, which may be downloaded from
http://xmlrpc.usefulinc.com/php.html. We need to copy the library to a location from where it can be
accessed by a PHP application, for example under /usr/local/apache/htdocs/php:

```
$ cd /usr/local/apache/htdocs/php
$ unzip xmlrpc1_02.zip
```

On Microsoft Windows platforms, we could use any popular compression software, for instance Winzip,
to uncompress the file.

Installing the PHP Xindice Class Library

Finally, we need to download the PHP-Xindice class library from
http://phpxmlclasses.sourceforge.net/xindice.html (look for the item Xindice – the most current
version at the time of writing is class_xindice_1.2tgz) and copy the PHP file to a location from
where it can be accessed by a PHP application, for example, /usr/local/apache/htdocs/php:

```
$ cd /usr/local/apache/htdocs/php
$ gzip -cd class_xindice_1.2.tgz | tar xvf -
```

On Microsoft Windows platforms, we could use most of the popular compression software, for instance
Winzip, to uncompress the file to the **htdocs** directory of the Apache distribution.

Finally for the XML-RPC library and the Xindice class library to be made available to any PHP program, we include directives to the php.ini file, usually located under /usr/local/lib/php.ini:

```
include_path =
  ".:/usr/local/apache/htdocs/php/xindice:/usr/local/apache/htdocs/php/
  xmlrpc:/usr/local/apache/htdocs/php/class_xindice:/usr/local/apache/
  htdocs/php/class_xindice/xmlrpc"
```

On Microsoft Windows platforms, a typical configuration would look like:

```
include_path = ".;C:\apache\htdocs\php\xindice;
  C:\apache\htdocs\php\xmlrpc;C:\apache\htdocs\php\class_xindice;
  C:\apache\htdocs\php\class_xindice\xmlrpc"
```

Working with Xindice

xindiceadmin and xindice are command line utilities available under the bin directory of a Xindice installation. xindice can be used to perform various user-level tasks on the Xindice database. xindiceadmin can be used to perform administrative tasks, apart from which, it can also perform all tasks that could be performed with xindice. These are Java programs that use the XML:DB API to connect to a Xindice server to perform administrative tasks. The most common usage for these utilities follows the syntax:

```
$ xindice (or xindiceadmin) action -c collection arguments
```

Below is a syntactical breakdown of the command line:

- ❏ action indicates the action to be performed. This could be specified as a long form, for instance add_collection, rather than the short form:

  ```
  $ xindiceadmin ac -c /db -n employeedb
  ```

  There are more actions to list the collection, create new collections, and documents, and delete collections and documents.

- ❏ collection indicates the name of the collection to which the action should apply.

- ❏ arguments depend on the action to be performed and could be optional for some actions. A typical example of arguments is when using the add_document or ad action. For example, -f empdb.xml would indicate that the document to be inserted should be picked up from the file empdb.xml. And -n empdb would indicate that the document needs to be inserted with the key empdb.

We shall use the command line interface provided by Xindice to get a feel for the database and work with some of the concepts we discussed earlier in the chapter. To work with the examples in this section it is sufficient to perform a simple installation of Xindice as explained in Step 1 in the previous section. After installing Xindice, we start it by executing the start script (Unix) or startup.bat (Windows) in the bin directory of the Xindice installation. We will start by loading some sample data into the Xindice database.

Here is a sample XML document that we could load into the Xindice database. We shall name it empdb.xml, and save it in in the htdocs folder.

```xml
<?xml version="1.0"?>
<myorg>
  <floors>
    <floor id="1234">3</floor>
    <floor id="4567">2</floor>
    <floor id="7890">1</floor>
  </floors>
  <departments>
    <engineering>
      <employee id="99999">
        <name>Harry</name>
        <floor>1</floor>
      </employee>
      <employee id="66666">
        <name>Steve</name>
        <floor>2</floor>
      </employee>
      <employee id="77777">
        <name>Tara</name>
        <floor>1</floor>
      </employee>
    </engineering>

    <accounting>
      <employee id="88888">
        <name>Bob</name>
        <floor>3</floor>
      </employee>
      <employee id="44444">
        <name>Sam</name>
        <floor>3</floor>
      </employee>
      <employee id="33333">
        <name>Minnie</name>
        <floor>3</floor>
      </employee>
    </accounting>
  </departments>
</myorg>
```

Let's see how we can get the data in this document into our database.

Try It Out – Inserting XML Documents

Before we insert the sample document listed above, we need to create a collection in the database and then insert the file under this collection. Like so:

```
$ xindiceadmin ac -c /db -n employeedb
Created : /db/employeedb
```

Now the collection is created, we are ready to upload the document saved in a file, in our case empdb.xml:

```
$ xindice ad -c /db/employeedb -f empdb.xml -n empdb
Added document /db/employeedb/empdb
```

To verify that the document has been inserted under the right collection, we could list all the documents under the `/db/employeedb` collection:

```
$ xindice ld -c /db/employeedb

  empdb
Total documents: 1
```

We can view the document through Xindice as follows:

```
$ xindice rd -c /db/employeedb -n empdb
<?xml version="1.0"?>
<myorg>
  <floors>
    <floor id="1234">3</floor>
    <floor id="4567">2</floor>
    <floor id="7890">1</floor>
  </floors>
  <departments>
    <engineering>
    <employee id="99999">
    <name>Harry</name>
. . . . .
```

We can delete the collection and therefore all the documents under it:

```
$ xindiceadmin dc -c /db -n employeedb
Are you sure you want to delete the collection employeedb ? (y/n)
y
Deleted: /db/employeedb
```

Finally we shut down the Xindice database

```
$ xindiceadmin shutdown -c /db
```

How it Works

Initially, we created a collection specifying `ac` as the action:

```
$ xindiceadmin ac -c /db -n employeedb
```

We could use the long form, `add_collection`, which would have worked the same. Using the `-c` switch, we specify the collection under which the new collection is to be created. In this case, a new collection called `employeedb` is created under the root collection `/db`. The root collection is available by default when installed. New collections are added under the root collection or under other collections below the root collection.

We then inserted the document `empdb.xml` with the key `empdb` under the collection `/db/employeedb`:

```
$ xindice ad -c /db/employeedb -f empdb.xml -n empdb
```

The action was specified as ad, which is the equivalent of add_document.

Next, we listed the documents under the collection /db/employeedb by specifying the ld or list_documents action:

```
$ xindice ld -c /db/employeedb
```

We retrieved the document that was inserted using the rd or retrieve_document action:

```
$ xindice rd -c /db/employeedb -n empdb
```

Then we queried the Xindice database using the xpath_query action:

```
$ xindice xpath_query -c /db/employeedb -q '/myorg/departments/engineering'
```

The –q option was used to specify the query string. The query string is specified in the *XPath* format, which we shall look at in some detail soon.

Finally, we removed the collection and consequently the document(s) under it by specifying the dc or delete_collection action:

```
$ xindiceadmin dc -c /db -n employeedb
```

Xindice User's Guide at http://www.dbxml.org/docs/UsersGuide and Administrator's Guide at http://www.dbxml.org/docs/AdministratorsGuide.html, provide a detailed description of the Xindice command line utilities.

Accessing Xindice from PHP

In the previous section, we briefly saw how we could use the command line utilities supplied with the Xindice distribution to access the Xindice database and manage it. In this section we shall take a comprehensive look at how these tasks can be achieved using PHP scripts.

Try It Out – Accessing Xindice from PHP

The script below performs various administrative and user-level tasks by calling the various methods on the Xindice class supplied in the Xindice-PHP distribution. This following example is intended to be more illustrative than to perform any one particular task. Save the following script as usexindiceclass.php in a directory from where PHP can load scripts, for example /usr/local/Apache/htdocs/php/xindice.

Next, follow the sequence of steps:

1. Instantiate an object of the class:

```
<?php
//Ensure that class_xindice.php resides in a directory which PHP will search
//for scripts to load, using the include_path directive in php.ini.
```

```
//Alternative is to use the absolute path to class_xindice.php

include_once('class_xindice.php');

//These need to be set to the right values for a particular installation
//Or localhost if Xindice is running on the same machine as PHP
$xindice_server = "penguin.myorg.com";

$xindice_port = 4080;

//Create an instance of the Xindice class
$xindice = new Xindice($xindice_server, $xindice_port);

if (!$xindice) {
 die("Failed to create Xindice object");
} else {
 //Turn off XML-RPC debugging
 $xindice->setXmlRpcDebug(false);
 echo "<b>Created Xindice object</b>";
 echo "<br><br>";
}
```

2. Create a new collection under which we can add documents:

```
//Create a new collection to add documents
$base_collection = "/db";
$new_collection = "employeedb";
$ret = $xindice->createCollection($base_collection, $new_collection);
if ($ret) {
 $err_mesg = $xindice->getError($xindice_server, $xindice_port);
 die("Failed to create collection. Error returned is: " . $err_mesg);
} else {
 echo "<b>Successfully created the collection </b>" . $new_collection . "<b> under
</b>" . $base_collection . "</b>";
 echo "<br><br>";
}
```

3. List the collections under the parent collection to see if our collection actually got created:

```
//List the collections under the parent collection
$collection = "/db";
$list = $xindice->listCollections($collection);
if (!$list) {
 $err_mesg = $xindice->getError($xindice_server, $xindice_port);
 die("Failed to list collection. Error returned is: " . $err_mesg);
} else {
 echo "<b>Following collections are present under </b>" . $collection;
 echo ":<br>";
 foreach ($list as $coll) {
  echo $coll;
  echo "<br>";
 }
 echo "<br><br>";
}
```

4. Insert a document under the new collection. This is the same document, which in the previous section, we used to illustrate the Xindice command line utilities:

```
//Add/insert a document under the new collection
$collection = "/db/employeedb";
$key = "empdb";
//Note: Ensure that the file empdb.xml is in the same directory as the
//this script or use the absolute path to the XML file
$xml_file = join(' ', file('./empdb.xml'));
$ret = $xindice->insertDocument($collection, $key, $xml_file);
if (!ret) {
 $err_mesg = $xindice->getError($xindice_server, $xindice_port);
 die("Failed to insert a new document under " . $collection . " Error returned: "
 . $err_mesg);
} else {
 echo "<b>Succesfully inserted a new document under </b>" . $collection;
 echo "<br><br>";
}
```

5. List all the documents under this collection to make sure that the new document did indeed get created:

```
//List the documents under this collection
$collection = "/db/employeedb";
$list = $xindice->listDocuments($collection);
if (!$list) {
 $err_mesg = $xindice->getError($xindice_server, $xindice_port);
 die("Failed to list the documents under " . $collection . " Error returned is: "
 . $err_mesg);
} else {
 echo "<b>Following documents are present under </b>" . $collection;
 echo ":<br>";
 foreach ($list as $document) {
  echo $document;
  echo "<br>";
 }
 echo "<br><br>";
}
```

6. Attempt to count the number of documents under the newly created collection:

```
//Get a count of the documents under this collection
$collection = "/db/employeedb";
$count = $xindice->getDocumentCount($collection);
echo "<b>Number of documents under </b>" . $collection . ": " . $count;
echo "<br><br>";
```

7. Attempt to retrieve the document that we had previously inserted:

```
//Retrieve the document from the collection
$collection = "/db/employeedb";
$key = "empdb";
$document = $xindice->getDocument($collection, $key);
echo "<b>Retrieved document</b>: <br>";
echo $document;
echo "<br><br>";
```

8. Create an index on the collection. An index speeds up queries that match the pattern specified in the index.

```
//Create an index on the collection
$collection = "/db/employeedb";
$index_name = "empname";
$index_pattern = "name";
$ret = $xindice->createIndexer($collection, $index_name, $index_pattern);
if ($ret) {
 $err_mesg = $xindice->getError($xindice_server, $xindice_port);
 die("Failed to create a new index on " . $collection . " Error returned: " .
$err_mesg);
} else {
 echo "<b>Succesfully created a new index on </b>" . $collection;
 echo "<br><br>";
}
```

9. Query the newly created collection, searching for employees in the Engineering department:

```
//Query the collection
$collection = "/db/employeedb";
$query_type = "XPath";
$query = "/myorg/departments/engineering/employee/name";
$result = $xindice->queryCollection($collection, $query_type, $query);
if (!$result) {
 $err_mesg = $xindice->getError($xindice_server, $xindice_port);
 die("Failed to query " . $collection . " Error returned: " . $err_mesg);
} else {
 echo "<b>Query result (querying the collection):</b><br>";
 echo $result;
 echo "<br><br>";
}
```

10. Query the newly inserted document itself, searching for employees in the Engineering department. In this particular case, it is essentially the same as querying the collection in the previous step, since the collection contains just one document.

```
//Query the newly inserted document
$collection = "/db/employeedb";
$query_type = "XPath";
$query = "/myorg/departments/engineering/employee/name";
$document_key = "empdb";
$result = $xindice->queryDocument($collection, $query_type, $query,
$document_key);
if (!$result) {
 $err_mesg = $xindice->getError($xindice_server, $xindice_port);
 die("Failed to query " . $document_key . " Error returned: " . $err_mesg);
} else {
 echo "<b>Query result (querying the document):</b><br>";
 echo $result;
 echo "<br><br>";
}
```

11. Delete the index on the collection:

```
//Delete the index on this collection
$collection = "/db/employeedb";
$index_name = "empname";
$ret = $xindice->dropIndexer($collection, $index_name);
if ($ret) {
 $err_mesg = $xindice->getError($xindice_server, $xindice_port);
 die("Failed to delete the index on " . $collection . " Error returned: " .
$err_mesg);
} else {
 echo "<b>Deleted the index on </b>" . $collection;
 echo "<br><br>";
}
```

12. Delete the inserted document:

```
//Remove the newly inserted document
$collection = "/db/employeedb";
$document_key = "empdb";
$ret = $xindice->removeDocument($collection, $document_key);
if ($ret) {
 $err_mesg = $xindice->getError($xindice_server, $xindice_port);
 die("Failed to remove document with the key " . $document_key . " Error returned:
" . $err_mesg);
} else {
 echo "<b>Deleted the document with the key </b>" . $document_key;
 echo "<br><br>";
}
```

13. Delete the collection that we created:

```
//Remove the newly inserted collection
$collection_path = "/db/employeedb";
$ret = $xindice->dropCollection($collection_path);
if ($ret) {
 $err_mesg = $xindice->getError($xindice_server, $xindice_port);
 die("Failed to remove the collection " . $collection_path . " Error returned: " .
$err_mesg);
} else {
 echo "<b>Deleted the collection </b>" . $collection_path;
 echo "<br><br>";
}
?>
```

We need to save the script to a location accessible by the web server. The following screenshots show the script in action:

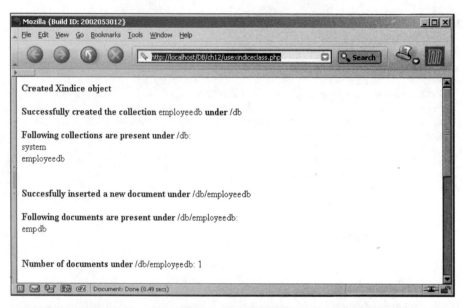

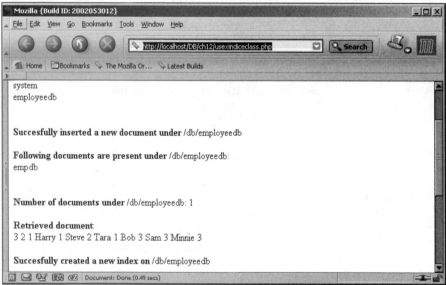

How It Works

In the first step, we included the PHP script, which contains the Xindice-PHP class. We also set the value of the Xindice server host name and port number to point to our local installation. We then instantiated a `Xindice` object by calling the `Xindice()` constructor, which takes the Xindice server name and port number as arguments.

```
$xindice = new Xindice($xindice_server, $xindice_port);
```

On successfully creating the object, we turned off XML-RPC debugging. Since PHP clients talk to a Xindice server using XML-RPC, turning this on during the development phase is useful in debugging any issues that arise. However, in a production environment, it is best to turn it off.

In Step 2, we created a new collection by calling the `createCollection()` method of the Xindice object:

```
$ret = $xindice->createCollection($base_collection, $new_collection);
```

This method takes two arguments, `new_collection`, and its parent class, `base_collection`.

Then, we listed the collections under the parent collection, `/db`. This helps us verify that the new collection was indeed created. We called the `listCollection()` method for this, passing the name of the collection.

```
$list = $xindice->listCollections($collection);
```

Next, we inserted a new document under the collection supplying a key that is required later on when referring to the document. We inserted the new document by calling the `insertDocument()` method, which takes the name of the collection, the document key, and the XML file to be uploaded for arguments, concatenated as a string:

```
$ret = $xindice->insertDocument($collection, $key, $xml_file);
```

The key can be randomly generated using the `rand()` function of PHP or any other unique name that is intuitive in the context of the application. We need to ensure that the `empdb.xml` file is present in the same directory as the script or if present in a different directory, the correct location must be specified in the script.

In Step 5, we listed the documents under the new collection so that we could verify that the new document indeed got created. We listed all the documents under the collection by calling the `listDocuments()` method, which takes the name of the collection as the argument.

```
$list = $xindice->listDocuments($collection);
```

After that, we counted the number of documents under the collection. There should just be one, since we inserted just one document. To count the number of documents under the collection, we invoked the `getDocumentCount()` method passing the name of the collection as an argument.

```
$count = $xindice->getDocumentCount($collection);
```

In step 7, we retrieved the document that was previously inserted by us. We did this by invoking the `getDocument()` method, passing the name of the collection and the document key specified at the time of insertion:

```
$document = $xindice->getDocument($collection, $key);
```

Next, we created an index on the new collection. An index can be specified using a pattern, which may include specific element names or attributes or use wildcards. Queries that match the pattern enjoy improved performance. Here is a list of examples for index patterns and sample queries that might benefit from adding an index using that pattern. The examples can be even better appreciated once we get to a subsequent section where we discuss XPath in some detail.

Index pattern	Description	Example	Sample matching query
ElementName	Name of a specific element	Name	/myorg/departments /engineering/ employee/name
ElementName@attrName	Name of a particular attribute of an element	name@id	/myorg/departments /engineering/emplo yee[@id='99999']
*	All elements	*	/myorg/floors
*@attrName	Name of a particular attribute applicable to all elements	*@id	/myorg/floors/floo r[@id='1234']
ElementName@*	All attributes of a particular element	employe e@*	/myorg/departments /engineering/emplo yee[@id='99999']
@	All attributes of all elements	*@*	/myorg/floors

> It is always best to create as specific an index as possible. Indexes with a very broad scope may actually hinder query performance.

The index is created by invoking the createIndexer() method, passing the name of the collection, name of the index, and the index pattern as arguments:

```
$ret = $xindice->createIndexer($collection, $index_name, $index_pattern);
```

In step 9, we queried the newly created collection, to list the name sub-elements of all employee elements in the Engineering department. We did this by invoking the queryCollection() method, passing the name of the collection, query type, and the query itself. The query is an XPath query, which describes the path leading to the element that we intend to query. The only supported query type is XPath, though in future, support for XQuery or other query mechanisms may be supported.

```
$result = $xindice->queryCollection($collection, $query_type, $query);
```

In the next step, we queried the newly inserted document using the queryDocument() method to list the name sub-elements of all employee elements in the Engineering department:

```
$result = $xindice->queryDocument($collection, $query_type, $query,
$document_key);
```

The query is the same as before. Since we just inserted one document in the collection, the result should be the same as with the previous query.

The query results in the browser are not properly formatted, with the names bunched together. This is because the query result is in XML, which was not properly formatted by the browser. However, if we looked at the source of this page from the browser, we should see the following query result (other content is deleted for brevity):

```
<?xml version="1.0"?>
<result count="3">
  <name xmlns:src="http://xml.apache.org/xindice/Query" src:col="/db/employeedb"
src:key="empdb">Harry</name>
  <name xmlns:src="http://xml.apache.org/xindice/Query" src:col="/db/employeedb"
src:key="empdb">Steve</name>
  <name xmlns:src="http://xml.apache.org/xindice/Query" src:col="/db/employeedb"
src:key="empdb">Tara</name>
</result>
```

Noticeably, there is a `result` element, which encapsulates the result and indicates the number of elements that constitute the result. Also, three new attributes are present in each of the result elements: `xmlns:src`, `src:col`, and `src:key`. The `xmlns:src` attribute indicates the XML namespace of the other two new attributes. XML namespace, very loosely defined, indicates a certain context in which elements and attributes of a particular type have a certain meaning. In this case, the context is the query result and the attributes `src:col` and `src:key` indicate the collection (`/db/employeedb`) and key (`empdb`) of the document to which the elements belong. This is particularly useful when we query a collection with several documents and we need to establish the origin document of each of the query results.

In step 11, we deleted the index that we had created. We do this by invoking the `dropIndexer()` method, specifying the name of the collection and the index name, which was specified at the time the index was created:

```
$ret = $xindice->dropIndexer($collection, $index_name);
```

Next, we deleted the document that was inserted by invoking the `removeDocument()` method, passing the name of the collection and the document key that was specified when the document was inserted for the first time:

```
$ret = $xindice->removeDocument($collection, $document_key);
```

Finally, we proceeded to delete our collection, by invoking the `dropCollection()` method, passing the path leading to the collection, in this case `/db/employeedb`:

```
$ret = $xindice->dropCollection($collection_path);
```

Deleting the collection quite obviously results in the deletion of associated documents and indexes also.

XPath

In the previous sections, we have often referred to XPath as a mechanism to specify queries. XPath has much more significance than fashioning XML queries out of it. By definition, XPath can be used to refer to various parts of an XML document – to elements, attributes, and text nodes. Some of us might have already observed that XPath uses paths similar to file system paths to define XML elements. However, the expression syntax used to define a path is quite powerful. In fact, the power of XPath derives from the extensive constructs and functions it provides to address various aspects of an XML document. As we shall soon see, XPath is also used to identify elements and attributes in XML documents when they are transformed using XSLT.

With Xindice, XPath is used to query both documents and collections. In this section we shall look at some examples in PHP that will clarify the function of XPath.

Note: For all the Try It Out examples in this section, the previously mentioned `empdb.xml` file should be loaded as `/db/employeedb/empdb` after creating the `/db/employeedb` collection:

```
$ xindiceadmin ac -c /db -n employeedb
$ xindice ad -c /db/employeedb -f empdb.xml -n empdb
```

Try It Out – Querying with the Complete Path

We are going to execute a query which returns a list of the `name` elements corresponding to all employees in the Engineering department under the `myorg` document.

```php
<?php
include_once('class_xindice.php');

$xindice_server = "localhost";
$xindice_port = 4080;

//Create an instance of the Xindice class
$xindice = new Xindice($xindice_server, $xindice_port);

if (!$xindice) {
  die("Failed to create Xindice object");
} else {
    //Turn off XML-RPC debugging
    $xindice->setXmlRpcDebug(false);
  }

//Query the collection using XPath

//Query string - '//departments/engineering/employee/name'
$collection = "/db/employeedb";
$query_type = "XPath";
$query = "//departments/engineering/employee/name";
$result = $xindice->queryCollection($collection, $query_type, $query);
if (!$result) {
  $err_mesg = $xindice->getError($xindice_server, $xindice_port);
```

```
      die("Failed to query " . $collection . " Error returned: " . $err_mesg);
  } else {
     echo $result;
  }

?>
```

How it Works

We created a `Xindice` object as before and turned off the XML-RPC debugging. We then specified the collection that we intended to query and also the query type, which in this case is `XPath`. Xindice also supports the `XUpdate` query type, which we shall look at in a later section. We then specified the query as `/myorg/departments/engineering/employee/name`, which returns a list of the `name` elements corresponding to all employees in the Engineering department in the `myorg` document.

Try It Out – Querying for any Element with a Given Name

Now, we are going to execute a query which returns a list of elements corresponding to all employees in all the departments:

```php
<?php
include_once('class_xindice.php');

$xindice_server = "localhost";
$xindice_port = 4080;

//Create an instance of the Xindice class
$xindice = new Xindice($xindice_server, $xindice_port);

if (!$xindice) {
  die("Failed to create Xindice object");
} else {
   //Turn off XML-RPC debugging
   $xindice->setXmlRpcDebug(false);
}

//Query the collection using XPath

//Query string - '//name'
$collection = "/db/employeedb";
$query_type = "XPath";
$query = "//name";
$result = $xindice->queryCollection($collection, $query_type, $query);
if (!$result) {
   $err_mesg = $xindice->getError($xindice_server, $xindice_port);
   die("Failed to query " . $collection . " Error returned: " . $err_mesg);
} else {
   echo $result;
}

?>
```

How it Works

We specified the query as `//name`, which returns a list of the `name` elements corresponding to all employees in all the departments.

Try It Out – Querying with a Wildcard

In this example, we are going to execute a query which returns a list of all the department elements and their sub-elements.

```php
<?php
include_once('class_xindice.php');

$xindice_server = "localhost";
$xindice_port = 4080;

//Create an instance of the Xindice class
$xindice = new Xindice($xindice_server, $xindice_port);

if (!$xindice) {
  die("Failed to create Xindice object");
} else {
   //Turn off XML-RPC debugging
   $xindice->setXmlRpcDebug(false);
  }
```

```php
//Query the collection using XPath

//Query string - '/myorg/departments/*'
$collection = "/db/employeedb";
$query_type = "XPath";
$query = "/myorg/departments/*";
```

```php
$result = $xindice->queryCollection($collection, $query_type, $query);
if (!$result) {
  $err_mesg = $xindice->getError($xindice_server, $xindice_port);
  die("Failed to query " . $collection . " Error returned: " . $err_mesg);
} else {
   echo $result;
  }

?>
```

How it Works

This time we specified the query as /myorg/departments/*, which returns a list of all the department elements and their sub-elements. This is a typical example of superfluous data shortcomings, where the querying for departments returns the list of all the employees working under all departments.

Try It Out – Querying with a Wildcard and Terminating in a Fixed Element

This time we are going to execute a query which returns a list of the names of all employees working in all the departments.

```php
<?php
include_once('class_xindice.php');

$xindice_server = "localhost";
$xindice_port = 4080;
```

```
//Create an instance of the Xindice class
$xindice = new Xindice($xindice_server, $xindice_port);

if (!$xindice) {
  die("Failed to create Xindice object");
} else {
    //Turn off XML-RPC debugging
    $xindice->setXmlRpcDebug(false);
  }


//Query the collection using XPath

//Query string - '/myorg/departments/*/employee/name'
$collection = "/db/employeedb";
$query_type = "XPath";
$query = "/myorg/departments/*/employee/name";
$result = $xindice->queryCollection($collection, $query_type, $query);
if (!$result) {
  $err_mesg = $xindice->getError($xindice_server, $xindice_port);
  die("Failed to query " . $collection . " Error returned: " . $err_mesg);
} else {
    echo $result;
  }

?>
```

How it Works

We specified the query as /myorg/departments/*/employee/name, which returns a list of the names of all employees working in all the departments. The asterisk acts as a wildcard that matches all the departments.

Try It Out – Querying for the *n*th Child

Now, we are going to execute a query that returns the second element in the list of employee elements under engineering.

```
<?php
include_once('class_xindice.php');

$xindice_server = "localhost";
$xindice_port = 4080;

//Create an instance of the Xindice class
$xindice = new Xindice($xindice_server, $xindice_port);

if (!$xindice) {
  die("Failed to create Xindice object");
} else {
    //Turn off XML-RPC debugging
    $xindice->setXmlRpcDebug(false);
  }


//Query the collection using XPath
```

```
//Query string - '/myorg/departments/engineering/employee[2]'
$collection = "/db/employeedb";
$query_type = "XPath";
$query = "/myorg/departments/engineering/employee[2]";

$result = $xindice->queryCollection($collection, $query_type, $query);
if (!$result) {
  $err_mesg = $xindice->getError($xindice_server, $xindice_port);
  die("Failed to query " . $collection . " Error returned: " . $err_mesg);
} else {
    echo $result;
  }

?>
```

How it Works

Here, we specified the query as /myorg/departments/engineering/employee[2], which returns the second element in the list of employee elements under engineering. It is worthwhile to note that the first element has an index of 1 and not 0, as in some programming languages.

Try It Out – Querying for the Last Child

We are executing a query which returns the last employee element under engineering.

```
<?php
include_once('class_xindice.php');

$xindice_server = "localhost";
$xindice_port = 4080;

//Create an instance of the Xindice class
$xindice = new Xindice($xindice_server, $xindice_port);

if (!$xindice) {
  die("Failed to create Xindice object");
} else {
    //Turn off XML-RPC debugging
    $xindice->setXmlRpcDebug(false);
}
```

```
//Query the collection using XPath

//Query string - '/myorg/departments/engineering/employee[last()]'
$collection = "/db/employeedb";
$query_type = "XPath";
$query = "/myorg/departments/engineering/employee[last()]";

$result = $xindice->queryCollection($collection, $query_type, $query);
if (!$result) {
  $err_mesg = $xindice->getError($xindice_server, $xindice_port);
  die("Failed to query " . $collection . " Error returned: " . $err_mesg);
} else {
    echo $result;
  }
?>
```

How it Works

We specified the query as `/myorg/departments/engineering/employee[last()]`, which returns the last employee `element` under `engineering`.

Try It Out – Querying for an Attribute Match

Now, we are going to execute a query which returns the `employee` element with an `id` attribute whose value is `99999`.

```php
<?php
include_once('class_xindice.php');

$xindice_server = "localhost";
$xindice_port = 4080;

//Create an instance of the Xindice class
$xindice = new Xindice($xindice_server, $xindice_port);

if (!$xindice) {
  die("Failed to create Xindice object");
} else {
    //Turn off XML-RPC debugging
    $xindice->setXmlRpcDebug(false);
  }


//Query the collection using XPath

//Query string - '/myorg/departments/engineering/employee[@id='99999']'
$collection = "/db/employeedb";
$query_type = "XPath";
$query = "/myorg/departments/engineering/employee[@id='99999']";
$result = $xindice->queryCollection($collection, $query_type, $query);
if (!$result) {
  $err_mesg = $xindice->getError($xindice_server, $xindice_port);
  die("Failed to query " . $collection . " Error returned: " . $err_mesg);
} else {
    echo $result;
  }

?>
```

How it Works

In this query, we specified the query as `/myorg/departments/engineering/employee[@id='99999']`, which returns the `employee` element with an `id` attribute whose value is `99999`. The @ symbol is used to refer to attributes.

Try It Out – Querying for an Attribute Match with a Wildcard in the Path

We are going to execute a query that returns a list of all the `employee` elements corresponding to employees who work on the second floor.

```php
<?php
include_once('class_xindice.php');

$xindice_server = "localhost";
$xindice_port = 4080;

//Create an instance of the Xindice class
$xindice = new Xindice($xindice_server, $xindice_port);

if (!$xindice) {
  die("Failed to create Xindice object");
} else {
    //Turn off XML-RPC debugging
    $xindice->setXmlRpcDebug(false);
}

//Query the collection using XPath

//Query string - '/myorg/departments/*/employee[floor="2"]'
$collection = "/db/employeedb";
$query_type = "XPath";
$query = '/myorg/departments/*/employee[floor="2"]';

$result = $xindice->queryCollection($collection, $query_type, $query);
if (!$result) {
  $err_mesg = $xindice->getError($xindice_server, $xindice_port);
  die("Failed to query " . $collection . " Error returned: " . $err_mesg);
} else {
    echo $result;
  }

?>
```

How it Works

We specified the query as /myorg/departments/*/employee/[floor="2"], which returns a list of all the employee elements corresponding to employees who work on the second floor.

This is only an introduction and by no means an exhaustive coverage of the functions and functionality that XPath provides. In fact XPath is a W3C Standard and the XPath specification is available at http://www.w3.org/TR/xpath. For further reading on XPath, *Professional XML: 2nd Edition*, Wrox Press; *ISBN: 1861005059,* is an excellent resource.

XUpdate

While XPath is used to query data existing in the Native XML Database, it has no means to update existing data. The XUpdate specification addresses this requirement. XUpdate operations are defined as complete XML documents that describe the location within the document where the operation should be performed and what the operations are.

XUpdate uses XPath to select elements, which are then updated or processed as per the operations specified in the XUpdate document. Operations range from inserting new elements, to deleting existing ones, and to modifying attributes. An update is represented by a top-level Xupdate:modifications element in an XML document. This element requires a mandatory version attribute, which is currently set to 1.0.

The `Xupdate:modifications` element in turn may contain the following types of sub-elements:

Sub-element name	Description
`Xupdate:insert-before`	Inserts elements, attributes, or text-nodes before the selected element(s) or attribute(s).
`Xupdate:insert-after`	Inserts elements, attributes, or text-nodes after the selected element(s) or attribute(s).
`Xupdate:append`	Appends elements, attributes, or text-nodes to the selected element(s) or attribute(s).
`Xupdate:update`	Updates elements, attributes, or text-nodes of children of the selected element(s) or attribute(s).
`Xupdate:remove`	Removes elements, attributes, or text-nodes of the selected element(s).
`Xupdate:rename`	Renames selected elements, attributes, or text-nodes.
`Xupdate:variable`	Defines variables within the scope of the XUpdate XML fragment, which are then used in conjunction with any of the modifiers defined earlier.
`Xupdate:value-of`	Enumerates the value of a particular expression.
`Xupdate:if`	Used for conditional statements in the update logic.

Both `Xupdate:insert-before` and `Xupdate:insert-after` are used to insert elements into the document. These elements require a `select` attribute specifying the node selected by an XPath expression, before or after which the insertion will happen. The `Xupdate:insert-before` and `Xupdate:insert-after` elements may in turn contain the following types of sub-elements:

Sub-element name	Description
`Xupdate:element`	Defines a new element in the target document. It has a `name` attribute, which defines the name of the new element.
`Xupdate:attribute`	Defines a new attribute in the target document. It has a `name` attribute, which defines the name of the new attribute.
`Xupdate:text`	Defines a new text node in the target document.
`Xupdate:processing-instruction`	Defines a new XML-processing instruction in the target document.
`Xupdate:comment`	Defines a new XML comment in the target document.

Without further ado, we shall dive into some examples that will clarify the syntax better.

Try It Out – Inserting After a Selection

To begin with, we are going to execute a query which inserts an employee element.

```php
<?php

include_once('class_xindice.php');

$xindice_server = "localhost";
$xindice_port = 4080;

//Create an instance of the Xindice class
$xindice = new Xindice($xindice_server, $xindice_port);

if (!$xindice) {
  die("Failed to create Xindice object");
} else {
    //Turn off XML-RPC debugging
    $xindice->setXmlRpcDebug(false);
  }
```

```php
//Query the collection using XUpdate to update the document
$collection = "/db/employeedb";
$query_type = "XUpdate";
$query = '<xu:modifications version="1.0"
xmlns:xu="http://www.xmldb.org/xupdate">';
$query = $query . '<xu:insert-after
select="/myorg/departments/engineering/employee[last()]">';
$query = $query . '<xu:element name="employee">';
$query = $query . '<xu:attribute name="id">45678</xu:attribute>';
$query = $query . '<name>Bryce</name>';
$query = $query . '<floor>3</floor>';
$query = $query . '</xu:element>';
$query = $query . '</xu:insert-after>';
$query = $query . '</xu:modifications>';

//XUpdate query
$ret = $xindice->queryCollection($collection, $query_type, $query);
if (!$ret) {
  $err_mesg = $xindice->getError($xindice_server, $xindice_port);
  die("Failed to update " . $collection . " Error returned: " . $err_mesg);
}
```

```php
//XPath query to see if update worked
//Query string - '/myorg/departments/engineering/employee'
$query_type = "XPath";
$query = "/myorg/departments/engineering/employee";
$result = $xindice->queryCollection($collection, $query_type, $query);
if (!$result) {
  $err_mesg = $xindice->getError($xindice_server, $xindice_port);
  die("Failed to query " . $collection . " Error returned: " . $err_mesg);
} else {
    echo $result;
  }

?>
```

How it Works

We specified the collection to be queried and set the query type as XUpdate. Strange as it may sound, we continue to use the queryDocument() method to update an existing document; the differences from an Xpath query being that the query type is XUpdate and that the query itself is in the XUpdate format. In the query we used xu:element to define an additional element that corresponds to a new employee. We also used the xu:attribute element to set the id for the aforementioned element. Submitting the query creates a new employee element in the document below the element that is currently last. This new element can now be seen when the document is fetched using the queryCollection() method.

Try It Out – Inserting Before a Selection

Here, we are inserting a new employee element before a selected element.

```php
<?php

include_once('class_xindice.php');

$xindice_server = "localhost";
$xindice_port = 4080;

//Create an instance of the Xindice class
$xindice = new Xindice($xindice_server, $xindice_port);

if (!$xindice) {
  die("Failed to create Xindice object");
} else {
    //Turn off XML-RPC debugging
    $xindice->setXmlRpcDebug(false);
  }
```

```php
//Query the collection using XUpdate to update the document
$collection = "/db/employeedb";
$query_type = "XUpdate";
$query = '<xu:modifications version="1.0"
xmlns:xu="http://www.xmldb.org/xupdate">';
$query = $query . '<xu:insert-before
select="/myorg/departments/engineering/employee[2]">';
$query = $query . '<xu:element name="employee">';
$query = $query . '<xu:attribute name="id">1234</xu:attribute>';
$query = $query . '<name>Danielle</name>';
$query = $query . '<floor>2</floor>';
$query = $query . '</xu:element>';
$query = $query . '</xu:insert-before>';
$query = $query . '</xu:modifications>';

//XUpdate query
$ret = $xindice->queryCollection($collection, $query_type, $query);
if (!$ret) {
 $err_mesg = $xindice->getError($xindice_server, $xindice_port);
```

```
    die("Failed to update " . $collection . " Error returned: " . $err_mesg);
}
```

```
//XPath query to see if update worked
//Query string - '/myorg/departments/engineering/employee'
$query_type = "XPath";
$query = "/myorg/departments/engineering/employee";
$result = $xindice->queryCollection($collection, $query_type, $query);
if (!$result) {
  $err_mesg = $xindice->getError($xindice_server, $xindice_port);
  die("Failed to query " . $collection . " Error returned: " . $err_mesg);
} else {
    echo $result;
  }

?>
```

How it Works

In the query, we used the `select` attribute of the `xu:insert-before` element to specify the selection as the second `employee` element in the list of `employee` elements under `engineering`. The `xu:element` is used to define an additional element that corresponds to a new employee. We also used the `xu:attribute` element to set the `id` for the aforementioned element. Submitting the query creates a new `employee` element in the document below the element that is currently the second one under `engineering`. This new element can now be seen when the document is fetched using the `queryCollection()` method.

Try It Out – Appending to a Selection

This script appends a new `employee` element to the document below the element that is currently the last `employee` element under `engineering`:

```
<?php

include_once('class_xindice.php');

$xindice_server = "localhost";
$xindice_port = 4080;

//Create an instance of the Xindice class
$xindice = new Xindice($xindice_server, $xindice_port);

if (!$xindice) {
  die("Failed to create Xindice object");
} else {
    //Turn off XML-RPC debugging
    $xindice->setXmlRpcDebug(false);
```

```
        }

        //Query the collection using XUpdate to update the document
        $collection = "/db/employeedb";
        $query_type = "XUpdate";
        $query = '<xu:modifications version="1.0"
        xmlns:xu="http://www.xmldb.org/xupdate">';
        $query = $query . '<xu:append select="//engineering" child="last()">';
        $query = $query . '<xu:element name="employee">';
        $query = $query . '<xu:attribute name="id">6732</xu:attribute>';
        $query = $query . '<name>Chris</name>';
        $query = $query . '<floor>1</floor>';
        $query = $query . '</xu:element>';
        $query = $query . '</xu:append>';
        $query = $query . '</xu:modifications>';

        //XUpdate query
        $ret = $xindice->queryCollection($collection, $query_type, $query);
        if (!$ret) {
          $err_mesg = $xindice->getError($xindice_server, $xindice_port);
          die("Failed to update " . $collection . " Error returned: " . $err_mesg);
        }

        //XPath query to see if update worked
        //Query string - '/myorg/departments/engineering/employee'
        $query_type = "XPath";
        $query = "/myorg/departments/engineering/employee";
        $result = $xindice->queryCollection($collection, $query_type, $query);
        if (!$result) {
          $err_mesg = $xindice->getError($xindice_server, $xindice_port);
          die("Failed to query " . $collection . " Error returned: " . $err_mesg);
        } else {
            echo $result;
        }

    ?>
```

How it Works

In the query, we used the `select` and `child` attributes of the `xu:append` element to specify the selection as the second `employee` element in the list of `employee` elements under `engineering`. The `xu:element` is used to define an additional element that corresponds to a new employee. We also used the `xu:attribute` element to set the `id` for the aforementioned element. Submitting the query appends a new `employee` element to the document below the element that is currently the last `employee` element under `engineering`. This new element can now be seen when the document is fetched using the `queryCollection()` method.

Try It Out – Updating a Selection

In this script, we change the value of the `name` attribute of the second employee in the engineering department:

```php
<?php

include_once('class_xindice.php');
```

```
$xindice_server = "localhost";
$xindice_port = 4080;

//Create an instance of the Xindice class
$xindice = new Xindice($xindice_server, $xindice_port);

if (!$xindice) {
  die("Failed to create Xindice object");
} else {
    //Turn off XML-RPC debugging
    $xindice->setXmlRpcDebug(false);
  }
```

```
//Query the collection using XUpdate to update the document
$collection = "/db/employeedb";
$query_type = "XUpdate";
$query = '<xu:modifications version="1.0"
xmlns:xu="http://www.xmldb.org/xupdate">';
$query = $query . '<xu:update
select="/myorg/departments/engineering/employee[2]/name">';
$query = $query . 'Daniel';
$query = $query . '</xu:update>';
$query = $query . '</xu:modifications>';

//XUpdate query
$ret = $xindice->queryCollection($collection, $query_type, $query);
if (!$ret) {
  $err_mesg = $xindice->getError($xindice_server, $xindice_port);
  die("Failed to update " . $collection . " Error returned: " . $err_mesg);
}
```

```
//XPath query to see if update worked
//Query string - '/myorg/departments/engineering/employee'
$query_type = "XPath";
$query = "/myorg/departments/engineering/employee";
$result = $xindice->queryCollection($collection, $query_type, $query);
if (!$result) {
  $err_mesg = $xindice->getError($xindice_server, $xindice_port);
  die("Failed to query " . $collection . " Error returned: " . $err_mesg);
} else {
    echo $result;
  }

?>
```

How it Works

In this query, we used the select attribute of the xu:update element to specify the selection as the name of the second employee in the list of employee elements under engineering. We specified a different spelling for the name attribute (substituting Daniel for Danielle) under the xu:update element. Submitting the query changes the value of this name element. This modified element can be seen when the document is fetched using the queryCollection() method.

Try It Out – Renaming a Selection

In this script, we change the name of the element corresponding to engineering from engineering to codecrew:

```php
<?php

include_once('class_xindice.php');

$xindice_server = "localhost";
$xindice_port = 4080;

//Create an instance of the Xindice class
$xindice = new Xindice($xindice_server, $xindice_port);

if (!$xindice) {
  die("Failed to create Xindice object");
} else {
    //Turn off XML-RPC debugging
    $xindice->setXmlRpcDebug(false);
}

//Query the collection using XUpdate to update the document
$collection = "/db/employeedb";
$query_type = "XUpdate";
$query = '<xu:modifications version="1.0"
xmlns:xu="http://www.xmldb.org/xupdate">';
$query = $query . '<xu:rename select="/myorg/departments/engineering">';
$query = $query . 'codecrew';
$query = $query . '</xu:rename>';
$query = $query . '</xu:modifications>';

//XUpdate query
$ret = $xindice->queryCollection($collection, $query_type, $query);
if (!$ret) {
  $err_mesg = $xindice->getError($xindice_server, $xindice_port);
  die("Failed to update " . $collection . " Error returned: " . $err_mesg);
}

//XPath query to see if update worked
//Query string - '/myorg/departments'
$query_type = "XPath";
$query = "/myorg/departments";
$result = $xindice->queryCollection($collection, $query_type, $query);
if (!$result) {
  $err_mesg = $xindice->getError($xindice_server, $xindice_port);
  die("Failed to query " . $collection . " Error returned: " . $err_mesg);
} else {
    echo $result;
}

?>
```

How it Works

In the query we use the `select` attribute of the `xu:rename` element to specify the selection as the element corresponding to the `engineering` department. We changed the name of the element itself, from `engineering` to `codecrew`, under the `xu:rename` element. Submitting the query changes the name of this element. This modified element can now be seen when the document is fetched using the `queryCollection()` method.

Try It Out – Removing a Selection

In this script, we are attempting to remove an element corresponding to an employee:

```php
<?php

include_once('class_xindice.php');

$xindice_server = "localhost";
$xindice_port = 4080;

//Create an instance of the Xindice class
$xindice = new Xindice($xindice_server, $xindice_port);

if (!$xindice) {
  die("Failed to create Xindice object");
} else {
    //Turn off XML-RPC debugging
    $xindice->setXmlRpcDebug(false);
}
```

```php
//Query the collection using XUpdate to update the document
$collection = "/db/employeedb";
$query_type = "XUpdate";
$query = '<xu:modifications version="1.0"
xmlns:xu="http://www.xmldb.org/xupdate">';
$query = $query . '<xu:remove
select="/myorg/departments/engineering/employee[last()]"/>';
$query = $query . '</xu:modifications>';

//XUpdate query
$ret = $xindice->queryCollection($collection, $query_type, $query);
if (!$ret) {
 $err_mesg = $xindice->getError($xindice_server, $xindice_port);
 die("Failed to update " . $collection . " Error returned: " . $err_mesg);
}
```

```php
//XPath query to see if update worked
//Query string - '/myorg/departments/engineering/employee'
$query_type = "XPath";
$query = "/myorg/departments/engineering/employee";
$result = $xindice->queryCollection($collection, $query_type, $query);
if (!$result) {
  $err_mesg = $xindice->getError($xindice_server, $xindice_port);
```

```
        die("Failed to query " . $collection . " Error returned: " . $err_mesg);
    } else {
        echo $result;
    }

?>
```

How it Works

In the query we use the `select` attribute of the `xu:remove` element to specify the selection as the last of the `employee` elements in the list of `employee` elements under `engineering`. Submitting the query deletes this `employee` element. The modified set of elements can now be seen when the document is fetched using the `queryCollection()` method.

We did not cover the complete functionality offered by the XUpdate specification. In fact the specification is currently still a working draft and may be subject to significant changes in the future. The XML:DB API working group home page at http://www.xmldb.org/xupdate/index.html has more details on the progress of this specification. The XUpdate working draft also serves as an API reference and can be found at http://www.xmldb.org/xupdate/xupdate-wd.html.

Transforming XML

We know XML to be a fantastic tool for representing data. However, to do more with the data, we need to have some mechanisms to filter, sort, and order the data in an XML document. There should also be mechanisms to refer to the various parts of an XML document. This is where XSL comes into the picture. XSL (e**X**tensible **S**ty**L**esheets) is an umbrella technology for three other inter-related technologies, namely XPath, XSL:FO or XSL Formatting Objects, and XSLT or XSL Transformations.

XSLT

For our purposes, we need to transform the XML data obtained from the Native XML Database into HTML or some other markup language that browsers can understand (for instance, WML for certain wireless phones). Therefore, XSLT is of particular interest to us since it can be used to transform an XML document to another markup language. In general, transformations allow programmers to map an existing XML document to another form. This mapping is defined by a set of rules that constitute an XSLT stylesheet.

We shall look at an example that uses an XSLT stylesheet to transform our employee database represented in XML to HTML.

Try It Out – Transforming to HTML

1. We instantiate an object of the `Xindice` class to perform various operations on Xindice:

```php
<?php
include_once('class_xindice.php');
```

```
$xindice_server = "localhost";
$xindice_port = 4080;

//Create an instance of the Xindice class
$xindice = new Xindice($xindice_server, $xindice_port);

if (!$xindice) {
  die("Failed to create Xindice object");
} else {
    //Turn off XML-RPC debugging
    $xindice->setXmlRpcDebug(false);
  }
```

2. Fetch the document specifying the collection and the document key specified at installation:

```
//Fetch the document

$collection = "/db/employeedb";
$document_key = "empdb";
$emp_xml = $xindice->getDocument($collection, $document_key);
if (!$emp_xml) {
  $err_mesg = $xindice->getError($xindice_server, $xindice_port);
  die("Failed to get document from " . $collection . " Error returned: " .
$err_mesg);
}
```

3. Fetch the XSLT stylesheet that is required to transform the document:

```
$emp_xsl = join(' ', file('./emp.xsl'));
$arguments = array('/_xml' => $emp_xml, '/_xsl' => $emp_xsl);
$xh = xslt_create();
```

4. Apply the transformer on the XML and display the results:

```
$result = xslt_process($xh, 'arg:/_xml', 'arg:/_xsl', NULL, $arguments);
echo $result;
?>
```

5. Specify the XSL namespace:

```
<?xml version="1.0" encoding="UTF-8"?>
<xsl:stylesheet version="1.0" xmlns:xsl="http://www.w3.org/1999/XSL/Transform"
xmlns:src="http://xml.apache.org/xindice/Query">

  <xsl:output method="html"/>
```

6. The top-level template match is for the /myorg element:

```
<xsl:template match="/myorg">
  <html><head>
    <title>YetAnotherCompany - copmany non-grata</title>
    <h2>YetAnotherCompany - a profile</h2>
  </head><body>
  <p>
    An ode to a company of unsung gearheads. YetAnotherCompany is based
    out of Silicon slough, ushering in the 'modern times'. Here is a brief
    profile of the company.
  </p>
```

7. We use the xsl:variable and xsl:value-of elements to ascertain the number of floors:

```
  <p>
    <xsl:variable name="num_floors" select="floors/floor"/>
    YetAnotherCompany is based out of a building with
    <xsl:value-of select="count($num_floors)"/>
    floors firmly rooted in suburbia.
  </p>
```

8. We use the xsl:variable and xsl:for-each elements to list the employees working in Engineering:

```
  <p>
    These are the employees that work in Engineering:<br/>
    <xsl:variable name="coder" select="departments/codecrew/employee"/>
    <ul>
    <xsl:for-each select="$coder">
      <li>
        <xsl:value-of select="name"/>
        (employee-id: <xsl:value-of select="@id"/>) works on floor
        <xsl:value-of select="floor"/>
      </li>
    </xsl:for-each>
    </ul>
  </p>
  </body></html>

</xsl:template>
</xsl:stylesheet>
```

This produces the following screenshot when the script is accessed from a browser:

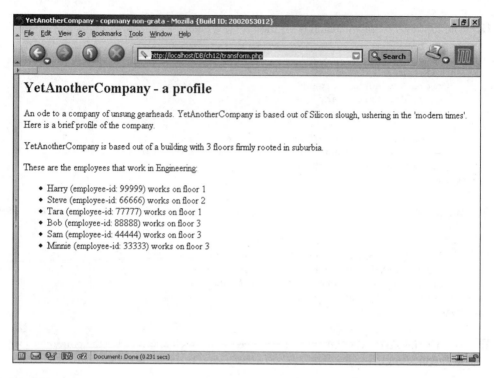

How It Works

First, we instantiated the Xindice class and performed other familiar initialization tasks. Then, we fetched the actual XML document from the database using the getDocument() method. We read in the stylesheet, emp.xsl, using the file() function and used the join() function to concatenate it as a string. Of course, we need to ensure that the emp.xsl file is present in the same directory as the script.

We then went on to apply the transformer using the xslt_process() function. This function takes a handle with the Sablotron XSLT processor as the first argument; in this case the one created by xslt_create(). The second and third arguments represent the indices of an associative array whose first and second values are the XML and XSL documents respectively. This is a technique to allow the Sablotron XSLT processor to load the XML and XSL documents from a script. Once the transformation is performed, we displayed the result, which is in HTML.

Next, we looked at the stylesheet that was used to effect this transformation. The top-level element is the xsl:stylesheet element that specifies the namespace of the XSL stylesheet. The xsl:output element indicates that the transformed output is HTML. We defined the xsl:template element, which matches the element /myorg. All the elements under this xsl:template element have /myorg as their context and therefore, may define paths or expressions relative to it. We used xsl:variable to define the XSLT variable num_floors, which contains the set of nodes that match the expression floors/floor (relative to /myorg and hence /myorg/floors/floor). Then we used the xsl:value-of element and in the select attribute of this element, we used the count() function to count the number of elements in the set of nodes held by the num_floors variable. Finally, we used this count to display HTML indicating the number of floors.

In the last step, we defined another XSLT variable `coder`, which represents the list of all employee elements under `engineering`. We used the `xsl:for-each` element to display the name, employee id (an attribute of the `employee` element), and floor of each of the employees working in Engineering.

This is by no means an exhaustive coverage of the functionality that XSLT provides. It would take an entire book by itself to do justice to the myriad of functions that XSLT provides. *XSLT Programmer's Reference 2nd Edition, Wrox Press Inc; ISBN: 1861005067,* is an excellent reference. XSLT is a W3C Standard and the specification is available at http://www.w3.org/TR/xslt.

XQuery

XQuery is among the latest in the line of query mechanisms for XML data. XQuery is meant to replace XPath as the XML query language of the future. However, at the time of writing, this is still very much a nascent technology and is not supported by most of the Native XML Database vendors. Xindice, for instance, does not yet support XQuery, although this might soon change. This section introduces XQuery very briefly from a conceptual and syntactic standpoint.

XQuery is essentially a vastly improved upon form of XPath. In fact, most of the existing XPath queries will be valid XQuery statements. In addition, XQuery introduces much more powerful SQL-like syntax that vastly improves the querying capabilities. Using XQuery, it is possible to query documents, collections or other abstract groupings of XML documents. In fact, the specification does not dictate the exact type of XML documents, as long as the entity queried upon is represented in XML. This accords vendors lots of freedom in bringing out competitive solutions.

Here is a simple Xpath-like query to return a list of the names of all employees in Accounting:

```
/myorg/departments/accounting/employees/name
```

The FLWR (pronounced as *flower*) query mechanism is the SQL-like syntax referred to in the previous paragraph. This stands for FOR, LET, WHERE, and RETURN. What this means is that we can construct queries of the form:

```
FOR expression WHERE expression
RETURN expression
```

And:

```
LET expression WHERE expression
RETURN expression
```

The previous query to return the list of employees names in accounting can be expressed as, either:

```
FOR $employee WHERE /myorg/departments/accounting/employees
RETURN $employee/name
```

or:

```
LET $employee WHERE /myorg/departments/accounting/employees
RETURN $employee/name
```

The difference between the FOR and LET statement is that the FOR statement iterates over each of the nodes returned, where as the LET statement treats them as a node-set. In this simple example, both constructs do not have a difference. The RETURN statement returns its value only once regardless of whether it is executed multiple times (as in a FOR construct) or once (as in a LET construct).

XQuery is a W3C standard and the specification is available from http://www.w3.org/TR/xquery/.

Summary

In this chapter, we learnt about the various characteristics of Native XML Databases and how they compare with traditional database solutions. We briefly reviewed the workings of Native XML Databases by discussing their storage and grouping models. We also discussed issues and strategies for migrating existing data in a relational database to a Native XML Database.

While observing some of the shortcomings of Native XML Databases in their current shape, we also concluded that these are by no means a panacea to all data storage issues; in fact they are well-suited for certain applications and ill-suited for certain others. We also briefly reviewed the various vendor offerings, before looking in depth at Xindice, an opensource solution.

Using Xindice as our typical Native XML Database, we explored the functionality it provides and also explored the various technologies involved – XPath, XUpdate, XSLT, and the nascent XQuery technology. This chapter provides us with a firm footing for moving on to the next chapter in which we design a full-blown application.

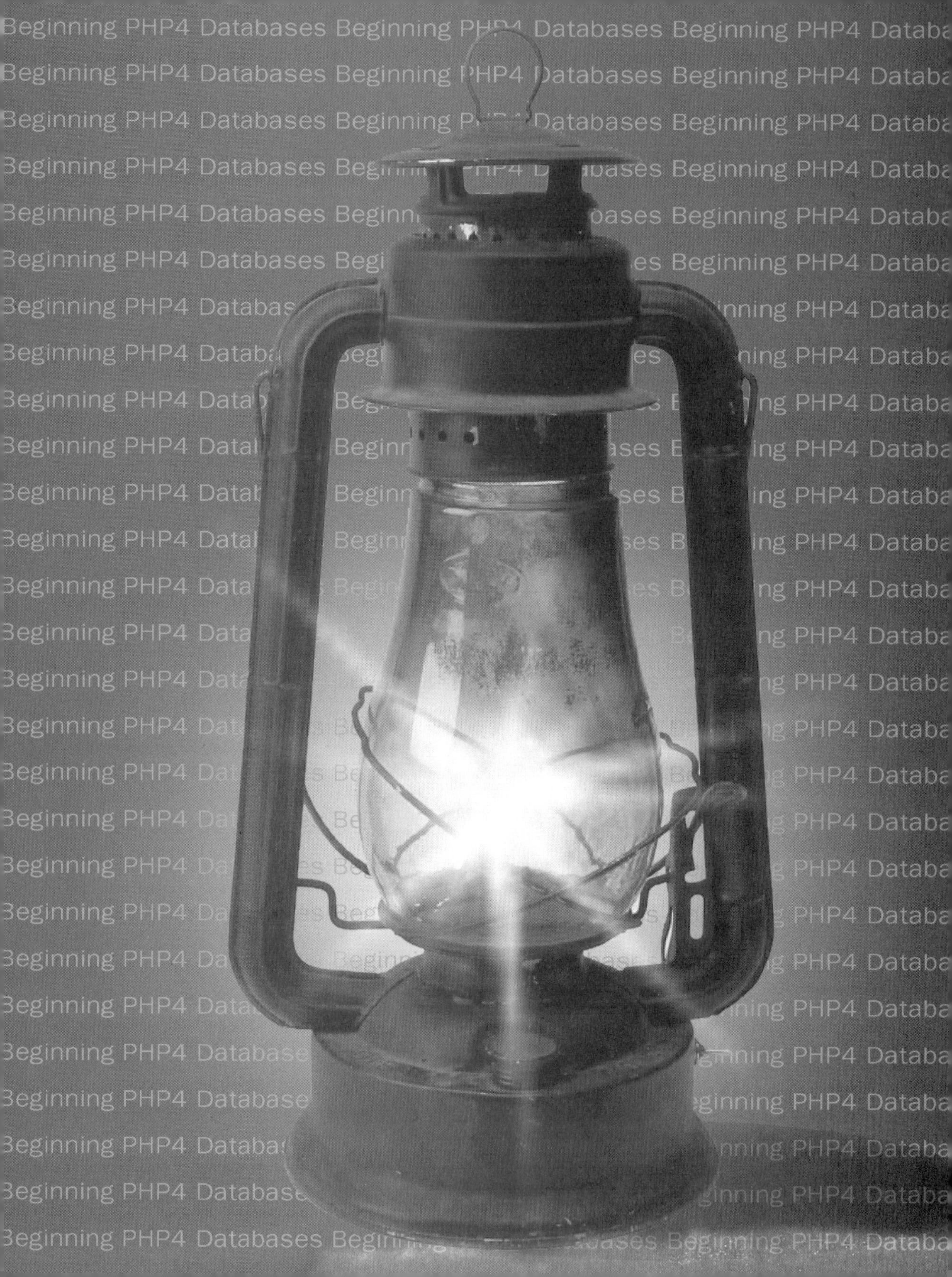
Beginning PHP4 Databases

Case Study: Using Xindice – A Recipe Exchange

In the last chapter, we were introduced to the world of Native XML Databases. In this chapter, we go a little further than that by actually creating a full-fledged application based on the native XML technologies that were introduced in the previous chapter. We shall use Xindice, the Apache software foundation's Native XML Database as our back - end data store.

Native XML Databases are most suited for application, like publishing and interacting with catalogued content. We shall design and implement a web application from scratch that will allow:

- ❑ All users to exchange recipes of their favorite dishes with other users
- ❑ All users to add new recipes to the database
- ❑ All users to rate and comment upon existing recipes
- ❑ All users to search for recipes and browse categories of recipes
- ❑ Administrators to edit existing recipes and ones contributed by users

Recipe Exchange Overview

In the course of designing and implementing our recipe exchange application, we shall use technologies and concepts that allow manipulation of XML content through PHP applications. For instance, these include:

- ❑ **XML**
- ❑ The storage of XML in a Native XML Database
- ❑ **Xindice** – a Native XML Database
- ❑ **XPath** for querying the XML database
- ❑ **XUpdate** for updating documents in the XML database

- **PHP-XML** SAX parsing routines
- **XSLT** (XSL Transformation) – an extension of XSL or eXtensible Stylesheet Language
- **PHP-Xindice** class library

We will look at the specifications of the application, the database organization, and then the class design before coding the application.

Specifications

Among the first things we need to do in the course of creating the application is to gather all possible requirements for the application. We should list all the desired and expected functionality of the application. By doing this first, we are less likely to run into unforeseen design and implementation problems later.

We are going to look at the specifications of the application from the perspective of the two types of users of this application:

- **End users**
  We will refer to them as **User**(s) henceforth. These users may search for, browse through, or add new recipes, and may also leave comments on recipes in the database.

- **Privileged users**
  We shall refer to them as **Administrator**(s). An administrator can edit or delete recipes and user comments as well as mark recipes as *featured* recipes.

User Privileges

All the actions that an end user of the application can perform are:

- Browse a category of recipes and access individual recipes under that category
- Search for recipes under a category
- Search for featured recipes in the database
- Add new recipes to the recipe database
- Rate a recipe on a scale of 1 to 5 and also provide feedback as comments

Note: We would not require that users log in for any of the above-mentioned activities.

Here is a use-case representation of the actions that a user may perform.

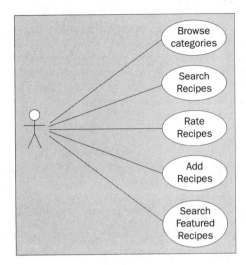

Administrator Privileges

An administrator, other than possessing the basic privileges given to a user, is also provided options to:

❑   Edit any recipe ingredient and the name associated with it

❑   Designate recipes as featured

❑   Edit names and mailing addresses of contributors of recipes

❑   Remove existing recipes

Here are the administrator use cases:

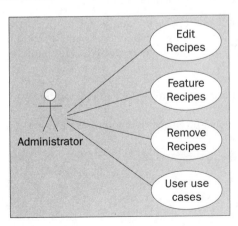

Designing the Application

The application consists of the following major entities: **Recipes**, **Categories**, and **Users**. A recipe comprises a list of a fixed number of attributes associated with the recipe such as its name, ingredients, and preparation instructions. A recipe may also have a variable number of feedback items associated with it. Recipes are organized into categories; a recipe can belong to a single category only. Users may add recipes or browse recipes. Administrators may perform all the tasks as a regular user, but in addition may delete or edit recipes and feedback items.

Recipe Structure

As mentioned earlier, a recipe consists of multiple attributes and a variable list of feedback items associated with it. The following are the attributes of a recipe:

- ❑ `Recipe Name`: This is the name of the recipe and is specified at the time of adding the recipe.

- ❑ `Category`: This attribute indicates the category a recipe belongs to, and is set by a user.

- ❑ `Featured`: This attribute indicates if the recipe is a *featured* recipe or not, and by default it is set to `false`. Possible values are `true` and `false`.

- ❑ `Submitter`: This corresponds to the details of the user who submitted this recipe. It as a compound attribute comprised of a name and e-mail attribute. The user sets it at the time of creation of the recipe.

- ❑ `Ingredients`: This is a variable-length list of ingredients necessary to prepare the item or dish described by the recipe.

- ❑ `Instructions`: This attribute represents the set of instructions to be followed during preparation. It is set by the user at the time of creation of the recipe and may be modified by an administrator.

- ❑ `Servings`: A value for the number of people the item or dish can serve is contained in this attribute. It is also set at the time of creation of the recipe.

- ❑ `Feedback`: This is a list of feedback items, which in turn comprises a `rating` attribute and a `comment` attribute. The `rating` attribute represents a rating rank given to the recipe by a user on a scale of 1 to 5. The user when specifying a rank may also specify optional comments on the recipe.

The administrator has the authority to modify the values in all the attributes given above.

Let us examine a typical recipe with the above-mentioned attributes represented as an XML document:

```
<?xml version="1.0" encoding="UTF-8"?>
<recipe>
  <name categoryid="entrees" recipeid="3728738232_3032">
    Pan-seared trout in lemon-caper sauce
  </name>
  <submitter>
    <name>Deepak Thomas</name>
```

```
            <email>deepak@deepakthomas.org</email>
        </submitter>
        <ingredients>
            <ingredient>2 pounds of firm-fleshed trout</ingredient>
            <ingredient>4 ounces extra virgin olive-oil</ingredient>
            <ingredient>2 stalks of celery</ingredient>
            <ingredient>6 cloves of garlic</ingredient>
            <ingredient>2 tea spoons of ground black pepper</ingredient>
            <ingredient>3 ounces of capers in brine</ingredient>
            <ingredient>1 small lemon</ingredient>
            <ingredient>5 small cherry tomatoes</ingredient>
        </ingredients>
        <instructions>
            Cut the fish in 4" squares and set aside. Prepare the sauce by chopping
            the tomatoes, garlic, and lemon juice. Marinade and refrigerate the fish
            in the sauce for 2 hours. Heat the oil in a non-stick pan for a minute.
            Sprinkle the ground pepper on the fish pieces while searing it in the
            pan for 5 minutes. Add salt to taste and serve with chopped celery.
        </instructions>
        <servings>2</servings>
        <feedback>
            <feedback-item id="3466">
                <rating>5</rating>
                <comment>
                    Tantalizing - the cat actually licked the plate clean
                </comment>
            </feedback-item>
            <feedback-item id="6772">
                <rating>4</rating>
                <comment>Ahem !!</comment>
            </feedback-item>
        </feedback>
        <featured>true</featured>
    </recipe>
```

The top level element is the recipe element. Below it are the submitter, name, ingredients, instructions, servings, feedback, and featured elements. The submitter element in turn contains name and email sub-elements, which contain the names and e-mail IDs of the submitting user. The ingredients element contains a variable number of ingredient sub-elements. The instructions element contains the text for the preparation instructions. The feedback element contains a variable number of feedback-item sub-elements, each of which in turn contain a rating and comment sub-element.

Some of you may have noticed that the name and feedback-item elements have some extra attributes – categoryid, recipeid, and id respectively. The recipeid attribute of a name element uniquely identifies a recipe. Using just the name may not work very well as two recipes may have the same name, for instance *Apple Pie*. The feedback-item element has an id attribute that uniquely identifies a feedback item that applies to a recipe. This is required because we allow the editing of individual feedback items, as we shall soon see. The categoryid is a unique way to refer to the category that the recipe belongs to. We shall see more on the categoryid in the next section.

Category Structure

The category entity is quite straightforward in that it associates a category name with a category identification (category id):

```xml
<?xml version="1.0"?>
<categories>
  <category id="appetizers">Appetizers</category>
  <category id="entrees">Entrees</category>
  <category id="saucesndips">Sauces &amp; Dips</category>
  <category id="desserts">Desserts</category>
  <category id="snacks">Snacks</category>
</categories>
```

The top level element is the categories element, which in turn contains a variable number of category sub-elements. The category sub-elements contain text denoting the name of the category. It also has an attribute called the id, which is essentially a short form or canonical key that refers to the category in question. A recipe refers to the category it belongs to by the id of the category. The categoryid attribute of the name sub-element, which we saw in the section describing the recipe, should have a value corresponding to the id attribute of one of the category sub-elements. Further, the id attribute allows the administrator to modify the name of a category without having to modify the recipes listed under it.

User Structure

User attributes are mainly used for authentication purposes. The user attributes represent a user's name, password, and if the user has administrator privileges. In our Recipe Exchange, we will restrict ourselves to an administrator user as entry only, and we will treat all other users as end users who do not require authentication. However, enhancements to the application may involve support for registering users and therefore, making entries for each of the end users in the users document.

Below is an XML representation of a user list:

```xml
<?xml version="1.0"?>
<users>
  <user admin="true" name="Administrator" password="foobar123" />
</users>
```

The top level element is the users element, which contains multiple user sub-elements, each representing a user. The user element has three attributes – admin, name, and password. The admin attribute is set to true if a user has administrator privileges. The name attribute defines the name of the user. Such a scheme allows multiple users to have administrator privileges. The password attributes defines the clear-text representation of the user's password.

Database Design

As seen in the previous section, the user information, in the form of recipes and categories, and also the administrative data is represented as XML documents. It is much easier to design the database using a Native XML Database since the data is inherently represented in XML. It might by worthwhile to note that hierarchical organization of data comes naturally to XML and therefore to a Native XML Database. Further, it is easier to solve the problem of variable length vectors, as is the case with the list of ingredients or the list of feedback items. The following case illustrates how easy it is to design a Xindice Native XML Database to organize XML data.

Collections

Let us recap the concepts from the previous chapter that we need to use here. Xindice considers documents to be contained in **collections**. A collection is essentially a group of XML documents that can be queried as a whole, and may contain other collections as well (apart from XML documents).

We shall organize our Recipe Exchange data in to collections. Look at the diagram below, and then refer to the explanation that follows.

In the figure below, the shadowed boxes represent collections and the plain boxes represent XML documents. Names of the category collections containing the recipes, for example /db/recipex/recipes/**entrees**, have a one-to-one relationship with the id attribute of the category element in the categories document:

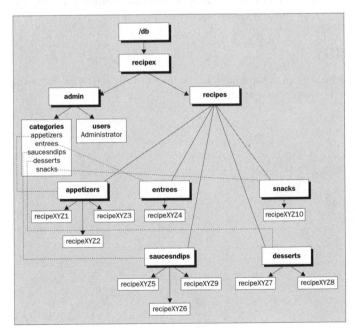

At the top-most level is a `recipex` collection that essentially is the collection of all documents that belong to the Recipe Exchange application. Below this collection, we create two other collections, the `admin` collection comprising the administrative metadata and a `recipes` collection. There are just two documents present under the `admin` collection – the `categories` document and the `users` document.

The `recipes` collection is a group of a variable number of recipe documents grouped under the categories collection. Under the `recipes` collection there are as many collections as there are categories. Each of these collections has the same name as the `id` of the category. Recipes are XML documents grouped under each of these collections.

Since the `recipex` document is created under the default root of the Xindice database, at the location `/db`, the `recipex` collection can be referred to by the collection path `/db/recipex`. Similarly, the `admin` collections, `categories` and `users`, can be referred to as `/db/recipex/admin/categories` and `/db/recipex/admin/users` respectively. Also, the recipes collection can be referred to as `/db/recipex/recipes`. A recipe belonging to the appetizers category with a recipe id *1234567_7890* is referenced as `/db/recipex/recipes/appetizers/1234567_7890`.

Class Design

To design and implement the application with an object-oriented approach, it is necessary to have data structures implementing the design in terms of interacting objects . These objects, such as the `Recipe` object or the `User` object, would be functionally instantiated from web pages, with the adding of a new recipe and the editing of an existing one being instances of this.

Class Hierarchy

We consider all the entities of the applications in terms of objects. The following diagram shows all the objects that will be used in our application.

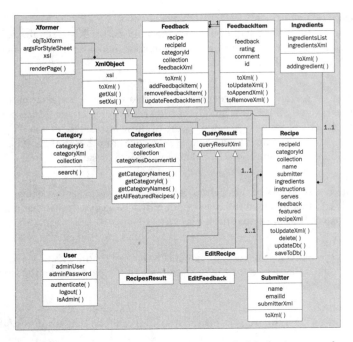

In the diagram, each box represents a class with its name in bold, for instance the `XmlObject` class. Below the name is a list of data members of the class, for example the `xsl` data member of the `XmlObject` class. Lastly, below this is a list of methods of the class. The method names end in a pair of parentheses, for instance the `toXml()` method of the `XmlObject` class.

An arrow with a triangular head indicates a parent-child relationship between two classes. The line originates from the child class and the arrowhead points at the parent class. Thus in the diagram, the `Recipe` class is a child of the `XmlObject` class. A line without arrowheads indicates a simple association relation between two classes. For instance, the `Submitter` class is related to the `Recipe` class since the `submitter` data member of the `Recipe` class refers to an instance of the `Submitter` class.

Purposely, only public data members and methods of classes are indicated, the ones that are used by the objects to interact with each other. We shall see more about the inner workings of these classes in the code section.

Classes and Members

Here is a detailed discussion on each of these classes:

❑ **XmlObject**
This class represents a generic object, which has the functionality to convert itself into XML. It also defines a stylesheet associated with it. Stylesheets as discussed in the last chapter, are essentially a set of rules to convert the XML into a particular format like HTML. The `XmlObject` class is actually an abstract class in that it does not have complete implementation of all its methods. In particular, the `toXml()` method is left empty for child classes (also known as sub-classes) to implement.

❑ **QueryResult**

This class represents the result of a query executed on the XML database. The QueryResult class is a child of the XmlObject class. The response to a query performed on an XML database is in the XML form.

❑ **Recipe**

The Recipe class represents a recipe that is either currently existent in the system or one that needs to be created afresh. It is a child of the XmlObject class and has several data members, which are the attributes of the recipe. Some of these attributes such as ingredients, feedback, and submitter are actually references to other objects. The Recipe class has several methods including those to delete and update or save itself to the XML database.

❑ **Category**

This is another sub-class of the XmlObject class and represents a category. It has a categoryid attribute used to uniquely identify a category. It also has a search() method, which is used to search recipes under it.

❑ **Categories**

This class represents a collection of categories. However, the primary use of this class is to provide methods that can return information about the categories and also perform operations that span multiple categories.

❑ **Ingredients**

This is a simple class that represents the list of ingredients that are part of the recipe.

❑ **Feedback**

The feedback provided by visitors to the site for the recipes is represented by this class. This class has methods to add, delete, and update feedback items.

❑ **FeedbackItem**

This class represents an individual feedback item in a feedback object associated with a recipe. It has an identifier associated with it, which is used to uniquely identify it within a recipe. Also, it has methods to convert itself into XML in XUpdate format that can be submitted to the XML database to add, delete, or update itself in the database. More on this when we discuss the code listing for this class.

❑ **Submitter**

A Submitter object stores the details of the user who submitted the recipe. It has data members representing the name and e-mail ID of the user and also a method to convert itself into XML.

❑ **User**

The User class represents a user. Its main function is to authenticate administrator users and to log out a currently logged-in administrator user. It fetches the admin user name and password from the XML databases and compares it with the value entered by the user during authentication.

❑ **Xformer**

This is a class representing a document transformer. Given an XML document and the stylesheet associated with it, in other words an XmlObject object, it converts the XML document to a format prescribed by the stylesheet. It takes an XmlObject and queries it to obtain the XML document and the XSL stylesheet associated with it, and then performs the actual transformation operation on the document.

❏ **`RecipesResult`, `EditFeedback` and `EditRecipe`**
These classes are sub-classes of the `QueryResult` class. The `RecipesResult` class represents a list of recipe names that could've been returned as the result of a query, for example, all the recipes under a category or all featured recipes. The `EditFeedback` class represents a result from a query seeking a particular feedback item. It is used to display the feedback item for editing. The `EditRecipe` class represents the result of a query seeking a particular recipe. It is used to display a recipe so that an administrator can edit it.

Implementation

In this section, we shall discuss the implementation of our design from the previous sections. We shall look at some preliminary set-up steps to be performed followed by the code listing itself.

Installation

As several new technologies will be used in this application, it is necessary to ensure that the following softwares are installed and configured before proceeding. Detailed instructions on how to install and configure them were provided in the previous chapter. This listing should be treated as a checklist to ensure all essential software is installed:

❏ Xindice Native XML Database

❏ Xindice XML-RPC libraries

❏ eXpat XML parser

❏ Sablotron XSLT processor

❏ PHP 4.2 or later, compiled with the following flags: `--with-xml`, `--enable-xslt`, and `--with-xslt-sablot`

❏ PHP XML-RPC library

❏ PHP Xindice class library

References to installation procedures for all of these are included under the *Installations* section in the *Native XML Databases* chapter (Chapter 12).

Preliminary Set-up

In this section, we perform certain set-up tasks that are necessary for us to deploy the application. We first set-up the code directories and then perform some administrative tasks on the database.

1. Create a directory, `/usr/local/apache/htdocs/phpxindice/recipex` (Unix) or `C:\Apache\htdocs\phpxindice` (Windows), to copy the code into. Use the `include_path` directives, which can be located under the heading 'Paths and Directories'.

2. Modify the local PHP configuration file, `/usr/local/lib/php.ini`. Use the `include_path` directives. Include the following paths:

   ❑ The install location of the PHP XML-RPC library,
   `/usr/local/htdocs/phpxindice/xmlrpc` (Unix) or
   `C:\Apache\htdocs\phpxindice\xmlrpc` (Windows)

   ❑ The PHP Xindice class library,
   `/usr/local/htdocs/phpxindice/class_xindice` (Unix) or
   `C:\Apache\htdocs\phpxindice\class_xindice` (Windows)

   ❑ The directory containing the application code,
   `/usr/local/htdocs/phpxindice/recipex` (Unix) or
   `C:\Apache\htdocs\phpxindice\recipex` (Windows)

3. Now we are ready to create a collection for the `recipex` application:

```
$ xindiceadmin ac -c /db -n recipex
Created : /db/recipex
```

4. We shall also create a `recipes` collection and an `admin` collection:

```
$ xindiceadmin ac -c /db/recipex -n admin
Created : /db/recipex/admin

$ xindiceadmin ac -c /db/recipex -n recipes
Created : /db/recipex/recipes
```

5. We shall load the initial data for the admin collection, which is just the user data:

```
$ xindice ad -c /db/recipex/admin -f ./users.xml -n users

Added document /db/recipex/admin/users
```

6. Now we shall create the recipe collections under `/db/recipex/recipes` and an index-document of all recipes under `/db/recipex/admin`:

```
$ xindiceadmin ac -c /db/recipex/recipes -n appetizers
Created : /db/recipex/recipes/appetizers

$ xindiceadmin ac -c /db/recipex/recipes -n entrees
Created : /db/recipex/recipes/entrees

$ xindiceadmin ac -c /db/recipex/recipes -n saucesndips
Created : /db/recipex/recipes/saucesndips

$ xindiceadmin ac -c /db/recipex/recipes -n desserts
Created : /db/recipex/recipes/desserts
```

```
$ xindiceadmin ac -c /db/recipex/recipes -n snacks
Created : /db/recipex/recipes/snacks

$ xindice ad -c /db/recipex/admin -f categories.xml -n categories

Added document /db/recipex/admin/categories
```

7. To optimise database queries, we shall create indexes for the most commonly queried parameters. This step needs to be repeated every time a new category is added.

```
$ xindiceadmin add_indexer -c /db/recipex/recipes/entrees -n nindex -p name
CREATED : nindex

$ xindiceadmin add_indexer -c /db/recipex/recipes/entrees -n ncindex -p
name@categoryid
CREATED : ncindex
```

Code Listing

The code is comprised of PHP classes and PHP pages that use these classes, along with XSL stylesheets that are used to transform XML. Also included are common *include* files and images. The classes are organized under the `recipex` directory in a sub-directory called `classes`. The PHP pages and common include files are under the `recipex` directory itself. Images go into the images sub-directory. The XSL stylesheets go into the `xsl/html` sub-directory.

Common Include File

This is a file named `common.inc`, which includes some essential classes and routines used by most classes and pages:

```php
<?php
  //File name - common.inc
  include_once('../class_xindice/class_xindice.php');
  $xindice_server='localhost'; //your server location, say xindice.my.org
  $xindice_port='4080';

  $xindice = new Xindice($xindice_server, $xindice_port);
  if (!$xindice) {
    die("Could not create Xindice object");
  }
  $xindice->setXmlRpcDebug(0);

?>
```

In the code above, the first three lines indicates installation specific changes that need to be made. The argument to `include_once` should be the actual location of the `class_xindice.php` file. Also the `$xindice_server` variable should be set to the hostname of the machine running the Xindice server and `$xindice_port` should be set to the port number at which the Xindice server is listening (by default 4080).

We create a Xindice object that will be used by most classes and pages.

Displaying the First Page

Here is a screen-shot of the first page of the application:

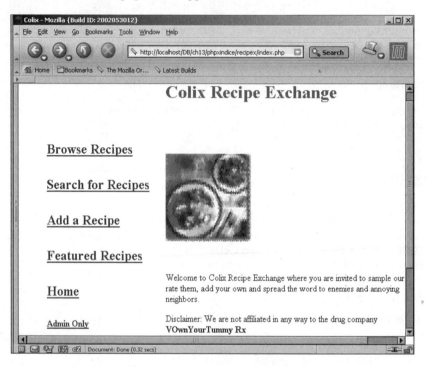

Here is the php-section of the opening file index.php, which produced the page shown above. Of course, readers are at liberty to choose a less ghastly layout and content for the first page:

```php
<?php
    //index.php - displays the first page of the application
    include_once('common.inc');
        include_once('classes/User.php');


        $isAdmin = false;
    $user = new User($xindice);
    $isAdmin = $user->isAdmin();
?>
```

In the code above, we are including two files: the common include file common.inc, which we just defined, and the User class that is also defined later in this chapter. We then instantiate the User class and check to see if the current user is an administrator or not. We will look at the details of how this is done later in the implementation. Below is the html section, ascontinuation to the above php file:

```
<!doctype html public "-//w3c//dtd html 4.0 transitional//en">
<html>
  <head>
    <title>Recipe Exchange application</title>
  </head>
  <body link="#0000FF" vlink="#800080">
     
    <table BORDER=0 CELLSPACING=0 CELLPADDING=7 WIDTH="763" >
      <tr>
        <td VALIGN=TOP COLSPAN="5" ROWSPAN="10"></td>
      </tr>

      <tr>
        <td VALIGN=CENTER WIDTH="29%" HEIGHT="63"></td>
        <td VALIGN=TOP ROWSPAN="7" WIDTH="66%" HEIGHT="63">
         <b><font color="#008080"><font size=+3>Colix Recipe Exchange</font>
         </font></b>
         <br> 
         <br> 
         <br> 
         <br> 
         <p>
           <img SRC="images/colix.gif" height="156" width="156">
           <br> 
           <br> 
           <p>Welcome to Colix Recipe Exchange where you are invited to
              sample our recipes, rate them, add your own and spread the
              word to enemies and annoying neighbors.
           <p> Disclaimer: We are not affiliated in any way to the drug
              company<b>VOwnYourTummy Rx</b>
        </td>
      </tr>

      <tr>
        <td VALIGN=CENTER WIDTH="29%" HEIGHT="30"><b>
           <font color="#008080"><font size=+2>
             <a href="browse.php">Browse Recipes</a>
           </font></font></b>
        </td>
      </tr>

      <tr>
        <td VALIGN=CENTER WIDTH="29%" HEIGHT="19"><b>
          <font color="#008080"><font size=+2>
            <a href="searchRecipes.php">Search for Recipes</a>
          </font></font></b></td>
      </tr>

      <tr>
        <td VALIGN=CENTER WIDTH="29%" HEIGHT="28">
          <b><font color="#008080"><font size=+2>
            <a href="addRecipe.php">Add a Recipe</a>
          </font></font></b></td>
```

```
      </tr>

      <tr>
        <td VALIGN=CENTER WIDTH="29%" HEIGHT="24">
        <b><font color="#008080"><font size=+2>
          <a href="featured.php">Featured Recipes</a>
        </font></font></b>
       </td>
      </tr>

      <tr>
        <td VALIGN=CENTER WIDTH="29%" HEIGHT="19">
          <b><font color="#008080"><font size=+2>
            <a href="index.php">Home</a>
          </font></font></b>
        </td>
      </tr>
```

In the PHP code fragment below, we display a link that would allow a user to log in as an administrator. An administrator who has already logged in is provided a link to log out:

```php
<?php
    function displayAuthenticationStatus($url, $message) {
          echo '<tr> <td VALIGN=CENTER WIDTH="29%" HEIGHT="19">
          <b><font color="#008080">
          <a href="' . $url . '">' . $message . '</a></font></b></td> </tr>';
    }
    if (!$isAdmin) {
          displayAuthenticationStatus("login.php", "Admin Only");
    } else {
          displayAuthenticationStatus("logout.php", "Logout");
    }
?>

  <tr>
    <td VALIGN=CENTER WIDTH="29%" HEIGHT="58"></td>
  </tr>
</table>

<br> 
<br> 
<br> 
</body>
</html>
```

Browsing for Recipes

As planned, we offer recipes under various categories for users to browse through. On clicking the Browse button on the first page, the user is shown a list of categories to choose from:

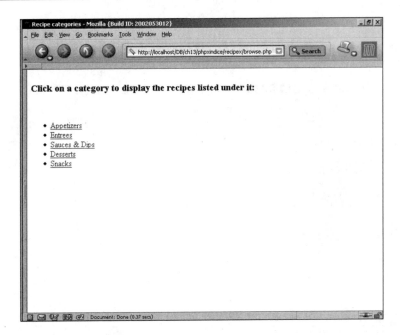

Here is the code that produced this page:

```php
<?php
//browse.php - browse categories

  include_once('common.inc');
  include_once('classes/Categories.php');
  include_once('classes/Xformer.php');
  include_once('classes/User.php');

  $allCategories = new Categories($xindice);

  $transformer = new Xformer($allCategories);

  $user = new User($xindice);
  if ($user->isAdmin()) {
    $result = $transformer->renderPage(true);
  } else {
    $result = $transformer->renderPage(false);
  }

  echo $result;

?>
```

In the PHP page above, we include a common include file and the definitions of three classes –
Categories, Xformer, and User. We instantiate a Categories object, which represents all the
categories in the system. We then pass this object to a freshly instantiated Xformer object, which is
defined later in the chapter. Finally, we render the page representing all the categories available in the
system by calling the renderPage() method of the Xformer object.

Adding a New Recipe

Users may add a new recipe to the database, by clicking the Add Recipe link on the first page. Here is a screenshot of a typical recipe being entered into the system:

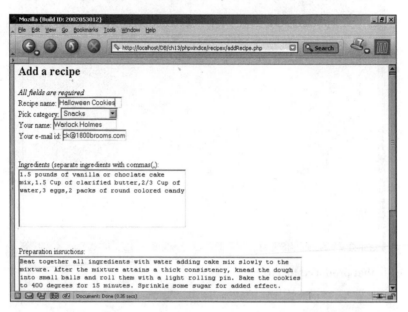

Here is the code that produced this page. We include the common include file and definitions for the Recipe, Categories, Submitter, and Ingredients classes:

```php
<?php
//addRecipe.php - Add a new recipe

    include_once('common.inc');
    include_once('classes/Recipe.php');
    include_once('classes/Categories.php');
    include_once('classes/Submitter.php');
    include_once('classes/Ingredients.php');
```

The below section of code gets executed when the page is accessed for the first time. It merely displays the form used by the end user to enter a new recipe. It creates form elements corresponding to the various recipe attributes allowing the user to enter information into these fields:

```php
    $categories = new Categories($xindice);

    if ($_POST["posted"] != "true")  {
```

We use a hidden field called `posted` in the HTML form for the new recipe. This field is obviously not set when the page is accessed for the first time. However, when the page is accessed a second time as a result of a form POST, this field is set, thereby helping us distinguish between the two cases:

```
echo "<h2>Add a recipe</h2>";
echo "<i>All fields are required</i>";
echo "<FORM METHOD=\"POST\" ACTION=\"addRecipe.php\">";
echo "<INPUT TYPE=\"hidden\" NAME=\"posted\" VALUE=\"true\">";
echo "Recipe name:  "; echo "<INPUT TYPE=\"text\" NAME=\"name\"><br>";
echo "Pick category: ";
echo "<SELECT NAME=\"categoryName\">";
```

Next, we list all the category names in this section:

```
$cat_array = $categories->getCategoryNames();
foreach($cat_array as $categoryId => $catName) {
  echo "<OPTION> " . $catName;
}
```

The below code gets executed when the form is posted with information pertaining to the new recipe:

```
echo "</SELECT><br>";
echo "Your name: ";
echo "<INPUT TYPE=\"text\" NAME=\"submitterName\"><br>";
echo "Your e-mail id: ";
echo "<INPUT TYPE=\"text\" NAME=\"submitterEmail\"><br>";
echo "<br><br>Ingredients (separate ingredients with commas(,):<br>";
echo "<TEXTAREA NAME=\"ingredients\" ROWS=6 COLS=40>";
echo "</TEXTAREA><br>";
echo "<br><br>Preparation insructions:<br>";
echo "<TEXTAREA NAME=\"instructions\" ROWS=10 COLS=70>";
echo "</TEXTAREA><br><br>";
echo "Serves: ";
echo "<INPUT TYPE=\"text\" NAME=\"serves\"><br>";
echo "<br><br><INPUT TYPE=\"submit\" VALUE=\"Submit Recipe\">";
echo "</FORM>";

} else {
```

In this section, the recipe details are extracted from form variables and used to create a new `Recipe` object:

```
$name = $_POST["name"];
$categoryName = $_POST["categoryName"];
$submitterName = $_POST["submitterName"];
$submitterEmail = $_POST["submitterEmail"];
$ingredientsStr = $_POST["ingredients"];
$instructions = $_POST["instructions"];
```

```
        $serves = $_POST["serves"];

if ( trim($name) == "" || trim($categoryName) == "" ||
    trim($submitterName) == "" ||
    trim($submitterEmail) == "" || trim($ingredientsStr) == "" ||
    trim($instructions) == "" || trim($serves) == "") {
        echo "<h3>Incomplete submission - " .
    "hit the back button on your brwoser and fill in all fields </h3>";
} else {
        $name = strtoupper($name);
        $categoryId = $categories->getCategoryId($categoryName);

        $submitter = new Submitter($submitterName, $submitterEmail);
        $ingredients = new Ingredients($ingredientsStr);
```

A new `Recipe` object is created and various attributes are set on this object:

```
        $recipe = new Recipe($xindice, $categoryId);
        $recipe->setName($name);
        $recipe->setSubmitter($submitter);
        $recipe->setIngredients($ingredients);
        $recipe->setInstructions($instructions);
        $recipe->setServes($serves);
```

After the attributes are set, the new recipe is saved to the database:

```
        $recipe->saveToDb();
```

After adding the recipe to the database, we redirect the user to a page that displays the newly added recipe:

```
        header("Location: displayRecipe.php?recipeId=" . $recipe->getRecipeId()
    . "&categoryId=" . $categoryId);
        //Printing a message as some browsers may not redirect
        //to the recipe page
        echo 'Recipe added';
    }
}
?>
```

Searching for Recipes

Users may search for recipes by clicking on the Search Recipe link on the first page and entering the search criteria:

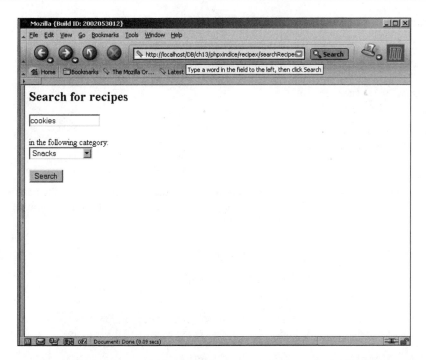

Submitting the search form returns a list of recipes that match the criteria. Users may view these recipes by clicking on the recipe links:

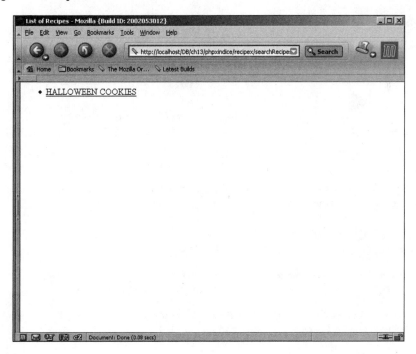

Here is the code to carry out the search:

```php
<?php
//searchRecipes.php - Search for recipes

    include_once('common.inc');
    include_once('classes/Categories.php');
    include_once('classes/Category.php');
    include_once('classes/Xformer.php');
    include_once('classes/RecipesResult.php');
    include_once('classes/User.php');
```

The code below is executed when the page is accessed for the first time. Form fields allow the user to enter search criteria. This conditional block handles the HTTP POST of the form above. It extracts form variables to create objects required for searching:

```php
if ($_GET["posted"] != "true")  {

    $categories = new Categories($xindice);

    echo "<h2>Search for recipes</h2>";
    echo "<FORM METHOD=\"GET\" ACTION=\"searchRecipes.php\">";
    echo "<INPUT TYPE=\"hidden\" NAME=\"posted\" VALUE=\"true\">";

    echo "<INPUT TYPE=\"text\" NAME=\"criteria\">";
    echo "<br><br>in the following category:<br>";
    echo "<SELECT NAME=\"categoryName\">";

    $cat_array = $categories->getCategoryNames();

    foreach($cat_array as $catId => $catName) {
       echo "<OPTION> " .  $catName;
    }

    echo "</SELECT>";
    echo "<br><br><INPUT TYPE=\"submit\" VALUE=\"Search\">";
    echo "</FORM>";

} else {
```

Then a `Category` object is instantiated by looking up the category and the `search()` method is invoked on the category using the criteria entered by the user:

```php
    $criteria = $_GET["criteria"];
    $categoryName = $_GET["categoryName"];

    $categories = new Categories($xindice);
    $categoryId = $categories->getCategoryId($categoryName);

    $category = new Category($xindice, $categoryId);
    $result_xml = $category->search($criteria);
```

The result of the query is used to construct a `RecipesResult` object, which is then passed as an argument to an `Xformer` user. Subsequently, the `renderPage()` method of the `Xformer` is invoked to render the page. We pass a Boolean flag to the `renderPage()` method to indicate if the page is to be rendered so that it exposes additional functionality reserved for administrators, such as editing and deleting recipes:

```
$query_result = new RecipesResult($result_xml);

$transformer = new Xformer($query_result);

$user = new User($xindice);
if ($user->isAdmin()) {
    $result = $transformer->renderPage(true);
} else {
    $result = $transformer->renderPage(false);
}
echo $result;

}
?>
```

Viewing a Recipe

Users may click on a recipe link listed as part of a category listing or a search result to view the recipe:

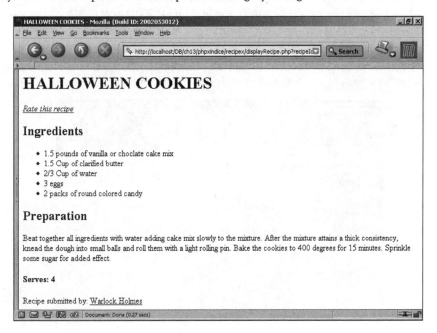

411

Here is the code that displays a recipe:

```php
<?php
//displayRecipe.php - Display an existing recipe

  include_once('common.inc');
  include_once('classes/Recipe.php');
  include_once('classes/Xformer.php');
  include_once('classes/User.php');

  $recipeId = $_GET["recipeId"];
  $categoryId = $_GET["categoryId"];

  $recipe = new Recipe($xindice, $categoryId, $recipeId);
  $transformer = new Xformer($recipe);

  $user = new User($xindice);
  if ($user->isAdmin()) {
    $result = $transformer->renderPage(true);
  } else {
    $result = $transformer->renderPage(false);
  }
  echo $result;

?>
```

We instantiate a `Recipe` object given the `categoryId` and the `recipeId` and pass it to an `Xformer` object. Finally, we invoke the `renderPage()` method on the `Xformer` to render the page.

Rating a Recipe

While on a recipe page, users may click on the **Rate this recipe** link to rate the recipe. They may provide a rating on a scale of 1 to 5 and optionally enter comments:

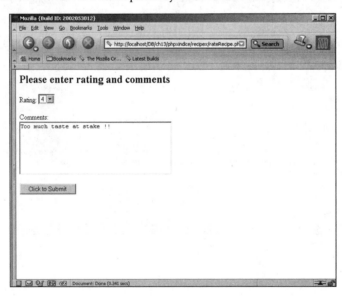

Here is the code that handles adding comments and a rating to a recipe:

```php
<?php
//rateRecipe.php - rate this recipe

include_once('common.inc');
include_once('classes/Recipe.php');
include_once('classes/Feedback.php');
include_once('classes/FeedbackItem.php');

if ($_POST["posted"] != "true") {
```

This conditional block starting above displays a form that allows the user to rank the recipe and enter comments. Alternatively, we could use a form generation and validation class like the *PHLib Form* available from http://www.ulf-wendel.de/docs/form/index2.html. This conditional block extract values of HTML form variables that will be used to create objects, as illustrated below:

```php
$recipeId = $_GET["recipeId"];
$categoryId = $_GET["categoryId"];
echo "<h2> Please enter rating and comments</h2>";
echo "<FORM METHOD=\"POST\" ACTION=\"rateRecipe.php\">";
echo "<INPUT TYPE=\"hidden\" NAME=\"posted\" VALUE=\"true\">";
echo "<INPUT TYPE=\"hidden\" NAME=\"recipeId\" VALUE=\"$recipeId\">";
echo "<INPUT TYPE=\"hidden\" NAME=\"categoryId\" VALUE=\"$categoryId\">";

echo "Rating: ";
echo "<SELECT NAME=\"rating\">";
echo "<OPTION SELECTED> 1";
echo "<OPTION> 2";
echo "<OPTION> 3";
echo "<OPTION> 4";
echo "<OPTION> 5";
echo "</SELECT>";
echo "<br><br>Comments:<br>";
echo "<TEXTAREA NAME=\"comment\" ROWS=6 COLS=40>";
echo "</TEXTAREA>";

echo "<br><br><INPUT TYPE=\"submit\" VALUE=\"Click to Submit\">";
echo "</FORM>";

} else {
```

A Recipe object can be created by looking up an existing recipe that matches the categoryId and recipeId. The last argument of the Recipe constructor below indicates whether the object has to be initialized by querying the database, which is the default behavior. Setting this argument to false will instruct the object not to initialize itself, which is what we want at this stage since we do not wan't to fetch the entire recipe again from the database just to add a feedback item to it:

```php
$recipeId = $_POST["recipeId"];
$categoryId = $_POST["categoryId"];
```

413

```
        $rating = $_POST["rating"];
        $comment = $_POST["comment"];

        $recipe = new Recipe($xindice, $categoryId, $recipeId, false);
```

A `Feedback` object representing the feedback for this recipe and a new `FeedbackItem` object representing the newly entered feedback are then instantiated. Plus the `rating` and `comment` attributes are set on the `FeedbackItem`. This object is then passed as an argument to the `Feedback` object's `addFeedbackItem()` method, causing the new comments and rating to be added to the recipe:

```
        $feedback = new Feedback($recipe);
        $feedback_item = new FeedbackItem($feedback);
        $feedback_item->setRating($rating);
        $feedback_item->setComment($comment);

        $feedback->addFeedbackItem($feedback_item);
```

The user is directed back to the original recipe page after the feedback item is added:

```
      header("Location: displayRecipe.php?recipeId=" . $recipeId . "&categoryId=" .
    $categoryId);

    }
    ?>
```

Logging In as an Administrator

The link **Admin only** on the front page prompts for the administrator's credentials. On verification, a user is logged in as an administrator:

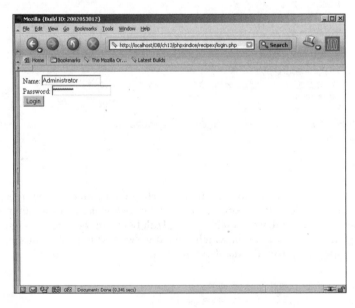

Once the user is logged in as administrator, he may browse or search recipes and perform all of the user level functions:

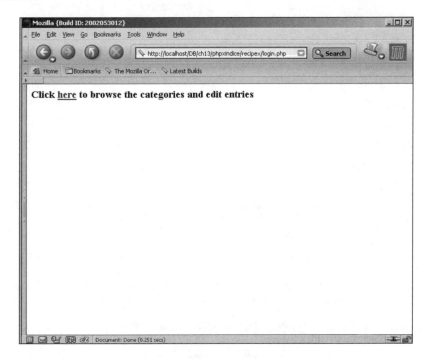

Here is the code that authenticates an administrator:

```php
<?php
//login.php - Authenticate an administrator

    include_once('common.inc');
    include_once('classes/User.php');

    $user = new User($xindice);
    $user->authenticate();
    echo '<h3>Click <a href="browse.php">here</a> to browse the categories and edit
entries</h3>';

?>
```

A User object is created and the `authenticate()` method called on it. The purpose of the `authentication()` method is to present the login page to the user until the correct user name and password are entered. After authentication, a link is displayed that allows browsing of recipes as an administrator.

Editing or Deleting a Recipe

Once an administrator has logged in, the recipe page is displayed with an additional couple of buttons, an EDIT button and a DELETE button. These are not be displayed for regular users:

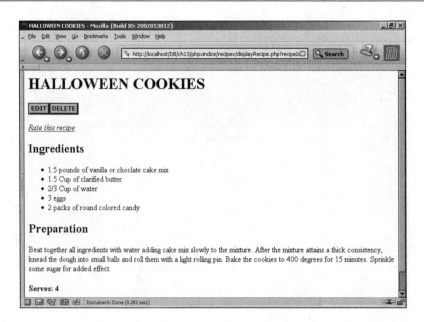

The EDIT and DELETE buttons are provided for deleting and editing recipes. An Edit Page is shown below. The user may make changes to any of these fields and click the Click to Submit button to submit the changes:

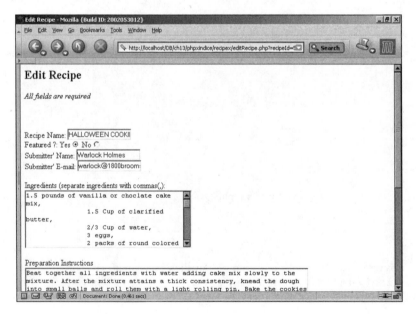

In the code below, the EDIT button on the recipe display page has a URL that points to this page. The URL has two attributes, recipeId and categoryId, which are used to lookup the recipe. This recipe is converted to XML, which is used to create a new EditRecipe object. This object is passed as an argument to the Xformer object and the renderPage() method is invoked on it to render the page presented to the user to edit the recipe:

```php
<?php
//editRecipe.php - Edit a recipe

  include_once('common.inc');
  include_once('classes/Recipe.php');
  include_once('classes/EditRecipe.php');
  include_once('classes/Xformer.php');
  include_once('classes/User.php');
  include_once('classes/Submitter.php');

  $user = new User($xindice);
  $user->authenticate();

  if ($_POST["posted"] != "true") {
    //Input form is generated here

    $recipeId = $_GET["recipeId"];
    $categoryId = $_GET["categoryId"];

    $recipe = new Recipe($xindice, $categoryId, $recipeId);
    $recipe_xml = $recipe->toXml();

    $query_result = new EditRecipe($recipe_xml);

    $transformer = new Xformer($query_result);

    $user = new User($xindice);
    if ($user->isAdmin()) {
      $result = $transformer->renderPage(true);
    } else {
      $result = $transformer->renderPage(false);
    }
```

A new Recipe object can be created without initializing it, thanks to the code above. Various attributes of the recipe submitted by the user are used to furnish this Recipe object. Finally, the updateDb() method is called on the Recipe object causing the changes to be committed to the database:

```php
    echo $result;
  } else {
    //Input form is processed here
    $name = trim($_POST["name"]);
    $recipeId = trim($_POST["recipeId"]);
    $categoryId = trim($_POST["categoryId"]);
    $isFeatured = (($_POST["featured"] == "true") ? true : false);
```

417

```php
        $submitterName = trim($_POST["submitterName"]);
        $submitterEmail = trim($_POST["submitterEmail"]);
        $ingredients_str = trim($_POST["ingredients"]);
        $instructions = trim($_POST["instructions"]);
        $serves = trim($_POST["serves"]);

        if ( $name == "" || $categoryId == "" || $submitterName == "" ||
             $submitterEmail == "" || $ingredients_str == "" ||
             $instructions == "" || $serves == "") {
            echo "<h3>Incomplete submission - hit the back button and fill in
                all fields</h3>";

    } else {

        $recipe = new Recipe($xindice, $categoryId, $recipeId, false);
        $recipe->setName($name);
        $recipe->setFeatured($isFeatured);

        $submitter = new Submitter($submitterName, $submitterEmail);
        $recipe->setSubmitter($submitter);

        $ingredients = new Ingredients($ingredients_str);
        $recipe->setIngredients($ingredients);

        $recipe->setInstructions($instructions);
        $recipe->setServes($serves);

        $recipe->saveToDb();
```

On successful completion of the update, the administrator is directed back to the page that displays the recipe:

```php
        header("Location: displayRecipe.php?recipeId=" . $recipeId . "&categoryId="
  . $categoryId);
    }
}
?>
```

We used an XSLT stylesheet to render the form for editing. An alternative approach is to present the form using form objects such as WebForm available at http://www.extremephp.org/.

Here is the code for deleting the recipe:

```php
<?php
//deleteRecipe.php - delete a recipe

include_once('common.inc');
include_once('classes/Recipe.php');
include_once('classes/User.php');
```

```php
$recipeId = $_GET["recipeId"];
$categoryId = $_GET["categoryId"];

//Create a Recipe object but do not initialize it since we just need to delete it
$recipe = new Recipe($xindice, $categoryId, $recipeId, false);

//Deletion is a priveleged operation - hence we authenticate first
$user = new User($xindice);
$user->authenticate();

$recipe->delete();

header("Location: listCategory.php?categoryId=" . $categoryId);

?>
```

Deleting a recipe is a simple matter of creating a `Recipe` object using the `categoryId` and `recipeId` to look up an existing recipe and calling the `delete()` method on it. After successful deletion of the recipe, the administrator is redirected to a page that lists all recipes under the category from which the recipe was originally deleted.

Editing or Deleting a Feedback Item

An administrator may edit or delete feedback items associated with a recipe. This can be done by clicking on the Edit or Delete links next to a feedback item in the Edit-Recipe page. Here is the code that does this:

```php
<?php
//editFeedback.php - Edit a feedback item

include_once('common.inc');
include_once('classes/Recipe.php');
include_once('classes/Feedback.php');
include_once('classes/FeedbackItem.php');
include_once('classes/EditFeedback.php');
include_once('classes/Xformer.php');
include_once('classes/User.php');

if ($_POST["posted"] != "true") {

//Input form is generated here
    $recipeId = $_GET["recipeId"];
    $categoryId = $_GET["categoryId"];
    $feedbackItemId = $_GET["feedbackItemId"];

    $recipe = new Recipe($xindice, $categoryId, $recipeId, false);
```

Below, we create a `Feedback` object associated with this recipe by passing the `Recipe` object to it. We also create a `FeedbackItem` object by looking up the feedback item by ID. This `FeedbackItem` object is converted to XML and used as an argument to create an `EditFeedback` object. An array of arguments are created to be passed on to the underlying stylesheet, which is then used to display the `FeedbackItem` for editing:

419

```
        $feedback = new Feedback($recipe);
        $feedback_item = new FeedbackItem($feedback, $feedbackItemId);

        $feedback_xml = $feedback_item->toXml();
        $query_result = new EditFeedback($feedback_xml);

        $argsForStyleSheet = array();
        $argsForStyleSheet['recipeId'] = $recipeId;
        $argsForStyleSheet['categoryId'] = $categoryId;
        $argsForStyleSheet['feedbackItemId'] = $feedbackItemId;
```

Further, a new FeedbackItem object is created and the rating and comments attributes set on it. The updateFeedbackItem() method is invoked to update the feedback item in the database:

```
        $transformer = new Xformer($query_result, $argsForStyleSheet);

        $user = new User($xindice);
        if ($user->isAdmin()) {
           $result = $transformer->renderPage(true);
        } else {
           $result = $transformer->renderPage(false);
        }

        echo $result;
} else {
        $recipeId = $_POST["recipeId"];
        $categoryId = $_POST["categoryId"];
        $feedbackItemId = $_POST["feedbackItemId"];
        $rating = $_POST["rating"];
        $comment = $_POST["comment"];

        $recipe = new Recipe($xindice, $categoryId, $recipeId, false);
        $feedback = new Feedback($recipe);
        $feedback_item = new FeedbackItem($feedback, $feedbackItemId);

        $feedback_item->setRating($rating);
        $feedback_item->setComment($comment);
        $feedback->updateFeedbackItem($feedback_item);
```

On success, the administrator is redirected to the Edit-Page of the recipe whose feedback item was modified:

```
        header("Location: " . "editRecipe.php?recipeId=" . $recipeId .
"&categoryId=" . $categoryId);
}
?>
```

Now is the code for deleting a feedback item:

```
<?php
//deleteFeedback.php - delete a feedback item
```

```
    include_once('common.inc');
    include_once('classes/Recipe.php');
    include_once('classes/Feedback.php');
    include_once('classes/FeedbackItem.php');

    $recipeId = $_GET["recipeId"];
    $categoryId = $_GET["categoryId"];
    $feedbackItemId = $_GET["feedbackItemId"];

    $recipe = new Recipe($xindice, $categoryId, $recipeId, false);
    $feedback = new Feedback($recipe);
    $feedback_item = new FeedbackItem($feedback, $feedbackItemId);
    $feedback->removeFeedbackItem($feedback_item);

    header("Location: editRecipe.php?recipeId=" . $recipeId . "&categoryId=" .
        $categoryId);
?>
```

A new `Feedback` object for the current recipe is created. A new `FeedbackItem` object is also created using the `feedbackItemId` to look up an existing feedback item. The `FeedbackItem` is passed as an argument to the `removeFeedbackItem()` method of the `Feedback` object to delete the feedback item. On successful deletion, the administrator is directed back to the Edit-Page of the recipe whose feedback item was deleted.

Displaying Featured Recipes

Users may search for featured recipes by clicking the **Featured Recipes** link on the first page.

Here is the code that displays a list of featured recipes:

```
<?php
//featured.php - Display a list of featured recipes

    include_once('common.inc');
    include_once('classes/Categories.php');
    include_once('classes/Xformer.php');
    include_once('classes/User.php');


    $categories = new Categories($xindice);

    $query_result = $categories->getAllFeaturedRecipes();

    $transformer = new Xformer($query_result);

    $user = new User($xindice);
    if ($user->isAdmin()) {
        $result = $transformer->renderPage(true);
    } else {
        $result = $transformer->renderPage(false);
    }

    echo $result;
?>
```

We create a new `Categories` object and call the `getAllFeauredRecipes()` method on it. The query result is supplied as an argument to an `Xformer` object. Finally, we call the `renderPage()` method to render the list of featured recipes.

Logging Out an Administrator

An administrator may log out by clicking the Logout link on the first page:

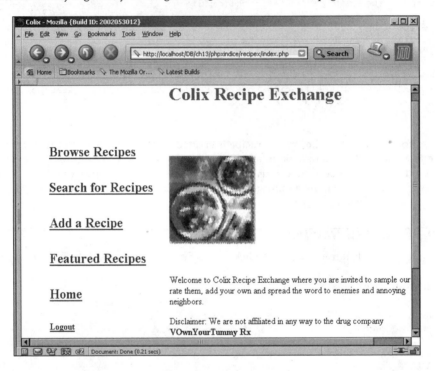

Here is the code for logging out an administrator:

```php
<?php
//logout.php - log out an administrator

    include_once('common.inc');
    include_once('classes/User.php');

    $user = new User($xindice);
    $user->logout();

    header("Location: index.php");
?>
```

Logging out an administrator is a simple task of a creating a `User` object and invoking the `logout()` method on it.

Classes

In this section we will discuss the actual classes that implement the bulk of the functionality.

XmlObject Abstract Class

The `XmlObject` class is an abstract class representing an object that can convert itself into XML and can also associate itself with a stylesheet that can process the XML. It is considered an abstract class because the sub-classes implement the `toXml()` method, which returns the XML:

```php
<?php
//XmlObject.php

//Generic XML object abstract class
//Subclasses must implement the abstract methods

  class XmlObject {

      var $xsl;

      //Constructor - empty place-holder
      function XmlObject() { }

      //Method to marshal itself to XML - abstract method
      function toXml() { }


      //Public method returns the XSL stsylesheet associated with this
      //XmlObject
      function getXsl() {
         return $this->xsl;
      }

      //Private method sets the XSL stsylesheet associated with this
      // XmlObject
      function setXsl($xslFile) {
         $this->xsl = join(' ', file($xslFile));
      }

  }
?>
```

Recipe Class

The `Recipe` class encapsulates a single recipe entity. It has methods to set and retrieve various recipe attributes and also methods to update, delete, and save itself to the database. It is a sub-class of `XmlObject` and hence can convert itself into XML:

```php
<?php
//Recipe.php
```

```
//The Recipe class - object representation of a recipe
//Methods to create, display, edit and delete a recipe

//Define the style-sheet relative to the document root
  define ("RECIPE_XSL",  "/phpxindice/recipex/xsl/html/recipe.xsl");

  include_once('classes/Ingredients.php');
  include_once('classes/Feedback.php');
  include_once('classes/XmlObject.php');
  include_once('classes/Id.php');

  define ("PARENT_COLLECTION", "/db/recipex/recipes");

  class Recipe extends XmlObject {
     var $xindice;

     var $recipeId = "";
     var $categoryId;
     var $collection;

     var $name;
     var $submitter; //Instance of Submitter object
     var $ingredients; //Instance of Ingredients object
     var $instructions;
     var $serves;
     var $feedback; //Instance of Feedback object
     var $featured = false;

     var $recipeXml;
```

Above are the various attributes of the Recipe object. $submitter, $ingredients, and $feedback are actually instances of the Submitter, Ingredients, and Feedback classes respectively.

```
     //Some constants

     var $xmlProlog = '<?xml version="1.0" ?>';
     var $rootCollection = '/db/recipex/recipes';


     //Public constructor used to construct a new Recipe object
     //or lookup an existing one

  function Recipe($xindice, $categoryId, $recipeId="", $initialize=true)      {
        $this->xindice = $xindice;
        $this->setXsl($_SERVER['DOCUMENT_ROOT'] . RECIPE_XSL);
        $this->setCategoryId($categoryId);

        if ($recipeId != "") { //Lookup case
           $this->setRecipeId($recipeId);
        if ($initialize) {
           $this->recipeXml = $this->xindice->getDocument($this->collection,
              $recipeId);
        }
      }
    }
}
```

The `$initialize` argument of the `Recipe` constructor determines if the object has to be initialized by querying the database. Several times we may have to create a `Recipe` object but never really have to use all of its attributes, which causes significant performance overhead on account of having to unnecessarily initialize the object. Setting the `$initialize` argument to `false` prevents the object from being initialized.

```
//Public method marshals this Recipe into XML
  function toXml() {
    if (!isset($this->recipeXml)) {
      $this->recipeXml = $this->xmlProlog;
      $this->recipeXml = $this->recipeXml . '<recipe>';
      $this->recipeXml = $this->recipeXml . '<name categoryid="'.
      $this->getCategoryId() . '" recipeid="' .
      $this->getRecipeId() . '">';
      $this->recipeXml = $this->recipeXml . $this->getName() . '</name>';
      $this->recipeXml = $this->recipeXml . '<ingredients>' .
                          $this->ingredients->toXml() . '</ingredients>';
      $this->recipeXml = $this->recipeXml . '<instructions>' .
                          $this->getInstructions() .'</instructions>';
      $this->recipeXml = $this->recipeXml . '<serves>' .
                          $this->getServes() . '</serves>';

      if (isset($this->feedback)) {
        $this->recipeXml = $this->recipeXml . $this->feedback->toXml();
      } else {
        $this->recipeXml = $this->recipeXml . "<feedback/>";
      }

      if ($this->isFeatured()) {
        $this->recipeXml = $this->recipeXml . '<featured>true</featured>';
      } else {
        $this->recipeXml = $this->recipeXml . '<featured>false</featured>';
      }

      $this->recipeXml = $this->recipeXml . '<submitter>' .
                          $this->submitter->toXml();
      $this->recipeXml = $this->recipeXml . '</submitter>' . '</recipe>';
      }

    return $this->recipeXml;
  }
```

The above toXml() method converts the object to an XML representation of this `Recipe` object.

```
//Public method marshals this Recipe into XUpdate format XML
  function toUpdateXml() {
    $updateXml = '<xu:modifications version="1.0"
                  xmlns:xu="http://www.xmldb.org/xupdate">';
    $updateXml = $updateXml . '<xu:update select="/recipe/name">' .
                  $this->getName() . '</xu:update>';

    $updateXml = $updateXml . '<xu:remove select="//ingredients"/>';
    $updateXml = $updateXml . '<xu:append select="/recipe"
                  child="last()">' . '<xu:element name="ingredients">' .
                  $this->ingredients->toXml() . '</xu:element>' .
```

```
                                '</xu:append>';

        $updateXml = $updateXml . '<xu:update select="//instructions">'
                        . $this->getInstructions() . '</xu:update>';

        $updateXml = $updateXml . '<xu:update select="//serves">' .
                        $this->getServes() . '</xu:update>';

          if ($this->isFeatured()) {
            $updateXml = $updateXml . '<xu:update select="//featured">' .
                        "true" . '</xu:update>';
          } else {
              $updateXml = $updateXml . '<xu:update select="//featured">' .
                          "false" . '</xu:update>';
          }

          $updateXml = $updateXml .  '<xu:remove select="//submitter"/>';
          $updateXml = $updateXml .  '<xu:append select="/recipe"
                        child="last()">' . '<xu:element name="submitter">' .
                        $this->submitter->toXml() . '</xu:element>' .
                        '</xu:append>';

          $updateXml = $updateXml . '</xu:modifications>';

          return $updateXml;
    }
```

Next, the method toUpdateXml() shown above generates XML in the Xupdate format for updating an existing recipe in the database.

```
        //Public method to delete this Recipe - admin only
        function delete() {
            $this->xindice->removeDocument($this->collection, $this->recipeId);
        }

        //Public method to update this Recipe - admin only
        function updateDb() {
              $collection = $this->getCollection();
              $recipeId = $this->getRecipeId();
              $updateXml = $this->toUpdateXml();

              $ret = $this->xindice->queryDocument($collection,
                                  "XUpdate", $updateXml, $recipeId);
        }
```

The above delete() method deletes an existing recipe.

```
//Persists this Recipe to the databas
  function saveToDb() {
    $this->toXml();
    $ret = $this->xindice->insertDocument($this->collection,
                          $this->recipeId, $this->recipeXml);
    if ($ret != $this->recipeId) {
      die("Failed to add recipe to recipe database. Error: " . join( ' ', $ret));
    }
  }
```

The method above converts the `Recipe` object to XML and uses the `insertDocument()` method of the `Xindice` object to insert the document into the database.

```
//Get/set methods for various Recipe data members
 function getRecipeId() {
      return $this->recipeId;
 }

 function setRecipeId($recipeId="") {
      if ($recipeId == "") {
          $this->recipeId = Id::generate($this->name);
      } else {
          $this->recipeId = $recipeId;
      }
 }

 function getXindice() {
      return $this->xindice;
}

function getCategoryId() {
      return $this->categoryId;
}

function getCollection() {
      return $this->collection;
}

function getParentCollection() {
      return PARENT_COLLECTION;
}

function setCollection($categoryId) {
      $this->collection = $this->rootCollection . "/" . $categoryId;
}

function setCategoryId($categoryId) {
      $this->categoryId = $categoryId;
      $this->setCollection($categoryId);
}

function getName() {
      return $this->name;
}

function setName($name) {
      $this->name = $name;
      if ($this->recipeId == "") {
          $this->setRecipeId();
      }
}
```

```php
    function getSubmitter() {
          return $this->submitter;
    }

    function setSubmitter($submitter) {
          $this->submitter = $submitter;
    }

    function getIngredients() {
          return $this->ingredients;
    }

    function setIngredients($ingredients) {
          $this->ingredients = $ingredients;
    }

    function getInstructions() {
          return $this->instructions;
    }

    function setInstructions($instructions) {
          $this->instructions = $instructions;
    }

    function getServes() {
          return $this->serves;
    }

    function setServes($serves) {
          $this->serves = $serves;
    }

    function getFeedback() {
          return $this->feedback;
    }

    function setFeedback($feedbackItem) {
          $feedback->add($feedbackItem);
    }

    function isFeatured() {
          return $this->featured;
    }

    function setFeatured($featured) {
          $this->featured = $featured;
    }
}

?>
```

Id Class

The Id class is used to generate and manage unique identifiers for the system. In our case we specifically use it to generate unique identifiers for new recipes:

```php
<?php
//Id.php

//The Id class - manages unique identifiers

class Id {
    //Method to generate an Id
    function generate($key=0) {
        if ($key == 0) {
            return rand(1000, 9999);
        } else {
            return md5($key) . "_" . rand(1000, 9999);
        }
    }
}

?>
```

Category Class

The Category class represents a category of recipes. It has methods to search for recipes listed under it. Since it inherits from the XmlObject class, it also has a toXml method to convert itself into XML.

```php
<?php
//Category.php

include_once('classes/XmlObject.php');

//The Category class is the object representation of a recipe category

//Define the style-sheet relative to the document root
define ("RECIPES_XSL",  "/phpxindice/recipex/xsl/html/recipes.xsl");

class Category extends XmlObject {

    var $xindice;

    var $categoryId;
    var $categoryXml;
    var $collection;
    var $query;


    //Public constructor to create and initialize a Category object
    function Category($xindice, $categoryId) {
        $this->xindice = $xindice;
        $this->setXsl($_SERVER['DOCUMENT_ROOT'] . RECIPES_XSL);
```

```
            $this->categoryId = $categoryId;
            $this->collection = sprintf("/db/recipex/recipes/%s",
                    $this->categoryId);
            $this->query = sprintf("/recipe/name[@categoryid=\"%s\"]/../name",
                    $this->categoryId);
    }


    //Public method to marshal this object into XML
    function toXml() {
        $categoryXml = $this->xindice->queryCollection($this->collection,
"XPath", $this->query);
        $this->categoryXml = $categoryXml;

        return $this->categoryXml;
    }


    //Pubic method to search this category
    function search($criteria) {
      $query_array = explode(" ", $criteria);
      $i = 0;
        foreach ($query_array as $criterion) {
          $criterion = strtoupper($criterion);
          $query_array[$i++] = "/recipe/name[contains(text(),
                            \"$criterion\")]";
      }

        //This query string selects all documents with at least one of the words
matching
        $query = join('|', $query_array);
        $collection = "/db/recipex/recipes/" . $this->categoryId;
        $recipes_xml = $this->xindice->queryCollection($collection, "XPath",
$query);

        return $recipes_xml;
    }
}
?>
```

The search() method is implemented by concatenating all the search criteria into an XPath query
and submitting the query to the database by calling the queryCollection() method on the
Xindice object.

Categories Class

The categories class represents the set of all categories. It has several utility methods that operate on
the categories as a whole:

```
<?php
//Categories.php

  include_once('classes/XmlObject.php');
  include_once('classes/Recipe.php');
  include_once('classes/RecipesResult.php');
```

```php
// The Categories  class is the object representation for a collection of
// Category objects

// Define the style-sheet relative to the document root
  define ("CATEGORIES_XSL",  "/phpxindice/recipex/xsl/html/categories.xsl");

  class Categories extends XmlObject {

    var $xindice;
    var $categoriesXml;
    var $current_id = "";
    var $current_buffer = "";
    var $attr_array = array();

    var $categoriesDocumentId = "categories";
    var $collection = '/db/recipex/admin';

    //Variables used while parsing the categories XML
    var $current_id = "";
    var $current_buffer = "";
    var $attr_array = array();

    //Public constructor to create a Categories object
    function Categories($xindice) {
      $this->xindice = $xindice;
      $this->setXsl($_SERVER['DOCUMENT_ROOT'] . CATEGORIES_XSL);
      $this->categoriesXml = $this->xindice->getDocument($this->collection,
          $this->categoriesDocumentId);

    }

    //Public method to marshal the Categories object into XML
    function toXml() {
      return $this->categoriesXml;
    }

    //Public method returns all category names as an array
    function getCategoryNames() {
      global $attr_array;
      $xml_parser = xml_parser_create();
      xml_parser_set_option($xml_parser, XML_OPTION_CASE_FOLDING, false);
      xml_set_object($xml_parser, &$this);

      xml_set_element_handler($xml_parser, "categoriesStartElement",
                          "categoriesEndElement");

      xml_set_character_data_handler($xml_parser, "categoriesCharacterData");

      if (!xml_parse($xml_parser, $this->categoriesXml, true)) {
        echo xml_error_string(xml_get_error_code($xml_parser));
        echo xml_get_current_line_number($xml_parser);
        die("Parsing failed");
      }

      return $attr_array;
    }
```

The `getCategoryNames()` method returns a list of category names in the system. It does this by fetching the `categories` XML document (`/db/recipex/admin/categories`) and parsing it. To parse the document, it uses the PHP XML routines. Before parsing certain handlers are set to handle events encountered by the parser. These handlers are essentially functions that are listed at the bottom of the file containing this class.

```php
//Public method returns a category ID, given a category name
function getCategoryId($categoryName) {
  $cat_array = $this->getCategoryNames();
  $categoryId = "";
  foreach($cat_array as $id => $name) {
    if (trim($name) == trim($categoryName)) {
      $categoryId = $id;
    }
  }
  return $categoryId;
}
```

`getCategoryId()` is a utility method that returns a category ID given a category name.

```php
//Public method returns all featured recipes as a QueryResult object
function getAllFeaturedRecipes() {
  $query = '/recipe/featured[text()="true"]/../name';
  $result = "<?xml version=\"1.0\" encoding=\"UTF-8\"?><allfeatured>";
  $categories = $this->getCategoryNames();
  foreach ($categories as $category) {
    $collection = Recipe::getParentCollection() .
                  "/" . $this->getCategoryId($category);

    $categoryResult = $this->xindice->queryCollection($collection,
                  "XPath", $query);

    $categoryResult = str_replace("<?xml version=\"1.0\"?>",
                  " ", $categoryResult);

    $result = $result . $categoryResult;
  }

  $recipes_xml = $result . "</allfeatured>";

  $query_result = new RecipesResult($recipes_xml);

  return $query_result;
}
```

The `getAllFeaturedRecipes()` method returns an XML document listing all the featured recipes from all categories.

```php
//XML parser handler methods (call-back functions)
//for parsing categories XML
```

```
        function categoriesStartElement($parser, $name, $attrs) {
          global $current_id;
          if ($name == "category") {
            $current_id = $attrs["id"];
          }
        }

        function categoriesEndElement($parser, $name) {
          global $current_id;
          global $current_buffer;
          global $attr_array;
          if ($name == "category") {
            $attr_array[$current_id] = $current_buffer;
            $current_buffer = "";
          }
        }

        function categoriesCharacterData($parser, $data) {
          global $current_buffer;
          $current_buffer = $current_buffer . $data;
        }

      }
    ?>
```

These functions are handlers invoked by the parser when it encounters certain events when parsing an XML document. Typical events include the start of an element and the end of an element.

FeedbackItem Class

The FeedbackItem class represents a single feedback item associated with a recipe. This class has methods to generate XML in the XUpdate format allowing it to be updated, deleted, and added to a recipe existing in the database.

```php
<?php
//FeedbackItem.php
//The FeedbackItem class represents a single feedback item

include_once('classes/Id.php');

class FeedbackItem {

  var $feedback; //instance of the parent Feedback
  var $rating;
  var $comment;
  var $id;

  var $topElementOpen = '<xu:modifications version="1.0"
                         xmlns:xu= "http://www.xmldb.org/xupdate">';

  var $topElementClose = '</xu:modifications>';

  //Public constructor used when creating a new feedback-item
  function FeedbackItem($feedback, $id=0) {
```

```
    $this->feedback = $feedback;

    if ($id != 0) {
      //Looking up an existing feedback-item
      $this->id = $id;
    } else {

    //Creating a new feedback-item
    $this->id = Id::generate();
  }

  //Public method marshals this object into XML in the
  //XUpdate 'append' format
  function toAppendXml() {
    if (!isset($this->rating)) { //Comment is optional
      die("Must set rating before invoking toAppendXml() .
      rating = " . $this->rating);
    }

    $feedbackItemAppendXml = $this->topElementOpen .
                      '<xu:append select="//feedback" child="last()">' .
                      '<xu:element name="feedback-item">' .
                      '<xu:attribute name="id">' .
                       $this->id .
                      '</xu:attribute>' .
                      '<rating>' . $this->rating . '</rating>' .
                      '<comment>' . $this->comment . '</comment>' .
                      '</xu:element>' . '</xu:append>' .
                      $this->topElementClose;

    return $feedbackItemAppendXml;
  }
```

The method above converts this `FeedbackItem` object into XUpdate XML that can be used to append itself to a recipe.

```
  //Public method marshals this object into XML
  //in the XUpdate 'update' format
  function toUpdateXml() {
    if (!isset($this->rating)) { //Comment is optional
      die("Must set rating before invoking toUpdateXml()");
    }

    $feedbackItemUpdateXml = $this->topElementOpen .
                      '<xu:update select="//feedback-item[@id=\'' .
                      $this->id . '\']/rating">' .
                      $this->rating .
                      '</xu:update>' .
                      '<xu:update select="//feedback-item[@id=\'' .
                      $this->id . '\']/comment">' .
                      $this->comment .
                      '</xu:update>' .
                      $this->topElementClose;

    return $feedbackItemUpdateXml;
  }
```

The method `feedbackItemUpdateXml()` above converts this `FeedbackItem` object into XUpdate XML that can be used to update itself.

```
//Public method marshals this object into XML
//in the XUpdate 'remove' format
function toRemoveXml() {
  $feedbackItemRemoveXml = $this->topElementOpen .
                    '<xu:remove select="//feedback-item[@id = \'' .
                    $this->id . '\']"/>' .
                    $this->topElementClose;

  return $feedbackItemRemoveXml;
}

//Public method to marshal this object into XML
function toXml() {
  $xindice = $this->feedback->xindice;
  $collection = $this->feedback->recipe->getCollection();
  $recipeId = $this->feedback->recipe->getRecipeId();
  $query = '//feedback-item[@id="' . $this->id . '"]';
  $feedbackItemXml = $xindice->queryDocument($collection,
                    "XPath", $query, $recipeId);

  return $feedbackItemXml;
}
```

The method `feedbackItemRemoveXml()` above converts this `FeedbackItem` object into XUpdate XML that can be used to remove itself.

```
//Public method to set rating
function setRating($rating) {
  $this->rating = $rating;
}

//Public method to set comment
function setComment($comment) {
  $this->comment = $comment;
}
}

?>
```

The methods above are used to set the rating and comment attribute respectively for this `FeedbackItem`.

Feedback Class

This class represents the complete set of feedback for a recipe. It also has the added function of acting as a go-between for the `Recipe` and `FeedbackItem` classes, which therefore do not have to know about each other.

```php
<?php
//Feedback.php

//The Feedback class encapsulates feedback in the form of rating & comments for a
//recipe
//Methods to display, add, delete and edit feedback

include_once('classes/Recipe.php');

class Feedback {

  var $recipeRootCollection;

  var $recipe; //parent Recipe object
  var $xindice;
  var $recipeId;
  var $categoryId;
  var $collection;
  var $feedbackXml;

  //Public constructor - no arguments
  function Feedback($recipe) {
    $this->recipeRootCollection = Recipe::getParentCollection();
    $this->recipe = $recipe;
    $this->xindice = $recipe->getXindice();
    $this->categoryId = $recipe->getCategoryId();
    $this->recipeId = $recipe->getRecipeId();
    $this->collection = $recipe->getCollection();
  }

  //Public method marshals object into XML
  function toXml() {
    $xpathQuery = '//feedback';
    $this->feedbackXml = $xindice->queryDocument($this->collection,
          "XPath", $xpathQuery, $this->recipeId);

    if (trim($this->feedback) == " ") {
      $this->feedback = "<feedback></feedback>";
    }
    return $this->feedbackXml;
  }

  //Public methods to add a new feedback item
  function addFeedbackItem($feedbackItem) {
    $feedbackItemXmlToAdd = $feedbackItem->toAppendXml();
    $this->xindice->queryDocument($this->collection, "XUpdate",
                  $feedbackItemXmlToAdd, $this->recipeId);

  }

  //Public methods to delete a feedback item
  function removeFeedbackItem($feedbackItem) {
```

```
      $feedbackItemXmlToRemove = $feedbackItem->toRemoveXml();
      $this->xindice->queryDocument($this->collection, "XUpdate",
$feedbackItemXmlToRemove, $this->recipeId);

    }

    //Public methods to update a new feedback item
    function updateFeedbackItem($feedbackItem) {
      $feedbackItemXmlToUpdate = $feedbackItem->toUpdateXml();
      $this->xindice->queryDocument($this->collection, "XUpdate",
          $feedbackItemXmlToUpdate, $this->recipeId);

    }

    //Public method returns the Xindice object associated with the asociated Recipe
    //object
    function getXindice() {
      return $this->recipe->getXindice();
    }
}
?>
```

Ingredients Class

The `Ingredients` class represents a list of ingredients for a recipe. It maintains individual ingredients as a list of strings and handles conversion of a list of ingredients passed to it as a string into a list of ingredients. Also, it does the reverse conversion that involves reconstituting the list as a string of comma-separated ingredients.

```
<?php
//Ingredients.php
//The Ingredients class encapsulates the array of ingredients for a recipe

class Ingredients {
  var $ingredientsList;
  var $ingredientsXml;

  //Public constructor - takes a string of comma-delimited ingredients
  function Ingredients($ingredientsStr) {
    $this->ingredientsList = explode(",", $ingredientsStr);
  }

  //Public method to add an ingredient to the list of ingredients
  function addIngredient($ingredient) {
    $this->ingredientsList[] = $ingredient;
  }
```

The method `addIngredient()` above adds an ingredient to the list of ingredients maintained by this class.

```
   //Public method marshals object into XML
   function toXml() {
     if (!isset($this->ingredientsXml)) {
       foreach ($this->ingredientsList as $ingredient) {
         if (trim($ingredient) != "") {
           $ingredientsXml = $ingredientsXml . "
<ingredient>$ingredient</ingredient>";
         }
       }
     }

     return $ingredientsXml;
   }
}
?>
```

User Class

The User class is a wrapper for user authentication utility methods. It also has a method to check if the current user is an administrator or not.

```
<?php
//User.php
//The User class - object representation of a user - admin or regular,
//interacting with the recipex system.
//Methods to authenticate and test if a user is an admin user or a regular user

define ("ADMIN_COLLECTION", "/db/recipex/admin");
class User {

  var $xindice;
  var $adminUser;
  var $adminPassword;

  //Public constructor to create a User object
  function User($xindice) {
    $this->xindice = $xindice;
  }

  //Public method to authenticate a user - usually before accessing admin-only
resources
  function authenticate() {
    session_start();

    //Testing for the case where the user is already authenticated
    if ($_SESSION['isAuthenticated'] == "yes") {
      return;
    }
```

A PHP session is started and checked to see if the isAuthenticated session parameter is set to yes. If yes, then we assume that authentication has already been done; otherwise a login page is displayed.

```
      //First attempt or failed attempt to login - display form
   if ($_POST['auth_posted'] != 'true') {
     if ($_GET['failed'] == "true") {
       echo "<h3>Authentication failed - please try again</h3>";
     }
     echo '<form method="post" action="'. $_SERVER['PHP_SELF'] . '">';
     echo '<input type="hidden" name="auth_posted" value="true"/>';
     echo 'Name: <input type="text" name="user"/><br>';
     echo 'Password: <input type="password" name="password"/><br>';
     echo '<input type="submit" value="Login"/>';
     echo '</form>';
     exit;
   } else {
       //Form posted with user/password
       $user = $_POST['user'];
       $password = $_POST['password'];


       //Authenticate here
       $adminCollection = ADMIN_COLLECTION;
       $query = '//user[@admin="true"]';
       $result = $this->xindice->queryDocument($adminCollection,
                  "XPath", $query, "users");
       $this->parseResult($result);
       if ($user != $this->adminUser || $password != $this->adminPassword) {
       //Authentication failed
         header("Location: " . $_SERVER['PHP_SELF'] . "?failed=true");
         echo 'Authentication failed'; exit;
       } else {
         //Authentication succeeded
         $_SESSION['isAuthenticated'] = "yes";
         return;
       }
     }
   }
}
```

The actual authentication involves fetching the administrator user name and password from the
/db/recipex/admin/users document in the database and comparing it with the values entered by
the user.

```
   //Public method to logout the admin user
   function logout() {
     session_start();
     $_SESSION['isAuthenticated'] = 'no';
   }
```

The administrator is logged out by setting the value of the session parameter isAuthenticated to no.

```
   //Public method returns the user mode, i.e. admin or regular
   function isAdmin() {
     session_start();
```

```
        //Testing for the case where the user is already authenticated
        if ($_SESSION['isAuthenticated'] == "yes") {
          return true;
        } else {
            return false;
          }
      }
```

The above isAdmin() method returns true if the current user is an administrator and false otherwise.

```
      //Private method extracts the admin user name and password from an XML result
      function parseResult($result) {
        $arr = explode(' ', $result);
        foreach ($arr as $item) {
          $nv = explode('=', $item);
          if ($nv[0] == 'name') {
            $name = $nv[1];
          }
          if ($nv[0] == 'password') {
            $password = $nv[1];
          }
        }

        $name = str_replace('"', '', $name);
        $password = str_replace('"', '', $password);

        $this->adminUser = trim($name);
        $this->adminPassword = trim($password);
      }
    }
    ?>
```

The above parseResult() method parses the users XML from the database and extracts the administrator user name and password.

> **In the User class above, we use PHP4 sessions to set authentication status. Therefore it is important to ensure that PHP4 session functionality is set up right and working. On Microsoft Windows platforms, the default setting of** session.save_path = /tmp **in the** php.ini **file will not work. This has to be set to some directory that is writeable by PHP (in other words, the web server), for example.** session.save_path = C:\temp. **The web server needs to be restarted for this to take effect.**

Submitter Class

This class represents a user who is submitting a recipe. It has two attributes – the name of the user and the e-mail id of the user:

```php
<?php
//Submitter.php
//The Submitter class encapsulates the name and email ID of
// a recipe submitter

class Submitter {
  var $name;
  var $emailId;
  var $submitterXml;

  //Public constructor
  function Submitter($name, $emailId) {
    $this->name = $name;
    $this->emailId = $emailId;
  }

  //Public method marshals object into XML
  function toXml() {
    if (!isset($this->submitterXml)) {
      $submitterXml = '<name>' . $this->getName() . '</name>';
      $submitterXml = $submitterXml . '<email>' .
                      $this->getEMailId() . '</email>';

      $this->submitterXml = $submitterXml;
    }

    return $this->submitterXml;
  }

  //Public get/set functions for this class' data members
  function setName($name) {
    $this->name = $name;
  }

  function getName() {
    return $this->name;
  }

  function setEmailId($emailId) {
    $this->emailId = $emailId;
  }

  function getEmailId() {
    return $this->emailId;
  }

}
?>
```

QueryResult Class

The QueryResult class is a sub-class of XmlObject. It represents the result of a database query, which in this case is always an XML document because the back-end database is a Native XML Database. Sub-classes of this class attach the appropriate stylesheet required for rendering the sub-class.

441

```php
<?php
//QueryResult.php
include_once('classes/XmlObject.php');

//The QueryResult class - object representation of the result of a query

class QueryResult extends XmlObject {
  var $queryResultXml;

  //Public constructor to create a QueryResult object
  function QueryResult($queryResultXml) {
    $this->queryResultXml = $queryResultXml;
  }

  //Public method to marshal a QueryResult object into XML
  function toXml() {
    return $this->queryResultXml;
  }
}
?>
```

RecipesResult Class

This class is a sub-class of the `QueryResult` class. It represents a list of recipes obtained as a result of a query, by listing recipes under a category or searching for featured recipes:

```php
<?php
//RecipesResult.php
//The RecipesResult class - object representation of a query result
//returning a list of recipes


include_once('classes/QueryResult.php');

//Define the style-sheet relative to the document root
define ("RECIPES_XSL",  "/phpxindice/recipex/xsl/html/recipes.xsl");

class RecipesResult extends QueryResult {

  function RecipesResult($queryResultXml) {
    QueryResult::QueryResult($queryResultXml);
    $this->setXsl($_SERVER['DOCUMENT_ROOT'] . RECIPES_XSL);
  }
}
?>
```

EditRecipe Class

This class is a sub-class of the `QueryResult` class. It represents a recipe obtained as a result of a query for a particular recipe. It associates a stylesheet with the recipe, which can render it in a format that allows users to edit it.

```php
<?php
// EditRecipe.php
//The EditRecipe class - object representation of a query result returning
//a Recipe to be edited
include_once('classes/QueryResult.php');

//Define the style-sheet relative to the document root
define ("EDITRECIPE_XSL",  "/phpxindice/recipex/xsl/html/editrecipe.xsl");

class EditRecipe extends QueryResult {

  function EditRecipe($queryResultXml) {
    QueryResult::QueryResult($queryResultXml);
    $this->setXsl($_SERVER['DOCUMENT_ROOT'] . EDITRECIPE_XSL);
      }
}
?>
```

EditFeedback Class

This class is another sub-class of the `QueryResult` class. It represents a feedback item obtained as a result of a query for a particular feedback item. It associates a stylesheet with the results that can render them in a format that allows users to edit them.

```php
<?php
//EditFeedback.php
//The EditFeedback class - object representation of a query result returning
//a Feedback item to be edited
include_once('classes/QueryResult.php');

//Define the style-sheet relative to the document root
define ("EDITFEEDBACK_XSL", "/phpxindice/recipex/xsl/html/editfeedback.xsl");

class EditFeedback extends QueryResult {

  function EditFeedback($queryResultXml) {
    QueryResult::QueryResult($queryResultXml);
    $this->setXsl($_SERVER['DOCUMENT_ROOT'] . EDITFEEDBACK_XSL);
  }
}
?>
```

Xformer Class

The `Xformer` class represents an entity that can take an `XmlObject` object as an argument. It converts the `XmlObject` into XML and also obtains the stylesheet associated with the `XmlObject`. It then applies the stylesheet on this XML. This class can also take an array of arguments that can be passed to the stylesheet.

```php
<?php
//Xformer.php
//The Xformer class - object representation of a transformer
//Operates on objects to produce the appropriate markup to display
```

```
class Xformer {

  var $objToXform;
  var $argsForStyleSheet;
  var $xsl;

  //Public constructor to create an Xformer object for a recipex object
  function Xformer($objToXform, $argsForStyleSheet="") {
    $this->setObjToXform($objToXform);
    $this->setArgsforStyleSheet($argsForStyleSheet);
  }

  //Public method to render a page - in admin mode or user mode
  function renderPage($isAdmin) {
    $obj_xml = $this->objToXform->toXml();
    $obj_xsl = $this->objToXform->getXsl();
    $arguments = array('/_xml' => $obj_xml, '/_xsl' => $obj_xsl);
    $xh = xslt_create();

    if ($isAdmin) {
      if (!isset($this->argsForStyleSheet)) {
        $this->argsForStyleSheet = array();
      }
      $this->argsForStyleSheet['isAdmin'] = true;
    }

    if (isset($this->argsForStyleSheet)) {
      $result = xslt_process($xh, 'arg:/_xml', 'arg:/_xsl', NULL,
                             $arguments, $this->argsForStyleSheet);

    } else {
      $result = xslt_process($xh, 'arg:/_xml', 'arg:/_xsl', NULL, $arguments);

    }

    xslt_free($xh);
    return $result;
  }
```

If the rendering mode is administrator-specific, an isAdmin parameter is set to true and passed to the stylesheet, which allows the stylesheet to render content specific to the administrator.

```
  //Get/set methods for various Xformer data members
  function setObjToXform($objToXform) {
    $this->objToXform = $objToXform;
  }

  function setArgsForStyleSheet($argsForStyleSheet) {
    if ($argsForStyleSheet != "") {
      $this->argsForStyleSheet = $argsForStyleSheet;
    }
```

```
    }

    function getArgsForStyleSheet() {
      return $this->argsForStyleSheet;
    }

    function getObjToXform() {
      return $objToXform;
    }
  }
  ?>
```

HTML Stylesheets

In this section we will see the various stylesheets used to transform objects from their XML representation to HTML. Stylesheets promote the separation of XML data from formatting.

recipe.xsl

This stylesheet is used to transform an XML document that represents an individual recipe. It formats various attributes of the recipe in HTML.

```
<?xml version="1.0" encoding="UTF-8"?>
<xsl:stylesheet version="1.0" xmlns:xsl="http://www.w3.org/1999/XSL/Transform"
xmlns:s
rc="http://xml.apache.org/xindice/Query">

  <xsl:param name="isAdmin"/>
```

The isAdmin parameter is tested to customize rendering for administrator users.

```
    <xsl:template match="/recipe">
    <html><head>
      <title><xsl:value-of select="name"/></title>
      </head>

      <body>
        <h1><xsl:value-of select="name"/></h1>
        <xsl:if test="boolean($isAdmin)">
        <a href="editRecipe.php?recipeId={name@recipeid}
                &amp;categoryId={name@categoryid}">
        <img src="images/edit.gif" height="20" width="41" align="absbottom"/>
        </a>
        <a href="deleteRecipe.php?recipeId={name@recipeid}
                &amp;categoryId={name@categoryid}">
        <img src="images/delete.gif" height="20" width="57" align="absbottom"/>
        </a><br/>
        </xsl:if>
```

```
        Recipe submitted by: <a href="mailto:{submitter/email}"><xsl:value-of
select="submitter/name"/></a><br/>
      <xsl:variable name="ingredients" select="ingredients/ingredient"/>
      <p><h2>Ingredients</h2></p>
      <ul>
      <xsl:for-each select="$ingredients">
        <li><xsl:value-of select="."/></li>
      </xsl:for-each>
      </ul>

      <p><h2>Preparation</h2></p>
      <p><xsl:value-of select="instructions"/></p>

      <p><h4>Serves: <xsl:value-of select="serves"/></h4></p>

      <xsl:variable name="ratingsTotal"
                        select="sum(feedback/feedback-item/rating)"/>
      <xsl:variable name="numRatings"
                        select="count(feedback/feedback-item/rating)"/>
      <xsl:if test="$numRatings > 0">
      <p><h4>Overall Rating (out of 5):
          <xsl:value-of select="$ratingsTotal div $numRatings"/></h4></p>
```

The overall rating of a recipe is calculated at the time of rendering by averaging all ratings attributed to this recipe:

```
      <p><h4>Comments:</h4></p>
      <xsl:variable name="feedback-items" select="feedback/feedback-item"/>
      <ul>
      <xsl:for-each select="$feedback-items">
      <li><xsl:value-of select="comment"/> <i> Rating:
          </i><xsl:value-of select="rating"/></li>
      </xsl:for-each>
      </ul>
      </xsl:if>
      <p>
      <a
href="rateRecipe.php?recipeId={name@recipeid}&amp;categoryId={name@categoryid}"><i
>Rate this recipe</i></a>
      </p>
    </body>
  </html>
  </xsl:template>
</xsl:stylesheet>
```

recipes.xsl

This stylesheet is used to transform an XML document that is a list of recipes potentially obtained as a result of a search for recipes, a listing of recipes under a category or a list of featured recipes. Each recipe is listed as a hyper-link that can display the contents of the recipe:

```
<?xml version="1.0" encoding="UTF-8"?>
<xsl:stylesheet version="1.0" xmlns:xsl="http://www.w3.org/1999/XSL/Transform">
<xsl:output method="html"/>

<xsl:template match="/">
<html><head><title>List of Recipes</title></head>
  <body>
    <xsl:variable name="resultSet" select="//name"/>
    <xsl:if test="count($resultSet)=0">
    <p>Sorry, no recipes match this category/criteria</p>
    </xsl:if>

  <ul>
    <xsl:for-each select="$resultSet">
    <li><a
href="displayRecipe.php?recipeId={@recipeid}&amp;categoryId={@categoryid}">
    <xsl:value-of select="."/>
    </a>
    </li>
    </xsl:for-each>
    </ul>
  </body></html>
</xsl:template>
</xsl:stylesheet>
```

categories.xsl

This stylesheet is used to render the categories of recipes. Categories are listed as links to URLs that list all the recipes under them:

```
<?xml version="1.0" encoding="UTF-8"?>

<xsl:stylesheet version="1.0" xmlns:xsl="http://www.w3.org/1999/XSL/Transform">

<!-- This template is used to display recipe categories -->
  <xsl:template match="//categories">
  <xsl:variable name="categoryName" select="category"/>
  <html><head><title>Recipe categories</title></head>
    <body>
    <p>
    <h3>Click on a category to display the recipes listed under it:</h3>
    </p>
    <br/>
    <ul>
    <xsl:for-each select="$categoryName">
    <li><a href="listCategory.php?categoryId={@id}">
    <xsl:value-of select="."/></a></li>
    </xsl:for-each>
    </ul>
    </body></html>
  </xsl:template>
<!-- End of template used to display recipe categories -->

</xsl:stylesheet>
```

447

editrecipe.xsl

This stylesheet generates the HTML form that is used to edit a recipe:

```
<?xml version="1.0" encoding="UTF-8"?>
<xsl:stylesheet version="1.0" xmlns:xsl="http://www.w3.org/1999/XSL/Transform">

  <xsl:template match="/recipe">
    <html><head>
      <title>Edit Recipe</title>
      </head>

    <body>
      <h2>Edit Recipe</h2>
      <i>All fields are required</i>
      <FORM METHOD="POST" ACTION="editRecipe.php">
        <INPUT TYPE="HIDDEN" NAME="posted" VALUE="true"/><BR/>
        <INPUT TYPE="HIDDEN" NAME="recipeId" VALUE="{name@recipeid}"/><BR/>
        <INPUT TYPE="HIDDEN" NAME="categoryId" VALUE="{name@categoryid}"/><BR/>

        Recipe Name:
        <INPUT TYPE="text" NAME="name" VALUE="{name}"/><BR/>

        Featured ?:
        Yes<INPUT TYPE="radio" NAME="featured" VALUE="true"/>
        No<INPUT TYPE="radio" NAME="featured" VALUE="false"/><BR/>

        Submitter&apos; Name:
        <INPUT TYPE="text" NAME="submitterName" VALUE="{submitter/name}"/><BR/>
        Submitter&apos; E-mail:
        <INPUT TYPE="text" NAME="submitterEmail" VALUE="{submitter/email}"/>

        <br/><br/>Ingredients (separate ingredients with commas(,):<br/>
        <xsl:variable name="ingredients" select="ingredients/ingredient"/>
          <TEXTAREA NAME="ingredients" ROWS="6" COLS="40">
          <xsl:for-each select="$ingredients">
           <xsl:value-of select="."/>,
          </xsl:for-each>
          </TEXTAREA>

        <br/><br/>Preparation Instructions<br/>
        <TEXTAREA NAME="instructions" ROWS="10" COLS="70">
        <xsl:value-of select="instructions"/>
        </TEXTAREA><br/>

        Serves: <INPUT TYPE="text" NAME="serves" VALUE="{serves}"/><BR/>

        <br/><br/>Comments:<br/>
        <xsl:variable name="feedback-item" select="feedback/feedback-item"/>
        <ul>
        <xsl:for-each select="$feedback-item">
          <li><xsl:value-of select="comment"/>
          <i> Rating: </i><xsl:value-of select="rating"/>
          <a href="editFeedback.php?recipeId={../../name@recipeid}&amp;
          categoryId={../../name@categoryid}&amp;
          feedbackItemId={@id}">[Edit]
          </a>
```

```
                    <a href="deleteFeedback.php?recipeId={../../name@recipeid}&amp;
                    categoryId={../../name@categoryid}&amp;
                    feedbackItemId={@id}">[Delete]
                    </a>
                    </li>
                </xsl:for-each>
                </ul>

                <INPUT TYPE="submit" VALUE="Click to Submit"/><BR/>
            </FORM>
        </body></html>
    </xsl:template>
</xsl:stylesheet>
```

editfeedback.xsl

The editfeedback.xsl stylesheet generates the HTML form that is used to edit a feedback item.

```
<?xml version="1.0" encoding="UTF-8"?>
<xsl:stylesheet version="1.0" xmlns:xsl="http://www.w3.org/1999/XSL/Transform">
  <xsl:output method="html"/>

    <xsl:param name="recipeId"/>
    <xsl:param name="categoryId"/>
    <xsl:param name="feedbackItemId"/>

    <xsl:template match="//feedback-item">
    <html><head>
      <title>Edit Feedback</title>
    </head>

    <body>
      <h2>Edit Feedback</h2>
      <i>All fields are required</i>
      <FORM METHOD="POST" ACTION="editFeedback.php">
          <INPUT TYPE="HIDDEN" NAME="posted" VALUE="true"/>
          <INPUT TYPE="HIDDEN" NAME="recipeId" VALUE="{$recipeId}"/>
          <INPUT TYPE="HIDDEN" NAME="categoryId" VALUE="{$categoryId}"/>
          <INPUT TYPE="HIDDEN" NAME="feedbackItemId" VALUE="{$feedbackItemId}"/>
          Rating: <INPUT TYPE="TEXT" NAME="rating" LENGTH="2" VALUE="{rating}"/>

          <br/><br/>Comments:<br/>
          <TEXTAREA NAME="comment" ROWS="10" COLS="70">
          <xsl:value-of select="comment"/>
          </TEXTAREA><BR/>

          <INPUT TYPE="SUBMIT" VALUE="Submit"/>
      </FORM>
    </body></html>
    </xsl:template>
</xsl:stylesheet>
```

449

Potential Enhancements

The application that we developed in this chapter demonstrates several key XML technologies, most importantly the storage and retrieval of XML documents in a Native XML Database. Here are some suggestions for potential enhancements to this application:

❑ The current implementation does not allow for the editing, addition, or deletion of categories from the application. These steps need to be performed using the Xindice command-line tools. This is acceptable most of the times because categories are not that frequently changed. However, for an application where such changes are frequent, it might be worthwhile to implement creation, deletion, and editing of categories.

❑ Currently the system recognizes only two users – a regular user or an administrator user. This functionality could be enhanced by allowing users to register themselves. Users could be grouped into classes such as administrators, designers, and end users.

❑ The current implementation assumes that all access to the application is from HTML browsers. It might be worthwhile to modify the application and add support for stylesheets that render wireless markup languages. For such an approach, the application needs to be written such that the presentation logic, or the markup language, is cleanly isolated from the objects involved.

❑ Another enhancement could be to add pictures to recipe items submitted.

Summary

In this chapter we leveraged off our understanding of the previous chapter where we dealt with XML databases and various associated technologies, by building a Recipe Exchange application from the ground up. We started by defining the specifications for the application and then designing the application based on the various entities involved and their attributes. After having designed the database organization and also the class hierarchy, we created collections, set up indexes, and performed setup tasks for the application. Lastly, we discussed the code comprising of the PHP pages, classes, and XSL stylesheets, that together made up our application.

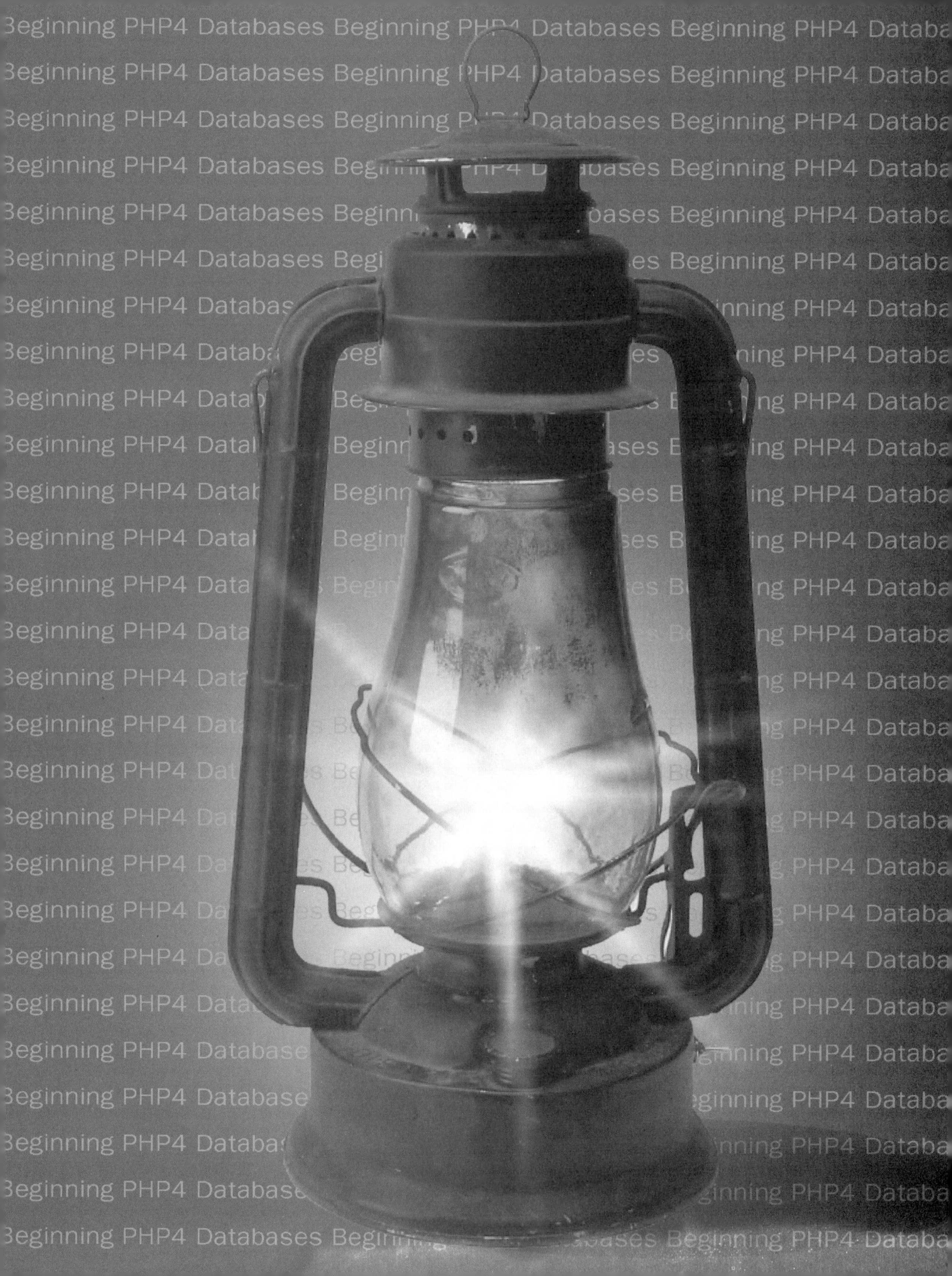
Beginning PHP4 Databases

Administration

Backup and Recovery

A backup is, in basic terms, a copy of your data. Why would you need a copy of your data? Perhaps you need to move your data to another database. Or perhaps one of your disks suffers a failure and your database is no longer usable. You need to have a spare copy of it because your data is important to you, your employer, your customers, or whoever needs it. That spare copy needs to be usable so that the recovery process will actually yield a working database.

> *If you aren't backing up your data in a way that allows you to recover it, then the data is not important to you.*

Most likely the database was created for some purpose. How would that purpose be served if all of the data were gone? If it would have absolutely no impact on that purpose, then we would guess that you have no need for the database, or that it is a development or testing database. If this is not the case, then you need to have a method of being able to reproduce your data when the inevitable occurs.

This appendix will provide you with the basic knowledge of how a backup and recovery system works. It would be impossible to cover all of the variations given that each database vendor has their own unique methods for this important task. Once you have a basic understanding of how a backup and recovery system functions, you will then need to understand the particular methodology for your chosen database management system.

It is recommended that you gain an understanding of the backup and recovery systems in place for a particular vendor's product prior to purchasing. A lower-cost product may cost you more in the long run if it is unable to perform these functions in a manner that is consistent with the needs of your environment.

The Basics

Your chosen database management system will most likely provide you with the basic tools to back up your databases. This may not be sufficient to meet your needs. Some backup systems require you to lock out users from the database, or severely impact database performance during the backup process. While this is okay in some environments, this is not acceptable when your database is required to be online all the time. If you find yourself in this situation, you may be able to find a product from your database vendor or another vendor that will allow you to work around this, you may be able to develop your own process for doing this, or you may need to change to another database management system (DBMS).

Many database systems have two types of backups: full database dumps, and transaction log dumps. The former is quite straightforward. The database simply creates a file or set of files that can be used to recreate the database. This can be as simple as a file that has CREATE and INSERT statements to recreate the database structure and fill your tables, or it can be a more complex and proprietary file.

For some database products, you only have a database dump as described above. In others, you have transaction log dumps in addition. For example, let's say that you dump the full database every day at 11:00. What happens to the data that is inserted, updated, and deleted between that full dump and the crash that happens at 2:23 the following morning? If you are only doing full dumps, those changes are lost. Transaction log dumps are incremental dumps, and they allow you to recover the transactions (hence data) closer to the time of a failure without the time and storage space required by more frequent full dumps.

A database server stores data in tables. During the normal course of operation, users are adding new data, changing existing data, and removing existing data. Rather than constantly update the data that exists in the tables, which would consume resources and degrade performance, the DBMS will store these data changes in a transaction log. When the server has less user requirements, the housekeeping processes will take these changes and apply them to the tables.

In a recovery process, the server first reads the data dump, which is the copy of the data as it existed in the tables at the time of the dump. Once this is completed, it will read through the transaction log and apply the changes. After this process is complete, the database should be an exact copy of what it looked like when the dump was taken, and it should be ready for use. The diagram below shows a simple dump timeline:

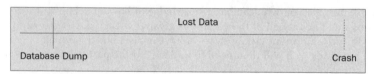

Let us now examine this figure. The administrator only performs a full database dump. When the server crashes at the time indicated by the dotted line, all data that has been inserted, updated, or deleted after the database dump (indicated by the straight line) is lost. By adding transaction dumps, as seen in the diagram below, less data is lost when the server crashes:

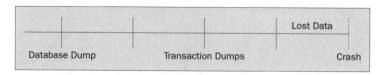

If you do your full database dumps daily at 11:00 and you do a transaction dump every other hour of the day, then when your system crashes at 2:23 the following morning (assuming that you lose your database), you will only lose the data between the 2:00 transaction dump and the 2:23 crash. This is, of course, assuming that your dump process yields dumps that are able to be reloaded. You can adjust the timing of the transaction dumps to fit your environment. You may need them every 20 minutes, every 3 hours, or perhaps you need them every 30 minutes between 9:00 and 17:00 and then every 2 hours between 17:00 and 9:00.

If you are thinking about database security, and you probably should be, then do you really want a database dump that anyone can come along and read? We won't go into too much detail about security at this point. However, it is important to keep this in mind. Anyone who has access to your dumps probably has the ability to read or copy your data.

Creating a Backup Strategy

When creating your backup strategy, it has to result in a process that is able to provide you with a working database with no referential integrity issues, minimize lost data to an acceptable level, and it should alert you if there are failures in the process.

While in some systems such as banking systems there is no room for any lost data, in other systems it is acceptable to lose data. While this sounds counter-intuitive, it really is not. Your database may be used as a library system for a tape library. If 20 minutes of data is lost, the cost is quite low to have someone re-enter the lost data. The decision of how frequently to perform transaction log dumps is usually a business decision.

As you wouldn't like to lose any data, the preference is for more frequent dumps during the hours of higher transaction loads, and reduce the frequency during the slower hours. After two or three failures, you will get a feel for what management feels is an appropriate interval, and often they are happy to provide any additional budget to meet their needs.

The basic questions you need to ask are:

- ❑ Does the backup process require downtime, and if it does, will this work in your environment?
- ❑ Where will you place your backups (disk, tape, CD, or a combination)?
- ❑ When is the best time to make backups?

Servers That Require Downtime

The question of your environment allowing for database downtime should be a pretty easy one to answer. Either it does or it doesn't. If your database has any users at all, often the answer is *no*. Users want their information available all of the time. However, you can get away with a little downtime in some environments. If you are in the group that doesn't allow database downtime, then you should look for a database system that can properly handle backups while the system is running.

Some database systems do allow you to make backups while the system is still running, and produce a backup that has inconsistent referential integrity. Let's say that you are backing up your database. Your backup system writes table A to the backup file. During that process, a user performs a DELETE that removes data from table A and table C. After this DELETE, the backup process then writes table B and then table C to the backup file. The backup goes well and you feel safe.

An hour later, your database becomes corrupt and the only way to fix it is to rebuild your server. So you rebuild your server and then load your dump. The load goes fine, but all is not good with your data. If you will recall from above, table A was written before the DELETE was executed, so the data was already in the dump file. After your recovery, table A still has that row of data. How will the affect the referential integrity of your application? From this example, we don't know. It may not cause a problem at all, it may cause some minor problems, or it may really cause a lot of problems for your application.

The lesson here is that you need a backup system that will ensure that your data is written in a way that it is recoverable. Data consistency is very important here. If you find yourself in the above situation, you either need to build a process that will remove user access, or switch to a DBMS that is able to perform on-the-fly backups.

Servers That Use Physical Files

Some database environments are set up to use physical files to store live data. The system administrator usually has a file system backup process that will archive important files. When the system administrator or a user looks to verify that all the files have been backed up and are safe, it will appear that all is well.

Now that you understand the previous scenario, you should realize the potential here. The backup system is archiving the data file(s). During this archive process, the file is still being used; data is being inserted, updated, and deleted. Writing these files to the backup system is just like writing the tables in the previous example, and will result in a backup that is not able to be recovered into a correctly operating database.

A Simple Backup Solution

If your vendor provides a simple backup system, then you'll need a simple solution. Stop all user activity in the database and make your backup. When the backup process is complete, you can then allow users to continue their work. If this is not acceptable in your working environment, then you need a database system with a more complex backup process, or a backup product from another vendor.

On-the-Fly

In many of the more major database products, there is a backup process that reads data into memory, or some other location, using the tables and the transaction log, so that it take a "snapshot" or picture of the data at a particular point in time. The advantage of this type of backup process is that it produces a backup that is consistent and recoverable. Some vendors implement this in a way that minimally impacts users of the system to the point that they are completely unaware that the backup is being performed.

Storing a Dump

Is it best to place your backups directly onto tape, just keep them on a disk, or should they be burned onto CD? Like every other aspect of the backup/recovery process, it depends on the needs of your particular environment.

One preferred method is to back up to disk. These online backups are fast and available as long as you don't suffer a failure of the dump disk. You can program your backup process to store several days of backups online and this gives you more of a likely chance that you can quickly recover a good backup. This combined with a tape-or-CD type of archive process allows for a good bit of flexibility.

Also something to keep in mind is that although technology is getting better, media failures do still happen. This is the reason dumps are stored in several different places. If we keep several days online, and then we archive to tape, we are able to restore from tape should the dump file system fail. In addition, you can have online tape storage, and offline and even off-site storage of tapes. Many Internet Service Providers today offer an off-site disk storage system. Housed in a secure location far away from your main production systems, this is like having an online backup system that is close at hand. These facilities are physically secure and usually have a high bandwidth connection to their general facilities.

When To Back Up

When is the best time to back up your data? This really does depend on your backup process. If you have to stop all user activities to perform your backup process, then it is probably something you will do when your users don't need the database, or at least when fewer users need the data. If you are able to back up your database on-the-fly, then you can really do them anytime. In a previous environment, we did all of our backups in the middle of the night so that we would minimize the impact on our users. Our backup process was completely automated and would alert us if there was a failure. Unfortunately, if you are running your backups in the middle of the night and there is a failure (which will happen quite often when you have more than 500 databases), the DBA will be awakened in the middle of the night.

The smart DBA gets tired of this after 2 or 3 years and decides to look for a better way. Our better way came when the database vendor released a new version of their software. The dump processes were made so that they minimally impacted the users. We changed our strategy to do the majority of the backups during the day while we were in the office or at least awake. This greatly reduced the number of times we needed to wake up in the middle of the night. Problems are usually fixed a lot faster if the DBA is awake.

Third-Party Products

There are many products developed by other companies that can be used to back up your database. Often these products will incorporate tools and features that your database vendor will not include in their products. Some tools allow you to back up your database, migrate your data from one DBMS to another, and even dump the database schema to a file. Other tools are traditional file system backup software with added modules or plug-ins that allows the software to interact directly with the database software to dump the database.

Using the type of tool that has the ability to dump the schema of your database and then export the data from your database is quite similar to the simple dump method mentioned earlier. Another feature of some of these tools is the ability to look at the individual transactions that are in your transaction log. This can aid in recovering data that may have been accidentally changed or deleted.

DBA Thoughts

Something to keep in mind here is that often a more complex process will have many more features, however the trade-off is that there are many more areas for failure. A simple process usually has simple problems. A script that connects to the database, dumps the database, and disconnects from the database doesn't have a lot of room for fail, although it will fail from time to time. When this process fails, it is quite simple to find the problem.

Some added features are nice. With some dump process, we could have it insert information into an administrative database so that we can track the dump process over time. We can see how long each dump takes, how large the dumps are, and can also look at the historical perspective.

With this information, we have the ability to see the growth pattern of each database and we can better anticipate when we will need to add space to the database or the dump directory. By doing this in advance, we are able to keep from filling the disks and suffering failures as a result.

Another advantage of this tracking is that we are better able to see the effects of the dump process on the timing of all of the maintenance processes. There are more processes for a DBA to administer than just dumps. As the database grows, the length of the dump process also grows, in fact, most, if not all of the maintenance processes increase in time as the database grows. By knowing when the dumps complete, we can ensure other processes that rely on the dump (say the load of a reporting server) are timed properly.

Plan for Failures

Let us now look at some of the plans in case there is a failure of backup.

Test the Process

It has been emphasized that you need to create a system that will produce a backup that is recoverable. How do you know that you have such a system? The only way is to test it. You need to test this on a regular basis to verify that all backup systems are working properly, so that you have additional practice at recovering your databases from what your backup process provides you with, and so that you can document this process.

If you practice this on a regular basis, chances are you will make a lot of mistakes when you are practicing and what better time to make them? And it can be fun. The DBA job can be a monotonous one at times. Fixing something that is broken gives one a great feeling. Practice will help you to make sure that you react quickly and correctly when there is a failure, and you can bet that if you are functioning as a DBA for more than ten minutes, there will be some kind of failure.

Safety in Distance

Disasters really do happen, sometimes disks and tapes really are unreadable, and sometimes you are unable to find the storage medium where you carefully saved a copy of your database. For these reasons alone, it is strongly recommended that you periodically archive your database to an off-site location. The more geographically dispersed your operational database and your off-site backup the better, as long as you are still able to recover it in a reasonable timeframe.

If you are lucky, you have an office that is on another continent and you have a good network connection between the two locations. There are many companies that have safe facilities for the storage of archive tapes. If you lose all of your data, this service is well worth the cost. Often someone will just take a copy of the archive and keep it in their home. While this idea brings up a significant number of security issues, it is better than losing all of your data.

Some companies will make an agreement with another non-competing company to swap archive space. This allows you both to have an off-site backup with reasonable costs. Whatever off-site storage system you use, keep in mind that your archive is probably not encrypted and therefore you should guard it well.

While distance is good when you are thinking in terms of a disaster, it can also be a struggle when you think of it in terms of security. The battle of ease-of-use versus security has probably been raging on since the first implementation of security. We recommend that you weigh the security risk against the risk of losing your data and then allow those who make the business decisions decide what the best risk for your particular situation is.

Getting it in Writing

The importance of documentation cannot be stressed enough. If you happen to be out on a holiday and something fails, you want to make sure that your replacement is able to restore the environment to its proper working order. This will minimize the number of calls you receive while on holiday, and it will help you to find your environment in working order when you return.

The best way to do this is to write down (or cut/paste into an editor) every command that you issue while doing one of your recovery practices. Then go back and add comments and reasoning to the list of commands. The best test of your documentation is to have another person walk through them without you helping. Take notes of where the process doesn't work and then add to your documentation. If you can get your manager or one of your users to help you in this step, they will likely have a lot more respect for the work you do.

When All Else Fails

What if the most horrible event happens and for whatever reason, there is no good backup? Well there are still a few steps that might help you. First is to contact the support department of your DBMS software to determine whether or not they can assist you in any way to recover any of your data. Normally you will contact them and then wait for a return phone call. This is actually a great thing for you personally, as it will give you time to update your resume. Hold on to it, as you'll likely need it in the final step.

If the vendor support team is unable or unwilling to help you, you may be able to find a third-party company that is able to assist you in data recovery. Be prepared, as these services are quite expensive. Another possible option is to look at the files, or raw disk partitions with something like the UNIX strings command to see if you can recover any data.

Third-Party Backup Products

If you aren't satisfied with your available backup/recovery options, the following products may provide for your needs. The functionality of some of these products to back up both the file system and directly connect with the DBMS to control database backups makes them quite attractive:

- ❏ Legato Networker
- ❏ Veritas NetBackup
- ❏ IBM's Tivoli Storage Manager
- ❏ ManageIT Backup and Recovery

Redundancy (Fault Tolerance)

The idea of redundancy is great. While your main server is working, you essentially copy over the transactions that are executed in it to another server or to more than one server. If your main server fails, you are then able to work on the redundant server. Another use of replication is for reporting servers. If your reporting is done on a server other than your main server, this frees the resources of your main server to perform better for your main processing.

Basic replication provides read-only tables that can be queried, but not written to. Advanced replication allows data to be updated on any available server. If you need a truly fault-tolerant database solution, you will certainly want to find a product that supports this advanced level or replication.

Replication in Action

The simplest form of replication is fine for applications that do not have quickly changing data. If you think of a chain of stores, they could use this type of replication to push product and pricing information from their headquarters to their sales locations on a specified basis. This could be nightly, weekly, or whatever is appropriate. This is not information that the store would need to update in this case.

In the more advanced version, typical applications include sales applications which are geographically dispersed. Let's say a retailer has their Internet site with points of presence in San Jose and London. If the San Jose site goes down when there is a disruption in their connection to the internet, all of the companies' customers are able to shop via the London site. Once communication is re-established with the San Jose site, data is synchronized.

As you see, the more advanced strategy is good for an application that is distributed, needs to increase performance, or is experiencing rapid growth and needs to add additional servers to handle the load. Another good use is the field sales organizations. They are out in the field and from time to time they connect with the home office to download the latest pricing and product information, and to upload their sales data.

How It Works

In the simple form of replication as shown below, it is easy to see that there is one primary database and one or more redundant databases as seen in the successive diagram. Data is moved (usually in the form of transactions) from the primary to the redundant database(s). The diagram below shows a simple replication with one primary database:

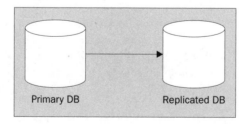

The diagram below shows a simple replication with more than one replicated database.

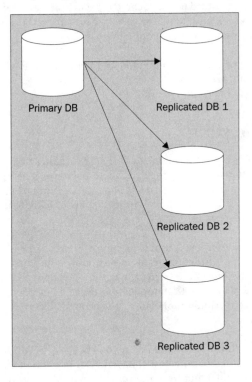

In the more advanced version or the two-way replication, databases can serve as primary and redundant databases:

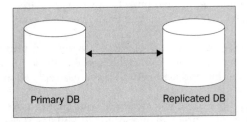

Strategies

If you decide that you want to implement a replication strategy, be prepared to do your homework. While the marketing information will lead you to believe it is easy to implement, the reality of running a replication system is that you will need to do your homework. This means a lot of planning in advance, and as mentioned in the earlier sections, you need to document your installation and practice recovering from failures. It is preferable that you do this in a testing environment.

In planning for your replication system, you really need to take the time to map out the reasons you feel you need to replicate. Look at your database schema, decide on what data will be replicated, and draw out a map of your hardware, network, and any external connections to the system. Take a look at what might possibly fail and how that will affect your system.

Once you have all of this information documented and you really know the reasons for needing to replicate your data, you can then go about deciding which replication product works best for you. This step will also take a significant amount of work.

Realities of Replicating

Many database vendors offer a process that is dedicated to reading the primary database's transaction log. It then executes those transactions in the redundant database. The best aspect of this type of replication is that it doesn't noticeably degrade application performance, as replication is performed in the background. In general, your transactions replicate quite quickly and the replicated database is ready to take over should the primary fail.

If you have a failure and you then need to run on the replicated database, you can, with most replication software, reverse the direction of the replication so the transactions performed on the replicated database are replicated to the primary when it is again available. If the failure is a serious one, then you will likely have to restart the replication process before you do this. If your replication system is configured for bi-directional replication, this is not as big an issue for you as you already replicate in both directions.

This means that if you suffer a catastrophic loss on your primary database and you switch to run your application on the replicated database, you will have to dump the replicated database, load it into the primary database, and start replicating from the replicated database to the primary database. Once you have got to this point, you can decide to either continue to run in this manner, or you can switch back to the primary database. If both machines and servers are the same size and are configured the same, it's easier to just keep running on the replicated (now the primary) database. However, if your primary database is running on a faster machine, then you would certainly want to switch back.

If you have a failure, you can quickly fill the transaction log in your primary database. This will cause your server to stop functioning and wait for available space in the log. It is strongly recommended that you implement a good monitoring and alert system if you use replication.

If you use the bi-directional replication, you can write your application to automatically determine what server or servers are available and direct all queries to an available server.

Optimization

Optimization is one of the most interesting aspects of database interaction. For example, an application developer had some performance issues with a report.

With a few changes, the report, which originally took 14 hours to run, was now running in about 30 minutes. The developer couldn't believe this was possible, until he ran both versions and realized the resultset was identical.

In this example, the original report was using row-by-row processing, which means that it selected one row of data from the database, processed it, and then selected the next row. While it makes sense from the development point of view that this would provide the desired report, from a performance point of view this is horribly wasteful.

The new version of the report used set-based transaction processing and the difference could be seen clearly. Instead of acting on each row of data, set-based transaction processing works on the data in a large chunk. Most documentation dealing with database performance will strongly urge not to use cursors and other row-by-row methods of processing.

There is so much more to performance optimization, and it really is a field all by itself. As with many other aspects of database operation, performance issues vary across the various database management systems (DBMS). So it is recommended that you attend a performance (also known as performance and tuning) training session dedicated to your particular database system.

We will cover some of the more generic issues here. Keeping these in mind can really help you to build applications that perform better.

What Level of Performance Should You Expect?

Before you can make your application perform better, you need to know what you can realistically expect your performance to be. If a query takes one second to provide the results to a query, is that good? Is half a second acceptable? Are you expecting a certain response time, or are you focusing on the server's throughput (the amount of data that can be transferred in a particular length of time)?

Actually, good performance begins at the beginning. When you are designing your database structure, this is when you need to take performance into account. You need to design your queries in a way that will allow them to best use your indexes and you need to build the proper indexes.

In reality, performance includes the operating system, hardware, network, DMBS server, database, and application. Any one of these can become a bottle-neck for your application. To decrease the response time of a query, you can upgrade your hardware, tune queries so they execute more quickly, and you can decrease the time that a query must wait for the resources to execute it.

Performance Analysis

First you need to get a baseline of your current performance. Many times your application or some component of your system will allow you to log the run-time of queries in your system. This will give you the historical perspective to determine if the changes you make increase or decrease overall performance. It is recommended that you monitor overall performance in addition to specific performance. If you make changes so that a single query executes as quickly as possible, those changes may have also caused 5 other queries to perform horribly slow.

Make sure you analyze the perceived problem. Try to determine what part of the system may be causing the problem. Take this information and compare it with your overall performance goals. Is this a query that is run quite frequently? Is it for a special report that the CEO needs every morning? Or is it a query that is run monthly? What is the expected execution time for this query? Are these expectations achievable?

Once you have a good idea of what the real problem is, make the changes necessary and again monitor performance both on the individual level and the overall level to determine the effects of the changes. Remember, it is easier to know which change is the correct one if you make the changes one at a time. It is also highly recommended that you make the change in a development environment prior to making the change in the production environment.

Normal Form

In a relational database, we use the term **normalized** for a table that has all its non-key data dependent on its primary key (we have seen this in detail in Chapter 3). This provides for ease of database maintenance and is called Third Normal Form. This is a term anyone working in databases will hear frequently. It is taught in almost every database course and most people who work with databases will know this well.

From the performance point of view, Third Normal Form is not the best table layout for performance. Often a developer or DBA will denormalize the data. This means they purposely combine tables, which will cause there to be redundant data stored in the table. The performance gain here is that a query isn't required to join the combined tables and this will decrease the time the query takes to execute.

A database that is normalized will have smaller tables, smaller indexes, and less data since there are no or fewer redundancies. If indexed well, joins can be made quickly.

The most common forms of denormalization are to combine multiple tables into fewer tables (or one table), simply add a column or columns from other tables to a particular table, and adding tables that are the result of operations performed on multiple columns.

> The decision to denormalize data should be made when you know it will solve a particular performance problem and you also know that it will not cause other performance problems that result in a net degradation in performance. Consult the performance and tuning specifics of your particular DBMS.

Indexing

Indexes are the most significant tool to performance. If there are no indexes on a table, then every query that uses that particular table must do a table scan, which means that it must read every row of data in the table to provide the query results. Indexes allow a server to quickly locate the data rows required to resolve a query. If the index is properly written, the server doesn't need to read the data, as the index will contain all the data the query needs to provide the resultset.

Although indexes can provide such significant improvements in performance, if used wrongly, they can also degrade performance. While indexes speed the reading of data, they slow the writing of data, as the index needs to be maintained in addition to the data.

You can think of an index as a small table that has a pointer to a row of data along with information from that row. If you have a base table `Table 1`, you can index the last name and the first name to speed queries that use those columns to search for particular rows of data. The index includes a pointer to the data row (shown in `Table 2` as `id`). Notice the index is sorted in `last_name`, `first_name` order. Without changing the order of the base table, the query can use the index to quickly find a particular row. Most database systems will use a pointer to the data rather than an `id`. The `id` is used in this case to simplify the example.

The base table `Table 1` is as follows:

id	last_name	first-name	sex	status
1	Hubbard	Mary	f	1
2	Ogborn	Geoff	m	4
3	Thrift	Ken	m	23
4	Jones	Mike	m	5
5	Hubbard	Jim	m	3
6	Johnson	Peter	m	5
7	Schollo	Christopher	m	6
8	Scholenvogt	Claire	m	7
9	Scholenvogt	Ellen	f	2
10	DeRuyter	Nick	m	45
11	Dyer	Bob	m	8
12	Brouillard	Bugs	m	65
13	Coit	Gregory	m	99
14	Kelley	Scott	m	7
15	Burwell	Helene	f	8
16	Cosgrove	Nancy	f	12
17	Hubbard	Cindy	f	45
18	Simpson	Dave	m	33
19	Crider	Kevin	m	76
20	Keating	Matthew	m	5
21	Niessner	Andreas	m	8

Table 2 is as follows:

last_name	first-name	id
Brouillard	Bugs	12
Burwell	Helene	15
Coit	Gregory	13
Cosgrove	Nancy	16
Crider	Kevin	19
DeRuyter	Nick	10
Dyer	Bob	11
Hubbard	Cindy	17
Hubbard	Jim	5
Hubbard	Mary	12
Johnson	Peter	6
Jones	Mike	4
Keating	Matthew	20
Kelley	Scott	14
Niessner	Andreas	21
Ogborn	Geoff	2
Scholenvogt	Claire	8
Scholenvogt	Ellen	9
Schollo	Christopher	7
Simpson	Dave	18
Thrift	Ken	3

A Sample Query

How does your DBMS find the data you need? Let's take a simple query where you are looking for one particular row of data. For this example, we will assume there are no indexes on the table:

```
select *
from table 1
where id = 21
```

For this query, the DBMS will have to look through the table row by row trying to find the row or rows that have an id of 21. If you have a table with 10,000 rows of data, your query will require the reading of all 10,000 rows. This is because the server has no way of knowing if the first, last, or any row in between has an id of 21.

Adding an index to a table is a method for speeding up queries in a database. It is a way of quickly locating specific values for a given column or columns. In the above query, let's add an index on the column ID.

The query can now execute a lot faster. Since the index knows where the row or rows of data are that have an id of 21, the server will read significantly fewer data pages. Perhaps the results are returned in one thousandth of the time of the same query with no index.

So how is an index able to retrieve the data so quickly? In the above example, an index was created on the ID column of Table 1. For each row in Table 1, an entry is made into the index, along with a pointer to the data page that contains that row. The index is then structured in a hierarchical manner so that it can quickly locate specific IDs.

When a query needs to find a specific ID, or a set of IDs, it only needs to find the correct ID(s) in the index and then read the associated data pages. This saves from having to read the entire table, which is the worst possible performance for a given query.

This sounds great, so why not put an index on every column so that every query is really fast? Well in some cases, this is done. Indexes take additional space in the database, and they cause additional overhead when data is inserted, updated, and deleted. Any time there is a change to the data in a table, the indexes must be maintained, and this means that data in the index may need to be moved around, data pages may need to be added or removed. All of this takes time.

It is mentioned that in some cases having a lot of indexes is a good thing. This is most often seen in a reporting server. A Decision Support System (DSS) is the first type of server that comes to mind. Usually this server is loaded with data from an On Line Transaction Processing (OLTP) server. Once the dump has been loaded into the DSS server, many indexes can be added to speed the queries used to generate reports. The DBA must balance the time required to create the indexes with the time required to generate the reports.

In an OLTP environment, such as you would find in many web sites, you really need to watch the balance between too many and not enough indexes. It is easy to tune if you only run three queries. When an application has hundreds of queries, it is important to start planning your schema and standards in advance.

Search Arguments

The key to a query's performance is the use of search arguments. Search arguments are found in the WHERE clause of a query. These are the statements that limit the number of rows returned by a particular query. They use the greater than, less than, and similar operators, as well as the is null operator. Some examples of search arguments are:

```
Id > 25
first_name = "Mary"
time_in_prison is null
```

While these help the server to limit the number of rows, they can also improve performance if written in such a way as to properly use the indexes on a particular table. It must be noted here that different DBMS's can handle performance in different ways, so make sure you are aware of the methods your particular software is tuned to. The information below is of a generic nature to give you a better understanding of how search arguments affect performance.

In the list of examples before, the statement `first_name = "Mary"` is focused on looking for a very particular set of rows. If there is an index on the column `first_name`, then this query will use the index to quickly find the matching rows. If however we were to use wildcards, the query may or may not use the index. Again, learn the particulars of your chosen DBMS.

If we change that statement to be `first_name like "%ary%"`, the query will still return all rows that have a first name of Mary, along with any row that has `ary` in this field. However, by using the wildcards in the statement, the server must do a table scan (read every row of data in the table) because there is no other way to determine which rows will match the statement. As you know, this will result in a horribly performing query.

As a side note, the statement `first_name like "Mar%"` may be able to use the index as the index would be able to find all rows that start with `Mar` and return those rows.

Parallel Processing

The idea of parallel processing isn't a new one. If you break down a task into steps and are then able to perform some of the tasks at the same time, then the time that it takes to perform that task from start to finish is decreased. This ability is available in many of the larger DBMS packages.

Like so many of the performance issues, each vendor is likely to have differences as to how this is implemented. At this point, you should be aware that it is possible to decrease the execution time of a query using this method. Check the documentation for your DBMS product to see if you can use this in writing your queries.

Stored Procedures

A stored procedure is a set of SQL statements that are grouped together much like a function. You call the stored procedure, and it returns the results. Instead of sending the entire SQL query across the network to your server, you just send the name of the stored procedure along with any arguments. In really big queries, this can save you lots of network traffic and increase performance.

There are more benefits to using stored procedures. Stored procedures are compiled the first time they are run. Subsequent calls to the stored procedure are quicker as the stored procedure doesn't need to be recompiled. Raw SQL would need to be compiled before being executed. Another benefit is the ability to change the database structure or the stored procedure without needing to change the application. If you call the stored procedure 50 times in your application, you would need to update the SQL query in all 50 places if you did not use stored procedures. This can considerably ease the maintenance of your application code.

If you decide to use stored procedures, and it is recommended that you do, you will need to work out a process for making sure you keep them updated in your sourcecode storage area.

eginning PHP4 Databases Beginning PHP4 Databases Beginning PHP4 Databas

PHP Database Functions

Database Abstraction Layer (DBA) Functions

Defined in ~/ext/dba/dba.c:

Function	Returns	Description
dba_close(handle)	Void	Closes the database specified by handle
dba_delete (key, handle)	Boolean	Deletes the entry specified by key from the database specified by handle
dba_exists (key, handle)	Boolean	Checks if the specified key exists in the database specified by handle
dba_fetch(key, handle)	String	Returns the data specified by key from the database specified by handle
dba_firstkey(handle)	String	Returns the first key in the database specified by handle and resets the database pointer to the first entry
dba_insert(key, value, handle)	Boolean	Inserts an entry with the specified key and value into the database specified by handle
dba_nextkey(handle)	String	Returns the next key from the database specified by handle and increments the database pointer
dba_open(path, mode, handler [, string])	Integer	Opens a database instance for path with mode using handler
dba_optimize(handle)	Boolean	Optimizes the database with the specified handle and returns true on success

Table continued on following page

Function	Returns	Description
dba_popen(path, mode, handler[, string])	Integer	Establishes a persistent database instance for path with mode using handler and returns False if it fails
dba_replace(key, value, handle)	Boolean	Replaces or inserts the entry specified by key and value into the database specified by handle and returns true on success
dba_sync(handle)	Boolean	Synchronizes the database with the specified handle and returns true on success

DBM Functions

These functions allow you to work with DBM-style (key/value) databases. These are defined in ~/ext/db/db.c:

Function	Returns	Description
dblist()	String	Describes the DBM-compatible library in use
dbmclose(dbm_id)	Boolean	Closes the DBM database specified by dbm_id
dbmdelete(dbm_id, key)	Integer	Deletes the value specified by key from the DBM database
dbmexists(dbm_id, key)	Integer	Indicates whether a value exists for the specified key in the DBM database specified by dbm_id
dbmfetch(dbm_id, key)	String	Returns the value for the specified key from the DBM database
dbmfirstkey(dbm_id)	String	Returns the first key in the DBM database
dbminsert(dbm_id, key, value)	Integer	Inserts the specified key/value pair into the DBM database
dbmnextkey(dbm_id, key)	String	Returns the next key after the specified key in the DBM database
dbmopen(filename, mode)	Integer	Opens a DBM database with the specified filename and returns an identifier for the database
dbmreplace(dbm_id, key, value)	Integer	Replaces with value the value associated with the specified key in the DBM database

dBase Functions

Defined in ~/ext/dbase/dbase.c:

Function	Returns	Description
Dbase_add_record (dbase_id, record)	Boolean	Adds a record to the dBase database
Dbase_close(dbase_id)	Boolean	Closes the dBase database specified by dbase_id
Dbase_create(filename, fields)	Integer	Creates a dBase database specified by filename with the field formats specified by fields and returns an identifier (dbase_id) for the database on success
Dbase_delete_record (dbase_id, record)	Boolean	Marks the specified record for deletion from the dBase database
Dbase_get_record (dbase_id, record)	Array	Returns the specified record from the dBase database in an array
Dbase_get_record_with_n ames(dbase_id, record)	Array	Returns the specified record from the dBase database in an associative array
Dbase_numfields (dbase_id)	Integer	Returns the number of fields in the dBase database
Dbase_numrecords (dbase_id)	Integer	Returns the number of records in the dBase database
Dbase_open(filename, flags)	Integer	Opens the dBase database specified by filename in the mode specified by flags and returns an identifier (dbase_id) for the database on success
Dbase_pack(dbase_id)	Boolean	Packs (deletes records marked for deletion) the dBase database specified by dbase_id
Dbase_replace_record(db ase_id, record, record_num)	Boolean	Replaces the data specified by record_num in the dBase database with the data specified by record

dbx Functions

Defined in ~/ext/dbx/dbx.c:

Function	Returns	Description
Dbx_close(link_id)	Boolean	Closes an open connection/database
Dbx_compare(row_a, row_b, column_key, [flags])	Integer	Compares two rows for sorting purposes
Dbx_connect(module, host, database, username, password, [persistent])	Object	Opens a connection/database
Dbx_error(link_id)	String	Reports the error message of the latest function call in the module (not just in the connection)
Dbx_query(link_id, sql_statement, [flags])	Object	Sends a query and fetches all results (if any)
Dbx_sort(result_id, user_compare_function)	Boolean	Sorts a result from a dbx_query by a custom sort function

FilePro Plus Functions

Defined in ~/ext/filepro/filepro.c:

Function	Returns	Description
filepro(directory)	Integer	Reads and verifies the filepro map file
filepro_fieldcount()	Integer	Counts the number of fields in the database that's currently open
filepro_fieldname(field_num)	String	Returns the name of field number field_num
filepro_fieldtype(field_num)	String	Returns the edit type of field number field_num
filepro_fieldwidth(field_num)	Integer	Returns the width of field number field_num
filepro_retrieve(row_num, field_num)	String	Returns the data stored in the database at row number row_num and field number field_num
filepro_rowcount()	Integer	Counts the number of rows in the database that's currently open

FrontBase Functions

Defined in ~/ext/fbsql/php_fbsql.c:

Function	Returns	Description
fbsql_affected_rows([link_id])	Integer	Gets number of affected rows in previous FrontBase operation
fbsql_autocommit(link_id, [True/False])		Enables or disables autocommit
fbsql_change_user(user, password, [database][link_id])		Changes logged-in user of the active connection
fbsql_close([link_id])	Boolean	Closes FrontBase connection
fbsql_commit([link_id])	Boolean	Commits a transaction to the database
fbsql_connect ([hostname, [username, password]]])	Integer	Opens a connection to a FrontBase Server
fbsql_create_blob(blob_data, [link_id])	Integer	Creates a BLOB
fbsql_create_clob(clob_data, [link_id])	Integer	Creates a CLOB
fbsql_create_db(database_name, [link_id])		Creates a FrontBase database
fbsql_data_seek(result_id, row_number)	Boolean	Moves internal result pointer
fbsql_database_password(link_id , [database_password])	String	Sets or retrieves the password for a FrontBase database
fbsql_database(link_id, [database_name])		Gets or sets the database name used with a connection
fbsql_db_query(database_name, query, [link_id])	Integer	Sends a FrontBase query
fbsql_db_status(database_name, [link_id])	Integer	Gets the status for a given database
fbsql_drop_db(database_name, [link_id])	Boolean	Drops (deletes) a FrontBase database
fbsql_errno([link_id])	Integer	Returns the numerical value of the error message from previous FrontBase operation

Table continued on following page

475

Function	Returns	Description
fbsql_error([link_id])	String	Returns the text of the error message from the previous FrontBase operation
fbsql_fetch_array(result_id, [array_type])	Array	Fetches a result row as an associative array, a numeric array, or both
fbsql_fetch_assoc(result_id)	Array	Fetches a result row as an associative array
fbsql_fetch_field(result_id, [offset])	Object	Gets column information from a result and returns as an object
fbsql_fetch_lengths([result_id])	Array	Gets the length of each output in a result
fbsql_fetch_object (result_id, [result_type])	Array	Fetches a result row as an object
fbsql_fetch_row(result_id)	Array	Gets a result row as an enumerated array
fbsql_field_flags(result_id, offset)	String	Gets the flags associated with the specified field in a result
fbsql_field_len(result_id, offset)	Integer	Returns the length of the specified field
fbsql_field_name(result_id, field_index)	String	Gets the name of the specified field in a result
fbsql_field_seek(result_id, offset)		Sets result pointer to a specified field offset
fbsql_field_table(result_id, offset)	String	Gets name of the table the specified field is in
fbsql_field_type(result_id, offset)	String	Gets the type of the specified field in a result
fbsql_free_result(result_id)		Frees result memory
fbsql_get_autostart_info(link_id)		No description given yet
fbsql_hostname(link_id, [host_name])	String	Gets or sets the hostname used with a connection
fbsql_insert_id([link_id])	Integer	Gets the ID generated from the previous INSERT operation

Function	Returns	Description
fbsql_list_dbs(link_id)	Integer	Lists databases available on a FrontBase server
fbsql_list_fields(database_name, table_name, [link_id])	Integer	Lists FrontBase result fields
fbsql_list_tables(database_name, [link_id])	Integer	Lists tables in a FrontBase database
fbsql_next_result(result_id)	Boolean	Moves the internal result pointer to the next result
fbsql_num_fields(result_id)	Integer	Gets number of fields in result
fbsql_num_rows(result_id)	Integer	Gets number of rows in result
fbsql_password(link_id, [string])		Gets or sets the user password used with a connection
fbsql_pconnect([hostname], [username], [password])	Integer	Opens a persistent connection to a FrontBase Server
fbsql_query(query, [link_id])	Boolean	Sends a FrontBase query
fbsql_read_blob(blob_handle, [link_id])	String	Reads a BLOB from the database
fbsql_read_clob(clob_handle, [link_id])	String	Reads a CLOB from the database
fbsql_result(result_id, row, [field])	String	Gets result data
fbsql_rollback(link_id)	Boolean	Rolls backs a transaction to the database
fbsql_select_db(database_name, [link_id])	Boolean	Selects a FrontBase database
fbsql_set_lob_mode(result_id, database_name)	Boolean	Sets the LOB retrieve mode for a FrontBase resultset
fbsql_set_transaction(link_id, locking_level, isolation_level)		Sets the transaction locking and isolation
fbsql_start_db(database_name, [link_id])	Boolean	Starts a database on local or remote server
fbsql_stop_db(database_name, [link_id])	Boolean	Stops a database on local or remote server

Table continued on following page

477

Function	Returns	Description
`fbsql_tablename(result_id, index)`	String	Gets table name of field
`fbsql_username(link_id, [username])`		Gets or sets the host user used with a connection
`fbsql_warnings([On/Off])`	Boolean	Enables or disables FrontBase warnings

Hyperwave Functions

Defined in `~/ext/hyperwave/hw.c`:

Function	Returns	Description
`hw_Array2Objrec(obect_array)`	Object	Converts attributes from object array to object record
`hw_changeobject(link_id, objectID, attributes)`		Changes attributes of an object (obsolete)
`hw_Children(connection_id, objectID)`	Array	Object IDs of children
`hw_ChildrenObj(connection_id, objectID)`	Array	Object records of children
`hw_Close(connection_id)`	Boolean	Closes the Hyperwave connection
`hw_Connect(host, port, [username, [password]])`	Integer	Opens a connection
`hw_connection_info(link_id)`		Prints information about the connection to the Hyperwave server
`hw_Cp(connection_id, object_id_array, destination_id)`		Copies objects
`hw_Deleteobject(connection_id, objectID)`	Boolean	Deletes object
`hw_DocByAnchor(connection_id, anchorID)`	Integer	Object ID object belonging to anchor
`hw_DocByAnchorObj(connection_id, anchored)`	Object	Object record object belonging to anchor

Function	Returns	Description
hw_Document_Attributes (hw_document)	Object	Object record of hw_document
hw_Document_BodyTag (hw_document)	String	Body tag of hw_document
hw_Document_Content (hw_document)	String	Returns content of hw_document
hw_Document_SetContent (hw_document, content)	String	Sets/replaces content of hw_document
hw_Document_Size (hw_document)	Integer	Size of hw_document
hw_dummy(link_id, id, msgid)		Hyperwave dummy function
hw_EditText(connection_id, hw_document)		Retrieves text document
hw_Error (connection_id_	Integer	Error number
hw_ErrorMsg(connection_id)	String	Returns error message
hw_Free_Document(hw_document)		Frees hw_document
hw_GetAnchors(connection_id, objectID)	Array	Object IDs of anchors of document
hw_GetAnchorsObj(connection_id, objectID)	Array	Object records of anchors of document
hw_GetAndLock(connection_id, objectID)	Object	Returns object record and lock object
hw_GetChildColl(connection_id, objectID)	Array	object IDs of child collections
hw_GetChildCollObj(connection_id, objectID)	Array	Object records of child collections
hw_GetChildDocColl(connection_id, objectID)	Array	Object IDs of child documents of collection
hw_GetChildDocCollObj(connection_id, objectID)	Array	Object records of child documents of collection
hw_GetObject (connection_id, objectID, query)	Object	Object record
hw_GetObjectByQuery(connection_id, query, max_hits)	Array	Searches object

Table continued on following page

Function	Returns	Description
hw_GetObjectByQueryColl (connection_id, objectID, query, max_hits)	Array	Searches object in collection
hw_GetObjectByQueryCollObj (connection_id, objectID, query, max_hits)	Array	Searches object in collection
hw_GetObjectByQueryObj(connection_ id, query, max_hits)	Array	Searches object
hw_GetParents(connection_id, objectID)	Array	Object IDs of parents
hw_GetParentsObj(connection_id, objectID)	Array	Object records of parents
hw_getrellink(link_id, rootid, sourceid, destid)		Gets link from source to destination relative to rootid
hw_GetRemote(connection_id, objectID)	Object	Gets a remote document
hw_GetRemoteChildren(connection_ id, object_record)	Object	Gets children of remote document
hw_GetSrcByDestObj(connection_id, objectID)	Array	Returns anchors pointing at object
hw_GetText(connection_id, objectID, rootID/prefix)	String	Retrieves text document
hw_getusername(connection_id)	String	Name of currently logged-in user
hw_Identify(username, password)		Identifies as user
hw_InCollections(connection_id, object_id_array, collection_id_array, return_collections)	Array	Checks if object IDs in collections
hw_Info(connection_id)	String	Info about connection
hw_InsColl(connection_id, objectID, object_array)		Inserts collection
hw_InsDoc(connection_id, parented, object_record, text)		Inserts document
hw_insertanchors(hwdoc, anchorecs, dest, [urlprefixes])		Inserts only anchors into text

Function	Returns	Description
hw_InsertDocument(connection_id, parent_id, hw_document)	Integer	Uploads any document
hw_InsertObject(connection_id, object_rec, parameter)		Inserts an object record
hw_mapid(connection_id, server_id, objectID)		Maps global ID on virtual local ID
hw_Modifyobject(connection_id, object_to_change, remove, add, mode)	Boolean	Modifies object record
hw_Mv(connection_id, object_id, source_id, destination_id)	Integer	Moves objects
hw_New_Document(object_record, documents_data, document_size)	Object	Creates new document
hw_Objrec2Array(object_record, [array format])	Array	Converts attributes from object record to object array
hw_Output_Document(hw_document)	String	Prints hw_document
hw_pConnect(host, port, username, password)	Integer	Makes a persistent database connection
hw_PipeDocument(connection_id, objectID)	Object	Retrieves any document
hw_Root()	Integer	Root object ID
hw_setlinkroot(link_id, root_id)		Sets the ID to which links are calculated
hw_stat(link_id)	String	Returns status string
hw_Unlock(connection_id, objectID)		Unlocks object
hw_Who(connection_id)	Array	Lists of currently logged-in users

Informix Functions

Defined in ~/ext/informix/ifx.ec:

Function	Returns	Description
ifx_affected_rows (result_id)	Integer	Returns the number of rows affected by the query
ifx_blobinfile_mode (mode)	Nothing	Sets the default BLOB mode for SELECT queries
ifx_byteasvarchar(mode)	Nothing	Sets the default byte mode for SELECT queries
ifx_close ([link_identifier])	Integer	Closes the connection
ifx_connect([database] [, userid] [, password])	Integer	Opens a connection to an Informix database and returns a connection identifier
ifx_copy_blob(bid)	Integer	Copies the specified BLOB object
ifx_create_blob(type, mode, param)	Integer	Creates a BLOB object
ifx_create_char(param)	Integer	Creates a char object
ifx_do(result_id)	Integer	Executes a previously prepared SQL statement
ifx_error()	String	Returns the last occurring error
ifx_errormsg ([error_code])	String	Returns the error message for the last occurring error or for the specified error_code
ifx_fetch_row(result_id [, position])	Array	Fetches a row as an enumerated array
ifx_fieldproperties (result_id)	Array	Returns an associative array of the field names and the SQL field properties
ifx_fieldtypes(result_id)	Array	Returns an associative array of the field names and the SQL field types
ifx_free_blob(bid)	Integer	Deletes the BLOB object specified by bid
ifx_free_char(bid)	Integer	Deletes the char object specified by bid
ifx_free_result(result_ id)	Integer	Frees the resources used by the specified query
ifx_free_slob(bid)	Integer	Deletes the specified SLOB object
ifx_get_blob(bid)	Integer	Returns the content of the specified BLOB object

Function	Returns	Description
`ifx_get_char(bid)`	Integer	Returns the content of the specified char object
`ifx_getsqlca(result_id)`	Array	Returns the contents of `sqlca.sqlerrd[0..5]` after a query
`ifx_htmltbl_result (result_id [, html_table_options])`	Integer	Formats the rows of a query specified by `result_id` as an HTML table
`ifx_nullformat(mode)`	Nothing	Sets the default return value for `Null` values on a fetched row
`ifx_num_fields(result_id)`	Integer	Returns the number of fields in the query
`ifx_num_rows(result_id)`	Integer	Returns the number of rows already fetched for the query
`ifx_pconnect([database] [, userid] [, password])`	Integer	Opens a persistent connection to an Informix database and returns a link identifier
`ifx_prepare(query [, link_identifier] [, cursor_type] [, blobidarray])`	Integer	Prepares a SQL statement for execution, returns a `result_id` for use by `ifx_do()`
`ifx_query(query, [, link_identifier] [, cursor_type], [, blobidarray])`	Integer	Executes the specified `query` against the Informix database
`ifx_textasvarchar(mode)`	Nothing	Sets the default text mode for `SELECT` queries
`ifx_update_blob(bid, content)`	Integer	Updates the content of the specified BLOB object
`ifx_update_char(bid, content)`	Integer	Updates the specified char object with `content`
`ifxus_close_slob(bid)`	Integer	Deletes the specified SLOB object
`ifxus_create_slob(mode)`	Integer	Creates and opens a SLOB object
`ifxus_free_slob(bid)`	Integer	Deletes the SLOB object
`ifxus_open_slob(bid, mode)`	Integer	Opens the specified SLOB object
`ifxus_read_slob(bid, bytes)`	Integer	Reads the specified number of bytes of the specified SLOB object

Table continued on following page

Function	Returns	Description
ifxus_seek_slob(bid, mode, offset)	Integer	Sets the current position of the specified SLOB object to offset
ifxus_tell_slob(bid)	Integer	Returns the current position of the SLOB object specified
ifxus_write_slob(bid, content)	Integer	Writes the specified content into the specified SLOB object

Ingres II Functions

Defined in ~/ext/ingres_ii/ii.c:

Function	Returns	Description
ingres_autocommit([link])	Boolean	Turns autocommit on or off
ingres_close([link])	Boolean	Closes a connection to an Ingres II database
ingres_commit([link])	Boolean	Commits a transaction
ingres_connect([database [,username [,password]]])	Resource	Opens a connection to an Ingres II database
ingres_fetch_array ([array_type [,link]])	Array	Fetches a row into an array of type array_type
ingres_fetch_object ([result_type [,link]])	Array	Fetches a row into an object of type result_type
ingres_fetch_row([link])	Array	Fetches a row into an enumerated array
ingres_field_length (index [,link])	String	Returns the length of a field number index in a query result
ingres_field_name(index [,link])	String	Returns the name of a field name index in a query result
ingres_field_nullable (index [,link])	String	Returns true if a field is nullable and false if it is not
ingres_field_precision (index [,link])	String	Returns the precision of a field in a query result
ingres_field_scale (index [,link])	String	Returns the scale of a field in a query result
ingres_field_type(index [,link])	String	Returns the type of a field in a query result

Function	Returns	Description
ingres_num_fields([link])	Int	Returns the number of fields returned by the last query
ingres_num_rows([link])	Int	Returns the number of rows affected or returned by the last query
ingres_pconnect ([database [,username [,password]]])	Resource	Opens a persistent connection to an Ingres II database
ingres_query(query [,link])	Boolean	Sends an SQL query to Ingres II
ingres_rollback([link])	Boolean	Rolls back a transaction

InterBase Functions

Defined in ~/ext/interbase/interbase.c:

Function	Returns	Description
ibase_blob_add(bid, data)	Integer	Adds the data into the specified BLOB
ibase_blob_cancel(bid)	Integer	Cancels the creating of the BLOB
ibase_blob_close(bid)	Integer	Closes the BLOB
ibase_blob_create([link_id])	Integer	Creates a blob for adding data. Returns the BLOB ID.
ibase_blob_echo(bid)	Integer	Echoes the contents of the blob to the browser
ibase_blob_get(bid, len)	Integer	Returns len bytes of data from the specified BLOB
ibase_blob_import([link_id,] file_id)	String	Creates a BLOB, imports the contents of the file into it and then closes it
ibase_blob_info(bid)	Object	Returns information about the specified BLOB
ibase_blob_open(bid)	Integer	Opens a BLOB for retrieving data
ibase_close([connection_id])	Integer	Closes a connection to the specified InterBase database, or the last opened link
ibase_commit([link_identifier,] trans_number)	Integer	Commits the specified transaction

Table continued on following page

Function	Returns	Description
`ibase_connect(database [, username [, password [, charset [, buffers [, dialect [ ,role]]]]]])`	Integer	Opens a connection to an InterBase database
`ibase_errmsg()`	String	Returns the last error message generated by Interbase
`ibase_execute(query [,bind_args])`	Integer	Executes a query prepared by `ibase_prepare()`
`ibase_fetch_object(result_ id[, blob_flag])`	Object	Returns a row as an object from `result_id`
`ibase_fetch_row(result_id [, blob_flag])`	Array	Returns the next row specified by `result_id` (obtained from `ibase_query`)
`ibase_field_info(result, field_num)`	Array	Returns information relating to the given field
`ibase_free_query(query)`	Integer	Frees a prepared query
`ibase_free_result(result_ id)`	Integer	Frees the resultset specified by `result_id`
`ibase_num_fields(result_ id)`	Integer	Returns the number of fields in the specified resultset
`ibase_pconnect(database [, username [, password [, charset [, role]]]])`	Integer	Creates a persistent connection to an InterBase database
`ibase_prepare([link_ identifier, query])`	Integer	Prepares a query for later binding of parameter placeholders and execution
`ibase_query([link_ident ifier, query] [, bind_args])`	Integer	Executes a query on an InterBase database and returns a `result_identifier`
`ibase_rollback([link_id entifier,] trans_number)`	Integer	Rolls back the specified transaction
`ibase_timefmt(format)`	Integer	Sets the format of timestamp, date-or time-type columns returned from queries
`ibase_trans([trans_args [, link_identifier]])`	Integer	Starts a new transaction on the database

LDAP Functions

Defined in ~/ext/ldap/ldap.c:

Function	Returns	Description
ldap_8859_to_t61(string)		Translates 8859 characters to t61 characters
ldap_add(link_id, dn, entry)	Boolean	Adds entries to LDAP directory
ldap_bind(link_id, [bind_rdn, [bind_password]])	Boolean	Binds to LDAP directory
ldap_close(link_id)	Boolean	Closes link to LDAP server
ldap_compare(link_id, dn, attribute, value)	Boolean	Compares value of the attribute found in entry specified with DN
ldap_connect(hostname, [port])	Integer	Connects to an LDAP server
ldap_count_entries(link_id, result_id)	Integer	Counts the number of entries in a search
ldap_delete(link_id, dn)	Boolean	Deletes an entry from a directory
ldap_dn2ufn(dn)	String	Converts DN to User Friendly Naming format
ldap_err2str(error_number)	String	Converts LDAP error number into string error message
ldap_errno(link_id)	Integer	Returns the LDAP error number of the last LDAP command
ldap_error(link_id)	String	Returns the LDAP error message of the last LDAP command
ldap_explode_dn(dn, with_attrib)	Array	Splits DN into its component parts
ldap_first_attribute(link)id, result_entry_id, ber_id)	String	Returns first attribute
ldap_first_entry(link_id, result_id)	Integer	Returns first result ID
ldap_first_reference(link_id, result_id)		Returns first reference
ldap_free_result(result_id)	Boolean	Frees result memory
ldap_get_attributes(link_id, result_entry_identifier)	Array	Gets attributes from a search result entry

Table continued on following page

Function	Returns	Description
`ldap_get_dn(link_id, result_entry_id)`	String	Gets the DN of a result entry
`ldap_get_entries(link_id, result_id)`	Array	Gets all result entries
`ldap_get_option(link_id, option, retval)`	Boolean	Gets the current value for a given option
`ldap_get_values_len(link_id, result_entry_id, attribute)`	Array	Gets all binary values from a result entry
`ldap_get_values(link_id, result_entry_id, attribute)`	Array	Gets all values from a result entry
`ldap_list(link_id, base_dn, filter, [attributes, [attrsonly, [sizelimit, [timelimit, [deref]]]]])`	Integer	Single-level search
`ldap_mod_add(link_id, dn, entry)`	Boolean	Adds attribute values to current attributes
`ldap_mod_del(link_id, dn, entry)`	Boolean	Deletes attribute values from current attributes
`ldap_mod_replace(link_id, dn, entry)`	Boolean	Replaces attribute values with new ones
`ldap_modify(link_id, dn, entry)`	Boolean	Modifies an LDAP entry
`ldap_next_attribute(link_id, result_entry_id, ber_id)`	String	Gets the next attribute in a result
`ldap_next_entry(link_id, result_entry_id)`	Integer	Gets next result entry
`ldap_next_reference(link_id, entry)`		Gets next reference
`ldap_parse_reference(link_id, entry_id, referrals)`		Extracts information from a reference entry
`ldap_parse_result(link_id, result_id, errcode, matcheddn, errmsg, referrals)`		Extracts information froma result
`ldap_read(link_id, base_dn, filter, [attributes, [attrsonly, [sizelimit, [timelimit, [deref]]]]])`	Integer	Reads an entry

Function	Returns	Description
ldap_rename(link_id, dn, newrdn, newparent, deleteoldrdn)	Boolean	Modifies the name of an entry
ldap_search(link_id, base_dn, filter, [attributes, [attrsonly, [sizelimit, [timelimit, [deref]]]]])	Integer	Searches LDAP tree
ldap_set_option(link_id, option, newval)	Boolean	Sets the value of the given option
ldap_set_rebind_proc(link_id, callback)		Sets a callback function to do rebind
ldap_sort(link_id, result_id, sortfilter)		Sorts LDAP result entries
ldap_start_tls(link_id)		Starts TLS
ldap_t61_to_8859(value)		Translates t61 characters to 8859 characters
ldap_unbind(link_id)	Boolean	Unbinds from LDAP directory

Lotus Notes Functions

Defined in ~/ext/notes/php_notes.c:

Function	Returns	Description
notes_body(server, mailbox, msg_number)		Opens the message msg_number in the specified mailbox on the specified server
notes_copy_db(from_database_name, to_database_name)		Creates a note using form form_name
notes_create_db(database_name)		Creates a Lotus Notes database
notes_create_note(database_name, form_name)		Creates a note using form form_name
notes_drop_db(database_name)		Drops a Lotus Notes database
notes_find_note(database_name, name, [type])		Returns a note ID found in database_name. Specifies the name of the note leaving type blank

Table continued on following page

Function	Returns	Description
notes_header_info(server, mailbox, msg_number)		Opens the message msg_number in the specified mailbox on the specified server (leave server)
notes_list_msgs(database_name)		Returns the notes from a selected database_name
notes_mark_read(database_name, user_name, note_id)		Marks a note_id as read for the User user_name
notes_mark_unread(database_name, user_name, note_id)		Marks a note_id as unread for the User user_name
notes_nav_create(database_name, name)		Creates a navigator name, in database_name
notes_search(database_name, keywords)		Finds notes that match keywords in database_name
notes_unread(database_name, user_name)		Returns the unread note IDs for the current User user_name
notes_version(database_name)		Gets the version of Lotus Notes

Microsoft SQL Server Functions

Defined in ~/ext/mssql/php_mssql.c:

Function	Returns	Description
Mssql_close([link_id])	Boolean	Closes the specified SQL Server connection
Mssql_connect([server_name] [, username] [, password])	Integer	Opens an SQL Server connection and returns a link_id
Mssql_data_seek(result_id, row_number)	Boolean	Moves to the specified row_number in the resultset
Mssql_fetch_array (result_id)	Array	Returns the next row in the resultset as an array
Mssql_fetch_batch (result_index)	Integer	Returns the next batch of records for the result
Mssql_fetch_field(result_id [, field_offset])	Object	Returns an object representing the specified field
Mssql_fetch_object (result_id)	Object	Returns the next row in the resultset as an object

Function	Returns	Description
Mssql_fetch_row (result_id)	Array	Returns the next row in the resultset as an enumerated array
Mssql_field_length(result_ id [, offset])	Integer	Returns the length of a field
Mssql_field_name(result [, offset])	Integer	Returns the name of a field
Mssql_field_seek(result_ id, field_offset)	Integer	Moves to the field specified in field_offset
mssql_field_type(result_ id [, offset])	String	Returns the field type
mssql_free_result(result_ id)	Integer	Frees the memory used by the resultset
mssql_get_last_message()	String	Returns the last message from the server
mssql_min_error_severity (severity)	Nothing	Sets the lower error severity
mssql_min_message_ severity(severity)	Severity	Sets the lower message severity
mssql_next_result (result_id)	String	Moves the internal result pointer to the next result
mssql_num_fields(result_ id)	Integer	Returns the number of fields in the specified resultset
mssql_num_rows (result_id)	Integer	Returns the number of rows in the specified resultset
mssql_pconnect([servern ame][, username] [, password])	Integer	Opens a persistent SQL connection and returns a link_id
mssql_query(query, [link_id[, batch_size]])	Integer	Executes the specified query and returns a result_id
mssql_result(result_id, row, field)	Integer	Fetches the contents of the cell specified by the row and field arguments
mssql_rows_affected (link_id)	Integer	Returns the number of rows affected by the query
mssql_select_db(database [, link_id])	Integer	Sets the specified SQL Server database as the current database

mSQL Functions

Defined in ~/ext/msql/php_msql.c:

Function	Returns	Description
msql(database, query, link_id)	Integer	Alias for msql_db_query()
msql_affected_rows (query_id)	Integer	Returns the number of rows affected by the specified query
msql_close(link_id)	Boolean	Closes the mSQL connection
msql_connect([hostname[: port]] [, username] [, password])	Integer	Opens a connection to the specified mSQL server and returns a link_id
msql_create_db(name, [link_id])	Integer	Creates an mSQL database with the specified name
msql_createdb(name, [link_id])	Integer	Alias for msql_create_db()
msql_data_seek(query_id, row_number)	Boolean	Moves to the specified row of a resultset
msql_db_query(dbname, query[, link_id])	Integer	Sends a SQL query on the given database to mSQL
msql_dbname(query_id, index)	String	Returns the name of the mSQL database with the specified index position
msql_drop_db(name, [link_id])	Boolean	Deletes the named mSQL database
msql_dropdb(name, link_id)	Boolean	Alias for msql_drop_db()
msql_error([link_id])	String	Returns any error message resulting from the last mSQL operation
msql_fetch_array(query_id [, result_type])	Array	Fetches the next row in the resultset as an array
msql_fetch_field(query_id [, field_offset])	Object	Returns an object representing the field with the specified position
msql_fetch_object(query_id [, result_type])	Object	Fetches the next row in the resultset as an object
msql_fetch_row(query_id)	Array	Fetches the next row in the resultset as an enumerated array

Function	Returns	Description
msql_field_flags(query_id, field)	String	Returns the flags for the specified field
msql_field_len(query_id, field)	Integer	Returns the length of the specified field
msql_field_name(query_id, field)	String	Returns the name of the specified field
msql_field_seek(query_id, field_offset)	Integer	Moves to the field specified by field_offset
msql_field_table(query_id, field)	Integer	Returns the name of the table that field was fetched from
msql_field_type(query_id, field)	String	Returns the field type for the specified field
msql_free_result(query_id)	Integer	Frees the memory used by the resultset
msql_freeresult(query_id)	Integer	Alias for msql_free_result()
msql_list_dbs([link_id])	Integer	Lists the database on the specified mSQL server; returns a result identifier
msql_listdbs([link_id])	Integer	Alias for msql_list_dbs()
msql_list_fields(database, table[, link_id])	Integer	Lists the fields in the specified table; returns a result identifier
msql_listfields(database, table[, link_id])	Integer	Alias for msql_list_fields()
msql_list_tables(database [, link_id])	Integer	Lists tables in the specified mSQL database; returns a result identifier
msql_listtables(database [, link_id])	Integer	Alias for msql_list_tables()
msql_num_fields(query_id)	Integer	Returns the number of fields in the resultset
msql_numfields(query_id)	Integer	Alias for msql_num_fields()
msql_num_rows(query_id)	Integer	Returns the number of rows in the resultset
msql_numrows(query_id)	Integer	Alias for msql_num_rows()
msql_pconnect([hostname[:port]] [, username] [, password])	Integer	Opens a persistent connection to the specified mSQL server and returns a link_id
msql_query(query, [link_id])	Integer	Executes the specified mSQL query and returns a query_id

Table continued on following page

Function	Returns	Description
`msql_result(query_id, row[, field])`	Integer	Fetches the contents of the cell specified by the `row` and `field` arguments
`msql_select_db(database, link_id)`	Boolean	Sets the current database to the one specified
`msql_selectdb(database, link_id)`	Boolean	Alias for `msql_select_db()`
`msql_tablename(query_id, field)`	String	Returns the table name for the specified field

MySQL Functions

Defined in `~/ext/mysql/php_mysql.c`:

Function	Returns	Description
`mysql`		Alias for `mysql_db_query()`
`mysql_affected_rows ([link_id])`	Integer	Returns the number of rows affected by the query
`mysql_change_user(user, password [, database] [, link_id])`	Integer	Changes the logged-in user of the active connection
`mysql_close([link_id])`	Boolean	Closes the MySQL connection
`mysql_connect([hostname [:port] [:path]] [, username] [, password])`	Integer	Opens a connection to the specified MySQL server at the given address
`mysql_create_db(database [, link_id])`	Integer	Creates a MySQL database with the name `database`
`mysql_createdb`		Alias for `mysql_create_db()`
`mysql_data_seek(result_id, row_number)`	Boolean	Moves to the specified row of a resultset
`mysql_db_name(result_id, row [, field])`	Integer	Obtains result data
`mysql_dbname`		Alias for `mysql_db_name()`
`mysql_db_query(database, query [, link_id])`	Integer	Executes the specified `query` on the specified `database` and returns a `result_id`

Function	Returns	Description
`mysql_drop_db(database_ name [, link_id])`	Integer	Deletes the specified MySQL database
`mysql_dropdb`		Alias for `mysql_drop_db()`
`mysql_errno([link_id])`	Integer	Returns the error number for the previous MySQL operation
`mysql_error([link_id])`	String	Returns the error message for the previous MySQL operation
`mysql_escape_string ([string])`	Character	Sets the `escape_string` for a MySQL query to `string`
`mysql_fetch_array(result_ id, [result_type])`	Array	Fetches the next row in the resultset as an array
`mysql_fetch_assoc (result_id)`	Array	Returns a recordset as an associative array
`mysql_fetch_field(result_ id [, field_offset])`	Object	Returns an object representing the specified field
`mysql_fetch_lengths (result_id)`	Array	Returns an array consisting of the length of each field in the resultset
`mysql_fetch_object(result_ id [,result_type])`	Object	Fetches the next row in the resultset as an object
`mysql_fetch_row(result_id)`	Array	Fetches the next row in the resultset as an enumerated array
`mysql_field_flags(result_ id, field)`	String	Returns the field flags of the specified field
`mysql_fieldflags`		Alias for `mysql_field_flags()`
`mysql_field_len(result_ id, field)`	Integer	Returns the length of the specified field
`mysql_fieldlen`		Alias for `mysql_field_len()`
`mysql_field_name(result_ id, field)`	String	Returns the name of the specified field
`mysql_fieldname`		Alias for `mysql_field_name()`
`mysql_field_seek(result_ id, field_offset)`	Integer	Moves to the specified `field_offset`
`mysql_field_table(result _id, field)`	String	Returns the name of the table that the specified `field` is in

Table continued on following page

Function	Returns	Description
`mysql_fieldtable`		Alias for `mysql_field_table()`
`mysql_field_type(result_id, field)`	String	Returns the type of the specified `field`
`mysql_fieldtype`		Alias for `mysql_field_type()`
`mysql_free_result(result_id)`	Integer	Frees the memory used by the resultset
`mysql_freeresult`		Alis for `mysql_free_result()`
`mysql_get_client_info()`	String	Returns the version string of the MySQL client software installed on the client machine
`mysql_get_host_info([link_id])`	String	Returns a status report on the host and link connection
`mysql_get_proto_info([link_id])`	Integer	Returns the protocol version being used by the connection
`mysql_set_server_info([link_id])`	String	Returns the version string of the MySQL server software being referenced
`mysql_insert_id([link_id])`	Integer	Returns the ID generated by an `AUTO_INCREMENT` field in a previous `INSERT` query
`mysql_list_dbs([link_id])`	Integer	Lists the database on the specified MySQL server and returns a `result_id`
`mysql_list_fields(database, table, [link_id])`	Integer	Lists the fields in the specified table and returns a `result_id`
`mysql_listfields`		Alias for `mysql_list_fields()`
`mysql_list_tables(database)`	Integer	Lists the database in the specified MySQL database; returns a `result_id`
`mysql_listtables`		Alias for `mysql_list_tables()`
`mysql_num_fields(result_id)`	Integer	Returns the number of fields in the resultset
`mysql_numfields`		Alias for `mysql_num_fields()`
`mysql_num_rows(result_id)`	Integer	Returns the number of rows in the resultset
`mysql_numrows`		Alias for `mysql_num_rows()`
`mysql_pconnect([hostname [:port] [:path]] [, username] [, password])`	Integer	Opens a persistent connection to the specified MySQL server

Function	Returns	Description
mysql_query(query, [link_id])	Integer	Executes the specified MySQL query
mysql_result(result_id, row, [field])	Mixed	Fetches the contents of the cell specified by the row and field arguments
mysql_select_db(database, [link_id])	Boolean	Sets the current database to the one specified
mysql_selectdb		Alias for mysql_select_db()
mysql_tablename(result_id, index)	String	Returns the table name from which the specified field was taken

(Unified) ODBC Functions

Defined in ~/ext/odbc/php_odbc.php:

Function	Returns	Description
odbc_autocommit (connection_id, OnOff])	Boolean	Sets or returns the auto-commit behavior for the specified connection
odbc_binmode(result_id, mode)	Integer	Sets the mode for converting binary data
odbc_close(connection_id)	Nothing	Closes the specified ODBC connection
odbc_close_all()	Nothing	Closes all ODBC connections
Odbc_columnprivileges(c onnection_id [, qualifier [, owner [, table_name [, column_name]]]])	Integer	Lists columns and associated privileges for the specified table and returns a result_id
odbc_columns(connection _id [, qualifier] [, owner] [, table_name] [, column_name])	Integer	Lists all columns in the specified range and returns a result_id
odbc_commit(connection_ id)	Integer	Commits all pending transactions on the specified connection
odbc_connect(DSN, userID, password [, cursor_type])	Integer	Connects to the ODBC data source with the specified Data Source Name and returns a connection_id

Table continued on following page

Function	Returns	Description
`odbc_cursor(result_id)`	String	Returns the cursorname for the specified resultset
`odbc_do(connection_id, query)`	Integer	Prepares and executes the specified SQL query
`odbc_error([connection_id])`	String	Returns the error number for the last error that occurred
`odbc_errormsg ([connection_id])`	String	Returns the error message for the last error that occurred
`odbc_exec(connection_id, query[, flags])`	Integer	Prepares and executes the specified SQL query and returns a `result_id`
`odbc_execute(result_id, [parameters])`	Integer	Executes a prepared SQL statement
`odbc_fetch_array(result_id[, row_number])`	Array	Fetches a result row as an associative array
`odbc_fetch_into(result_id [, row_number], result)`	Integer	Fetches the specified row from the resultset into the `result` array
`odbc_fetch_object(result_id[, row_number])`	Object	Fetches a result row as an object
`odbc_fetch_row(result_id [, row_number])`	Boolean	Fetches the specified row from the resultset
`odbc_field_len(result_id, field_number)`	Integer	Returns the length of the specified field
`odbc_field_name(result_id, field_number)`	String	Returns the name of the specified field
`odbc_field_num(result_id, field_name)`	Integer	Returns the column number for the specified `field_name`
`odbc_field_precision (result_id, field_number)`	Integer	Returns the length of the specified field
`odbc_field_scale(result_iod, field_number)`	String	Returns the scale of the specified field
`odbc_field_type(result_id, field_number)`	String	Returns the data type of the specified field

Function	Returns	Description
odbc_foreignkeys(connec tion_id, pk_qualifier, pk_owner, pk_table, fk_qualifier, fk_owner, fk_table)	Integer	Retrieves information about foreign keys in the specified table and returns a result_id
odbc_free_result(result_ id)	Boolean	Releases the resources used by the specified resultset
odbc_gettypeinfo (connection_id, [data_type])	Integer	Retrieves information about data types supported by the data source and returns a result_id
odbc_longreadlen(result_ id, length)	Integer	Determines the number of bytes returned to PHP from fields of type LONG
odbc_next_result(result_ id)	Boolean	Returns whether or not there is another resultset
odbc_num_fields(result_ id)	Integer	Returns the number of fields in the resultset
odbc_num_rows(result_id)	Integer	Returns the number of rows in the resultset
odbc_pconnect(DSN, userID, password, [cursor_type])	Integer	Opens a persistent connection to the ODBC data source with the specified Data Source Name
odbc_prepare(connection_ id, query)	Integer	Prepares the specified SQL statement for execution
odbc_primarykeys(connec tion_id, qualifier, owner, table)	Integer	Obtains the column names that comprise the primary key for a table and returns a result_id
odbc_procedurecolumns (connection_id [, qualifier [, owner [, proc [, column]]]])	Integer	Retrieves information about parameters for procedures and returns a result_id
odbc_procedures (connection_id [, qualifier [, owner [, name]]])	Integer	Obtains the list of procedures in the requested range and returns a result_id
odbc_result(result_id, field)	String	Returns the contents of the specified field
odbc_result_all(result_ id [, format])	Integer	Prints the entire resultset as an HTML table

Table continued on following page

Function	Returns	Description
odbc_rollback (connection_id)	Integer	Aborts all pending transactions on the specified connection
odbc_setoption(ID, function, option, parameter)	Integer	Sets the specified ODBC option
odbc_specialcolumns (connection_id, type, qualifier, owner, table, scope, nullable)	Integer	Returns either the optimal set of columns that uniquely identifies a table row, or columns that are automatically updated
odbc_statistics (connection_id, qualifier, owner, table_name, unique, accuracy)	Integer	Retrieves statistics about the specified table and its indexes and returns a result_id
odbc_tableprivileges (connection_id [,qualifier] [,owner] [,name])	Integer	Lists tables and privileges associated with each table and returns a result_id
odbc_tables (connection_id [,qualifier] [,owner] [,name] [,types])	Integer	Lists table names in the specified data source

Oracle Functions

Defined in ~/ext/oracle/oracle.c:

Function	Returns	Description
Ora_bind(cursor, variable_name, SQLparameter, length [,type])	Boolean	Binds the specified PHP variable to the specified Oracle parameter
Ora_close(cursor)	Boolean	Closes the specified Oracle cursor
Ora_columnname(cursor, column)	String	Returns the name of the specified column
Ora_columnsize(cursor, column)	Integer	Returns the size of the specified column
Ora_columntype(cursor, column)	String	Returns the data type of the specified column

Function	Returns	Description
Ora_commit(connection)	Boolean	Commits a transaction
Ora_commitoff(connection)	Boolean	Disables automatic committing of transactions
Ora_commiton(connection)	Boolean	Enables automatic committing of transactions
Ora_do(connection, query)	Integer	Parses and executes a statement, then fetches the first result row
Ora_error(cursor|connection)	String	Returns the message for the last occurring error
Ora_errorcode(cursor|connection)	Integer	Returns the code for the last occurring error
Ora_exec(cursor)	Boolean	Executes a parsed statement on the specified cursor
Ora_fetch(cursor)	Boolean	Fetches a row from the specified cursor
Ora_fetch_into(cursor, result [,flags])	Integer	Fetches a row into the specified result array
Ora_getcolumn(cursor, column)	Mixed	Returns the contents from the specified column for the current row
Ora_logoff(connection)	Boolean	Closes the specified Oracle connection
Ora_logon(user, password)	Integer	Opens a connection to Oracle and returns a connection index
Ora_numcols(cursor_ind)	Integer	Returns the number of columns in a resultset
Ora_numrows(cursor_ind)	Integer	Returns the number of rows in a resultset
Ora_open(connection)	Integer	Opens a cursor on the specified connection and returns a cursor_index
Ora_parse(cursor, SQL_statement [, defer])	Boolean	Validates the specified SQL statement
Ora_plogon(user, password)	Boolean	Opens a persistent connection to an Oracle database
Ora_rollback(connection)	Boolean	Aborts and rolls back a transaction

Oracle 8 Functions

Defined in ~/ext/oci8/oci8.c

Function	Returns	Description
ocibindbyname(statement, ph_name, variable, length [, type])	Integer	Binds the specified PHP variable to the Oracle Placeholder specified by ph_name
ocicancel(statement)	Integer	Cancels current fetch and gets the next row from the resultset instead
Ocicolumnisnull (statement, column)	Boolean	Indicates whether the specified column contains a Null value
ocicolumnname(statement, column)	String	Returns the name of the specified column_number
Ocicolumnprecision (statement, column)	Integer	Returns the precision of the specified column
ocicolumnscale(statement, column)	Integers	Returns the scale of the specified column
ocicolumnsize(statement, column)	Integer	Returns the size of the specified column
ocicolumntype(statement, column)	Mixed	Returns the data type of the specified column
Ocicolumntyperaw (statement, column)	Mixed	Returns the raw Oracle data type of the specified column
ocicommit(connection)	Integer	Commits all pending transactions on the specified connection
ocidefinebyname(statement, column_name, variable [, type])	Integer	Fetches the specified SQL column into the supplied PHP variable
ocierror ([statement|connection| global])	Integer	Returns the code for the last occurring error
ociexecute(statement, [mode])	Integer	Executes the specified SQL statement
Ocifetch(statement)	Integer	Fetches the next row from the resultset
ocifetchinto(statement, result, [mode])	Integer	Returns the next row from the resultset into the result array
ocifetchstatement(statement, result)	Integer	Returns all rows from the resultset into the result array

Function	Returns	Description
ocifreecursor(statement)	Boolean	Frees all resources used by the cursor for the specified statement
ocifreedesc(lob_id)	String	Frees up resources by deleting the description for the specified large object
Ocifreestatement (statement)	Integer	Frees all resources used by the specified statement
ociinternaldebug(onoff)	Nothing	Turns internal debugging on or off
ociloadlob(lob_id)	String	
ocilogoff(connection)	Integer	Closes the specified Oracle connection
ocilogon(username, password, [database])	Integer	Opens a connection to an Oracle database and returns a connection identifier
ocinewcursor(connection)	Integer	Returns a new cursor for the specified connection
ocinewdescriptor(connection [,type])	String	Initializes a new empty LOB (the default) or FILE descriptor
ocinlogon(username, password, [database])	Integer	Connects to an Oracle database using a new connection
ocinumcols(statement)	Integer	Return the number of columns in the resultset
ociparse(connection, query)	Integer	Validates the specified query
ociplogon(username, password, [database])	Integer	Opens a persistent connection to an Oracle database
ociresult(statement, column)	Mixed	Returns the data for the specified column for a fetched row
ocirollback(connection)	Integer	Aborts all pending transactions on the specified connection
ocirowcount(statement)	Integer	Returns the number of affected rows in the resultset
ocisavelob(lob_id)	String	Saves the specified large object
ocisavelobfile(lob_id)	String	Saves a large object file
Ociserverversion (connection)	String	Returns information about the server version
Ocisetprefetch (connection, query)	Integer	Sets a prefetch query

Table continued on following page

Function	Returns	Description
Ocistatementtype (statement)	String	Returns the type of the specified OCI statement
ociwritelobtofile(lob_id [, filename] [, start] [, length])	Void	Writes a large object into the named file

Ovrimos SQL Functions

Defined in ~/ext/ovrimos/ovrimos.c:

Function	Returns	Description
ovrimos_autocommit (connection_id, OnOff)	Integer	Toggles the transaction autocommit mode on or off
ovrimos_close(connection)	Void	Closes the specified connection, rolling back uncommitted transactions
Ovrimos_close_all()	Void	Closes all connections, rolling back uncommitted transactions
ovrimos_commit (connection_id)	Integer	Commits an Ovrimos transaction
ovrimos_connect(host, db, user, password)	Integer	Connects to the Ovrimos database with the parameters specified, returning a connection ID
ovrimos_cursor(result_id)	String	Gets the name of the cursor
ovrimos_exec(connection_id, query)	Integer	Prepares and executes a SQL statement, returning a result ID
ovrimos_execute(result_id [,parameters_array])	Integer	Executes a prepared statement
ovrimos_fetch_into (result_id, result_array [,how, [rownumber]])	Integer	Fetches one row from the resultset into an array
ovrimos_fetch_row(result_id [,how, [row_number]])	Integer	Fetches a row from the resultset
ovrimos_field_len(result_id, field_number)	Integer	Gets the length of a column specified by field_number in the resultset specified by result_id

Function	Returns	Description
ovrimos_field_name(result_id, field_number)	String	Gets the name of the column specified by field_number
ovrimos_field_num(result_id, field_name)	Integer	Returns the number of the column specified by field_name
ovrimos_field_type(result_id, field_number)	String	Gets the data type of the column specified by field_number
ovrimos_free_result (result_id)	Integer	Frees up the resources associated with the result specified by result_id
ovrimos_longreadlen (result_id, length)	Integer	Specifies how many bytes are to be returned from columns with a long data type
ovrimos_num_fields(result_id)	Integer	Gets the number of columns in the specified resultset
ovrimos_num_rows(result_id)	Integer	Gets the number of rows in the specified resultset
ovrimos_prepare (connection_id, query)	Integer	Prepares a statement for execution, returning a result ID
ovrimos_result(result_id, field)	String	Gets the data from the specified field in the resultset
ovrimos_result_all(result_id [,format])	Integer	Prints all the results in the specified resultset as an HTML table
ovrimos_rollback (connection_id)	Integer	Rolls back a transaction
ovrimos_setoption(conn_id|result_id, which, option, value)	Integer	Sets connection or statement options

PEAR DB Functions

Defined in ~/pear/DB/:

Function	Returns	Description
DB::connect(dsn, [options])	Object	Creates a new DB connection object and connects to the specified database
DB::disconnect()	Boolean	Logs out and disconnects from the database

Table continued on following page

Function	Returns	Description
`DB::isWarning()`	Boolean	Tells whether a result code from a DB method is a warning
`DB::isError()`	Boolean	Tells whether a result code from a DB method is an error
`DB::quote(string)`	String	Quotes a string so it can be safely used in a query
`DB::provides(feature)`	String	Tells whether a DB implementation or its back-end extension supports a given feature
`DB::setFetchMode(fetch mode, [object_class])`		Sets the fetch mode that should be used by default on queries on the connection
`DB::prepare(query)`	Object	Prepares a query for multiple execution with `execute()`
`DB::autoPrepare(table, table_fields, mode, [where])`	Object	Builds automatically an `insert` or an `update` SQL query and calls `prepare()` with it
`DB::execute(sql_ statement, data)`	Object	Executes a prepared SQL query
`DB::executeMultiple (sql_statements, data)`	Object	Executes several prepared SQL queries
`DB::query(query, [parameters])`	Object	Sends a query to the database
`DB::limitQuery(query, from, count)`	Object	Generates a limited query EXPERIMENTAL
`DB::getOne(query, [params])`	Array	Fetches the first column of the first row from a query
`DB::getRow(query, [params, [fetchmode]])`	Array	Fetches the first row from a query
`DB::getCol(query, [column, [params]])`	Array	Fetches a single column from a query
`DB::getAssoc(query, [force_array, params]])`	Array	Fetches the resultset as an associative array using the first column as the key
`DB::getAll(query, [params, [fetchmode]])`	Array	Fetches all the rows returned from a query
`DB::affectedRows()`	Integer	Returns the affected rows of a query

Function	Returns	Description
`DB::nextId(seq_name, on_demand)`	Integer	Returns the next free ID of a sequence
`DB::createSequence (seq_name)`	Mixed	Creates a new sequence
`DB::dropSequence(seq_name)`	Mixed	Deletes a sequence
`DB::getListOf(type)`	String	Lists internal DB info
`DB_Result`		Contains the result of a database query
`DB_Result::fetchRow([fetchmode, [rownum]])`	Array	Fetches and returns a row of data
`DB_Result::fetchInto (arr, [fetchmode, [rownum]])`	Mixed	Fetches a row of data into an existing variable
`DB_Result::numCols()`	Integer	Gets the number of columns in a resultset
`DB_Result::numRows()`	Integer	Gets the number of rows in a resultset
`DB_Result::nextResult()`	Boolean	Gets the next result if a batch of queries was executed
`DB_Result::free()`	Boolean/ Error Object	Frees the resources allocated for this resultset
`DB_Result::tableInfo (result, [mode])`	Mixed	Returns meta data about the resultset
`DB_Error`		Class for reporting portable database error messages
`DB_Warning`		Class for reporting portable database warning messages

PostgreSQL Functions

Defined in ~/ext/pgsql/pgsql.c

Function	Returns	Description
`Pg_client_encoding ([connection])`	String	Returns the client encoding as a string
`Pg_clientencoding`		Alias for `pg_client_encoding()`

Table continued on following page

Function	Returns	Description
Pg_close(connection)	Boolean	Closes a PostgreSQL connection
Pg_cmdtuples(result_id)	Integer	Returns the number of affected tuples
Pg_connect(host, port, options, tty, dbname)	Integer	Connects to a PostgreSQL database and returns a connection_index
Pg_dbname(connection)	String	Returns the name of the database for the specified connection
Pg_end_copy([connection])	Boolean	Syncs PostgreSQL front end with the back end after doing a copy operation
Pg_errormessage (connection)	String	Returns the error message for the specified connection
Pg_exec(connection, query)	Integer	Executes the specified query
Pg_fetch_array(result, row [,result_type])	Array	Fetches a row as an array
Pg_fetch_object(result, row [,result_type])	Object	Fetches a row as an object
Pg_fetch_row(result, row)	Array	Fetches a row as an enumerated array
Pg_fieldisnull(result_id, row, field)	Integer	Indicates whether the specified field in the given row has a Null value
Pg_fieldname(result_id, field_number)	String	Returns the name of the specified field
Pg_fieldnum(result_id, field_name)	Integer	Returns the number of the specified field
Pg_fieldprtlen(result_id, row_number, field_name)	Integer	Returns the printed length of the specified field
Pg_fieldsize(result_id, field_number)	Integer	Returns the internal storage size of the specified field
Pg_fieldtype(result_id, field_number)	String	Returns the type of the specified field
Pg_freeresult(result_id)	Integer	Frees the memory used by the resultset
Pg_getlastoid(result_id)	Integer	Returns the last object identifier
Pg_host(connection)	String	Returns the hostname associated with the connection

Function	Returns	Description
Pg_loclose(file_descriptor)	Nothing	Closes the large object specified by the file_descriptor
Pg_locreate(connection)	Integer	Creates a large object and returns the object_id
Pg_loexport(object_id, file [,connection_id])	Boolean	Exports a large object to the specified file
Pg_loimport(file, [connection_id])	Integer	Imports a large object from the specified file and returns an object_id
Pg_loopen(connection, object_id, mode)	Integer	Opens a large object and returns a file descriptor for the object
Pg_loread(file_descriptor, len)	String	Reads up to len number of bytes from the specified large object
Pg_loreadall(file_descriptor)	Nothing	Reads an entire large object and passes it through to the browser
Pg_lounlink(connection, object_id)	Nothing	Deletes the large object with the specified identifier
Pg_lowrite(file_descriptor, buf)	Integer	Writes to the specified large object from the variable buf
Pg_numfields(result_id)	Integer	Returns the number of fields in the specified resultset
Pg_numrows(result_id)	Integer	Returns the number of rows in the specified resultset
Pg_options(connection)	String	Returns the options associated with the specified connection
Pg_pconnect(connection)	Integer	Opens a persistent connection to a PostgreSQL database using the quoted string connection, and returns a connection index
Pg_port(connection)	Integer	Returns the port number for the specified connection
Pg_put_line([connection, data])	Boolean	Sends a Null-terminated string to the PostgreSQL back-end server
Pg_result(result_id, row_number, field_name)	Mixed	Returns values from a result identifier
Pg_set_client_encoding([connection, encoding])	Boolean	Sets the client encoding

Table continued on following page

Function	Returns	Description
Pg_setclientencoding		Alias for `pg_set_client_encoding()`
Pg_trace(filename [,mode [,connection]])	Boolean	Enables tracing of a PostgreSQL connection
Pg_tty(connection)	String	Returns the `tty` name associated with the `connection`
Pg_untrace([connection])	Boolean	Disables tracing of a PostgreSQL connection

SESAM Functions

PHP 3 Specific. Defined in `~/functions/sesam.c`:

Function	Returns	Description
sesam_affected_rows (result_id)	Integer	Gets number of rows affected by an immediate query
sesam_commit(void)	Boolean	Commits pending updates to the SESAM database
sesam_connect(catalog, schema, user)	Boolean	Opens SESAM database connection
sesam_diagnostic(void)	Array	Returns status information for last SESAM call
sesam_disconnect(void)	Always True	Detaches from SESAM connection
sesam_errormsg(void)	String	Returns error message of last SESAM call
sesam_execimm(string)	Integer	Executes an immediate SQL statement. Returns a result identifier on success or `False` on error
sesam_fetch_array(result_id, [whence],[offset])	Array	Fetches one row as an associative array
sesam_fetch_result(result_id, [max_rows])	Array	Returns all or part of a query result
sesam_fetch_row(result_id, whence, offset)	Array	Fetches one row as an array
sesam_field_array(result_id)	Array	Returns meta information about individual columns in a result

Function	Returns	Description
sesam_field_name(result_id, string)	String	Returns one column name of the resultset
sesam_free_result(result_id)	Boolean	Releases resources for the query
sesam_num_fields(result_id)	Integer	Returns the number of fields/columns in a resultset
sesam_query (query, [scrollable])	Integer	Performs a SESAM SQL query and prepares the result
sesam_rollback (void)	Boolean	Discards any pending updates to the SESAM database
sesam_seek_row (result_id, [whence],[offset])	Boolean	Sets scrollable cursor mode for subsequent fetches
sesam_settransaction (isolation_level, read_only)	Boolean	Sets SESAM transaction parameters

Sybase Functions

Defined in ~/ext/sybase/php_sybase_db.c and ~/ext/sybase_ct/php_sybase_ct.c:

Function	Returns	Description
sybase_affected_rows ([link_id])	Integer	Returns the number of rows affected by the query. Available only in the CT library
sybase_close(link_id)	Boolean	Closes the Sybase connection
sybase_connect(server_name, username, password)	Integer	Opens a connection to the specified Sybase server and returns a link_id
sybase_data_seek(result_id, row_number)	Boolean	Moves to the specified row of a resultset
sybase_fetch_array(result_id)	Integer	Fetches the next row in the resultset as an array
sybase_fetch_field(result_id, field_offset)	Object	Returns an object containing field information for the field with the specified position

Table continued on following page

Function	Returns	Description
sybase_fetch_object(result_id)	Object	Fetches the next row in the resultset as an object
sybase_fetch_row(result_id)	Array	Fetches the next row in the resultset as an enumerated array
sybase_field_seek(result_id, field_offset)	Integer	Moves to the specified field_offset
sybase_free_result(result_id)	Integer	Frees the memory used by the resultset
sybase_get_last_message()	String	Returns the last message from the Sybase DB server
sybase_min_error_severity(severity)	Void	Sets the minimum error-severity level
sybase_min_message_severity(severity)	Void	Sets the minimum message-severity level
sybase_num_fields(result_id)	Integer	Returns the number of fields in the resultset
sybase_num_rows(result_id)	Integer	Returns the number of rows in the resultset
sybase_pconnect(servername, username, password)	Integer	Opens a persistent connection to the specified Sybase server and returns a link_id
sybase_query(query, [link_id])	Integer	Executes the specified Sybase query
sybase_result(result_id, row, field)	Integer	Fetches the contents of the cell specified by the row and field arguments
sybase_select_db(database [,link_id])	Boolean	Sets the current database to the one specified

Velocis SQL Functions

Defined in ~/ext/odbc/velocis.c:

Function	Returns	Description
velocis_autocommit(conn)	Boolean	Sets the autocommit feature of the connected database to on
velocis_close(conn)	Boolean	Closes the named connection to the Velocis database
velocis_commit(conn)	Boolean	Commits the current transaction to the database
velocis_connect(server, username, password)	Integer	Creates a connection to the Velocis database and returns a handle to it
velocis_exec (conn, query)	Integer	Executes a SQL query on the given Velocis connection
velocis_fetch(conn)	Integer	Returns the resultset from the last query
velocis_fieldname(result, field_index)	String	Returns the name of the field in the resultset given its index number
velocis_fieldnum(result)	Integer	Returns the number of fields per result in the resultset
velocis_freeresult (result)	Boolean	Frees up the memory and resources used to store the given result
velocis_off_autocommit (conn)	Boolean	Sets the autocommit feature of the connected database to off
velocis_result(result, field)	Integer	Returns the value of the specified field in the resultset
velocis_rollback(conn)	Boolean	Rolls back the current transaction on the database

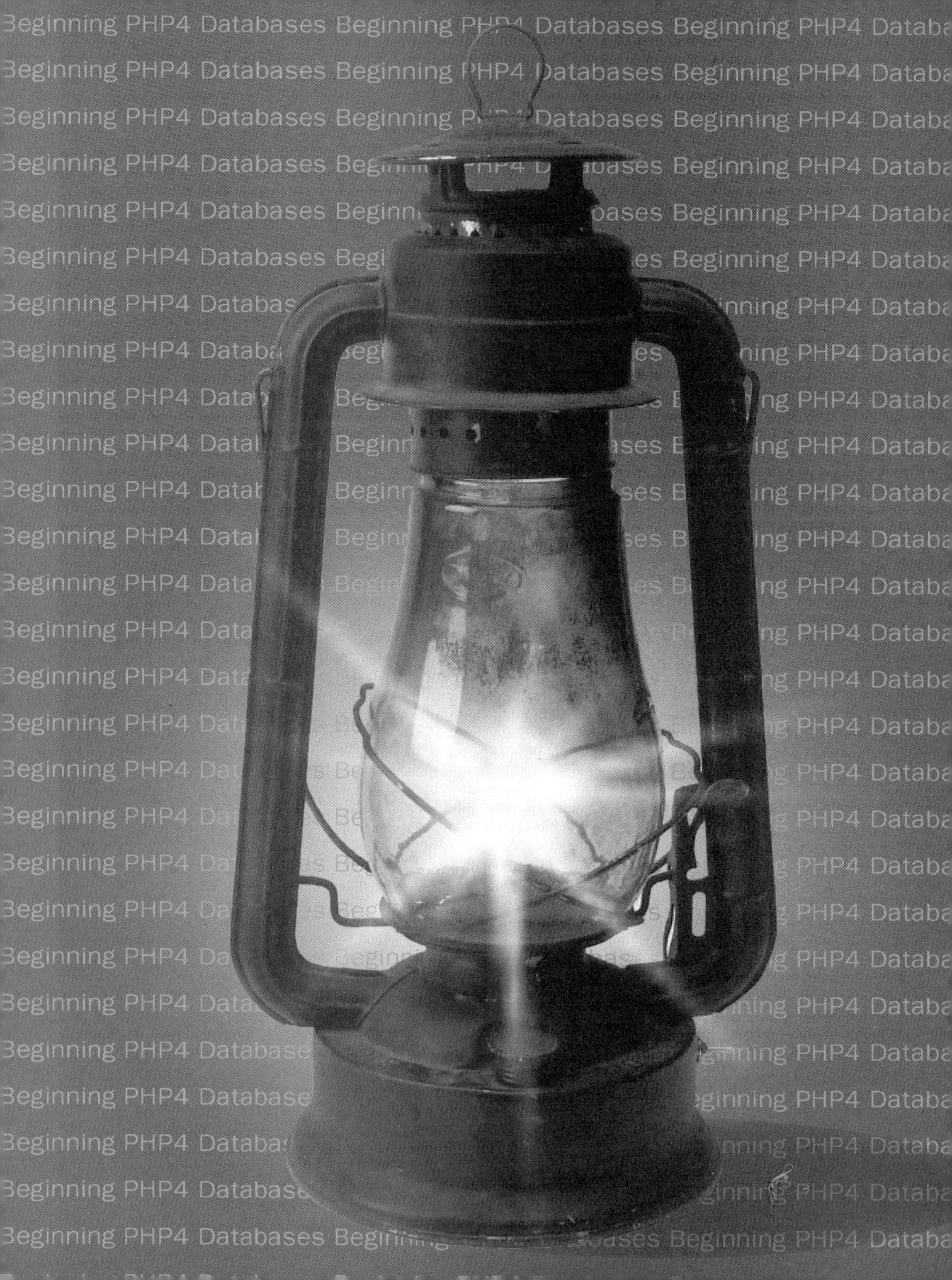
Beginning PHP4 Databases

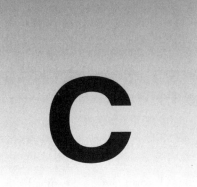

Installing PHP, Apache, and iODBC

To use ODBC drivers to connect to a database under UNIX platforms, PHP needs to be linked against an ODBC driver manager, which registers the drivers to be used, and holds sets of connection parameters called **DSNs (Data Source Names)**. These DSNs store information about the driver and the connection, and may be used for initiation of an ODBC connection. A mature ODBC driver manager, which is easily linked against PHP on most platforms, is the open source iODBC driver manager, freely available at http://www.iodbc.org.

Let's digress for a moment to show how to link the iODBC Driver Manager against PHP and Apache under UNIX platforms. Since Apache 2 is fairly mature as of this writing, we will use that for the example, but instructions for Apache 1.3.x are available from the iODBC site mentioned above.

Aside from the iODBC driver manager, you will also need an ODBC driver and database to complete the architecture.

If you need ODBC drivers to connect to a third-party database on the same or another machine, OpenLink ODBC Drivers are available, and may be downloaded from http://www.openlinksw.com.

The Virtuoso database may be downloaded from: http://www.openlinksw.com/virtuoso. Information on Virtuoso is available at: http://www.openlinksw.com/virtuoso/whatis.htm.

Both Virtuoso and OpenLink's Multi-Tier ODBC drivers download with a free 30-day license.

Support for setting up the OpenLink products may be obtained at:
http://www.openlinksw.com/support/suppindx.htm.

Compiling PHP with Linked iODBC Driver Manager As an Apache Shared Module

The process is fairly straightforward. You will need to be a user who has sufficient privileges to perform all of these steps as well. Root privileges can be gotten by su - root and entering your root password, but be forewarned that you can compromise your system as root. If you use root privileges please do so with care.

Set Up a Build Location, and Get the Latest Builds of iODBC, Apache, and PHP

Open a terminal window:

```
cd /usr/local/src
```

An iODBC `.taz` archive for your platform may be downloaded from: http://www.iodbc.org/opliodbc.htm. As of this writing the latest version is 3.0.6.

Copy that to your `/usr/local/src` and:

```
tar xzf <archive_name>.taz
```

Install the iODBC SDK, Apache, and PHP Sources

The `install.sh` file will install iODBC.

> If you are compiling iODBC from source and get `pthread` errors, you have obtained a threaded iODBC SDK and are using a non-threaded operating system, or vice-versa, and need to get the proper components for your system.

Apache may be downloaded here: http://httpd.apache.org/dist/httpd/. Copy that to your `/usr/local/src` and:

```
tar xzf httpd_x.x.x.tar.gz
```

PHP source is available here: http://www.php.net/downloads.php. Copy that to your `/usr/local/src` and:

```
tar xzf php-x.x.x.tar.gz
```

Set Some Environment Variables

At the command line, run the following:

```
export LD_LIBRARY_PATH=/usr/local/src/odbcsdk/lib
```

This tells the compiler where to find the driver manager. If you prefer to statically link iODBC then remove or rename `libiodbc.so` from the above path and `libiodbc.a` will be statically linked instead.

Alternatively, find the `openlink.sh` in your iODBC install directory and apply it to your shell:

```
./openlink.sh
```

(Notice the leading dot, this applies the `openlink.sh` to your current shell).

Look at the output of the `env` command to ensure that your `LD_LIBRARY_PATH` points to the `odbcsdk/lib/` directory.

Build Apache

First, move into the Apache directory with the command:

```
cd httpd_x.x.x
```

Then:

```
./configure --prefix=/www –enable-so
```

You may set the prefix controlling the Apache install location to anything you like. Then run:

```
make
```

After this:

```
make install
```

Build PHP

First move into the PHP directory and then run the `configure` command:

```
cd ../php-x.x.x
configure –with-iodbc=/usr/local/src/odbcsdk  \
--with-apxs2=/www/bin/apxs
```

Add any other configure commands you want here, from the list at:
http://www.php.net/manual/en/print/install.configure.php

Note: Using `–with-openlink` has been deprecated, use `–with-iodbc`.

Then run the following commands:

```
make
make install
```

Configure and Start Apache

Edit your `/www/conf/httpd.conf` and add or uncomment (remove the #) these lines below the AddType section:

```
AddType application/x-httpd-php .php
AddType application/x-httpd-php-source .phps
```

Also ensure that this line is present and uncommented, below the `Dynamic Shared Object (DSO)` `Support` section:

```
LoadModule php4_module modules/libphp4.so
```

Now you can start your new Apache:

```
/www/bin/apachectl start
```

PHP: Check Your Installation

Create a text file called `php.info` with the following in it:

```
<?php phpinfo(); ?>
```

To see an example of this, enter the following content in your text editor:

```
<?php
phpinfo();
?>
```

Save this as a file called `phpinfo.php` in your `htdocs` or other appropriate web-page directory.

Accessing the `phpinfo.php` page via your browser will show you an extremely useful set of information regarding your programming environment, as well as the configuration commands used to build PHP with your web server.

As with all information-rich tools that are publicly viewable, `phpinfo()` output can be used to compromise security, so don't leave it in a production directory unless you protect it with a `.htaccess` restriction or some other password trick.

Place this file in your `/www/htdocs/` directory. Point your browser to http://localhost/phpinfo.php to see your configuration setup.

You should see something like this:

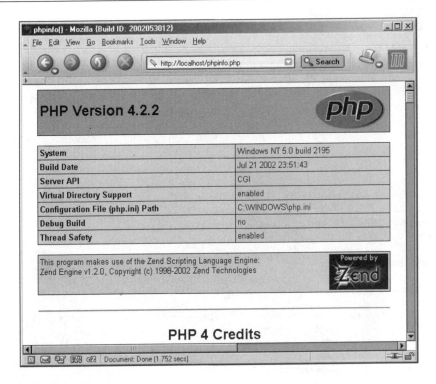

Additional iODBC Notes

When starting Apache in the future, you will need to have LD_LIBRARY_PATH set:

```
export LD_LIBRARY_PATH =/usr/local/src/odbcsdk/lib
```

The path in this statement indicates where you have kept libiodbc.so. An easy way to do this automatically is to place a setenv to it in your .login or .profile.

The location of your shared iODBC support is set by this environment variable. If it's not set, Apache will give an error when starting, as it cannot find libiodbc.so. Also, you can upgrade your iODBC version simply by updating to a newer file (overwriting).

To test a new libiodbc.so before overwriting the old one, you can temporarily set LD_LIBRARY_PATH to point to a new libiobc.so.

As of PHP 4.2, REGISTER_GLOBALS is now OFF by default.

Your php.ini is in /www/lib/php.ini you may wish to edit this setting, but please review the implications at http://www.php.net/manual/en/language.variables.predefined.php.

Sample Connection

Notice the `putenv`'s in the example below. These variables include ones necessary for an Openlink driver connection. Third-party drivers used with iODBC may require different environment variables. It's usually a good idea to put all the necessary variables in a `putenv.inc.php` file, and include them using `require_once()` at the beginning of each script that requires ODBC connectivity. This is not a huge issue for a small site with three `putenv`'s on each page, but in practice, you could have many pages with many environment variables on each one. It's cleaner to only be able to make mistakes in one place. This also allows you to apply different sets of `env`'s to different scripts, interchanging values with great flexibility:

```php
<?php
//Locations determined by your ODBC Driver and iODBC installations.
putenv("LD_LIBRARY_PATH=/path/to/odbcsdk/lib");
putenv("ODBCINSTINI=/path/to/odbcinst.ini");
putenv("ODBCINI=/path/to/odbc.ini"); //Contains your DSN

$dsn="OpenLink"; // Must be a valid DSN - test first with odbctest.
$usr="username";
$pwd="password";

$sql="SELECT * FROM table_name";  //Replace "table_name" as appropriate.
$connection=odbc_connect("$dsn","$usr","$pwd") or die (odbc_error());
echo "connected to DSN: $dsn <br>";

if($result=odbc_do($connection, $sql))
{
    echo "executing SQL: $sql <br>";
    echo "Results: <br>";
    odbc_result_all($result);
    echo "<br>Freeing result resource.<br>";
    odbc_free_result($result);
}else {
        echo "can not execute $sql<br> ";
    }
echo "Closing connection $connection<br>";
odbc_close($connection);
echo "Database connection closed.<br>";
?>
```

ODBC Troubleshooting

Here is a table of common issues you may encounter with ODBC and PHP:

Error	Description
DSN not found and no default driver specified	This may be the most common error. Under UNIX platforms, this means that your ODBCINI environment variable is not set, your DSN name is wrong, or the odbc.ini file where your ODBCINI is pointing cannot be read by PHP due to permission issues.
	Under Windows, this error typically means that you are trying to use a file or user DSN instead of a System DSN or, again, that you are passing a bogus DSN name.
	Either way, the odbc.ini file is read by the ODBC Driver Manager (iODBC or the Windows ODBC Administrator) and this error is that ODBC Driver Manager complaining.
SQL error: SQL State 01000 in SQLConnect	This is a General Error – your database (or driver) has failed. Verify that a connection works outside of PHP, either in the native database interface or in odbctest.
When starting Apache: libiodbc.so.x: cannot open shared object file: No such file or directory	This error occurs under UNIX platforms – it indicates that the odbcsdk/iodbc files linked into your PHP using the –with-iodbc configure switch cannot be found. Check permissions on the directory where the libiodbc file is and ensure that your putenvs for LD_LIBRARY_PATH (or DYLD_LIBRARY_PATH on Mac OS X) is pointing to that directory.
Syntax error or access, SQL State 37000 in SQLExecDirect (or other SQLExec)	Literally, an SQL syntax error. Check your SQL statement for errors and unescaped quotes and the like.
Fatal error: Call to undefined function odbc_xxxx()	ODBC is not installed or activated in your PHP install. Verify your PHP environment is set up to use ODBC via the phpinfo() function.

iODBC: Additional Sources of Information

- ❑ The PHP manual, install instructions: http://www.php.net/manual/en/installation.php
- ❑ The iODBC forum: www.iodbc.org
- ❑ The PHP mailing lists: http://www.php.net/support.php
- ❑ Openlink Software Online Support, at http://www.openlinksw.com/support/suppindx.htm

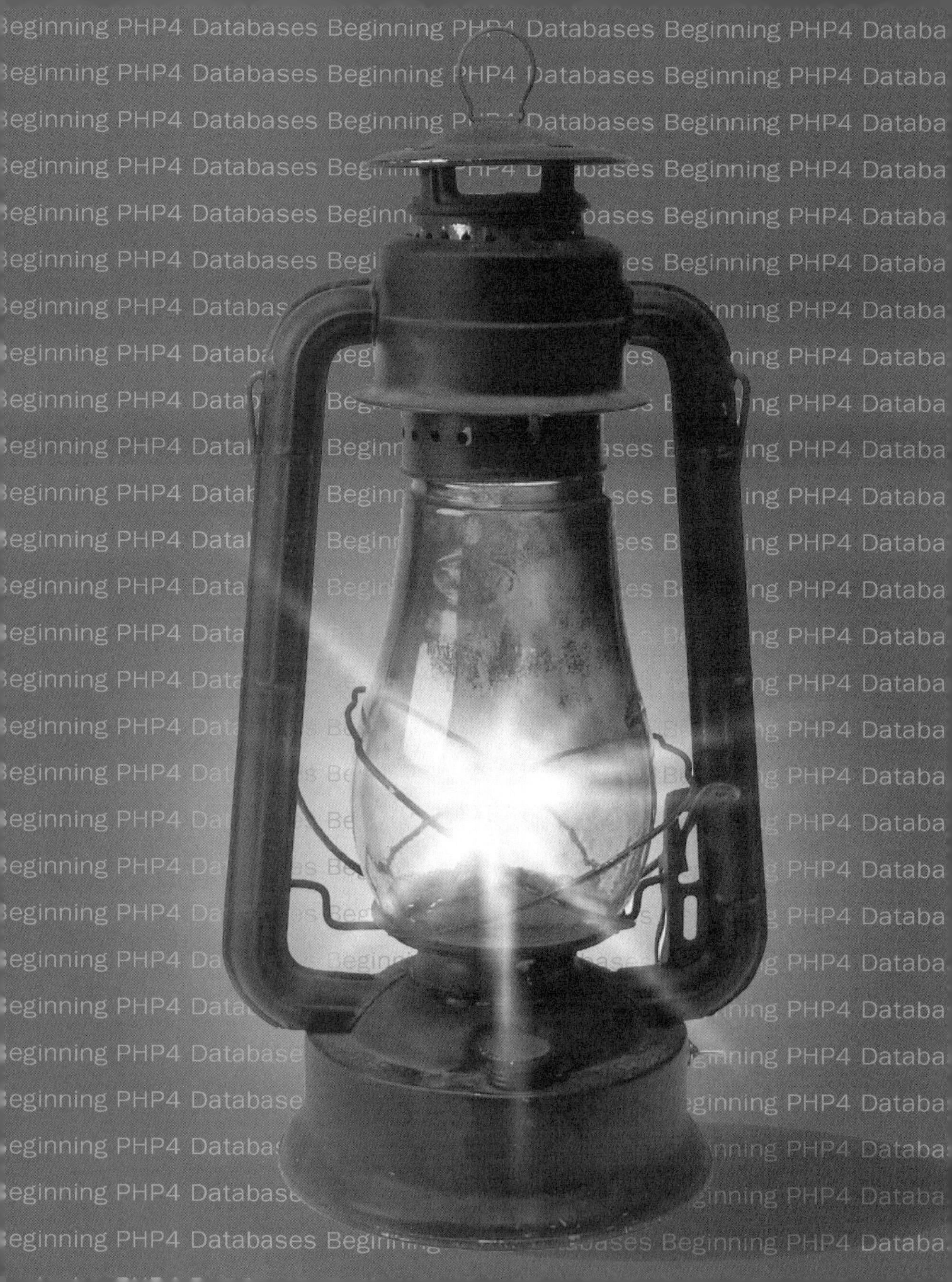
Beginning PHP4 Databases

Index

A Guide to the Index

The index is arranged hierarchically, in alphabetical order, with symbols preceding the letter A. Most second-level entries and many third-level entries also occur as first-level entries. This is to ensure that users will find the information they require however they choose to search for it.

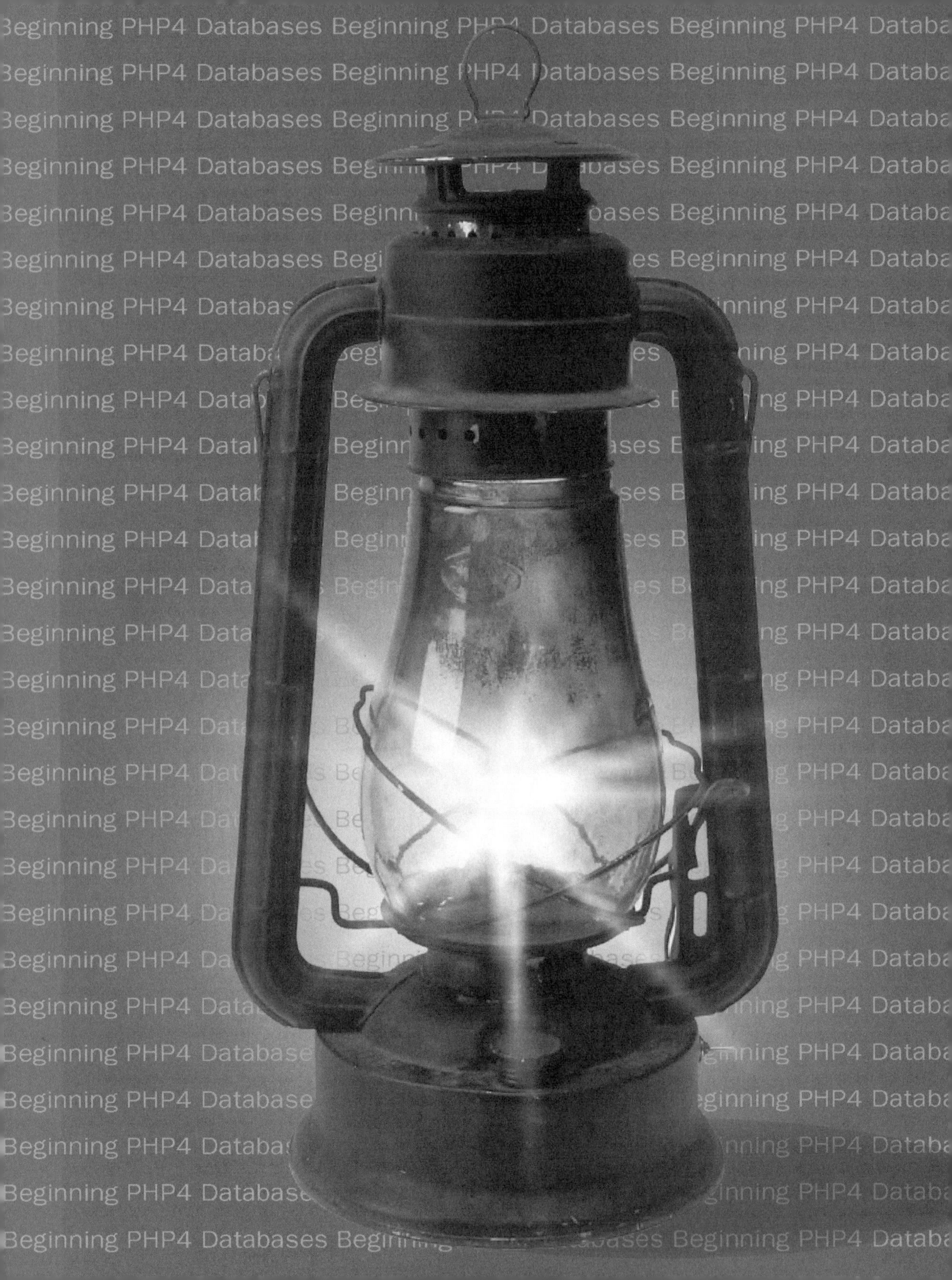
Beginning PHP4 Databases

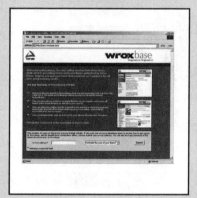
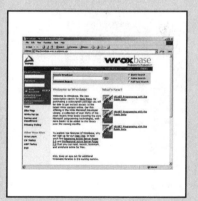